Communications
in Computer and Information Science   2047

Rationale

The CCIS series is devoted to the publication of proceedings of computer science conferences. Its aim is to efficiently disseminate original research results in informatics in printed and electronic form. While the focus is on publication of peer-reviewed full papers presenting mature work, inclusion of reviewed short papers reporting on work in progress is welcome, too. Besides globally relevant meetings with internationally representative program committees guaranteeing a strict peer-reviewing and paper selection process, conferences run by societies or of high regional or national relevance are also considered for publication.

Topics

The topical scope of CCIS spans the entire spectrum of informatics ranging from foundational topics in the theory of computing to information and communications science and technology and a broad variety of interdisciplinary application fields.

Information for Volume Editors and Authors

Publication in CCIS is free of charge. No royalties are paid, however, we offer registered conference participants temporary free access to the online version of the conference proceedings on SpringerLink (http://link.springer.com) by means of an http referrer from the conference website and/or a number of complimentary printed copies, as specified in the official acceptance email of the event.

CCIS proceedings can be published in time for distribution at conferences or as postproceedings, and delivered in the form of printed books and/or electronically as USBs and/or e-content licenses for accessing proceedings at SpringerLink. Furthermore, CCIS proceedings are included in the CCIS electronic book series hosted in the SpringerLink digital library at http://link.springer.com/bookseries/7899. Conferences publishing in CCIS are allowed to use Online Conference Service (OCS) for managing the whole proceedings lifecycle (from submission and reviewing to preparing for publication) free of charge.

Publication process

The language of publication is exclusively English. Authors publishing in CCIS have to sign the Springer CCIS copyright transfer form, however, they are free to use their material published in CCIS for substantially changed, more elaborate subsequent publications elsewhere. For the preparation of the camera-ready papers/files, authors have to strictly adhere to the Springer CCIS Authors' Instructions and are strongly encouraged to use the CCIS LaTeX style files or templates.

Abstracting/Indexing

CCIS is abstracted/indexed in DBLP, Google Scholar, EI-Compendex, Mathematical Reviews, SCImago, Scopus. CCIS volumes are also submitted for the inclusion in ISI Proceedings.

How to start

To start the evaluation of your proposal for inclusion in the CCIS series, please send an e-mail to ccis@springer.com.

M. A. Jabbar · Sanju Tiwari ·
Fernando Ortiz-Rodríguez · Sven Groppe ·
Tasneem Bano Rehman

Editors

Applied Machine Learning and Data Analytics

6th International Conference, AMLDA 2023
Lübeck, Germany, November 9–10, 2023
Revised Selected Papers

Springer

Editors
M. A. Jabbar (i)
Vardhaman College of Engineering
Hyderabad, India

Fernando Ortiz-Rodríguez (i)
Autonomous University of Tamaulipas
Ciudad Victoria, Mexico

Tasneem Bano Rehman (i)
Sage University
Bhopal, India

Sanju Tiwari (i)
Bharati Vidyapeeth's Institute of Computer
Applications and Management (BVICAM)
New Delhi, India

Sven Groppe (i)
University of Lübeck
Lübeck, Germany

ISSN 1865-0929   ISSN 1865-0937 (electronic)
Communications in Computer and Information Science
ISBN 978-3-031-55485-8   ISBN 978-3-031-55486-5 (eBook)
https://doi.org/10.1007/978-3-031-55486-5

This Springer imprint is published by the registered company Springer Nature Switzerland AG
The registered company address is: Gewerbestrasse 11, 6330 Cham, Switzerland

Paper in this product is recyclable.

Preface

This volume contains the main proceedings of the 2023 edition of the International Conference on Applied Machine Learning and Data Analytics (AMLDA 2023). AMLDA is established as a yearly venue for discussing the latest scientific results and technology innovations related to Machine Learning.

The International Conference on Applied Machine Learning and Data Analytics is the premier conference in this branch of artificial intelligence. AMLDA 2023 presented cutting-edge research on all aspects of machine learning as well as important application areas such as healthcare and medical imaging informatics, biometrics, forensics, precision agriculture, risk management, robotics, and satellite imaging. Participants at AMLDA 2023 were from academia and industrial researchers and engineers, graduate students, and postdocs.

AMLDA is convened annually to provide a platform for knowledge exchange of the most recent scientific and technological advances in the field of applied machine learning and data analytics. The main scientific program of the conference comprised 19 papers: 17 full research papers and two short research paper selected out of 76 reviewed submissions, which corresponds to an acceptance rate of 25% for the research papers submitted. The program also included two exciting, invited keynotes, Ralf Möller from University of Lübeck, Germany and Ketan Kotecha from Symbiosis Institute of Technology (SIU) Pune, India, with novel topics.

The General and Program Committee chairs would like to thank the many people involved in making AMLDA 2023 a success. First, our thanks go to the co-chairs of the main event and more than 50 reviewers for ensuring a rigorous review process that led to an excellent scientific program and an average of three reviews per article. AMLDA 2023 was kicked off with the speech of the president of the University of Lübeck, Prof. Gabriele Gillessen-Kaesbach, during the inauguration of the event.

Further, we are grateful for the kind support of all people from Universität zu Lübeck, particularly the hosting chair Sven Groppe and his team. We are thankful for the kind support of all people from Springer. We finally thank our sponsors, our community, and web master for their vital support of this edition of AMLDA 2023.

The editors would like to close the preface with warm thanks to our supporting keynotes, the program committee for their rigorous commitment in carrying out reviews, and finally, our enthusiastic authors who made this event truly international.

November 2023

M. A. Jabbar
Sanju Tiwari
Fernando Ortiz-Rodríguez
Sven Groppe
Tasneem Bano Rehman

Organization

General Chairs

M. A. Jabbar	Vardhaman College of Engineering, India
Sanju Tiwari	Bharati Vidyapeeth's Institute of Computer Applications and Management (BVICAM), India
Fernando Ortiz-Rodriguez	Universidad Autónoma de Tamaulipas, Mexico
Sven Groppe	University of Lübeck, Germany
Tasneem Bano	SAGE University Bhopal, India

Program Chairs

Millie Pant	IIT Roorkee, India
Shishir Kumar Shandilya	VIT Bhopal University, India
José Melchor Medina-Quintero	Universidad Autónoma de Tamaulipas, Mexico
Andries Engelbrecht	University of Stellenbosch, South Africa

Local Team

Jinghua Groppe	University of Lübeck, Germany
Hanieh Khorashadizadeh	University of Lübeck, Germany
Umut Çalikyilmaz	University of Lübeck, Germany
Tobias Groth	University of Lübeck, Germany
Nitin Nayak	University of Lübeck, Germany
Tobias Winker	University of Lübeck, Germany
Angela König	University of Lübeck, Germany
Nils Fußgänger	University of Lübeck, Germany

Publicity Chairs

Fatima Zahra Amara	University of Khenchela, Algeria
Patience Usoro Usip	University of Uyo, Nigeria
Vania V. Estrela	Universidade Federal Fluminense, Brazil
P. Sivakumara	University of Malaya, Malaysia

Workshop

Shikha Mehta   JIIT Noida, India
Yusniel Hidalgo Delgado   Universidad de las Ciencias Informáticas, Cuba
C. A. Dhawale   P R Pote Patil College of Engineering and
                               Management, India

Special Session

Tanima Datta   IIT BHU, India
David Hicks   Texas A&M University - Kingsville, Texas
Antonio De Nicola   ENEA, Italy
Patrice Boursier   International Medical University, Malaysia

Tutorial

Hari Prabhat Gupta   IIT BHU, India
Ayush Goyal   Texas A&M University - Kingsville, Texas, USA

Program Committee

Abhishek Hazra   NUS, Singapore
Anand Panchbhai   Logy.AI, India
Ajit Kumar   Soongsil University, South Korea
Anupkumar M. M. Bongale   Symbiosis Institute of Technology, Pune, India
Beyzanur Cayir Necmettin   Erbakan University, Turkey
Bidush Kumar Sahoo   G.I.E.T. University, India
Carlos F. Enguix   Universidad Autónoma de Tamaulipas, Mexico
Carlos Pereira   ISEC, Portugal
Debajyoty Banik   Kalinga Institute of Industrial Technology, India
Deepak Dharrao   Symbiosis Institute of Technology, Pune, India
Fatima Zahra Amara   University of Khenchela, Algeria
Fernando Ortiz-Rodriguez   Universidad Autónoma de Tamaulipas, Mexico
František Zbořil   Brno University of Technology, Czech Republic
Gloria Cerasela Crisan   Vasile Alecsandri University of Bacau, Romania
Gourav Shrivastava   SAGE University, Bhopal, India
Hanieh Khorashadizadeh   University of Lübeck, Germany
Himadri B. G. S. Bhuyan   GITAM University, India
Hirosato Seki   Osaka University, Japan

Ifiok James Udo	University of Uyo, Nigeria
Isaac Chairez	Tecnológico de Monterrey, Mexico
Isabel Jesus	Institute of Engineering of Porto, Portugal
Jerry Chun-Wei Lin	Western Norway University, Norway
Jolanta Mizera-Pietraszko	Military University of Land Forces, Poland
José Everardo B. Maia	Universidade Estadual do Ceará, Brazil
Joseph A. Brown	Innopolis University, Russia
Jude Hemanth	Karunya University, India
Karima Saidi	Batna 2 University, Algeria
Khushbu Doulani	IIIT Lucknow, India
Kusum Lata	Sharda University, India
Manoj Kumar	Directorate of Technical Education & Training, Odisha, India
Mansi Sharma	IIT Madras, India
M. A. Jabbar	Vardhaman College of Engineering, India
Meenakshi Srivastava	Amity University, Lucknow, India
Meriem Djezzar	University of Khenchela, Algeria
Mounir Hemam	University of Khenchela, Algeria
Müge Oluçoğlu Dokuz	Eylül University, Turkey
Namrata Nagpal	Amity University, Lucknow, India
N. D. Patel	VIT Bhopal, India
Neeranjan Chitare	Northumbria University, UK
Onur Dogan	İzmir Bakırçay University, Turkey
Ömer Faruk Gürcan	Sivas Cumhuriyet University, Turkey
Patience U. Usip	University of Uyo, Nigeria
Paulo Moura Oliveira	UTAD University, Portugal
Premananda Sahu	Lovely Professional University, India
Radu-Emil Precup	Politehnica University of Timisoara, Romania
Ritu Tanwar	NIT Uttarakhand, India
Ronald O. Ojino	Co-operative University of Kenya, Kenya
Sachinandan Mohanty	KIIT University, India
Sashikala Mishra	Symbiosis International University, India
Shankru Guggari	KLE Technological University, India
Shishir Kumar Shandilya	VIT Bhopal University, India
Sven Groppe	Universität zu Lübeck, Germany
Tasneem Bano Rehman	SAGE University, Bhopal, India
Sanju Tiwari	Bharati Vidyapeeth's Institute of Computer Applications and Management (BVICAM), India
Siddhartha Banerjee	Ramakrishna Mission Residential College, India
Sourav Banerjee	Kalyani Govt Engg College, India
Srikanta K. Mohapatra	Chitkara University, Punjab, India

Tanusree Dutta	Vardhaman College of Engineering, Hyderabad, India
Udit Chawla	University of Engineering & Management, Kolkata, India
Youssef Mourdi	Cadi Ayyad University, Morocco
Yusniel Hidalgo Delgado	Universidad de las Ciencias Informáticas, Cuba

Contents

Get It Right: Improving Comprehensibility with Adaptable Speech Expression of a Humanoid Service Robot

Thomas Sievers(✉) and Ralf Möller

Institute of Information Systems, University of Lübeck, 23562 Lübeck, Germany
{sievers,moeller}@ifis.uni-luebeck.de

Abstract. As humanoid service robots are becoming more and more perceptible in public service settings for instance as a guide to welcome visitors or to explain a procedure to follow, it is desirable to improve the comprehensibility of complex issues for human customers and to adapt the level of difficulty of the information provided as well as the language used to individual requirements. This work examines a case study using a humanoid social robot Pepper performing support for customers in a public service environment offering advice and information. An application architecture is proposed that improves the intelligibility of the information received by providing the possibility to translate this information into easy language and/or into another spoken language.

Keywords: Social Robot · Human-Robot Interaction · Easy Language · Comprehensibility · Translation

1 Introduction

As self-service technologies (SSTs), which allow customers to access a service without interaction with service staff, become more common in public services, the use of service robots, which can physically replace a human service worker, offers the opportunity to increase the level and availability of customer service while reducing costs [1]. Especially in times of an increasing shortage of professionals, the use of robots appears to be a practical way to relieve skilled workers. Moreover, in an unsettled world situation the requirements for dealing with people with a different cultural background and lack of language skills are increasing, especially for the authorities in public services. Therefore, it would be desirable that robots in this field are able to interact effectively with human clients across different cultural settings. These robots need social and cross-cultural skills to provide information and assistance in an adequate way. They should be able to respond to the client's linguistic and intellectual abilities.

Most of the people surveyed in a study by TU Darmstadt on the robotization of office and service professions [2] would accept robots as counterpart in a variety of service environments. More than 80% of respondents, however, prefer

© The Author(s), under exclusive license to Springer Nature Switzerland AG 2024
M. A. Jabbar et al. (Eds.): AMLDA 2023, CCIS 2047, pp. 1–14, 2024.
https://doi.org/10.1007/978-3-031-55486-5_1

human contact for sensitive, personal services such as complex financial advice, psychological or medical care. It is therefore important that a robot addresses people and engages with them in an appropriate manner, not least because many people are still surprised that they can communicate with a robot in a natural way using natural language [3]. Robots will be most successful in being accepted if they meet expectations through aesthetic characteristics that engage users within a clearly defined context [4]. Everything from the robots appearance to the visual design and the sound of voice hold semantic value. Previous work has also provided insights into the effects of language and cultural context on the credibility of robot speech [5]. The way robots express themselves to build credibility and convey information in a meaningful and compelling way is a key function in creating acceptance and usability.

A decisive factor for the success of the use of service robots in interaction with customers is the customers' trust or lack of trust respectively [6]. Trust is a multidimensional concept, reflecting the perceived competence, integrity and benevolence of another entity [7] and therefore a strong determinant of intention for customers to use a service robot. If they do not trust it they will not enjoy using it and therefore the potential of service robots is not exploited. In research a lack of trust in service robots is often cited as the main reason for customers not to have the intention to use the service robot [8,9]. Establishing trust and trying to create empathy toward the robot while the customers believe in the robot having empathy towards them is considered indispensable for a successful service and caring process [4].

In their research van Pinxteren et al. [6] focus on anthropomorphism as a central concept in human-robot interaction (HRI). According to theory, human-like features of the robot facilitate anthropomorphism [10]. More than 80 per cent of respondents surveyed by TU Darmstadt [2] believe that robots can show feelings. One recalls the Arthur C. Clarke quote that "any sufficiently advanced technology is indistinguishable from magic", and according to Diana [4] this phenomenon makes it all the more important for a robot creator to build a strategy that acknowledges limitations helping people to understand what to expect. An enlightenment of the average user assuming magical, sophisticated knowledge and perception of the robot will help to avoid miscommunication. It must be clear and understandable to the customer what can be expected from the service robot.

People tend to blame robots, when they experience them as social actors, for mistakes and annoyances to the degree they attribute to their autonomy [11]. Thus, especially when something fails in completing the desired task for example due to misunderstandings, the human perception of the service robot can be a critical component for the acceptance of robotic services in general. Greater autonomy of the robot can lead to greater blame if something goes wrong.

This paper discusses an approach to making communication between service robots and human clients easier to understand in order to reduce possible fears, barriers and misunderstandings and to enable successful and goal-oriented communication. We propose features for a humanoid social robot that can improve its intelligibility and thus the acceptance of such a service robot in environments that are sensitive and anxiety-provoking for humans.

2 Preliminaries

Especially in the public service, there is a need to facilitate access to important information. In Germany alone, more than 10 million people [12] (some speak of more than 17 million people [13]) require text in easily understandable language to access crucial information and successfully manage their daily lives. There are many different names and designations for easy language: Easy language, simple language, easily understandable language, barrier-free information and communication [14]. Easy language is defined as a language style with simpler sentence structure and additional explanations. The target group that can benefit from texts in easy language include people with learning difficulties, little knowledge of administrative language, reading difficulties, older people or people suffering from dementia, as well as people learning the official language as a second language. This results in the need to provide as much information as possible in easy language.

In order to avoid misunderstandings, it would also be a great advantage if the relevant content were offered in a language that the client understands well. This would usually be the client's mother tongue. Clients who turn to public services have a specific problem they want to solve and often do not know how to achieve the desired result. They are therefore in a state of uncertainty. In this state of mind, it is very easy to get upset when things are not going in the right direction, and then misunderstandings, angry reactions, and agitation often occur. To avoid this, it is better to communicate with clients in their own language because they can express themselves more easily, important bits of information won't get lost in translation and the client's anxiety of speaking another language is removed. If clients or customers are upset, they might not want the extra mental effort of communicating in a second language. As multicultural expert Michael Soon Lee states "Even if you only have a basic command of the customer's native language, it may take longer to get your point across, but the customer is much more likely to be receptive and understanding" [15].

The eGovernment MONITOR 2022 [16] shows that only 54% of the population in Germany uses eGovernment services at all. More than half of all citizens still use services for which they have a need in analog form (57%). Lack of knowledge of online availability is the central reason for the digital usage gap for many services. Under these circumstances, it cannot be assumed that advance information and preparation for a visit to a public authority with regard to necessary documents, requirements, etc. is always optimal. This is probably even more true for people with a migration background.

Misunderstandings, ignorance, and lack of understanding on the part of clients can also create stress for public service staff to deal with. Therefore, conflicts cannot be ruled out and a friendly and approachable interaction with each other is sometimes difficult. Despite its human-like appearance, the Pepper robot remains a little abstract and does not resemble a real human being in all facets, for example in a sometimes all too human unkind reaction to incomprehension. The service robot always remains calm, friendly and courteous, whatever happens. These skills make him a valuable service provider for clients when supporting service staff.

This leads to the conclusion that humanoid service robots equipped with the flexibility to present information in easy language and/or in another language if needed can be of great benefit to people seeking advice, information or help, especially if these people come from a different country or have difficulties in understanding for other reasons. The improvements we propose in the intelligibility and usability of public services are difficult to realise by human agents, but we will show that it is relatively easy to equip a robot with these features.

3   Related Work

We have not found many implementations for the use of easy language or translation by a humanoid robot to improve the comprehensibility of information for human counterparts. In particular, the use of easy language does not seem to have been the subject of research related to humanoid robots so far. A robot-bound speech-to-speech translation system is proposed in the domain of medical care as a one-way translation designed to help English speaking patients describe their symptoms to Korean doctors or nurses [17]. The use of a social robot to teach vocabulary to Turkish-Dutch children and the extent to which a bilingual robot or a monolingual robot promotes word learning is investigated by Leeuwestein et al. [18]. Santano [19] shows how to provide Pepper with translating capabilities using Google's ML Kit Translation API [20]. This works in offline mode as on-device translation and is intended for casual and simple translations only as it does not offer the same quality as Google's Cloud Translation API.

Meaningful and communicative robot actions expressed through body language interpretable by humans offer a further channel of communication with measurable effects on the interaction [21]. This implicit communication through movement has the potential to increase efficiency in collaborative tasks between robots and humans and is therefore very promising in terms of social interaction.

A reference framework adding intelligibility to the behavior of a robotic system for improvement of predictability, trust, safety, usability, and acceptance of autonomous robotic systems is proposed by van Deurzen et al. [22]. It comprises an interactive, online, and visual dashboard to help identify where and when adding intelligibility to the interface design is required so that developers and designers can customise the interactions to improve the experience for people working with the robot.

These approaches help to improve communication between humans and robots, or between humans with the help of robots, without simplifying the complexity of the language or the representation of the information itself. However, in such simplification lies a key to better understanding.

4 Humanoid Robot Pepper

The social humanoid robot Pepper [23] as seen in Fig. 1 was developed by Aldebaran and first released in 2015. The robot is 120 cm tall and optimized for human interaction. It is able to engage with people through conversation, gestures and its touch screen. Pepper is equipped with internal sensors, four directional microphones in his head and speakers for voice output. The robot is able to process images from its 3D camera and two HD cameras by shape recognition software for identification of faces and objects so that it can focus on, identify, and recognize people. Speech recognition and dialogue is available in 15 languages. Beyond, Pepper can perceive basic human emotions.

The robot features an open and fully programmable platform so that developers can program their own applications to run on Pepper using software development kits (SDKs) for programming languages like C++, Python or Java respectively Kotlin. This approach allows the development of robot applications for a wide variety of scenarios in a development environment familiar to most developers.

On Pepper's chest a tablet is located presenting a screen resolution of 1280 by 800 pixels. This tablet, which runs Google's Android system, can be equipped with applications to create interaction between the robot and a human user via a straightforward application programming interface (API). There is a Pepper SDK [24], which is an Android Studio plug-in and provides a set of graphical tools and a Java library when using Android Studio as an integrated development environment (IDE). The Pepper SDK contains an emulator for the tablet and a robot viewer that shows, among other things, a dialogue view with which the robot's speaking actions can be tested without needing the real robot.

Since research has generally shown that trust is the basis for successful communication tasks and trust in robots is increased by anthropomorphism, a humanoid social robot like Pepper is a good choice for service delivery in interaction with customers. A human face, the possibility of human-like expressions and body language, the use of voice and a name of its own are seen as beneficial for the trust of customers in the robot [25].

5 Case Study

Our case study relates to the scenario of a customer centre of a public service authority, where many people regularly pursue different concerns such as applying for identity cards, residence permits or work permits. Official procedures usually require knowledge about necessary requirements, documents needed, etc. Many procedures also require explanation for people who rarely have to deal with them, especially if they have a limited understanding of the language and/or belong to a different cultural group with different experiences and background. This can easily lead to uncertainties and tense situations that make it difficult to process the respective case together with the case worker in a stress-free and relaxed manner. Furthermore, it is unfavourable if, for example, the lack

Fig. 1. Humanoid Robot Pepper

of prerequisites or necessary documents is noticed only during the conversation with a human case worker. It would be better if an applicant was informed about everything necessary beforehand and in a way that is understandable and comprehensible to him or her. This would save frustration and unnecessary waiting time on the part of the customer, as well as needless time spent by the case worker on cases that cannot be processed directly due to a lack of sufficient prerequisites.

Such information and education about necessary prerequisites can be provided by a robot with social interaction capabilities. This robot, positioned in the waiting or reception area of an authority with personal customer contacts, can approach individual customers and ask about their concerns. Equipped with application-specific expertise, the robot can provide helpful information and clarification on the respective issue. Furthermore, a humanoid social robot can also provide additional general guidance and orientation in such a scenario.

This paper discusses a possible approach to automatically reduce the complexity of regulatory information or adapting it to the needs of individual customers by translating such content into easy language and/or a foreign language. We think that with such measures, an improvement of adequate information of the customers in terms of comprehensibility and preparation possibilities can be achieved, as well as an increase in the effectiveness of the processes in the conversation with the clerk. This would result in time savings, better preparation, reduction of anxieties and perhaps a more relaxed social intercourse.

6 Application Architecture

We developed our exemplary application to achieve this goal using Android Studio and the programming language Kotlin. We use the Pepper SDK for Android [24] which allows the robot to be controlled from our Android application on its tablet with existing functionalities of Pepper's operating system for focusing upon a person, listening, talking and chatting as well as movements of head and arm to underline what is said with appropriate movements. Every output the robot performs by voice is also displayed on its tablet for the purpose of redundancy serving those with hearing impairment. The tablet serves as a user interface showing the obtained information and offering the possibility to make a selection for easy language or translation as can be seen in Fig. 2. This selection can also be made by voice using a phrase containing predefined key words like "easy language" or "translation". A blue speech bar on the tablet indicates listening and an animation is shown when Pepper is receiving and processing information.

As a knowledge base in our case study for the case-specific complex expert knowledge that the robot should be able to provide information about, we use data from a MySQL database hosted on a web server with a self-programmed application programming interfaces (API) that returns text answers in JSON (JavaScript Object Notation) format. This API transmits a term or phrase that the robot has heard and recognised to the server via Wi-Fi connection. A PHP

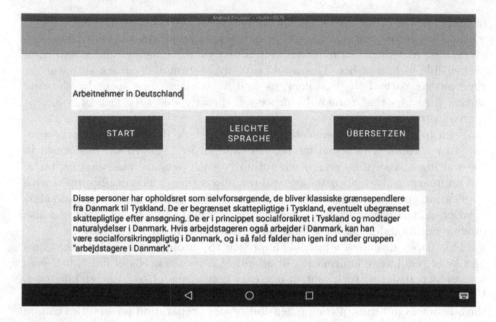

Fig. 2. Tablet as user interface displaying obtained information translated to Danish

script running on the web server then returns a corresponding response from the database. This basic example knowledge base could be something totally different in another case of application. It represents the initial information that needs to be simplified.

For translation into easy language and into a foreign language, we use services that are hosted on various external servers and are not proprietary. These services are also connected to the robot application via Wi-Fi and a corresponding API connection. We connect to the AI-powered translation tool for easy language of SUMM AI [26] and use the API of DeepL [27] for translation services. Text given to this APIs is automatically returned in a JSON format that is handed over to the voice and tablet output of the robot. This method and the use of the APIs is described in more detail by Sievers et al. [28]. SUMM AI currently supports easy language for German. DeepL provides translation to 27 languages. In our proof-of-concept application, we only use one foreign language, Danish. The Pepper robot has to be equipped with the appropriate language package for being able to pronounce used languages correctly.

6.1   Application Structure

The Android application with its *Main Activity* acts as a scaffold and control unit for the basic proceedings. It contains the program routines necessary for the usage of native robot resources like listening and talking and subroutines for calling the APIs as illustrated in Fig. 3. A subroutine for asking a customer after 10 s idling if the service robot could help with another topic is also implemented.

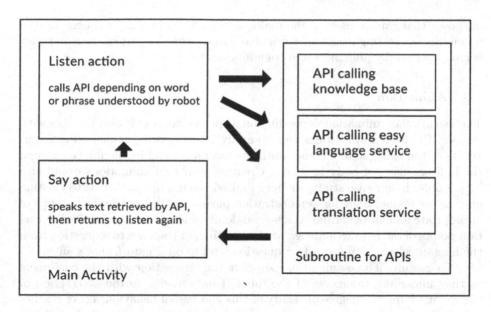

Fig. 3. Main Activity of our application

6.2   Listen and Say or Chat

Our first approach was to use the Pepper-specific *Listen* and *Say* functionalities [29,30] to realise a dialogue between robot and customer. The Pepper robot is able to react to words or phrases provided in the program code of the application. Real speech recognition in a general sense is not possible with Pepper's native abilities but the robot is able to spot a word or phrase known to him while listening. Our application contains the necessary vocabulary for the words and phrases that the robot should understand, divided into different phrases for different topics. These topics refer to the knowledge base stored in our database. For every topic we provide a set of words or phrases serving as keywords for the retrieval of the related information. Positively understood words or phrases are forwarded to a subroutine that processes the first API call to the knowledge base.

In a second approach, we used Pepper's *Chat* feature [31] to conduct the dialogue. This was found to bring a significant improvement in terms of spoken language recognition. Using *Listen* action the word or phrase of the topic is mostly only understood if it is said apart from the context of other words or a sentence. With the *Chat* function, individual words and short sentences of a topic are usually understood even if they are spoken as part of a longer sentence. Also a more natural flow of dialogue is possible using the *Chat* feature due to the flexible possibilities of using variables or randomly selected sentence components in the robot's responses as can be seen in Fig. 4.

By using pauses in speech, emphasis and modulation of the voice, intelligibility can be further improved. The Pepper SDK provides parameters for these purposes that can be used in the dialogue topics. All in all, this opens up the possibility of creating a customer-oriented dialogue on the part of the robot that is characterised by politeness and friendliness.

6.3   Animation

The use of robot animation depending on a specific context is also possible with Pepper. Predefined animations can be easily integrated depending on different events of the dialogue to enhance anthropomorphism and intelligibility through the indirect effect of body language. Creating your own animations would also be possible. In our case study, we have limited the use of animations to existing ones in the Pepper SDK for demonstration purposes. We have defined groups of appropriate animations, from which a randomly selected one is executed at certain points of the interaction, e.g., at the greeting, in response to a question from the human, when the robot asks a question, and so on. Figure 5 shows an example of a gesture. These animations support the interaction with the customers as they underline statements of the robot. However, due to the abstraction of the robot's form, the degree of reality of this non-verbal behaviour never reaches a level that would have a negative impact on the acceptance of the robot's behaviour with regard to the *uncanny valley* effect [32].

7   Conclusions

With this paper we propose a method to improve the comprehensibility of complex official information for human customers by adapting the level of content-related difficulties. We suggest that such content, when a customer asks for it, be automatically translated into easy language or a foreign language by a humanoid social robot. Our case study involves a customer-facing government agency where a Pepper robot does just that.

Workshops we did together with public service staff show that such features are seen as useful and that one can well imagine the use of such a robot in suitable public authorities. The use of the aforementioned functional APIs via an internet connection proves to be possible without any problems and without unreasonably long response times. An integration of external services via API into applications using the Pepper SDK in Android Studio is quite possible for experienced Android developers. Additional knowledge about the inner workings of the connected services is not required, which is particularly advantageous when integrating complex AI technologies and simplifies application development for such technologies. This approach is not limited to a specific robot model, but can be realised as an API connection for various models.

In future work, we hope to further improve the robot's capabilities in dialogue with human customers and make it less prone to errors. Using language models such as Generative Pre-trained Transformer 3 (GPT-3) or more recent versions to generate human-like text may be an option. Data protection concerns also require closer consideration.

```
●  ○  ●                    Dialog view
Robot: Hallo , was kann ich für Sie tun?
Human: Wer darf ein Haus kaufen (100%)
Robot: Lassen Sie mich überlegen.
Robot: Also , Wer darf in Dänemark ein Haus erwerben, ohne
gesonderte Zustimmung der Behörde „Civilstyrelsen"? Jeder,
der in Dänemark wohnt, jeder, der in Dänemark 5 Jahre
gewohnt hat, jeder, der die Immobilie geerbt hat, jeder, der die
Immobilie in gerader aufsteigender oder absteigender Linie
geschenkt bekommt. Jeder Bürger, der Arbeitnehmer in
Dänemark, einem Mitgliedsstaat der EU oder des EWR ist oder
selbständig in Dänemark arbeiten möchte. Zusätzlich muss die
Immobilie zur Ganzjahresnutzung bestimmt sein. Alle anderen
benötigen eine Genehmigung von Civilstyrelsen.  Möchten Sie
mehr zum Thema Wer darf ein Haus kaufen wissen?
Human: Leichte Sprache bitte (100%)
Robot: Kein Problem
Robot: Wer darf in Dänemark ein Haus kaufen?
Das muss die Behörde "Civilstyrelsen" entscheiden.
Diese Menschen dürfen ein Haus kaufen:
- wenn sie in Dänemark wohnen.
- wenn sie in Dänemark 5 Jahre gewohnt haben.
- wenn sie das Haus von einem Verstorbenen geerbt haben.
- wenn jemand das Haus Ihnen schenkt.
- wenn Sie Arbeit·nehmer in Dänemark sind.
- wenn Sie in einem Mitglieds·land von der EU oder dem EWR
arbeiten.
- wenn Sie selbständig in Dänemark arbeiten möchten.
Das Haus muss für den ganzen Jahres·gebrauch sein.
Möchten Sie vielleicht noch etwas wissen ?
Human: Und nun übersetzen (100%)
Robot: Gern
Robot: Hvem må købe et hus i Danmark?
Det er op til Civilstyrelsen at afgøre det.
Disse mennesker har lov til at købe et hus
- hvis de bor i Danmark.
- hvis de har boet i Danmark i 5 år.
- hvis de har arvet huset efter en afdød.
- hvis nogen giver dig huset i gave.
- hvis du er lønmodtager i Danmark.
- hvis du arbejder i et EU-land eller EØS-land.
- hvis du ønsker at arbejde som selvstændig i Danmark.
Huset skal kunne bruges hele året rundt.
Robot: Kann ich noch etwas für Sie tun?
Human: Nein (100%)
Robot: Womit kann ich Ihnen sonst noch helfen ?
```

Fig. 4. Robot emulation viewer showing dialogue between robot and human with knowledge base answer, translation to easy language, and translation to Danish

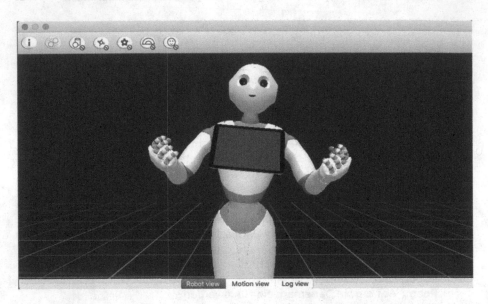

Fig. 5. Robot emulation viewer showing the gesture of an animation

Through further workshops with authorities and practical tests of our hypothesis in an environment corresponding to our case study, we will seek to gain a better understanding of how best to design our proposed application, overcome any limitations and improve human-robot interaction to achieve the goal of assisting individuals who have difficulty understanding complex content required in public service.

References

1. Allmendinger, G., Lombreglia, R.: Four strategies for the age of smart services. Harv. Bus. Rev. **83**, 131–143 (2005)
2. Stock-Homburg, R.: Denn sie wissen nicht, was sie tun - Studie der TU Darmstadt zur Robotisierung von Büro- und Dienstleistungsberufen. Transnational Study series "Robots@work4.0" [Online] (2016). https://www.tu-darmstadt.de/universitaet/aktuelles_meldungen/archiv_2/2016/2016quartal4/einzelansicht_162880.de.jsp
3. Gardecki, A., Podpora, M., Beniak, R., Klin, B.: The Pepper humanoid robot in front desk application. In: Conference Paper: Progress in Applied Electrical Engineering (PAEE) (2018). https://doi.org/10.1109/PAEE.2018.8441069
4. Diana, C.: My Robot Gets Me: How Social Design Can Make New Products More Human, pp. 218–228. Havard Business Review Press, Boston (2021). ISBN 9781633694422
5. Andrist, S., Ziadee, M., Boukaram, H., Mutlu, B., Sakr, M.: Effects of culture on the credibility of robot speech: a comparison between English and Arabic. In: Proceedings of the Tenth Annual ACM/IEEE International Conference on Human-Robot Interaction (HRI '15), pp. 157–164. Association for Computing Machinery, New York (2015). https://doi.org/10.1145/2696454.2696464

6. van Pinxteren, M.M.E., Wetzels, R.W.H., Rüger, J., Pluymaekers, M., Wetzels, M.: Trust in humanoid robots: implications for services marketing. J. Serv. Mark. **33**(4), 507–518 (2019)
7. Mayer, R.C., Davis, J.H., Schoorman, F.D.: An integrative model of organizational trust. Acad. Manag. Rev. **20**(3), 709–734 (1995). https://doi.org/10.2307/258792
8. Everett, J., Pizarro, D., Crockett, M.: Why are we reluctant to trust robots? [Online] (2017). https://www.theguardian.com/science/head-quarters/2017/apr/24/why-are-we-reluctantto-trust-robots
9. Morgan, B.:10 Things robots can't do better than humans [Online] (2017) . https://www.forbes.com/sites/blakemorgan/2017/08/16/10-things-robots-cant-do-better-than-humans
10. Epley, N., Waytz, A., Cacioppo, J.T.: On seeing human: a three-factor theory of anthropomorphism. Psychol. Rev. **114**(4), 864–886 (2007). https://doi.org/10.1037/0033-295X.114.4.864
11. Furlough, C., Stokes, T., Gillan, D.J.: Attributing blame to robots: I. The influence of robot autonomy. Hum. Factors **63**(4), 592–602 (2021). https://doi.org/10.1177/0018720819880641
12. Press and Information Office of the Federal Government (2021). Any complex content can be translated into easy language [Online]. https://www.bundesregierung.de/bregde/aktuelles/interview-anne-leichtfuss-1918176
13. Quatropus GmbH & Co. KG (2022). On the status quo of easy language in Germany [Online]. https://www.quatrolingo.com/status-quo-leichte-sprachedeutschland-2022/
14. capito. Easy-to-understand language and barrier-free information [Online]. https://www.capito.eu/en/what-is-easy-to-understand-language/
15. Michael Soon Lee. Driving Sales and Satisfaction with Multilingual Service [Online]. http://resources.rosettastone.com/CDN/us/pdfs/Biz-Public-Sec/Driving-Sales-and-Satisfaction-with-Multilingual-Service.pdf
16. Initiative D21 e. V (2022). eGovernment MONITOR [Online]. https://initiatived21.de/egovernment-monitor/
17. Shin, S., et al.: Speech-to-speech translation humanoid robot in doctor's office. In: 2015 6th International Conference on Automation, Robotics and Applications (ICARA), pp. 484–489 (2015). https://doi.org/10.1109/ICARA.2015.7081196
18. Leeuwestein, H., et al.: Teaching Turkish-Dutch kindergartners Dutch vocabulary with a social robot: does the robot's use of Turkish translations benefit children's Dutch vocabulary learning? J. Comput. Assist. Learn. **37**, 603–620 (2021). https://doi.org/10.1111/jcal.12510
19. Santano, S.: innovex GmbH (2023). How to Use Google's ML Kit to Enhance Pepper With AI (Part 5) [Online]. https://www.inovex.de/de/blog/how-to-use-googles-ml-kit-to-enhance-pepper-with-ai-part-5/
20. Google (2023). Translation [Online]. https://developers.google.com/ml-kit/language/translation
21. Lastrico, L., et al.: If you are careful, so am i! how robot communicative motions can influence human approach in a joint task (2022). https://doi.org/10.48550/ARXIV.2210.13290
22. van Deurzen, B., Bruyninckx, H., Luyten, K.: Choreobot: A reference framework and online visual dashboard for supporting the design of intelligible robotic systems. Proc. ACM Hum.-Comput. Interact. **6** (EICS), 24 (2022). https://doi.org/10.1145/3532201. Article 151
23. Aldebaran, United Robotics Group and Softbank Robotics (2022) . Pepper [Online]. https://www.aldebaran.com/en/pepper

24. Aldebaran, United Robotics Group and Softbank Robotics (2022). Pepper SDK for Android [Online]. https://qisdk.softbankrobotics.com/sdk/doc/pepper-sdk/index.html

25. Fink, J.: Anthropomorphism and human likeness in the design of robots and human-robot interaction. In: Ge, S.S., Khatib, O., Cabibihan, J.J., Simmons, R., Williams, M.A. (eds.) Social Robotics. Lecture Notes in Computer Science(), vol. 7621, pp. 199–208. Springer, Berlin (2012). https://doi.org/10.1007/978-3-642-34103-8_20

26. SUMM Ai GmbH (2022). Summ - easy language [Online]. https://summ-ai.com/en/

27. DeepL SE (2022). Translate with the deepl api [Online]. https://www.deepl.com/pro-api

28. Sievers, T., Bender, M., Möller, R.: Connecting AI technologies as online services to a humanoid service robot. In: 15th International Conference on Computer and Automation Engineering, (ICCAE 2023), March 3–5 2023

29. QiSDK (2022). Listen [Online]. https://qisdk.softbankrobotics.com/sdk/doc/pepper-sdk/ch4_api/conversation/reference/listen.html

30. QiSDK (2022). Say [Online]. https://qisdk.softbankrobotics.com/sdk/doc/pepper-sdk/ch4_api/conversation/reference/say.html

31. QiSDK (2022). Chat [Online]. https://qisdk.softbankrobotics.com/sdk/doc/pepper-sdk/ch4_api/conversation/reference/chat.html

32. Wikipedia contributers (2022). Uncanny valley [Online]. https://en.wikipedia.org/wiki/Uncanny_valley

Process Selection for RPA Projects with MDCM: The Case of Izmir Bakircay University

Ali Mert Erdogan(✉) [iD] and Onur Dogan [iD]

Department of Management Information Systems, Izmir Bakircay University, 35665 Izmir, Turkey
{alimert.erdogan,onur.dogan}@bakircay.edu.tr

Abstract. Robotic Process Automation (RPA) has emerged as a powerful technology for streamlining business operations by automating repetitive tasks. It is important for public universities as it helps streamline administrative processes, improve operational efficiency, and free up staff resources, allowing the institutions to focus more on delivering quality education and enhancing the overall student experience. However, selecting the right processes for RPA implementation poses a challenge due to the multitude of criteria involved. To address this issue, this paper proposes a multi-criteria decision-making (MCDM) approach for RPA process selection. The objective of this research is to develop a systematic methodology that enables decision-makers to evaluate and prioritize RPA processes based on multiple criteria, such as process complexity, ROI, and strategic importance. The proposed methodology incorporates two MCDM techniques, including the Analytic Hierarchy Process (AHP) and the Technique for Order of Preference by Similarity to Ideal Solution (TOPSIS), to assist decision-makers in effectively assessing and ranking alternative RPA processes. AHP helps determine the relative weights of criteria, while TOPSIS ranks alternatives based on their similarity to an ideal solution. A case study was conducted to validate the effectiveness of the proposed methodology. Empirical results showed that "Campus Event Management" is the most suitable alternative for RPA implementation, followed by "Campus Facility Management" and "Library Management". In the study, sensitivity analysis was also performed by changing the weight values given for three different experts. The findings of this research contribute to the field of RPA process selection by providing a structured framework that facilitates the evaluation and prioritization of RPA processes. The proposed methodology empowers organizations to maximize the benefits of RPA implementation by selecting processes that align with strategic goals, enhance operational efficiency, and optimize resource utilization.

Keywords: Robotic Process Automation (RPA) · Process selection · Smart campus · Multi-criteria decision making (MCDM) · ChatGPT Expert

© The Author(s), under exclusive license to Springer Nature Switzerland AG 2024
M. A. Jabbar et al. (Eds.): AMLDA 2023, CCIS 2047, pp. 15–28, 2024.
https://doi.org/10.1007/978-3-031-55486-5_2

1   Introduction

The Seyrek Campus of Izmir Bakircay University spans across an area of 58,898 m^2. It includes a computer and internet-supported library, occupying 1,350 m^2 and accommodating up to 350 students. The campus also features meeting and conference halls covering 2,170 m^2, sports facilities spanning 1,151 m^2, an exhibition hall with a capacity of 500 people and a size of 700 m^2, as well as 41 classrooms and amphitheaters of various sizes. With a total of 586 academic and administrative staff members, the university serves a student population of 6,573. These attributes highlight the advantages offered by Izmir Bakircay University, as discussed in the aforementioned source. Similar benefits can be anticipated for other universities in proportion to their respective dynamics. Establishing and embracing technological infrastructure will lead to significant economic and social benefits for public institutions and organizations.

A dedicated Smart University and Digital Transformation coordination office has been established at the university to implement and oversee the Smart University Project[1]. One of its primary goals is to ensure both ecological and financial sustainability, as well as the sustainability of data management and digitalization. A smart reporting system is being developed using centralized data management and cloud computing technologies to promote sustainability. Through this system, authorized users can access relevant reports instantly within their areas of responsibility, facilitating efficient decision-making processes [5]. One of the responsibilities of the coordination office is to digitize and automate the university processes.

Robotic Process Automation (RPA) has gained significant attention in recent years as organizations seek ways to improve operational efficiency, reduce costs, and enhance productivity. RPA enables the automation of repetitive tasks and processes through the use of software robots, freeing up human resources for more strategic and value-added activities. However, selecting the most suitable processes for RPA implementation presents a complex decision-making challenge, considering the multitude of criteria involved and the varying characteristics of different processes.

In order to address this challenge, organizations are increasingly turning to multi-criteria decision-making (MCDM) methods to support the RPA process selection process. MCDM approaches provide a structured framework for evaluating and prioritizing alternatives based on multiple criteria, taking into account the interdependencies and trade-offs between these criteria. Two widely used MCDM methods, namely the Analytic Hierarchy Process (AHP) and the Technique for Order of Preference by Similarity to Ideal Solution (TOPSIS), play a crucial role in this study.

The Analytic Hierarchy Process (AHP) serves as a powerful tool in determining the relative weights of criteria in the decision-making process. AHP allows decision-makers to systematically evaluate the importance of each criterion and derive meaningful priority weights, facilitating a more objective and consistent

---

[1] https://sudt.bakircay.edu.tr/.

approach to decision-making. By structuring the decision problem hierarchically and employing pairwise comparisons, AHP enables decision-makers to capture the relative importance of criteria and ensure a comprehensive evaluation.

On the other hand, the Technique for Order of Preference by Similarity to Ideal Solution (TOPSIS) aids in ranking alternatives based on their similarity to an ideal solution. This method quantifies the proximity of each alternative to an ideal state, considering both the positive (beneficial) and negative (undesirable) aspects of the decision criteria. By calculating the distances between alternatives and the ideal solution, TOPSIS provides a comprehensive ranking that allows decision-makers to identify the most favorable options.

This study aims to leverage the strengths of both AHP and TOPSIS in the context of RPA process selection. By integrating these MCDM methods, decision-makers can effectively evaluate and prioritize RPA processes based on their inherent characteristics, organizational goals, and operational requirements. The combination of AHP and TOPSIS offers a comprehensive decision-making framework that accounts for the relative importance of criteria and provides a systematic approach to rank alternatives.

Through the application of this integrated approach, organizations can make informed decisions regarding the selection of RPA processes, aligning them with strategic objectives, optimizing resource allocation, and maximizing the benefits of RPA implementation. By streamlining the decision-making process and enabling a more objective evaluation, the utilization of AHP and TOPSIS contributes to improved decision quality and enhances the likelihood of successful RPA implementations.

In the following sections of this paper, the study delvea into the methodology, presents a case study validating the effectiveness of the proposed approach, discusses the results and analysis, and provides insights for future research and practical implications.

2   Literature Review

In recent years, the adoption of Robotic Process Automation (RPA) in various industries, including the education sector, has gained significant attention [15]. Several studies have explored the challenges and opportunities associated with RPA implementation, particularly in the context of process selection [21].

Selecting the most suitable processes for automation is indeed a major challenge in RPA projects. The success of an RPA implementation heavily depends on identifying the right processes to automate [11]. Organizations operate on diverse architectures with processes that exhibit variations in various characteristics. These characteristics play a significant role in determining the automation potential of a process. Due to the impact of various process characteristics on their automation potential, RPA cannot be universally applied and requires a thoughtful assessment and informed decision-making process [6]. Therefore, it is crucial for organizations to gain a comprehensive understanding of their processes in order to ensure the overall success of their RPA projects.

One of the key challenges faced when implementing Robotic Process Automation (RPA) is the failure to achieve the anticipated cost savings [22]. This issue can often be traced back to inaccurate predictions regarding the economic value of RPA at the process level. To address this problem, it becomes crucial to establish a system that can accurately determine the economic benefits of automating specific processes. This calls for the development of a decision-support system that can assist in the selection of processes for automation and enable detailed cost-benefit analysis [2]. Such a system would provide valuable insights into the potential financial gains and help organizations make informed decisions about which processes to automate, ensuring that RPA initiatives are aligned with realistic cost-saving expectations [18].

Lacity et al. [10] focused on the dynamic nature of processes and their varying automation potential over time. By regularly assessing the suitability of processes for automation, organizations can identify any shifts in requirements and make necessary adjustments to their RPA strategies.

Numerous researchers have dedicated their effort to developing the best decision-making methodologies over the last decades. Different MCDM techniques have been applied to rank alternatives according to specific criteria in various areas [1,4,12,16]. Researchers often combine AHP and TOPSIS to take advantage of their complementary strengths [8,9,19,20]. AHP helps in structuring the decision problem and determining the relative weights of criteria, while TOPSIS provides a quantitative ranking of alternatives based on their proximity to the ideal solution. This combination enables decision-makers to consider both subjective judgments and objective measurements in their decision-making process.

Luqman et al. [13] conducted a study that aimed to assess the appropriate manufacturing process and proposed an approach utilizing the AHP. This approach assists decision-makers in identifying the most suitable process for a particular manufacturing area, with the objective of minimizing production costs. Ghaleb et al. [7] compared the performances of different MCDM approaches for the selection of manufacturing processes. The criteria utilized in identifying the optimal manufacturing process were divided into categories such as productivity, accuracy, complexity, flexibility, material utilization, quality, and operational cost. Five different manufacturing processes were considered as potential alternatives. The findings demonstrated that each approach proved to be suitable for addressing the challenges associated with manufacturing process selection, particularly in facilitating group decision-making and handling uncertainties. Costa et al. [3] presented a study that aimed to facilitate the accurate selection of generic business processes for automation. Their approach involved the integration of AHP and TOPSIS methods.

In the literature, it was seen that there was a lack of research presented concepts to support the selection of appropriate processes for RPA implementation in specific areas [14,21]. This study seeks to close this gap by developing a comprehensive framework by integrating the AHP and TOPSIS. The aim is to utilize this framework for the selection of RPA processes within the context of a

Smart University case. By applying AHP and TOPSIS, it was aimed to provide a systematic approach that considers various criteria and evaluates the potential of different processes for automation. This research intends to contribute to the existing knowledge by offering a practical methodology that can assist organizations in making informed decisions regarding RPA process selection in the Smart University domain.

3 Methodology

The selected MCDM methodology for RPA process selection in this study combines the Analytic Hierarchy Process (AHP) and the Technique for Order of Preference by Similarity to Ideal Solution (TOPSIS). This integrated approach allows decision-makers to systematically evaluate and prioritize RPA processes based on multiple criteria, facilitating a comprehensive and objective decision-making process. The methodology involves several key steps, as outlined in Fig. 1.

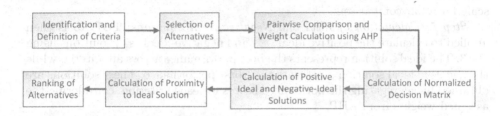

Fig. 1. Methodology steps

Step 1. Identification and Definition of Criteria: The first step is to identify and define the criteria that will be used to evaluate and compare the RPA processes. Criteria may include factors such as process complexity, return on investment (ROI), process stability, organizational impact, resource requirements, and scalability. It is essential to select criteria that are relevant to the specific context and objectives of the organization.

Step 2. Selection of Alternatives: A set of alternative RPA processes is selected for evaluation. These alternatives represent the different processes under consideration for automation. The alternatives should cover a range of processes that are representative of the organization's operational landscape and objectives.

Step 3. Pairwise Comparison and Weight Calculation using AHP: AHP is employed to determine the relative weights or importance of each criterion. Decision-makers are asked to make pairwise comparisons between criteria, assessing the relative importance of one criterion compared to another. These comparisons are made using a numerical scale (e.g., 1–5) to capture the degree of preference or importance. The AHP process ensures consistency and coherence in determining the relative importance of the criteria. In a consistent matrix,

w_j (weights vector) are calculated under a condition $\sum_{j=1}^{n} w_j$. The Consistency Index (CI) is calculated using Eq. 1.

$$CI = \frac{\lambda_{max} - n}{n - 1} \tag{1}$$

The Randomness Indicator (RI) depends on the size of the comparison matrix. For a 10-criterion matrix, RI is 1.49 [17]. After CI and RI values are calculated, consistency ratio (CR) is calculated by Eq. 2 To obtain a consistent comparison matrix, CR must be less than equal to 0,10.

$$CR = \frac{CI}{RI} \tag{2}$$

Step 4. Calculation of Normalized Decision Matrix: With the criteria weights established, the next step is to construct a decision matrix that represents the performance of each alternative with respect to the identified criteria. Decision-makers assign scores or ratings to each alternative based on how well they meet each criterion. These scores are often normalized to bring them to a common scale for a fair comparison.

Step 5. Calculation of Ideal and Negative-Ideal Solutions: TOPSIS is then applied to calculate the positive ideal (s_i^*) and negative-ideal (s_i^-) solutions using Eq. 3. The ideal solution represents the best performance across all criteria, while the negative-ideal solution represents the worst performance. These solutions are obtained by aggregating the normalized scores for each criterion, considering the assigned weights from AHP.

$$
\begin{aligned}
s_i^* &= \sqrt{\sum_{j=1}^{n} (v_{ij} - v_i^*)^2} \quad , i = 1, 2, \cdots, n \\
s_i^- &= \sqrt{\sum_{j=1}^{n} (v_{ij} - v_i^-)^2} \quad , i = 1, 2, \cdots, n
\end{aligned} \tag{3}
$$

Step 6. Calculation of Proximity to Ideal Solution: Using the ideal and negative-ideal solutions, the proximity of each alternative to these solutions is calculated. This proximity measurement reflects the similarity of each alternative to the ideal solution, taking into account both positive and negative aspects of the criteria. To obtain proximity to the ideal solution, relative closeness coefficients to the ideal solution are calculated by using Eq. 4.

$$C_i^* = \frac{s_i^*}{(s_i^* + s_i^-)} \quad i = 1, 2, \cdots, n \tag{4}$$

Step 7. Ranking of Alternatives: Based on the proximity calculations, the alternatives are ranked in descending order of their proximity to the ideal solution. The alternative with the highest proximity to the ideal solution is considered the most favorable and is ranked as the top choice for RPA process selection.

By following this methodology, decision-makers can systematically evaluate and prioritize RPA processes based on the identified criteria. The integration of AHP provides a consistent and structured approach to determine criteria weights, while TOPSIS enables a comprehensive ranking of alternatives based on their proximity to the ideal solution. This approach facilitates an informed decision-making process, supporting organizations in selecting the most suitable RPA processes for implementation.

4   Case Study

Step 1. Identification and Definition of Criteria

When selecting the best process for an RPA application, several criteria can be considered. The specific criteria may vary depending on the organization's goals, priorities, and industry. However, this study considers 10 commonly used criteria to assess the suitability of a process for RPA implementation.

- **Process Complexity (PC)**: Evaluate the complexity of the process in terms of the number of steps, decision points, variations, and dependencies. Less complex processes are generally more suitable for automation as they are easier to model and implement with RPA.
- **Repetitiveness and Rule-based Nature (RRN)**: Assess the extent to which the process involves repetitive tasks or follows predefined rules. Processes that involve high volumes of repetitive, rule-based activities are typically well-suited for RPA, as software robots can perform these tasks efficiently and accurately.
- **Transaction Volume (TV)**: Consider the volume of transactions or activities associated with the process. RPA is particularly effective in handling high-volume transactional processes, where human involvement can be time-consuming and prone to errors.
- **Data Standardization and Availability (DSA)**: Evaluate the availability and standardization of data required for the process. RPA relies on structured and consistent data inputs. Processes with well-defined and readily available data are more suitable for automation.
- **Exception Handling (EH)**: Assess the frequency and complexity of exceptions or deviations that occur within the process. RPA is best suited for processes with minimal exceptions or well-defined rules for handling them. Complex exception handling may require human intervention and can limit the effectiveness of RPA.
- **ROI and Cost-Benefit Analysis (RCBA)**: Consider the potential return on investment (ROI) and cost-benefit analysis associated with automating the process. Evaluate the expected cost savings, efficiency gains, error reduction, and productivity improvements that can be achieved through RPA implementation.
- **Process Stability (PS)**: Assess the stability and consistency of the process. Processes with a stable and predictable nature are more suitable for RPA, as they minimize the need for frequent modifications or adaptations in the automation setup.

- **Compliance and Regulatory Requirements (CRR)**: Consider any compliance or regulatory requirements associated with the process. Evaluate whether RPA implementation can help ensure compliance with regulations, improve auditability, and reduce the risk of non-compliance.
- **Strategic Importance (SI)**: Assess the strategic significance of the process to the organization's overall goals and objectives. Processes that align closely with strategic objectives, customer satisfaction, or competitive advantage may be prioritized for RPA implementation.
- **Scalability and Future Potential (SFP)**: Consider the scalability and future potential of the process. Evaluate whether the process is likely to grow or evolve in the future and whether RPA can accommodate such scalability. Processes with significant growth potential can provide long-term benefits through RPA.

Step 2. Selection of Alternatives

Under the smart campus application, several alternative processes can be considered for automation using RPA. These processes aim to enhance the efficiency, effectiveness, and overall experience within the campus environment. Here are some examples of alternative processes that can be targeted for RPA implementation:

- **Student Enrollment and Registration (SER)**: Automating the process of student enrollment and registration can streamline administrative tasks such as collecting student information, verifying documents, generating student IDs, and enrolling students in courses. RPA can facilitate seamless and error-free enrollment processes, reducing manual efforts and improving accuracy.
- **Course and Curriculum Management (CCM)**: Automating the process of course and curriculum management can involve activities such as scheduling classes, managing course catalogs, assigning instructors, and updating curriculum details. RPA can help ensure timely updates, optimize resource allocation, and facilitate efficient course planning.
- **Campus Facility Management (CFM)**: Automating facility management processes can include tasks such as managing maintenance requests, scheduling repairs, tracking inventory, and monitoring equipment. RPA can enable timely notifications, efficient resource allocation, and proactive maintenance, leading to improved facility management within the campus.
- **Library Services (LS)**: Automating library services can involve activities such as cataloging books, managing loan requests, sending overdue reminders, and tracking inventory. RPA can streamline these processes, ensuring accurate book records, efficient loan management, and improved access to library resources.
- **Financial Aid and Scholarship Processing (FASP)**: Automating the financial aid and scholarship processing process can include tasks such as verifying eligibility, processing applications, calculating awards, and disbursing funds. RPA can expedite the processing time, enhance accuracy, and provide a seamless experience for students applying for financial aid or scholarships.

- **Student Support Services (SSS)**: Automating student support services can involve tasks such as managing student queries, providing information about campus services, facilitating appointment scheduling with advisors, and tracking student progress. RPA can enhance the responsiveness of support services, improve communication channels, and ensure timely assistance to students.
- **Campus Event Management (CEM)**: Automating the process of campus event management can include activities such as event scheduling, venue booking, registration management, and communication with attendees. RPA can streamline event planning, automate event reminders, and improve the overall efficiency of organizing campus events.
- **Campus Security and Access Control (CSAC)**: Automating security and access control processes can involve tasks such as monitoring security systems, managing access permissions, and generating incident reports. RPA can enhance security measures, automate access control processes, and facilitate real-time monitoring of campus security systems.

Step 3. Pairwise Comparison and Weight Calculation using AHP

Pairwise comparisons are conducted to determine the relative importance or weights of each criterion, relying on expert judgments. In this study, a comparison matrix containing evaluations related to criteria has been created using twice ChatGPT as experts and one human expert. The pairwise comparison matrix containing the criterion evaluations of ChatGPT Expert 1 is given in Table 1.

Table 1. A sample criteria evaluation: ChatGPT Expert 1

	PC	RRN	TV	DSA	EH	RCBA	PS	CRR	SI	SFP
PC	1	3	2	4	3	4	2	3	2	3
RRN	0.33	1	0.33	3	2	3	2	2	2	3
TV	0.50	3.03	1	4	3	4	3	3	3	2.5
DSA	0.25	0.33	0.25	1	0.33	0.33	0.33	0.33	0.5	3
EH	0.33	0.50	0.33	3.03	1	1.5	2	2	2	4
RCBA	0.25	0.33	0.25	3.03	0.67	1	0.5	0.5	0.5	3
PS	0.50	0.50	0.33	3.03	0.50	2	1	2	2	2.5
CRR	0.33	0.50	0.33	3.03	0.50	2	0.50	1	2	3
SI	0.50	0.50	0.33	2.00	0.50	2	0.50	0.5	1	3.5
SFP	0.33	0.33	0.40	0.33	0.25	0.33	0.40	0.33	0.20	1

Expert weight: 0.30, CR 0.065 < 0.10

The three comparison matrices containing the evaluations of experts on criteria have been normalized, and then consistency ratios have been calculated. To aggregate these matrices, the opinions of the experts have been weighted. ChatGPT Expert 1, ChatGPT Expert 2 and human expert have weights of 0.30, 0.25, and 0.45, respectively. To bring all the values onto a common scale, allowing for meaningful comparisons and subsequent calculations, the comparison matrix is normalized. Table 2 presents the normalized comparison matrix.

Table 2. Aggregated and then normalized evaluations of criteria: ChatGPT Expert 1

	PC	RRN	TV	DSA	EH	RCBA	PS	CRR	SI	SFP	Weight
PC	0.259	0.406	0.357	0.263	0.228	0.214	0.188	0.188	0.136	0.137	**0.238**
RRN	0.086	0.135	0.197	0.197	0.173	0.181	0.146	0.137	0.125	0.110	**0.149**
TV	0.096	0.091	0.132	0.230	0.203	0.211	0.176	0.163	0.146	0.107	**0.155**
DSA	0.065	0.045	0.038	0.066	0.107	0.097	0.094	0.086	0.085	0.093	**0.078**
EH	0.113	0.077	0.064	0.061	0.099	0.126	0.146	0.137	0.125	0.121	**0.107**
RCBA	0.073	0.045	0.038	0.041	0.047	0.060	0.097	0.108	0.104	0.113	**0.072**
PS	0.082	0.055	0.045	0.042	0.040	0.037	0.060	0.095	0.085	0.071	**0.061**
CRR	0.070	0.050	0.041	0.039	0.037	0.028	0.032	0.051	0.134	0.111	**0.059**
SI	0.081	0.046	0.038	0.033	0.034	0.025	0.030	0.016	0.042	0.098	**0.044**
SFP	0.075	0.049	0.049	0.028	0.032	0.021	0.034	0.018	0.017	0.040	**0.036**

Just like the evaluation of criteria, three experts evaluated the alternatives with respect to the criteria. Table 3 shows the evaluations of ChatGPT Expert 1.

Table 3. A sample of alternatives evaluation: ChatGPT Expert 1

	PC	RRN	TV	DSA	EH	RCBA	PS	CRR	SI	SFP
SER	3	3	3	3	3	3	3	3	3	3
CCM	4	4	4	4	4	4	4	4	4	4
CFM	2	2	2	2	2	2	2	2	2	2
LS	3	3	3	3	3	3	3	3	3	3
FASP	4	4	4	4	4	4	4	4	4	4
SSS	4	4	4	4	4	4	4	4	4	4
CEM	3	3	3	3	3	3	3	3	3	3
CSAC	4	4	4	4	4	4	4	4	4	4

Step 4. Calculation of Normalized Decision Matrix
The three expert evaluations obtained for the alternatives have been aggregated considering the previously used weights and then normalized. Table 4 shows the normalized evaluations for ChatGPT Expert 1.

Step 5. Calculation of Positive-Ideal and Negative-Ideal Solutions
The best and worst possible values for each criterion are used as reference points to evaluate the alternatives. In this step, the distance values to the positive

Table 4. Aggregated and then normalized evaluations of alternatives: ChatGPT Expert 1

	PC	RRN	TV	DSA	EH	RCBA	PS	CCRR	SI	SFP
SER	0.37	0.30	0.46	0.36	0.27	0.38	0.32	0.40	0.38	0.39
CCM	0.32	0.39	0.33	0.32	0.35	0.28	0.37	0.30	0.36	0.32
CFM	0.27	0.35	0.36	0.31	0.32	0.25	0.37	0.33	0.29	0.36
LS	0.32	0.34	0.26	0.41	0.37	0.30	0.37	0.30	0.29	0.32
FASP	0.40	0.28	0.36	0.36	0.37	0.48	0.32	0.37	0.46	0.29
SSS	0.40	0.34	0.33	0.39	0.37	0.38	0.30	0.30	0.36	0.39
CEM	0.29	0.34	0.32	0.28	0.26	0.28	0.37	0.27	0.26	0.36
CSAC	0.43	0.46	0.38	0.38	0.47	0.41	0.40	0.50	0.38	0.39

Table 5. Positive and negative ideals

	PC	RRN	TV	DSA	EH	RCBA	PS	CCRR	SI	SFP
Positive Ideal (V+)	0.097	0.064	0.070	0.029	0.051	0.033	0.027	0.030	0.021	0.021
Negative Ideal (V-)	0.061	0.040	0.041	0.020	0.028	0.018	0.020	0.016	0.012	0.016

ideal and negative ideal solution values were obtained using the formulas in Eq. 3. Table 5 represents the positive and negative ideal values for each criterion.

Step 6. Calculation of Proximity to Ideal Solution

The calculation of proximity to the ideal solution involves comparing each alternative to the positive-ideal and negative-ideal solutions to determine the relative closeness of each alternative to the ideal solution. In this step, the closeness coefficients (CI) to the ideal solution were calculated using the formula in Eq. 4. The results of the relevant calculations can be seen in Table 6.

Step 7. Ranking of Alternatives

Alternatives are ranked according to the closeness index. Campus Event Management is the most suitable alternative for RPA implementation, followed by Campus Facility Management. "Campus Security" and "Financial Aid and

Table 6. Closeness coefficients

	Si+	Si-	Ci	Rank
SER	0.036	0.040	0.468	5
CCM	0.040	0.026	0.603	4
CFM	0.050	0.020	0.715	2
LS	0.047	0.022	0.676	3
FASP	0.033	0.041	0.442	7
SSS	0.032	0.038	0.458	6
CEM	0.052	0.015	0.782	1
CSAC	0.013	0.057	0.185	8

Table 7. Sensitivity analysis for decision makers' importance

Scenarios	Weights			Rankings							
	E1	E2	E3	1	2	3	4	5	6	7	8
1	0.30	0.25	0.45	CEM	CFM	LS	CCM	SE	SSS	FASP	CS
2	0.33	0.33	0.33	CEM	CFM	LS	CCM	SSS	SE	FASP	CS
3	0.25	0.25	0.50	CEM	CFM	LS	CCM	SE	SSS	FASP	CS
4	0.25	0.50	0.25	CEM	CCM	CFM	LS	SE	SSS	FASP	CS
5	0.50	0.25	0.25	CEM	CFM	LS	CCM	SSS	SE	FASP	CS
6	0.10	0.10	0.80	CFM	CEM	LS	CCM	SE	FASP	SSS	CS
7	0.10	0.80	0.10	CEM	CCM	LS	SE	CFM	SSS	FASP	CS
8	0.80	0.10	0.10	CFM	CEM	LS	CCM	SSS	SE	FASP	CS

Scholarship Processing" are the least significant alternatives for Izmir Bakircay University.

5   Sensitivity Analysis

The ranking results for seven different weight additional scenarios are provided in Table 7 o interpret the impact of expert weights on ranking. Scenario 1 indicates the initial scenario used in the study. Scenario 2 assumes what happens if three experts are equally weighted. The ranking has changed only for "Student Support Services (SSS)" and "Student Enrolment and Registration (SER)". The first four alternatives remained in the same ranking.

In Scenario 4 and Scenario 7, where ChatGPT Expert 2 has a higher weight compared to other scenarios, the 2nd alternative, "Course and Curriculum Management (CCM")", was ranked higher. It can be said that this alternative is relatively more important for ChatGPT Expert 2 in these scenarios.

In Scenario 6 and Scenario 8, where ChatGPT Expert 1 and Human Expert (Expert 3) were weighted at 0.80, "Campus Facility Management (CFM)" rises to the first rank. This indicates that the evaluations of these two experts have a stronger influence on the ranking of "Campus Facility Management". Therefore, it can be concluded that in these scenarios, where the weights differ, ChatGPT Expert 2 has a greater influence on the ranking of the "Course and Curriculum Management" alternative, while ChatGPT Expert 1 and Human Expert have a stronger impact on the ranking of the "Campus Facility Management".

6   Conclusion and Discussion

RPA has recently gained significant attention and has become a technology that is applied in various fields. Nevertheless, the successful implementation of this concept faces various challenges, one of which involves the lack of frameworks and methods. The significance of process selection in RPA lies in its ability to influence the effectiveness of automation projects. Thoughtful evaluation and choice of processes to automate are critical for attaining desired outcomes and maximizing the advantages of RPA implementation.

This study puts forward an essential contribution towards the implementation of RPA by taking the smart university domain as a case study. The approach involved devising a methodology that enables universities to acquire a set of processes ranked by their importance for RPA. In addition, obtaining evaluations from experts in real-life MDCM implementations can be challenging and time-consuming. In contrast to other studies, this research demonstrates that consistent evaluations ($CI < 0.10$) conducted at different times using ChatGPT indicate a decreased reliance on real experts.

As a result of the study, according to expert assessments, the ranking of the suitability of alternative processes for RPA projects in the context of Smart University was "Campus Event Management", "Campus Facility Management", "Library Services", and "Course and Curriculum Management", respectively.

In the sensitivity results obtained by changing the expert weights, it was observed that the "Campus Facility Management" alternative ranked first and the "Course and Curriculum Management" alternative ranked second in some scenarios. Apart from these, the rankings for different scenarios gave similar results.

Despite the method's contribution to assessing the potential for process automation, the outcomes of its application are still weak. Regarding limitations and future work, despite the promising outcomes demonstrated by this research, further empirical investigations are necessary to determine the usability of this method.

References

1. Abdel-Basset, M., Manogaran, G., Gamal, A., Smarandache, F.: A group decision making framework based on neutrosophic TOPSIS approach for smart medical device selection. J. Med. Syst. **43**, 1–13 (2019)
2. Akyol, S., Dogan, O., Er, O.: Process automation with digital robots under smart university concept. In: Abraham, A., Pllana, S., Casalino, G., Ma, K., Bajaj, A. (eds.) Intelligent Systems Design and Applications. Lecture Notes in Networks and Systems, vol. 646, pp. 242–251. Springer, Cham (2022). https://doi.org/10.1007/978-3-031-27440-4_23
3. Costa, D.S., Mamede, H.S., da Silva, M.M.: A method for selecting processes for automation with AHP and TOPSIS. Heliyon **9**(3) (2023)
4. Dewi, N.K., Putra, A.S.: Decision support system for head of warehouse selection recommendation using analytic hierarchy process (AHP) method. In: International Conference Universitas Pekalongan 2021, vol. 1, pp. 43–50 (2021)
5. Dogan, O., Cengiz Tirpan, E.: Process mining methodology for digital processes under smart campus concept. Bilecik Seyh Edebali Univ. J. Sci. **9**(2), 1006–1018 (2022)
6. Geyer-Klingeberg, J., Nakladal, J., Baldauf, F., Veit, F.: Process mining and robotic process automation: a perfect match. In: BPM (Dissertation/Demos/Industry), pp. 124–131 (2018)

7. Ghaleb, A.M., Kaid, H., Alsamhan, A., Mian, S.H., Hidri, L.: Assessment and comparison of various MCDM approaches in the selection of manufacturing process. Adv. Mater. Sci. Eng. **2020**, 1–16 (2020)
8. Jayant, A., Gupta, P., Garg, S., Khan, M.: TOPSIS-AHP based approach for selection of reverse logistics service provider: a case study of mobile phone industry. Procedia Eng. **97**, 2147–2156 (2014)
9. Kumar, R., Singh, K., Jain, S.K.: A combined AHP and TOPSIS approach for prioritizing the attributes for successful implementation of agile manufacturing. Int. J. Prod. Perform. Manage. **69**, 1395–1417 (2020)
10. Lacity, M., Willcocks, L.P., Craig, A.: Robotic process automation: mature capabilities in the energy sector. The Outsourcing Unit Working Research Paper Series 15/05 (2015)
11. Lindström, J., Kyösti, P., Delsing, J.: European roadmap for industrial process automation (2018)
12. Liu, F., Aiwu, G., Lukovac, V., Vukic, M.: A multicriteria model for the selection of the transport service provider: a single valued neutrosophic DEMATEL multicriteria model. Dec. Making: Appl. Manage. Eng. **1**(2), 121–130 (2018)
13. Luqman, M., Rosli, M., Khor, C., Zambree, S., Jahidi, H.: Manufacturing process selection of composite bicycle's crank arm using analytical hierarchy process (AHP). In: IOP Conference Series: Materials Science and Engineering, vol. 318, p. 012058. IOP Publishing (2018)
14. Marrella, A.: What automated planning can do for business process management. In: Teniente, E., Weidlich, M. (eds.) Business Process Management Workshops. Lecture Notes in Business Information Processing, vol. 308, pp. 7–19. Springer, Cham (2018). https://doi.org/10.1007/978-3-319-74030-0_1
15. Olucoglu, M., Dogan, O., Akkol, E., Keskin, B.: Digitized and automated a university process with robotic process automation. Erzincan Univ. J. Sci. Technol. **16**(1), 58–66 (2023)
16. Rahiminezhad Galankashi, M., Mokhatab Rafiei, F., Ghezelbash, M.: Portfolio selection: a fuzzy-ANP approach. Finan. Innov. **6**(1), 17 (2020)
17. Saaty, R.: The analytic hierarchy process-what it is and how it is used. Math. Model. **9**(3), 161–176 (1987)
18. Schmitz, M., Dietze, C., Czarnecki, C.: Enabling digital transformation through robotic process automation at deutsche telekom. In: Urbach, N., Roglinger, M. (eds.) Digitalization cases: How organizations rethink their business for the digital age, pp. 15–33. Springer, Cham (2019). https://doi.org/10.1007/978-3-319-95273-4_2
19. Sukmawati, M., Setiawan, A.D.: A conceptual model of green supplier selection in the manufacturing industry using AHP and TOPSIS methods. In: 2022 7th International Conference on Business and Industrial Research (ICBIR), pp. 659–664. IEEE (2022)
20. Vinodh, S., Prasanna, M., Prakash, N.H.: Integrated fuzzy AHP-TOPSIS for selecting the best plastic recycling method: a case study. Appl. Math. Model. **38**(19–20), 4662–4672 (2014)
21. Wanner, J., Hofmann, A., Fischer, M., Imgrund, F., Janiesch, C., Geyer-Klingeberg, J.: Process selection in RPA projects-towards a quantifiable method of decision making. In: Fortieth International Conference on Information Systems, Munich 2019, vol. 6 (2019)
22. Willcocks, L.P., Lacity, M., Craig, A.: The it function and robotic process automation. The Outsourcing Unit Working Research Paper Series 15/05 (2015)

The Metaverse: A Multidisciplinary Perspective on the Future of Human Interaction

Yuvraj Singh[1], Devangana Sujay[1(✉)], Shishir Kumar Shandilya[2],
and Smita Shandilya[3]

[1] VIT Bhopal University, Bhopal, India
devanganasujay@gmail.com
[2] Devi Ahilya Vishwavidyalaya, Indore, India
[3] Sagar Institute of Research and Technology, Bhopal, India

Abstract. As technology advances in the path to becoming smart cities, the Metaverse emerges as a dominant potential future. By utilizing affordable high-end devices, augmented reality offers immersive internet experiences with greater capabilities. The Metaverse fosters realism, facilitating remote cooperation, immersive digital environments, enhanced interactions, and more. This paper proposes that the metaverse needs to prioritize human-centricity. In the Metaverse, it is seen that the human population comprises the largest proportion. Consequently, this study begins with providing an introduction to the origins, characteristics, and related technologies of the metaverse, along with an exploration of the concept of the human-centric metaverse (HCM). Next, we will examine the expression of anthropocentrism inside the Metaverse. Subsequently, we will now address certain current issues about the development of HCM. This study presents a comprehensive examination of the utilization of human-centric technologies inside the metaverse, together with the corresponding application scenarios for the Human-Centric Metaverse (HCM). This document aims to offer academics and developers guidance and insights for the building of a human-centric Metaverse.

Keywords: Metaverse · Virtual Reality · Augmented Reality · Extended Reality · Human-centered Metaverse

1 Introduction

"Metaverse" is a terminology that has attained fresh fame and hype amongst the masses, most specifically belonging to academic and technological sectors. Its roots trace back to the year 1992 pointing out the name of Neal Stephenson, author of the novel, Snow Crash in which the depiction is of varied kinds and revolves around the Internet which is coupled with Virtual Reality (VR), Augmented Reality (AR) and Avatars. This innovative integration of the physical and digital realms employs avatars, blockchain technology, and HMDs. Much later,

M. A. Jabbar et al. (Eds.): AMLDA 2023, CCIS 2047, pp. 29–43, 2024.
https://doi.org/10.1007/978-3-031-55486-5_3

it was in 2003 when a multimedia platform named 'Second Life' was ideated and developed at Linden Lab which capacitated audiences to virtually make communications with one another and gain access to control of avatars, this was coined as the pioneer in this domain. The notable features of the 3D interactive atmospheres of Roblox and Fortnite were avatar creation and social interactions. There are setbacks that Metaverse is yet to overcome one of them being platform independence and integration into this gamified realm, but what almost nullifies its existence is its extremely extensive user base across the globe, which has been noted since the mid-2000s. Irrespective of the newly born technology's shortcomings, it has a long way to go in the direction of revolutionizing.

To effectively cater to the needs and well-being of individuals, Metaverse should adopt a human-centered approach. This entails placing humans at the forefront of its design and functionality, with a focus on facilitating meaningful connections while also ensuring the protection of privacy and safety. The ethical utilization of immersive technologies should aim to empower persons and effectively bridge physical divisions. The present moment calls for a transformative approach to enhancing connectivity, education, productivity, and leisure activities within the realm of digital technology, with a primary focus on serving the collective welfare of humanity. The adoption of a human-centered approach emphasizes the well-being, agency, and values of users, hence fostering ethical development and inclusivity. The metaverse can provide good influence by dismantling barriers, promoting collaboration, and enriching educational experiences. In essence, it converts the digital domain into a medium for fostering interpersonal relationships, individual development, and the advancement of society.

Considering the stage at which Metaverse is, it holds the potential to be cross-matched with various other technologies which find need to be used in correspondence with methodological implementations. Due to the degree of reliance of this technology on users, the growth, further evolution, and sustenance will be highly decisive for the human factor. [18] This points to the fact that any development scope must take into account the prioritization required for human participation. It should also be able to fortify secure spaces that ensure human rights. [10] Implementation strategizing should also have its focus point on the origin, which would be the human factor. In practical terms, creating such an immersive digital space endeavors to yield goods and services forging links between virtual realms with tangible ones catering towards societal advantages. By the utilization of a multitude of mediums, social interaction by virtualized means can appear seamless, a proof of the potentiality this possesses. Therefore, its foundational blueprint must follow principles originating from the core of human values by operating primarily with a proactive approach focused on the well-being and interests of individuals rather than self-indulgence [25].

Market data indicates that the global Metaverse industry attained a valuation of USD 38.85 billion in 2021, with projected growth to USD 47.48 billion in 2022 and an estimated worth of USD 829 billion by 2030 [33]. This trend has propelled organizations to evaluate strategies for assimilating the Metaverse into their extant business models [9]. Originally rooted in the discipline of Human-Computer Interaction (HCI), the Metaverse has evolved into a networked assemblage of virtual domains facilitating large-scale interactions among users. The realms within the Metaverse serve as arenas for multiplayer gaming, collaborative learning, remote work scenarios, and diverse other applications [15]. However, the large-scale development of the metaverse virtual worlds is now affected by the lack of necessary technology frameworks and infrastructure. Researchers are currently looking at how the metaverse will affect society and tackle issues with privacy, trust, and psychological aspects of its uptake. Unfortunately, there is still a dearth of studies examining the difficulties and possible uses of human-computer interaction in the metaverse. There are many obstacles standing in the way of a seamless HCI future for the metaverse due to the small body of scholarly work that is now available [2,34].

The strict maintenance and conformity to ethical regulations aiming to harmonize technical growth with the welfare of humans make the growth of Metaverse an ideal one. It points out the fact that apart from the entrepreneurship aspect, the human factor is the focus that should be paid the most attention. [37]. Rather than the concentration being stuck at the economic maximization criteria, it should make sure to approximate the probability of user grievances of any kind in this gamified platform to its bare minimum thus, reflecting on the human-centric goal attainment.

Additionally, instead of the idea of Metaverse being a singularly termed organization, it should be ruled upon by a comprehensible and ideal set of regulatory measures. Users should have the power to control the virtual world. This ensures the long-term success of this technical masterpiece [30].

The Metaverse places a high value on inclusiveness and accessibility. It needs to serve as a platform that promotes DEI (Diversity, Equity, and Inclusion). Anyone should be able to take part in various events in the metaverse, irrespective of their social status or financial situation. The Metaverse of the future is seen in this vision as a place where people from various backgrounds-such as race, nation, industry, position, or gender-can freely interact and communicate. The Metaverse has a lot of potential if it embraces a human-centric approach to the future. The Metaverse can bridge geographical gaps and allow people to join and communicate within this virtual environment with the right technology backing [29,36].

The structure of this paper is in such a way that there exist divisions of several sections each elaborating a specific concept, one notable one being MOE or Metaverse of Everything elaborately explained in Sect. 2. The area of focus of Sect. 3 is the provision of clear ideas of the literature used for the ideation. The Sect. 4 is the one that showcases the core concept of the Human-Centered Metaverse. The pivotal technologies of HCM and more are comprehensively detailed and discussed in Sect. 5. Finally, an extensive evaluation and applications of HCM are presented in Sect. 6. Section 7 focuses on future works for HCM and finally, in Sect. 8 we conclude this research.

2 Motivation, Foundational Technologies, and Essential Components

The metaverse, a virtual realm in the digital realm, offers a vision that prioritizes user well-being, inclusivity, and ethical considerations. This vision aims to create a space where users can express themselves freely, connect genuinely, and foster creativity (see Table 1).

Snow Crash, a novel by Neal Stephenson, introduced the concept of the metaverse in 1992. The term "Avatar" emerged as a result of this evolution, mirroring the maturation of immersive digital experiences. The metaverse's impact on Human-Computer Interaction (HCI) has been studied through a Scopus database search, revealing an increase in applicable publications and a trend in the occurrence of terms like "security" and "privacy" less frequently than expected. The distribution of these documents can be seen in Figs. 1 and 2.

Table 1. Development of Metaverse Terminology Year-wise

Year	Term	Description
1992	Metaverse	Coined by Neal Stephenson in his science fiction novel "Snow Crash" to describe a virtual world
1995	Avatar	Referring to digital representations of users in virtual environments
2004	Web 2.0	Not specific to metaverse, but marked a shift towards more interactive and collaborative web
2007	Augmented Reality	Technology blending digital content with the real world, relevant to metaverse discussions
2007	Virtual Reality	VR headsets and experiences gained attention as part of the metaverse conversation
2016	Mixed Reality	Combining aspects of both AR and VR, relevant to metaverse technologies
2021	Metaverse Economy	Emphasizing the economic aspects of virtual worlds and digital assets
2021	Non-Fungible Tokens	NFTs gained prominence for representing ownership of digital assets in the metaverse
2021	Decentralized Metaverse	Concepts related to Blockchain and Decentralized Technologies in the Metaverse

Here, the concept of major discussion will be, MoE or Metaverse of Everything. For a better understanding of the same, a three-layered architecture relevant to the newly transforming research exploration shall be utilized. The description deals with a comprehensive description that incorporates components that need to be addressed to define the concept (Fig. 3).

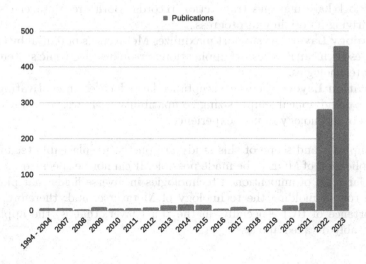

Fig. 1. Graph shows the Metaverse research article surge after Facebook rebrand.

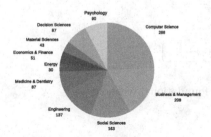

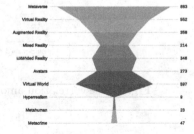

(a) The chart depiction presented showcases the volume of research articles focused on the subject of "Metaverse" published over the past few years. It provides a quantitative representation of the number of articles that specifically explore and investigate the concept of the Metaverse.

(b) The funnel chart presented illustrates the number of research articles mentioning the keyword associated with the "Metaverse" published over the past few years. This visualization offers a quantitative representation of the number of articles dedicated to exploring and investigating the concept of the Metaverse.

Fig. 2. Charts showcase Metaverse research trends, article volume, and keyword mentions.

1. **Infrastructure Layer:** AI is computer science replicating human functions, while Blockchain manages transaction records. Both are Metaverse's backbone, driving its origin and progress.
2. **Technology Layer:** AI support maximizes Metaverse's potential by enhancing its research capabilities. AI application personifies electronic systems with diverse technologies.
3. **Application Layer:** The user acceptance layer focuses on captivating interfaces for broad appeal, emphasizing compatibility with everyday devices and the role of technology in user experience.

The emphasis and scope of this study are on the irreplaceable technologies for the application of MOE to be made possible. It cannot be specified more that there is a large set of unmentioned technologies in diverse fields that play their respective role in molding the technology of Metaverse. and, therefore, MOE. The importance of HCI especially, in the third layer, that is, the application layer is notably detailed above.

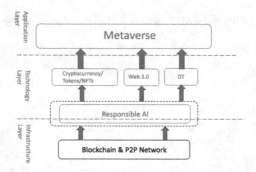

Fig. 3. The correlation among foundational technologies

2.1   Blockchain and NFTs

Blockchain's transformative impact stems from its decentralized, unchangeable ledger. Public blockchains enable open participation, influence various domains such as IoT, foster peer-to-peer networks, and reshape traditional paradigms. Several blockchain-based assets have use cases in the context of MoE (Metaverse of Everything) networks. Here are brief overviews of each definition.

1. **NFT 1.0:** These unique tokens are intricately connected to physical or digital objects, such as artwork, music albums, or office files. NFTs on the Ethereum platform follow the guidelines defined in the Ethereum Request for Comment (ERC-721). They possess immutable content and each NFT has a distinctive value that separates them as nonfungible assets [11].

2. **Dynamic non-fungible token (dNFT) or NFT 2.0:** The term "dynamic" refers to NFT headers that can be altered or modified. For instance, in a game, a character can enhance and acquire new abilities as the player progresses through different levels. Unlike standard NFTs, dNFTs show decreased levels of security [11].
3. **Cryptocurrency:** This digital currency operates on a specialized blockchain, and its value can fluctuate or remain stable. It gains strength from cryptographic tools [23].
4. **Tokens:** Tokens are cryptocurrencies developed on existing blockchains, typically public blockchains. They lack their independent blockchain and would become inaccessible if the underlying host blockchain were to disappear.

2.2 Responsible AI

The Metaverse is transforming the way AI is developed, requiring responsible governance mechanisms to ensure transparency, mitigate risks, and uphold user values. These mechanisms should foster interdisciplinary collaboration, prioritize user rights, and adhere to societal values, ensuring that Metaverse AI systems adhere to responsible principles [3].

2.3 Web 3.0

Web 3.0 embodies decentralization, enhancing user connectivity and accessibility. It incorporates various domains like Cryptocurrency, Blockchain, NFTs, and Tokenizations, ensuring decentralization and practicality. These features enable financial maximization through content creation, improving the overall Web experience [12].

2.4 Digital Twin

Digital twins, utilizing AI and IoT, offer a transformative framework for virtual representations of physical entities in the Metaverse realm. These digital replicas enable real-time data synchronization and interaction, providing a seamless connection between physical and virtual entities. Their hyperrealism and personalization have the potential to revolutionize various industries [14].

2.5 Metaverse

The Metaverse, a virtual world, allows users to engage in immersive activities using VR and advanced networks. This technology facilitates real-time interactions, information sharing, and resource utilization among diverse users. However, it requires complex system designs, data processing, and strong security frameworks to ensure authenticity and privacy (Fig. 4).

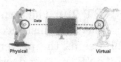

(a) The correlation between a physical   (b) The architecture of a
entity and its Digital Twin   Metaverse.

Fig. 4. The Metaverse's architecture, involving data synchronization, behavioral correspondence, and immersive experiences, is shaped by the correlation between physical entities and their Digital Twins. This intricate tapestry defines the complex ecosystem.

Architecture and Layers of the Metaverse: The metaverse is structured into a very complex and diverse seven-layer architecture, with each layer fulfilling a specific role and adding to the ecosystem's total effectiveness and complexity [32].

1. **Experience Layer:** The layer comprises fascinating and interactive metaverse experiences. These amazing experiences use cutting-edge technologies such as VR and AR to offer consumers immersive sensory experiences within the virtual world.
2. **Discovery Layer:** The discovery layer plans to simplify and customize content exploration throughout the metaverse. By implementing advanced algorithms and AI techniques, it analyzes user preferences, behavior, and contextual information. This enables the provision of personalized recommendations and facilitates effective search results.
3. **Creator Economy Layer:** This layer is dedicated to helping the economic aspects. It empowers both businesses and creators to effectively monetize their digital creations. This comprises various tools that involve intellectual property rights, revenue generation strategy, and digital assets ownership.
4. **Spatial Computing Layer:** The foundation of the metaverse is spatial computing, a technology that allows the seamless amalgamation of virtual and actual spaces. Real-time tracking, spatial awareness, and seamless interaction between the digital and physical worlds are made possible by this layer, which makes use of cutting-edge technologies including sensor networks, computer vision, and spatial mapping.
5. **Decentralization Layer:** The distributed and secure infrastructure for the metaverse is the primary goal of this layer. It makes use of decentralized protocols and blockchain technology to establish trust, transparency, immutability, robustness, and autonomy of the metaverse.
6. **Human Interface Layer:** User interfaces in the metaverse enable users to interact intuitively with the virtual world using natural language processing, gesture detection, and brain-computer interfaces.

7. **Infrastructure Layer:** The infrastructure layer, crucial for the enormous scale and complexity of the metaverse ecosystem, provides hardware, networking, computational resources, cloud services, and data storage capabilities.

The metaverse architecture consists of seven layers, enhancing user experiences, content discovery, economic opportunities, decentralization, security, and user-friendly interfaces.

3   Litrature Review

The Metaverse, based on AR and VR, offers vast potential for various sectors but poses risks like addiction and misinformation. Safety is crucial for global connections [25]. The article by Cheng Dai et al., "Sparse Attack Method for Metaverse Human Action Recognition," explores advanced computer science in Metaverse safety, enhancing user action recognition through strong attributes and mathematical functions. It highlights model vulnerabilities and promotes Metaverse for education and security awareness.

Lu et al. explore metaverse's medical applications, highlighting the International Association and Alliance of Metaverse in Medicine, MIOT, financial optimization, and potential VR, AR, MR involvement. Addressing security, ethics, and research-driven growth is crucial for this interdisciplinary field's promising future [24].

The article "Metaverse: Freezing the Time" by Qian, Yang, and Bai discusses how freezing time in the Metaverse can benefit various domains, addressing ethical and technical challenges. The article "Metaverse: Freezing the Time" by Qian, Yang, and Bai discusses how freezing time in the Metaverse can benefit various domains, addressing ethical and technical challenges [31].

Yihao et al. suggests self-powered sensing tech for enhancing Metaverse immersion via biosensors, offering a user-friendly and adaptive environment [43].

To succeed in user-dependent prototypes like the Metaverse, prioritize high-quality user experience (QoE) through mixed reality for immersive exploration. Consistency, authenticity, and smoothness matter. Prioritize QoE and MR for industrial Metaverse excellence [22].

Hyeonyeong et al. highlights the importance of perceived distance in the metaverse, affecting detachment and performance in a complex interplay of factors. Addressing this issue requires research into various dimensions, including safety, to enhance the performing arts [16].

Mattco et al.'s qualitative study highlights Metaverse accessibility challenges due to costly hardware, emphasizing the importance of inclusion, diversity, and ethical regulations [41].

Jeonghee et al.'s study reveals breast cancer patients found solace in the metaverse for anonymous peer support, positively impacting psychosocial well-being and expanding its usage [1].

4   Human-Centric Metaverse

While the presently rising popularity of the subject of human-centered AI notably throughout world-renowned academic institutions, to name a few, Stanford University, University of California, and Berkeley bearing a crucial role also need to address the indirect as well as negative consequences of the implementations and thereafter, the implication of AI. As per [40], there is a need for innovative expansion of the idea which is a purely human-based approach extending an endless array of opportunities by the combination of virtual and physical worlds. Augmented Reality or AR, is the immersive experience enhancing feature where the user stays in the physical world while experiencing the one which is computer-generated spanning in grades of visuals, audio, and more dynamics [6,20].

Human-centric Metaverse can be thought of as an extended version of Human-centred AI where there is natural input of human thought into the scope of this application. There is a strong advocacy for the fulfillment of human needs, out of which safety steps in as the first and foremost one. Humans are positioned at the nuclei of advancements, and the ethical as well as practical concerns over this are to be addressed. In the virtual environment, proving the safety of every user is thoroughly argued upon by [40]. There would be an assurance of an optimal system that holds satisfactory levels of human aspirations.

4.1   Why Human-Centric Metaverse Should Exist?

The Metaverse's growth prioritizes human-centricity, emphasizing immersiveness, quality of life, emotions, and intuitive interactions for happiness and convenience [4,40]. The shift towards the Metaverse is growing, emphasizing the importance of a human-centered approach for immersiveness, connections, knowledge, and real-world experiences. Tencent entrepreneurs emphasize tech serving people, focusing on enhancing QoE and life quality. Metaverse driven by human happiness aims to improve lives through virtual space [40].

The users' "digital avatar" in the Metaverse has a well-built connection with their senses, granting them personalized space. This highlights how human beings are inherently intuitive in their virtual space. For the Metaverse to develop, it must create innovative ways for humans to produce, live, and think. Human emotions will act as the most important factor for virtual spaces in the metaverse. It means human needs, QoE in metaverse will act as a catalytic function for its growth [4]. From its immersive nature to being an ultimate medium and following progressively vital, for the metaverse to adopt a human-centric approach (see Fig. 6).

4.2   Human-Centric Metaverse

Figure 5 Explores human-centric Metaverse framework, addressing tech, ethics, and applications comprehensively.

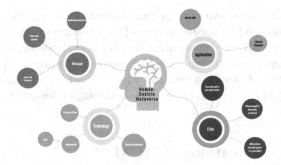

Fig. 5. Human-centric Metaverse.

1. **Human facet:** User-centric, gamified HCM empowers individuals for human progress and well-being.
2. **Technology facet:** VR, AR, haptic feedback, AI, cloud, networks for immersive realism.
3. **Application facet:** HCM integrates virtual reality into the real world, offering transformative experiences.
4. **Ethical facet:** HCM fosters ethics, collaboration, and rights in virtual environments for individuals.

The Fundamental Element of HCM Is Human. Metaverse with HCM model fosters human-tech-ethics mutualism, user empowerment, societal change [42].

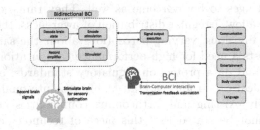

Fig. 6. Brain-Computer Interaction

The Key Attributes of HCM. The Human-Centric Metaverse promotes inclusivity, accessibility, and personalized experiences for all [5].

5   Pivotal Technologies of HCM

The Metaverse community is revolutionizing the virtual world through advanced technologies like Brain-Computer Interaction (BCI), VR, AR, and AI [35]. These technologies provide immersive sensory experiences, encompassing auditory and visual senses. The future Metaverse promises faster transmission speeds, seamless interconnection, and enhanced computing capabilities. However, ethical concerns surrounding AI usage must be addressed to ensure widespread acceptance. The Metaverse community is working towards a more inclusive virtual environment, promoting accessibility and interconnectedness through teleportation and remote services [18,28].

6 Principal Applications of HCM

The Metaverse, a virtual world that combines physical and virtual dimensions, has the potential to transform society through its human-centric approach [36,38]. It offers immersive experiences and tailored services, enhancing education, healthcare, and tourism. The Metaverse's human-centric approach prioritises students' needs, utilising technologies like augmented reality and artificial intelligence. The Industrial Metaverse, a close integration between the tangible and virtual worlds, focuses on products, businesses, and consumers, harnessing digitalization, blockchain-based production relationships, and artificial intelligence technologies [9,13].

7 Future Works

While numerous upcoming and ongoing innovations are in the path of disruption of tech, and hence every individual using them, the human-centric Metaverse of one and all holds a position that is unique, naturally different. This comes with a handful of challenges to be overcome as well. They range on an unexplored pavement to state a few, irregular distribution of awareness, the need for joining hands of multiple divisions, varying perceptions about the same entity, and so on. There also exists a need for high-performance computational competencies, following privacy and data protection regulatory standards, and non-technical needs, such as ethical constraints, are all highly resolute quality determinants. Unless all currently existing and forthcoming complexities are addressed and dealt with, it cannot be stated that this piece of technological work is at its finest, thus are the scope for future advancements.

8 Conclusion

This paper provides a comprehensive and concise overview of the metaverse, the evolving arena of digital growth with unexplored, newly found features, born in this age of technology. One peculiar indicator that is captivating is its human-centric nature. In a detailed fashion, it verbally proclaims the power of this digitalized prodigy. The description of how this technical embodiment can bear a human-centric innovation is clarified. It is highlighted and reflected upon, the overcoming of various setbacks that exist in physical reality using the integration and application of multiple layers of technological intricacies. The authors are also clear on the challenges that the currently existing systems are embedded with. How this could be a wave of transformation in fields of zero correlation ranging from education, medicine, and industrial practises to the performing arts is diverse in its distinct ways. This shall be an area with no restriction in the scope of research and development. There is an immaculate responsibility for reaching appropriate solutions to all currently existing and unforeseen complexities or constraints that, if not handled with caution, would later become setbacks for this domain itself. Therefore, in concluding remarks, this could be the platform of a revolutionising new horizon, thus a new world, or a catastrophic one.

References

1. Ahn, J., Lee, K.E.: Experiences of young women with breast cancer in peer support activities and the need for a metaverse-based peer support program: a qualitative study. Asia-Pac. J. Oncol. Nurs., 100253 (2023)
2. Alspach, K.: Why the fate of the metaverse could hang on its security (2022)
3. Arrieta, A.B., et al.: Explainable artificial intelligence (XAI): concepts, taxonomies, opportunities and challenges toward responsible AI. Inf. Fusion **58**, 82–115 (2020)
4. Bale, A.S., et al. A comprehensive study on metaverse and its impacts on humans. Adv. Hum.-Comput. Inter. (2022)
5. Balica, R.S., et al.: Metaverse applications, technologies, and infrastructure: predictive algorithms, real-time customer data analytics, and virtual navigation tools. Linguist. Philos. Invest. **21**, 219–235 (2022)
6. Bryson, J.J., Theodorou, A.: How society can maintain human-centric artificial intelligence. Hum.-Centered Digitalization Serv., 305–323 (2019)
7. Cai, Y., et al.: Compute-and data-intensive networks: the key to the metaverse. In: 1st International Conference on 6G Networking (2022), pp. 1–8. IEEE
8. Dai, C., Huang, Y., Chien, W.-C.: A sparse attack method on skeleton-based human action recognition for intelligent metaverse application. Futur. Gener. Comput. Syst. **143**, 51–60 (2023)
9. Dwivedi, Y.K., et al.: Metaverse beyond the hype: multidisciplinary perspectives on emerging challenges, opportunities, and agenda for research, practice and policy. Int. J. Inf. Manage. **66**, 102542 (2022)
10. George, A.H., et al.: Metaverse: the next stage of human culture and the internet. Int. J. Adv. Res. Trends Eng. Technol. **8**(12), 1–10 (2021)
11. Guidi, B., et al.: From NFT 1.0 to NFT 2.0: a review of the evolution of non-fungible tokens. Fut. Internet **15**(6), 189 (2023)
12. Hackl, C., et al.: Navigating the Metaverse: A Guide to Limitless Possibilities in a Web 3.0 World. John Wiley & Sons, Hoboken (2022)
13. Jiang, Y., et al.: Industrial applications of digital twins. Philos. Trans. R. Soc. A **379**(2207), 20200360 (2021)
14. Jones, D., et al.: Characterising the digital twin: a systematic literature review. CIRP J. Manuf. Sci. Technol. **29**, 36–52 (2020)
15. Katona, J.: A review of human-computer interaction and virtual reality research fields in cognitive info-communications. Appl. Sci. **11**(17), 2646 (2021)
16. Kim, H., Lee, H.: Performing arts metaverse: the effect of perceived distance and subjective experience. Comput. Hum. Behav. **146**, 107827 (2023)

17. Kozinets, R.V.: Immersive netnography: a novel method for service experience research in virtual reality, augmented reality and metaverse contexts. J. Serv. Manag. **34**(1), 100–125 (2023)
18. Laeeq, K.: Metaverse: why, how and what. How What (2022)
19. Leible, S., et al.: A review on blockchain technology and blockchain projects fostering open science. Front. Blockchain **16** (2019)
20. Lepri, B., et al.: Ethical machines: the human-centric use of artificial intelligence. IScience **24**(3), 102249 (2021)
21. Li, K., et al.: When internet of things meets metaverse: convergence of physical and cyber worlds. arXiv preprint: arXiv:2208.13501 (2022)
22. Liu, S., et al.: QoE enhancement of the industrial metaverse based on mixed reality application optimization. Displays **79**, 102463 (2023)
23. Liu, Y., et al.: Risks and returns of cryptocurrency. Rev. Finan. Stud. **34**(6), 2689–2727 (2021)
24. Lu, Y., et al.: MIoT integrates health, MM benefits humans: funding conference for international association and alliance of metaverse in medicine successfully held. Clin. eHealth **5**, 17–18 (2022)
25. Mourtzis, D., et al.: Human-centric platforms for personalized value creation in metaverse. J. Manufact. Syst. **65**, 653–659 (2022)
26. Mozumder, M.A.I., et al.: Overview: technology roadmap of the future trend of metaverse based on IoT, blockchain, AI technique, and medical domain metaverse activity. In: 24th International Conference on Advanced Communication Technology, pp. 256–261. IEEE (2022)
27. Neyer, G., et al.: Blockchain and payment systems: what are the benefits and costs? J. Payments Strategy Syst. **11**(3), 215–225 (2017)
28. Ning, H., et al.: A survey on metaverse: the state-of-the-art, technologies, applications, and challenges. arXiv e-prints (2021)
29. Njoku, J.N., et al.: Prospects and challenges of metaverse application in data-driven intelligent transportation systems. IET Intell. Transp. Syst. **17**(1), 1–21 (2023)
30. Ondrejka, C.: Escaping the gilded cage: user created content and building the metaverse. NYL Sch. L. Rev. **49**(1), 81 (2004)
31. Qian, P., et al.: Metaverse: freezing the time. Clin. eHealth (2023)
32. Rawat, D.B., El Alami, H.: Metaverse: requirements, architecture, standards, status, challenges, and perspectives. IEEE Internet Things Mag. **6**(1), 14–18 (2023)
33. Statista. Metaverse market size (2022)
34. Tan, Z.: Metaverse, HCI, and its future. Adv. Soc. Sci., Educ. Humanit. Res. **670**, 897–901 (2022)
35. Tang, F., et al.: The roadmap of communication and networking in 6G for the metaverse. IEEE Wireless Commun. (2023)
36. Tlili, A., et al.: Is metaverse in education a blessing or a curse: a combined content and bibliometric analysis. Smart Learn. Environ. **9**(1), 1–31 (2022)
37. Wang, Y., et al.: A survey on metaverse: fundamentals, security, and privacy. IEEE Commun. Surv. Tutorials (2022)
38. Wu, T.C., et al.: A scoping review of metaverse in emergency medicine. Australas. Emerg. Care **26**(1), 75–83 (2023)
39. Yang, B., et al.: Improving search in peer-to-peer networks. In: Proceedings 22nd International Conference on Distributed Computing Systems (2002), pp. 5–14. IEEE
40. Yu, G.: Metaverse: a future humanistic and amphibious social ecology. Shanghai Manage. Sci. **44**, 24–29 (2022)

41. Zallio, M., Clarkson, P.J.: Designing the metaverse: a study on inclusion, diversity, equity, accessibility and safety for digital immersive environments. Telematics Inform. **75**, 101909 (2022)
42. Zeb, S., et al.: Industry 5.0 is coming: a survey on intelligent nextG wireless networks as technological enablers. arXiv preprint: arXiv:2205.09084 (2022)
43. Zhou, Y., et al.: Self-powered sensing technologies for human metaverse interfacing. Joule **6**(7), 1381–1389 (2022)

Blockchain - A Secure and Transparent Solution to Detect Counterfeit Products

Ishaan Tyagi[1], Rajat Gupta[1], Divya Upadhyay[1], and Ashwani Kumar Dubey[2]([envelope])

[1] Department of Computer Science and Engineering, ABES Engineering College, Ghaziabad, UP, India
{ishaan.20b0101185,rajat.20b0101037}@abes.ac.in

[2] Department of Electronics and Communication Engineering, Amity School of Engineering and Technology, Amity University Uttar Pradesh, Noida, UP, India
dubey1ak@gmail.com

Abstract. Counterfeit products have had a massive impact on manufacturing industries in the past couple of years. This is affecting the company's name, sales, and profit. Blockchain innovation has acquired an interest in the course recently. The most important issue about this is currency exchange, but its application is not restricted to only Digital currency. This technology has the potential to influence different business sectors. Blockchain has brought high transparency and ease in how transactions are dealt with. Blockchain technology can be used to identify real products from fake ones. Using this technology, customers or users need not rely on third-party services for the product's safety. The proposed system's Quick Response (QR) code provides a robust technique to stop counterfeiting the products. Fake products can be detected using a Quick Response scanner, where a QR code is attached. This QR code is linked to the Blockchain network to identify the fake product. A block will be created to store the product-related information and its QR code, like product details, and generate a unique code for each block in the blockchain database. The user uploads and then compares the unique code of the product he intends to purchase with that stored in the blockchain network. If the code matches the code that the manufacturer generated, it will notify the customer, saying the QR code is matched; otherwise, it will notify the customer that the QR code is not matched and the product is fake.

Keywords: Block · Blockchain · Smart Contracts · Proof of Work (Pow) · Quick Response Code

1 Introduction

The global development of a product or technology always comes with risk factors such as counterfeiting and duplication, which can affect the company's name, revenue, and customer health. There are so many products that exist in the supply chain. To ensure that the product is real or fake. Because of counterfeit or fake products manufacturers face the biggest problem and losses. To find the genuineness of the product, The authors can use blockchain technology.

M. A. Jabbar et al. (Eds.): AMLDA 2023, CCIS 2047, pp. 44–53, 2024.
https://doi.org/10.1007/978-3-031-55486-5_4

Blockchain technology helps to solve the problem of counterfeiting a product. Blockchain technology is more secure [1]. Once the product is stored on the network hash code is generated for that product, it is possible to maintain all transaction records of the product, and its current owner as a chain will be created for that product's transactions. All the transaction records will be stored in the form of blocks in the blockchain. In the proposed system. The authors assign a generated QR code to a particular product, and the end customer can scan that QR code to get all the information about that product [2] after scanning the QR code. The authors can identify whether the product is real or fake.

Explosive growth in pharmaceuticals and other products worldwide has led to growth in large, globalized, digital supply chains. The structure of modern supply chains is mostly centralized, in which central authority stores and manages products' authentication records. In this typical structure, each node authenticates a product upon its arrival. This authentication is carried out by executing authentication protocols between a supply chain node and an authentication server. Track-and-trace-based supply chains function similarly, where a centralized tracking server tracks the physical locations of products and updates their records.

Blockchain was introduced to solve the problem of reaching agreements on a state among distributed nodes without a coordinating third party. These nodes are trusted less and may contain faulty nodes (e.g., malicious or crashed). Reaching a consensus on a proposed block in the presence of faulty nodes requires a consensus protocol executed by some selected nodes called validators or miners. In response to this, much research has been conducted to come up with robust yet efficient consensus protocols that guarantee consensus in the blockchain.

There is an obvious loss to companies due to identical products, but the user also feels cheated if the products he buys are forged/ fraudulent. Also, no one can afford to be cheated on products like medicines and cosmetics if the counterfeit injures health. To avoid this, the app uses a barcode/QR code unique to each packet to scan the product, which can say a lot about the product. Thus, the proposed system is of great use to end users as it helps to detect fake products in the supply chain.

Scanning a QR code that is assigned to a specific product can give all the information, like a current owner and transaction history, which tells the end users if their product is genuine or not. Counterfeiting of products happens everywhere in industries like fashion, clothing, Sports gear, Toys, and Vehicle accessories. In addition, legitimate firms suffering from huge revenue losses, and counterfeiting products could put lives at risk, for example, through auto parts of poor quality, medicines without relevant and required ingredients, and toys with unwanted components. Blockchain technology has become popular in recent times as it is the best solution to overcome these problems. It can create a trustworthy, transparent, and secure supply chain that avoids product counterfeiting. Information about the product cannot be manipulated or altered as information is permanently recorded in the blockchain network.

This paper is divided into multiple sections. Section 2 presents the motivation and literature survey which emphasis on the requirement of heart-diseases prediction system. Section 3 discusses the experiment setup and methodology opted to analyze the proposed model. Further sections present the result analysis and conclusion.

2 Literature Survey

A Survey of Counterfeit Product Detection by Prabhu Shankar, R. Jayavadivel is presented in [3]. Counterfeit products are growing exponentially with the enormous online and black market. So, there is a strong need to address the challenges of detecting counterfeit products and designing appropriate technology to improve detection accuracy. This is one of the active research areas to be explored in the current world. This paper discusses various techniques for identifying counterfeit products.

Smart Tags for Brand protection and anti-counterfeiting in the wine industry by steven, Marko [4]. This paper describes a brand protection and anti-counterfeiting solution for the wine industry based on smart tags and Cloud-enabled technologies. The main idea behind smart tags is to utilize quick response codes, functional inks supported by the Cloud system, and two-way communication between the winemaker and end-user.

A Blockchain-based Supply Chain Quality Management Framework by Si Chen, Rui Shi. In this paper, the authors propose a blockchain-based framework [5]. This framework will provide a theoretical basis for intelligent supply chain quality management based on blockchain technology. Furthermore, it provides a foundation for developing information resource management theories in distributed, virtual organizations.

In [6], authors suggested that using blockchain for real-time data management with monitoring and regulating data in a virtual environment includes less paperwork, increased supply chain visibility, increased efficiency with faster response times, and reduced geographic limits. Blockchain also lowers the risk of SCM attacks. The authors in the paper [7] also stated that traditional supply chains face issues, including misplaced shipment, delayed delivery, corruption, tampering, and counterfeiting products. Blockchain will help to overcome these issues.

Yaoming et al. [8] utilize blockchain technology to evaluate and generate a comprehensive life cycle for medical equipment that covers the entire process of supply, manufacturing, procurement, tendering, storage, usage, application, export, destruction, and traceability. In Indonesia, a Blockchain-enabled Medicine SCM system (MSCM) was projected by [9] to supply and distribute genuine medicines between public health centers. Musamih et al. [10] created an Ethereum-based pharmaceutical supply chain system using blockchain. Their proposed system was decentralised off-chain storage to monitor and trace medicines in a decentralised way. Uddin et al. [12] proposed a Hyperledger Fabric and Hyperledger Besu-based decentralised blockchain architectures that can fulfil security, privacy, accessibility, and transparency criteria.

The proposed blockchain architecture can also be used in various other applications [14] besides Counterfeit Products. They can manage time and synchronizations between various nodes in wireless sensor networks [11, 13, 15, 19]. It can also be used in Supply chain management [16], Smart world [17], and Intelligent Agriculture [18]. In future research, Blockchain technology can store sensor data, making it resistant to tampering securely. Utilizing blockchain instils confidence within a smart digital ecosystem for healthcare, agriculture etc. industries. It ensures that critical data about the tracking and distribution of pharmaceuticals is accessible to all participants within the blockchain network.

3   The Architecture of the Proposed Fake Product Detection System Using Blockchain

After going through multiple methodologies and techniques used in the market to ensure the authenticity of a product, it was observed that a decentralised solution to authenticate the products, whether they are real or fake, is the best solution to provide genuine products to customers. Blockchain is the best technology to provide a solution to this problem. Blockchain is an immutable, secure, and decentralised ledger. Once a block is added to the blockchain network, it can neither be modified nor deleted. One of the reasons behind opting for a decentralised system is that it is immutable, so there are no chances of tampering with the data, and they are public, so there is nothing like secrecy. It will provide complete transparency to the users, manufacturers, vendors and others.

Figure 1 Presents the workflow of the proposed system. This workflow was finalized after analyzing various research on the supply chain to find the requirements and to decide upon the workflow from the manufacturer to the customer. A smart contract structure is then created, creating a single manufacturer that accepts multiple distributors and consists of different entities: Manufacturer-Distributor-Customer. The contract deployer will be made by the manufacturer and the rest of the distributors and customers. Metamask was then integrated with the website, and based on the Metamask contact address, the nature of the user was decided. Only the deployer can open the Manufacturer part, which is determined by the user's contact address while anyone can access the distributor and customer part of the website. It is then integrated with ReactJs and Web3.js.

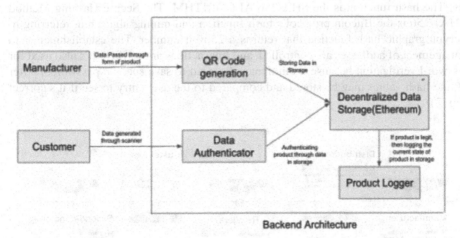

Backend Architecture

Fig. 1. Workflow for the proposed system of Fake Products Detection using blockchain

3.1   Methodology

The proposed approach ensures that fake products are detected in everyday life via a website. Customer or user android application, manufacturer or firm Android application, and Cloud/ Database are the three important components of the proposed system. The manufacturer or corporate side application is the first section of the website, where they must first register. After logging into the website and completing the registration process, they can choose from various possibilities. One alternative is to add a product and let the maker fill in the data. Another alternative is to display the order so they may see the details of the clients' orders before deciding whether to accept or reject the order. The manufacturer can also see whether or not the goods have been delivered. A QR code scanner can be used on this website to scan the QR code of a product and determine whether it is false or authentic. Another alternative is a blockchain, which shows the name of the generated block product quantity, the generated Hash Value, and whether or not the product is corrupted.

In the proposed system, the customer logs in and fills out the necessary information to order and book the product. The maker might be shown the product's order. The manufacturer determines whether or not the product request is acceptable. After a product's order is accepted, the manufacturer generates the product's unique QR code. Once a product order is saved on the network, a hash code for that product is generated, making it easy to keep track of the transaction. A QR code is created for a specific product in the proposed system. Customers can use their smartphone's QR code reader application or a QR code scanner on the customer's website to scan the QR code on the product or packaging. After scanning, the authors can determine whether the merchandise is genuine. Finally, the Blockchain system stores these product characteristics and transaction history, allowing product tracking along the distribution chain.

The Firebase cloud database stores all product details, block names, and hash values. The hash function is the SHA-256 ALGORITHM. The Secure Hashing Method (SHA)-256 is the Bitcoin protocol's hash function and mining algorithm, referring to a cryptographic hash function that returns a 256-bit number. The establishment and management of addresses are controlled, and transactions are verified. It's also used for password verification because it eliminates the need to save specific passwords. After all, the hash values may be stored and compared to the user entry to see if it's correct (Fig. 2).

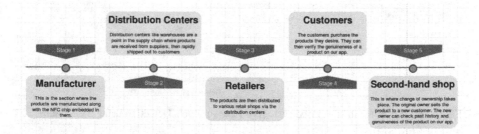

Fig. 2. Data Flow of the project

4   Results and Analysis

Ganache is a local blockchain simulator which can run blockchain for the proposed system. It can be developed, deployed and tested for proposed decentralised applications without buying ether. The Ganache interface includes various addresses and balances, which are fake ether. The proposed work can develop, deploy and test the smart contract using fake ether. It will also help get other information about Blocks, Transactions, Contracts, Events, and Logs.

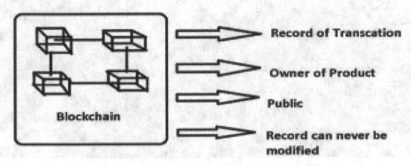

Fig. 3. Block Diagram of Blockchain System

Metamask is a software that makes interacting with any blockchain much easier. Metamask does all the code that the authors had to do automatically. Meta-masks act as a security layer as well as an accessibility layer. Nothing can go from our Metamask wallet to that website without permission. The account created in Metamask is shown in Fig. 3. The authors can deploy Smart contracts in solidity using Remix IDE. Remix IDE is a web application where authors must write their smart contracts in solidity. The authors can easily deploy our smart contracts to the test nets or the main nets, and then the authors can just test and verify the smart contracts within this environment.

Web3.js is the main JavaScript library for interacting with the Ethereum blockchain. When The authors are developing a website or a client of some kind that can actually talk to the blockchain, the web3.js library comes into play. The website talks to the blockchain with web3 with something called JSON RPC. RPC stands for remote procedure call protocol; this method allows us to talk to the Ethereum blockchain (Figs. 4, 5, 6 and 7).

Fig. 4. Ganache Interface

Fig. 5. Metamask Wallet

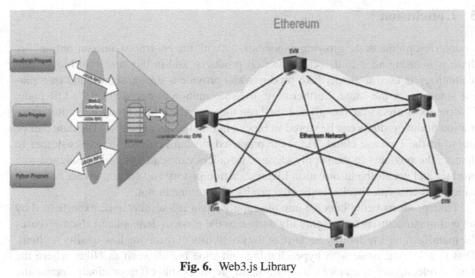

Fig. 6. Web3.js Library

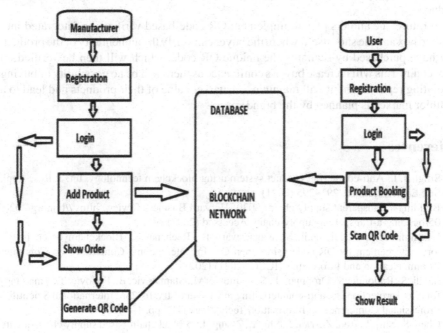

Fig. 7. Block Diagram of Blockchain Network

5 Conclusion

Counterfeit products are growing exponentially with the enormous amount online. So, there is a strong need to detect counterfeit products, and in this research, blockchain technology is used to detect fake products and provide a strong, secure and transparent solution for the same. Furthermore, the information is encoded into a QR code. Customers or users scan the QR code and can then detect the fake product. Digital information about products can be stored as blocks in blockchain networks. The data can be stored in the Firebase cloud. Thus, the proposed system is useful for the customer to detect fake products in the supply chain. Customers can scan QR codes assigned to a product and get all the information like transaction history and current owner based on which end-user can check whether the product is genuine or not.

Fake products being injected into the supply chain is a serious issue experienced by several manufacturers as it eventually decreases the product demand and also decreases the manufacturer's reliability because of the possibility of receiving low-quality replicas. This is a leading issue with hype clothing and shoe brands such as Nike, where the newest releases are often met with high-quality replicas sold off as originals, increasing the market supply or the market liquidity and thus reducing the asking price of other products.

In future, the authors plan to implement QR code-based verification integrated into the shoe box and the shoe itself, where the buyer can verify the authenticity of the product, they have purchased by scanning the unique QR code, which will then be verified on blockchain. This will increase buyer's confidence as there will be no possibility of buying or rotating replicas, and it will maintain the market value of their products and lead to a healthier market as planned by the brand.

References

1. Singhal, I.: Anti-counterfeit product system using blockchain technology. Int. J. Res. Appl. Sci. Eng. Technol. **9**, 291–295 (2021)
2. Building a transparent supply chain (2020) Harvard Business Review. https://hbr.org/2020/05/building-a-transparent-supply-chain. Accessed (2023)
3. Lakshmi, G.V., Gogulamudi, S., Nagaeswari, B., Reehana, S.: Blockchain based inventory management by QR code using open CV. In: International Conference on Computer Communication and Informatics (ICCCI-2021) (2021)
4. Sandi, S., Radonjic, S., Drobnjak, J., Simeunović, M., Stamatovic, B., Popovic, T.: Smart tags for brand protection and anti-counterfeiting in wine industry. In: 23rd International Scientific-Professional Conference on Information Technology (IT), pp. 1–5 (2018)
5. Chen, S., Shi, R., Ren, Z., Yan, J., Shi, Y., Zhang, J.: A blockchain-based supply chain quality management framework. In: IEEE 14th International Conference on e-Business Engineering (ICEBE), pp. 172–176 (2017)
6. Dede, S., Köseoğlu, M.C., Yercan, H.F.: Learning from early adopters of blockchain technology: a systematic review of supply chain case studies. Technol. Innov. Manage. Rev **2021**, 19–31 (2021)
7. Yadav, S., Singh, S.P.: Blockchain critical success factors for sustainable supply chain. Resour. Conserv. Recycl. **152**, 104505 (2020)

8. Yue, Y., Fu, X.: Research on medical equipment supply chain management method based on blockchain technology. In: Proceedings of International Conference on Service Science (ICSS), pp. 143–148 (2020)
9. Kumiawan, H., Kim, J., Ju, H.: Utilisation of the blockchain network in the public community health center medicine supply chain. In: Proceedings of 21st Asia-Pacific Network Operations and Management Symposium (APNOMS), pp. 235–238 (2020)
10. Musamih, A., et al.: A blockchain-based approach for drug traceability in healthcare supply chain. IEEE Access **9**, 9728–9743 (2021)
11. Upadhyay, D., Dubey, A.K.: Maximum probable clock offset estimation (MPCOE) to reduce time synchronization problems in wireless sensor networks. Wireless Pers. Commun. **114**, 1177–1190 (2020). https://doi.org/10.1007/s11277-020-07414-y
12. Uddin, M., Salah, K., Jayaraman, R., Pesic, S., Ellahham, S.: Blockchain for drug traceability: architectures and open challenges. Health Inform. J. **27**(2), 146045822110112 (2021). https://doi.org/10.1177/14604582211011228
13. Upadhyay, D., Dubey, A.K., Santhi Thilagam, P.: A probabilistic model of clock offset estimator (PMCOE) for clock synchronization in wireless sensor network. Wireless Pers. Commun. **108**, 995–1007 (2019). https://doi.org/10.1007/s11277-019-06447-2
14. Salama, R., Al-Turjman, F., Bhatla, S., Mishra, D.: Mobile edge fog, blockchain networking and computing-a survey. In: 2023 International Conference on Computational Intelligence, Communication Technology and Networking (CICTN), pp. 808–811 (2023). https://doi.org/10.1109/cictn57981.2023.10141348
15. Upadhyay, D., Dubey, A.K., Thilagam, P.S.: Application of non-linear gaussian regression-based adaptive clock synchronization technique for wireless sensor network in agriculture. IEEE Sens. J. **18**(10), 4328–4335 (2018). https://doi.org/10.1109/jsen.2018.2818302
16. Mishra, D., Singh, P., Singh, N.: Role of blockchain in achieving solutions in ambiguous supply chain operations. In: Blockchain in a Volatile-Uncertain-Complex-Ambiguous World, pp. 57–73 (2023). https://doi.org/10.1016/b978-0-323-89963-5.00012-5
17. Upadhyay, D., Sharma, S.: Convergence of artificial intelligence of things: concepts, designing, and applications. Towards Smart World 119–142 (2020). https://doi.org/10.1201/978100 3056751-8
18. Shrishti, R., Dubey, A.K., Upadhyay, D.: Precision agriculture using cloud-based mobile application for sensing and monitoring of farms. In: Hassanien, A.E., Bhattacharyya, S., Chakrabati, S., Bhattacharya, A., Dutta, S. (eds.) Emerging Technologies in Data Mining and Information Security. AISC, vol. 1300, pp. 417–425. Springer, Singapore (2021). https://doi.org/10.1007/978-981-33-4367-2_40
19. Singh, R., Dwivedi, A.D., Srivastava, G.: Internet of things based blockchain for temperature monitoring and counterfeit pharmaceutical prevention. Sensors **20**(14), 3951 (2020). https://doi.org/10.3390/s20143951

Data-Driven Approach to Network Intrusion Detection System Using Modified Artificial Bee Colony Algorithm for Nature-Inspired Cybersecurity

V. B. Gupta[1], Shishir Kumar Shandilya[2](✉) (iD), Chirag Ganguli[2](iD), and Gaurav Choudhary[3](iD)

[1] School of Data Science and Forecasting, Devi Ahilya University, Indore, Madhya Pradesh, India
[2] VIT Bhopal University, Bhopal, India
shishir.sam@gmail.com
[3] DTU Compute, Technical University of Denmark, 2800 Kongens, Lyngby, Denmark

Abstract. With ever-evolving cyberspace, adaptive defense is crucial. In this paper, we show the Adaptive Defense Mechanism to identify Anomalous hosts in a network using the Artificial Bees Colonization Algorithm. A self-driven metric has been defined to determine the performance of a network that would detect the behavior of its nodes. This algorithmic metric is inspired by the Nature-Inspired Artificial Bees Colonization Algorithm. The end result is randomly generated using a dimension index that gives the same result on the node's behavior which is then used to determine the probabilistic parametric fitness of the individual nodes. This helps to determine which nodes are getting affected the most or are nearer to the attack surface. The defense mechanism is based on the Nature Inspired Artificial Bees Colonization Algorithm, which is able to detect the nearest point/s of attack on nodes based on the experimental simulation of attacked nodes. It also shows the impact of the defense mechanism on the various topologies of the nodes as predefined in the testbed implementing a Distributed Denial-of-Service attack on the nodes. The proposed algorithm showcases the nodes that are affected due to the attack, providing the nearest point of the breach, which can provide a comprehensive way of examining the intrusion point. This algorithm outperformed in terms of stability and early identification of the malicious nodes.

Keywords: Nature Inspired Security Mechanism · Intrusion Detection · Artificial Bee Colony (ABC) algorithm · Robust Defense Approach

1 Introduction

With the growing advancements in the digital age, intrusions or unauthorized access to a network has become prevalent. For the effective suppression of these

M. A. Jabbar et al. (Eds.): AMLDA 2023, CCIS 2047, pp. 54–66, 2024.
https://doi.org/10.1007/978-3-031-55486-5_5

attacks, an effective step is to detect the point(s) of anomaly based on the behavior as early as possible and take the appropriate action to keep the network and critical assets safe. The nature-inspired artificial bees colonization (ABC) methodology is derived from the exploration technique of the honey bees [1–3]. The factor that influences the better performance of ABC is that it involves fewer control parameters. Therefore, ABC is considered to efficiently and optimally solve multi-dimensional and multi-modal optimization problems [4]. ABC is a meta-heuristic algorithm exhibiting collective intelligence made out of positive and negative feedback, multiple interactions, and fluctuations. Reports reveal that scout bees act as counterproductive and onlooker bees act with poor global search capability [5,6]. Therefore, it is considered to mention that the collection of behavioral patterns in animals presents a major part of communal interaction on the coordination and working behavior of large groups of animals that may be achieved through group-wide information flow, group decision-making, group motion, and activity synchronization [7]. Nature-Inspired Cyber Security is the model-based implication inflicted on a Security Attack to showcase a unique defensive mechanism. The nature-inspired defensive algorithm is used on the Distributed Denial-of-Service Attack on a pre-defined testbed using the ABC algorithm, which has the capability to perform anomaly detection in a robust and optimal manner, thereby safeguarding the efficiency and efficacy of a computer network [7–9]. This research aims to explore the application of nature-inspired principles and strategies to enhance cybersecurity measures. It involves studying natural systems to derive insights, developing advanced detection techniques, assessing their impact on digital system resilience and efficiency, and implementing these solutions in real-world scenarios to create more adaptive, efficient, and effective cybersecurity solutions. This research is driven by the critical need to revolutionize cybersecurity in response to evolving threats. Nature's adaptive strategies offer inspiration for more resilient, efficient, and effective cybersecurity solutions. The potential benefits include improved threat detection, reduced response times, and a safer digital ecosystem on a global scale.

Contribution of the Paper: In this paper, we propose a nature-inspired algorithm that can detect intrusions in a cyber-physical network. The major contributions of the paper can be summarized as follows: (i) Adaptively calculate Network Parameters to detect abnormal characteristics of the nodes present in the network, (ii) Determine the closest point of an attack origination (node or set of nodes in the network), (iii) Denial of Service detection by measuring fitness prospects of the connections in a defined network, (iv) Robust implementation of Network Intrusion Prevention Solutions.

2 Related Work

AI-assisted Computer Network Operations testbed provides a Nature Inspired Cyber Security based algorithm to provide an adaptive defense mechanism for implementing AI-assisted Computer Network Operations [10]. The Nature-Inspired Cyber Security (NICS) algorithm defined in this paper is based on the

Artificial Bees Colony Algorithm. According to [6], the ABC algorithm can be improved to overcome the shortcomings of the actual algorithm, which include slow convergence speed. Detection of Anomalies is defined to be the key issue to Intrusion Detection in which the probability of behavior indicates normal and under-attack situations [11]. According to [12], attacks occurring in distributed systems start at the network layer by collecting information on the network.

Table 1. Summary of Related Work and the Datasets used

PAPER	ALGORITHM IMPLEMENTED	DATASET	DOMAIN	CONTRIBUTIONS
A Network Intrusions Detection System based on a Quantum Bio Inspired Algorithm [1]	-Bio-Inspired Optimization Algorithm - Particle Swarm Optimization	KDD Dataset	Quantum Bio-Inspired Intrusion Detection System	The proposed algorithm seems to achieve high intrusions classification accuracy with the highest obtained accuracy of 94.8%
Application of artificial bee colony for intrusion detection systems [2]	- Swarm Intelligence Feature Selection - ABC Algorithm	KDD Cup 99 Dataset	ABC-Inspired Intrusion Detection System	ABC in the proposed algorithm that seems to have achieved an average accuracy rate of 97.5% for known attacks & 93.2% for overall known and unknown attacks.
Artificial Bee Colony Algorithm for Anomaly Based Intrusion Detection [3]	- PSO Algorithm - Clustering Algorithm (FFA)	KDD Cup 99 Dataset	ABC Inspired Intrusion Detection System	Proposed algorithm has an effective usage as an anomaly-based Intrusion Detection System
Lightweight intrusion detection for edge computing networks using deep forest and bio-inspired algorithms [13]	- Deep Forest Bio-Inspired Algorithm - Ant Lion Algorithm -ALO-FCM Algorithm	CICIDS 2017 Dataset	Mobile Edge Computing Based Intrusion Detection System	The applied approach can enhance the reliability of lightweight intrusion detection systems with respect to accuracy and execution time.
RNN-ABC: A New Swarm Optimization Based Technique for Anomaly Detection [14]	- Random Neural Network (RNN-ABC) - Gradient Descent Algorithm	NSL-KDD Dataset	ABC Inspired Swarm Optimization Based Intrusion Detection System	Overall accuracy of the algorithm is 95.02%. Performance estimates with respect to MMSE, SDMSE, BMSE, WMSE confirms the enhancement of this method over traditional ones.
Firefly algorithm based Feature Selection for Network Intrusion Detection [15]	- C4.5 and Bayesian Networks (BN) based classifier	KDD Cup 99 Dataset	Firefly Inspired Intrusion Detection System	The proposed algorithm presents that 10 features are enough to detect the intrusion thus providing improved accuracy.
A Modified Grey Wolf Optimization Algorithm for an Intrusion Detection System [16]	- Grey Wolf Optimization Algorithm (GWO) - Meta-heuristic algorithms	UNSWNB-15 dataset	Grey Wolf Inspired Intrusion Detection System	The proposed algorithm performed better than the traditional methods in limiting Crossover Error Rate and False Positive Rate to lower than 30%. Accuracy Score: 81% F1 Score: 78% G-Mean Measures: 84%
Modified Bio-Inspired Algorithms for Intrusion Detection System [17]	- Binary firefly optimization (BFA) - Binary swarm particle optimization (BPSO) - Cuttlefish optimization - Modified Cuttlefish algorithm (MCO)	CICIDS2017 dataset	Modified Cuttlefish Algorithm (MCO) Inspired Intrusion Detection System	Modified Cuttlefish Algorithm in the proposed paper has shown improved accuracy as compared to Binary Firefly optimization and Binary Swarm Particle Optimization
A Hybrid Model using Bio-Inspired Metaheuristic Algorithms for Network Intrusion Detection System [18]	- Hybridization bio-inspired metaheuristic algorithms - Particle Swarm Optimization (PSO) - Multi-verse optimizer (MVO) - Grey Wolf Optimizer (GWO) - Moth-flame optimization (MFO) - Whale Optimization Algorithm (WOA) - Firefly Algorithm (FFA) - Bat Algorithm (BAT)	UNSW-NB15 dataset	NIDS based on hybridization bio-inspired metaheuristic algorithms for detecting generic attacks	The proposed model in the paper presents that J48 is the better classifier as compared to SVM and RF for time-specific model building.
Bio-Inspired Search Optimization for Intrusion Detection System in Cognitive Wireless Sensor Networks [19]	- Bio-Inspired Algorithm - Search Optimization - Elephant Search Algorithm	NA	Elephant-Search Inspired Intrusion Detection System	The proposed concept in the paper has a CRN analysis for detecting DoS attack using network Performance Parameters (PDR, Bandwidth and E2E Delay)

Table 1 summarizes the applications of several Bio-Inspired Algorithms for Intrusion Detection Systems, Feature Selection and Optimization. It is evident from the proposed algorithms that Network Parameters play an important role in the analysis of several Optimization approaches in Network Intrusion Detection. In accordance with [1] and [12], the Artificial Bees Colonization Algorithm has improved the overall accuracy rate for both known and unknown attacks as compared to the traditional methods.

3   The Artificial Bees Colony Algorithm (ABC)

In the Artificial Bees Colonization algorithm, two types of bees exist - Employed and Unemployed Forager Bees, perform their own optimization to find an optimal food source with respect to their distance from the nest. The employed or

---

Algorithm 1: Basic ABC algorithm

Input: Target Function
Output: Best performing Bees (Solution)
1: Initialize the population of the bees in the hive
2: Calculate the fitness value of the entire population
3: Employed Bee Phase
4: Randomly select a food source location
5: Calculate the fitness value of the selected food source
6: Compare & update the new food source
7: **if** *all employed bees completed food positioning* **then**
  L   (GOTO 8)

  else
  L   [REPEAT FROM 3]
8: Onlooker Bee Phase
9: Calculate the probability for the optimal food source location
10: Select an optimized food source based on the probability
11: Compare & update it with the most optimal positions
12: **if** *all the onlooker bees have completed the process* **then**
  L   (GOTO 13)

  else
  L   (REPEAT FROM 8)
13: Scout Bee Phase
14: Evaluate the abandoned food source for a lower distance
15: Replace the discovered food source with the newly identified food source
16: Check whether all the criteria are fulfilled for the optimized food search process
    (YES): Store the position of the best optimal food source discovered (NO):
    (GOTO 3)

---

active bees are considered to be responsible for exploiting a food source, taking the nectar to the hive, and unloading it there. Thereafter, they can perform three activities: (1) abandon the food source due to them being in unfavorable conditions, (2) recruit unemployed bees for an optimized food source and return back to the hive, and (3) continue foraging the current source of food. The unemployed bees or the onlooker bees tend to follow the actively employed bees and begin a foraging approach to analyzing a source of food determined in context with the greedy nomination method, thereby selecting a prime food source for their hive, and the scout bees initiate a search impetuously to check if the sources of food discovered at a closer radius form the prime solution or a there is a requirement to find a better source [6, 10]. As indicated in the Algorithm 1, the population of the bees in the hive is randomly initialized, and then the fitness value of the population is calculated. In such a scenario, there are chances of false positives where the part of the population who is not fit enough may get approved for the first check as they might be the ones that were randomly selected. This could lead to slow sequential processing for larger node values. The study of a singular node (bees) would not have enough information about the entire cluster (a swarm of bees). Thereafter, different types of bees - both employed and unemployed bees (onlooker and scout bees) perform their own set of actions to get an optimized solution set, and the best solution is stored [3].

4   System Model and Methods

The proposed method discussed in this proposed paper is based on the idea on the Artificial Bees Colony Algorithm, which is altered to be implemented in the Intrusion Detection System Concept. The solution set can be generated using the set of nodes or the group of solutions prepared from the ABC algorithm. For generating the solution set, Eq. 1 is used:

$$sol_i = a_i + \phi_i * (a_i - a_j) \tag{1}$$

where sol forms a set in the array of solutions, ϕ can be any randomly generated floating point numeric value within $[-1,1]$. In the proposed methodology, the Gauss randomization procedure is implemented to determine the effective value of ϕ and direct the probable nodes under attack. And 'a' is considered as the combined average of Throughput (ATP), End-to-End Delay (E2E Delay), and Packet Delivery Ratio (PDR). This methodology can be combined to generate Eq. 2.

$$sol_i = \phi * ((ATP + (ATP - node['TP']))$$
$$+(AED + (AED - node['AED'])) \tag{2}$$
$$+(PDR + (PDR - node['PDR']))$$

The Eq. 2 is calculated for each of the nodes that are present in the network, and the solution set array is created. In Eq. 2, ϕ is the randomly generated arithmetic standard, the Average Throughput is denoted by ATP, the Average End-to-End Delay is presented as AED, and the Packet Delivery Ratio, denoted by PDR, is calculated from the connected nodes that are present in the said network. The solution set is generated for both normal and under-attack scenarios, and their parametric values or the value of the solution set sol for each node are noted. If the normal solution set value of a node is greater than the under-attack solution set value, then that particular node is least likely to the closer to the attack surface; otherwise, that node needs to be monitored and is hence selected to be a probable point of intrusion. The value of sol is hereby referred to as the parametric value of the nodes. Then the average fitness of the nodes is calculated in normal conditions and under attack. This process has been derived from the ABC Algorithm where after the array of solutions is determined of the current position for the food source (nodes in the network), the gathered information is shared with the onlooker bees, who in turn consider the nectar amount (fitness of a node in this case) and chooses a food source with the probabilistic ratio based on the pre-calculated nectar amount. This is implemented based on Eq. 3.

$$Probabilistic\ Fitness = \frac{fit_i}{fit_j} \tag{3}$$

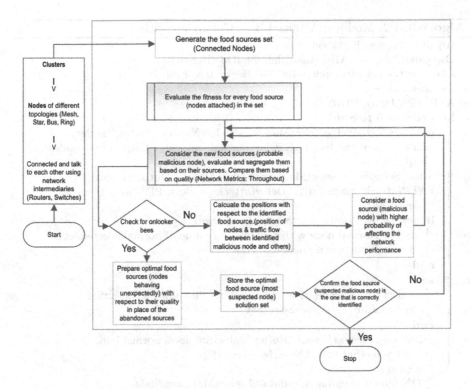

Fig. 1. Proposed Algorithm Diagram Flow

In Fig. 1, the nodes of different topologies are connected in clusters that are interconnected and talking to each other through several network intermediaries (routers and switches). A list of nodes is then randomly generated based on the network parameters and the fitness of all the nodes connected is evaluated. Then, the onlooker bees phase takes over where an optimal food source (probable malicious node) is selected in place of the set of probable solutions (malicious nodes). Then the optimal food source (suspected node) is stored in memory after which a confirmation set is executed on the optimal source by the scout bees phase. When confirmation is received about the optimal food source (malicious node) information, an alarm is generated stating the source of food (attack) before the attack has actually occurred.

The Algorithm 2 defines the functionality of the modified Artificial Bees Colony Algorithm for Optimized Intrusion Detection System where several network parameters (throughput, E2E Delay, and the nodes' Packet Delivery Ratio) are introduced in the defined network for determining the presence of a malicious node. It is similar to using several parameters for the solution set selection by the Employed and the Unemployed Bees. Therefore, the system is not dependent on a single parameter for randomly selecting nodes (one node at a time) therefore, increasing the accuracy of the algorithm as a whole.

Algorithm 2: Modified Artificial Bees Colony algorithm

Input: Targeted Equation
Output: Adaptive ABC Algorithm for IDS (Result)
1: Initialize the network nodes: Total 8 (Begin: 0 & End: 7)
2: $DeviceCluster \leftarrow$
3: ATP, E2E Delay, PDR
4: **for** $nodes \leftarrow 0$ **to** 8 **do**
5:      normalSelectedSet = selectMaliciousNodes(Normal_Output(nodes),
        ATP(normal_nodes), E2E delay(normal_nodes), PDR(normal_nodes),
        begin, end)
6:      attackSelectSet = selectMaliciousNodes(Attack_Output(nodes),
        ATP(attack_nodes), E2E Delay(attack_nodes), PDR(attack_nodes),
        begin, end)
7:      **if** $normalSelectedSet \geq attackSelectSet$ **then**
8:         Select Normal node with a parameter value of normalSelectedSet
9:         NormalSum += normalSelectedSet
     end
10:      **else**
11:         Select attack node with a parameter value of attackSelectSet
12:         AttackSum += attackSelectSet
     end
13:      $fitness \leftarrow fitnessProbability$(normalSelectedSet, normalSum,
        $attackSelectSet, attackSum, begin, end$)
14:      fitnessSum += fitness
15:      JSON filter the parametric data of selectMaliciousNode
16:      fitnessAverage = fitnessSum / Nodes
     selectMaliciousNode():
17:      $randomMetricValue \leftarrow gaussRandomization(-1, 1)$
18:      **for** $i \leftarrow begin$ **to** end **do**
19:         Append the Parametric generated Values
20:         sol = ϕ * ((ATP + (ATP - node['TP']) + (AED + (AED - node['AED'])
        + (PDR - node['PDR']))
21:         total += parametricValues
     end
22:      fitnessProbability():
23:      **for** $i \leftarrow begin$ **to** end **do**
24:         fitnessValue += (attackSelectSet / (attackSum + normalSum))
     end
end

---

5   Result

5.1   Network Architecture

In the network, 3 interconnected routers (Router 1, Router 2, Router 3) are present, which are further attached to the 5 network node clusters with contrasting topologies.

Table 2. Cluster Information

CLUSTER	DEVICE	TOPOLOGY	NO OF NODES
Node 0 (R1)	Router 1		
Node 1 (R2)	Router 2		
Node 2 (R3)	Router 3		
Node 3 (SW1)	Switch (Cluster 1)	Star	10
Node 4 (SW2)	Switch (Cluster 2)	Ring	10
Node 5 (SW3)	Switch (Cluster 3)	Star	10
Node 6 (SW4)	Switch (Cluster 4)	Tree	10
Node 7 (SW5)	Switch (Cluster 5)	Mesh	10

Table 2 showcases that each cluster is attached to the 10 nodes (end devices). In order to categorize the attack scenarios in the presented architecture, the malign node is connected internally to every network cluster node one after the other, and calculated outputs are noted on the basis of their actual, and the current composition of metrics using the trace analyzer python library. The proposed testbed has been modified based on its impact factor to adapt to the current working scenario of this experiment.

5.2 Scenario - 1

Using the proposed methodology, we have gathered experimental results by attaching the malign node to the network node clusters in a random order, to perform a Distributed Denial-of-Service (DoS) attack on the pre-determined network of endpoints. The "Affected Nodes" are defined by the under-attack metric values that show which could be the potential points of attack that need to be checked out of the several nodes attached to the network. In this case, the network is comprised of just 5 clusters and 3 routers but in a large network, there could be several clusters and this proposed algorithm could help reduce the search time of the attack surface by executing Artificial Bees Colonization Algorithm.

Table 3 displays the cases with the Clusters and Nodes that the malign node is attached along with the affected nodes with their types.

Case 1: The malign node is attached to Cluster 1 Network Node 9, whose packets are supposed to flow to Cluster 5 Network Node 9; therefore it has to go through Cluster 1 Switch, Router 1, Router 3, and Cluster 5 switch to reach Cluster 5 Node 9. This shows the attack surface and defines the devices that need to be checked for the attack. Figure 2 showcases the generated average attack throughput and the parametric graph.

Case 2: The malign node is attached to Cluster 2 Network Node 9, whose packets are supposed to flow to Cluster 4 Network Node 9, therefore it has to go through Router 3 to reach Cluster 4 Switch. This is detected to be the nearest

Table 3. Scenario 1 - Affected Nodes Chart

NO	MALICIOUS NODE ATTACHED	AFFECTED NODES	AFFECTED NODES TYPE
1	Cluster 1 - Node 9	Node 0, 2, 3, 7	R1, R3, SW1, SW5
2	Cluster 2 - Node 9	Node 2	R3
3	Cluster 3 - Node 4	Node 5	SW3
4	Cluster 4 - Node 6	Node 7	SW5
5	Cluster 5 - Node 9	Node 2, 3	R3, SW1

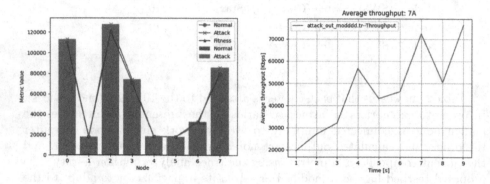

Fig. 2. Case 1: Parametric Graph and Average Throughput

point of attack and the router traffic can be monitored to detect the intrusion. Figure 3 showcases the generated average attack throughput and the parametric graph.

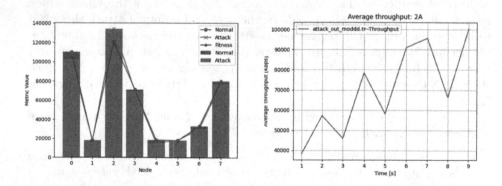

Fig. 3. Case 2: Parametric Graph and Average Throughput

Case 3: The malign node is attached to Cluster 3 Network Node 4, whose packets are supposed to flow to Cluster 1 Network Node 9; it has gone through the Cluster 3 switch, which is detected to be the nearest point of attack. The low rate of DoS would not be a parameter for the difference in results as, in this case, the rate was changed to 500 MB and the algorithm was tested again, and it received the same result as Cluster 3 Switch. Figure 4 showcases the generated average attack throughput and the parametric graph.

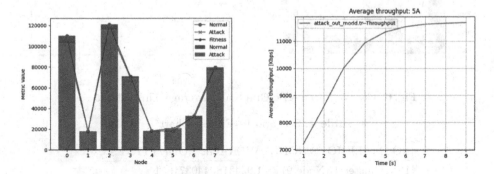

Fig. 4. Case 3: Parametric Graph and Average Throughput

Case 4: The malign node is attached to Cluster 4 Network Node 6, whose packets are supposed to flow to Cluster 3 Network Node 9, traffic flows to the Cluster 4 switch then to Router 3, and next to Cluster 5 switch which detected in this algorithm, after which the traffic flows to Router 2 and Cluster 3 Switch. Figure 5 showcases the generated average attack throughput and the parametric graph.

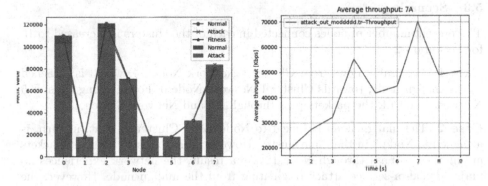

Fig. 5. Case 4: Parametric Graph and Average Throughput

Case 5: The malign node is attached to Cluster 5 Network Node 9, whose packets are supposed to flow to Cluster 1 Network, it has to go through Router 3 and Cluster 1 switch which is detected using the proposed algorithm. Figure 6 showcases the generated average attack throughput and the parametric graph.

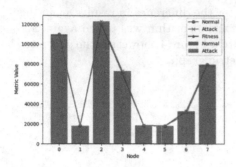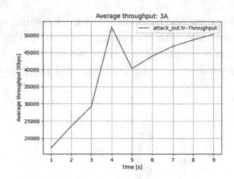

Fig. 6. Case 5: Parametric Graph and Average Throughput

Table 4. Scenario 1 - Fitness Chart

NO	MALICIOUS NODE	AVERAGE NODE FITNESS
1	Cluster 1 (Node 9)	1.9343186440371851
2	Cluster 2 (Node 9)	1.9356737321167585
3	Cluster 3 (Node 4)	1.9352716016032068
4	Cluster 4 (Node 6)	1.9368690483146382
5	Cluster 5 (Node 9)	1.9344092137626994

Table 4, showcases the average overall fitness of the network nodes, which range between 1.9343186440371851 to 1.9368690483146382, showing a precision to the third decimal.

5.3   Scenario - 2

The present number of nodes connected in each of the clusters is increased to 15 for Scenario - 2.

Case 1: The traffic flows from Cluster 1 Network Node 14, which is attached to the malign node, towards Cluster 1 Network Node 0. For reaching Cluster 5 Network Node 14, the packets pass through R3 and Network Switch 1.

Case 2: The malign node is linked to Node 12 in Cluster 2, that, in turn, is attached to Node 0 in the same cluster. However, due to restrictions, no packets are allowed to pass through Node 12. As a result, the network experiences no major denial-of-service attack originating from the malign node. However, the attack does impact the traffic flow through Router 3.

Case 3: In the mesh network, there is a malign node attached to Cluster 5 Network Node 10. This node is linked directly to Cluster 5 Network Node 11. As an overall output, the flow of traffic is affected in such a way that Switch 1 becomes a critical point of impact. This is because all the packets from Cluster 5 Network pass through Network Switch 1 before reaching Cluster 1 Network.

Hence, the successful flow of traffic is disrupted due to the presence of the malign node, leading to consequences for Switch 1.

6 Conclusions

This study presents an analysis of the behavior of nodes within a network that encompasses various network topologies and running diverse applications. This idea upon the findings of previous work [10] by demonstrating the attack scenario, that identifies the network nodes closest to the origin of the attack dependent on the determined network's topology and the speed at which malign traffic travels from the infected node. The main focus of this paper is to introduce Nature Inspired Cyber Defense in the context of Intrusion Detection Systems (IDS) in the overall defined network. The proposed method accurately evaluates the fitness of each node in relation to the overall network traffic, enabling early detection of malign nodes and facilitating prompt response from a firewall. Moreover, this research lays the groundwork for the development of a Nature-Inspired Network Intrusion Prevention System. The proposed algorithmic implementation can serve as an initial stage in the Network Intrusion Prevention System, effectively selecting and identifying potential malign nodes for further investigation.

Acknowledgement. The study does not hold any external funding.

Disclosure of Interests. The authors declare that they have no known competing financial interests or personal relationships that could have appeared to influence the work reported in this paper. The authors declare the following financial interests/personal relationships which may be considered as potential competing interests.

References

1. Soliman, O.S., Rassem, A.: A network intrusions detection system based on a quantum bio inspired algorithm
2. Aldwairi, M., Khamayseh, Y., Al-Masri, M.: Application of artificial bee colony for intrusion detection systems, Security and Communication Networks 8. https://doi.org/10.1002/sec.588
3. Celik, M., Kurban, R., Kurban, T.: Artificial bee colony algorithm for anomaly based intrusion detection
4. Mohammed, A., Yasir, A.: An understanding of artificial bee colony algorithm from the perspective of computation and applied mathematics: a comparative study. J. Phys: Conf. Ser. **1362**, 012132 (2019). https://doi.org/10.1088/1742-6596/1362/1/012132
5. Hussain, K., Salleh, M.N.M., Cheng, S., Shi, Y., Naseem, R.: Artificial bee colony algorithm: a component-wise analysis using diversity measurement. J. King Saud Univ.-Comput. Inf. Sci. **32**(7), 794–808 (2020)
6. Zhang, P., Liu, Y.: Application of an improved artificial bee colony algorithm. IOP Conf. Ser. Earth Environ. Sci. **634**, 012056 (2021). https://doi.org/10.1088/1755-1315/634/1/012056

7. Ramsey, M.-T., et al.: The prediction of swarming in honeybee colonies using vibrational spectra, Scientific Reports 10. https://doi.org/10.1038/s41598-020-66115-5

8. Wang, B., Mao, Z.: Outlier detection based on gaussian process with application to industrial processes. Appl. Soft Comput. **76**(1), 505–516 (2019). https://doi.org/10.1016/j.asoc.2018.12.029

9. Meira, J., et al.: Performance evaluation of unsupervised techniques in cyber-attack anomaly detection. J. Ambient Intell. Hum. Comput.11. https://doi.org/10.1007/s12652-019-01417-9

10. Shandilya, S.K., Upadhyay, S., Kumar, A., Nagar, A.: Ai-assisted computer network operations testbed for nature-inspired cyber security based adaptive defense simulation and analysis. Fut. Gener. Comput. Syst. 127. https://doi.org/10.1016/j.future.2021.09.018

11. Omar, S., Ngadi, M., Jebur, H., Benqdara, S.: Machine learning techniques for anomaly detection an overview. Int. J. Comput. Appl. **79**. https://doi.org/10.5120/13715-1478

12. Atighetchi, M., Pal, P., Webber, F., Jones, C.: Adaptive use of network-centric mechanisms in cyber-defense, pp. 179- (2003). https://doi.org/10.1109/ISORC.2003.1199253

13. Bangui, H., Buhnova, B.: Lightweight intrusion detection for edge computing networks using deep forest and bioinspired algorithms. Comput. Electr. Eng. **100**, 107901 (2022)

14. Qureshi, A., Larijani, H., Mtetwa, N., Javed, A., Ahmad, J.: RNN-ABC: a new swarm optimization based technique for anomaly detection. Computers **8**, 59 (2019). https://doi.org/10.3390/computers8030059

15. Selvakumar, B., Muneeswaran, K.: Firefly algorithm based feature selection for network intrusion detection. Comput. Secur. 81. https://doi.org/10.1016/j.cose.2018.11.005

16. Alzaqebah, A., Aljarah, I., Al-Kadi, O., Damasevicius, R.: A modified grey wolf optimization algorithm for an intrusion detection system. Mathematics 10. https://doi.org/10.3390/math10060999

17. Sharma, M., Saini, S., Bahl, S., Goyal, R., Deswal, S.: Modified bio-inspired algorithms for intrusion detection system 185–201 (2021). https://doi.org/10.1007/978-981-15-5113-0-14

18. Almomani, O.: A hybrid model using bio-inspired metaheuristic algorithms for network intrusion detection system. Comput. Mater. Continua **68**, 409–429 (2021). http://dx.doi.org/10.32604/cmc.2021.016113

19. Vinmathi, M.S., Josephine, M.S., Jeyabalaraja, V.E., Solanki, V.K., Kumar, R.: Bio-inspired search optimization for intrusion detection system in cognitive wireless sensor networks 33–41 (2021). https://doi.org/10.1007/978-3-030-57835-0-4

Forecasting User Payment Behavior Using Machine Learning

Deepali Vora[1]([✉]) [ID], Rupali Choudhary[1], Aman Kumar[1], and Payal Kadam[2] [ID]

[1] Symbiosis Institute of Technology, Pune Campus, Symbiosis International (Deemed University) Lavale, Pune, India
deepali.vora@sitpune.edu.in
[2] Bharati Vidyapeeth (Deemed to Be University) College of Engineering, Pune, India

Abstract. The payment prediction model is a software application that uses machine learning algorithms to predict future payments based on historical data. These models are crucial for organizations like credit card companies, banks, and other financial institutions that depend on recurring payments from their clients businesses may determine the possibility that consumers will miss their payments by utilizing payment prediction models, and they can then take action to either avoid or lessen the effects of any prospective non-payment. This system works on real-time data, data goes to different stages including data collection and storage, data pre-processing and cleaning, feature engineering, and model development. The system uses machine learning algorithms such as linear regression, decision trees, or XG boost to predict future payments based on historical payment data.

Keywords: Accounts Receivable-AR · Machine Learning-ML · Extreme Gradient boost-XG boost · React · User Interface

1 Introduction

Models for predicting payments can assist companies in enhancing their financial performance, lowering their risks, and strengthening customer connections. These advantages can help firms flourish by giving them the stability and resources they require to accomplish their objectives and expand their operations. Predicting payment behavior is crucial for businesses to manage cash flow, extend credit, and minimize the risk of financial loss. Businesses often rely on credit scores and past payment behavior to make decisions about extending credit to customers [2]. Machine learning algorithms can be used to analyze past payment behavior and demographic and credit information to predict payment behavior accurately. Accounts receivable (AR) is an accounting word that describes the money owing to a business or organization by its clients or customers for goods or services that are sold but have yet to be paid for. In other words, it is the sum of money the business anticipates receiving from its clients [4]. The app would collect and store historical payment data from subscribers, including information such as the amount paid, the frequency of payments, and any changes to the subscription over time. The data would then be pre-processed and cleaned to prepare it for use in machine learning algorithms.

M. A. Jabbar et al. (Eds.): AMLDA 2023, CCIS 2047, pp. 67–80, 2024.
https://doi.org/10.1007/978-3-031-55486-5_6

Next, the app would use feature engineering techniques to identify relevant features and create new features based on historical payment data. For example, features might include the duration of a subscription, the payment history of the subscriber, and any promotions or discounts offered to the subscriber.

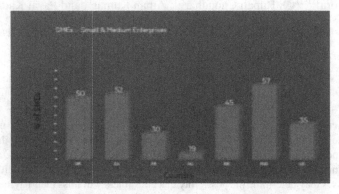

Fig. 1. Percentage of SMEs expecting impacts from late payment

The model utilizes machine learning algorithms and customer-related features to accurately predict the likelihood of a customer making a payment on time and has numerous practical applications in the business world. The motivation behind this project is to help businesses overcome the challenges of financial forecasting and improve their financial performance using machine learning technology. In the above-mentioned graph it has been found that the SMEs (Small and Medium enterprises) are the most affected due to the late payment behavior of the companies as shown in Fig. 1. Payment Prediction system can help SMEs better manage their finances, improve cash flow, reduce risk, and make more informed decisions in the following ways [3, 5]:

- It can help SMEs better understand their cash flow by predicting when payments are likely to be received.
- With a payment prediction system, SMEs can make more accurate financial forecasts, which can be helpful for planning and decision-making.
- By predicting when payments are likely to be received, SMEs can reduce the risk of late payments or non-payment. This can help them avoid cash flow problems and financial difficulties.

1.1 Need for Predicting User Payment Behavior

For many companies and organizations, particularly those involved in sectors like economics, online shopping, services for subscriptions, and others, predicting consumer payment behavior is crucial. Identifying and anticipating user payment behavior can provide a number of significant advantages as shown in Fig. 2 [6]:

- Risk Assessment: Predicting payment patterns aids in determining a user's or customer's trustworthiness. When deciding whether to authorize a loan or issue a credit

Fig. 2. Need for predicting user payment behavior.

card, financial institutions, lending organizations, and finance firms must consider this.

- Fraud Detection: Identifying and forecasting potentially fraudulent transactions or payment behavior are crucial. Machine learning algorithms can be utilized to identify unusual behavior and strange trends.
- Revenue Optimization: Forecasting payment patterns might help organizations increase their income. Forecasting when consumers will pay their bills or renew their subscriptions, for instance, can assist in designing marketing initiatives and offers to encourage prompt payments and extensions.
- Cash Flow Management: Cash flow management is aided by precise projections of payment behavior. It enables businesses to manage assets and plan for future revenue more effectively.
- Customer Engagement: Communication tactics can be more effectively tailored if payment behavior is understood. For instance, reminding users to make payments or rewarding those who consistently fail to do so might increase retention and involvement.
- Resource Allocation: Effective resource allocation can benefit from forecasting. Based on anticipated payment behavior patterns, businesses can staff their customer care, collections, and customer retention groups.
- Credit Risk Management: Forecasting aids in the efficient management of credit risk for businesses that issue credit to clients. Organizations can change credit limits or enact tighter terms for repayment by identifying clients who are more likely to default [5–8]

1.2 General Pipeline

Businesses and organizations aiming to maximize income, manage cash flow, and lower the risks associated with late or missed payments can greatly benefit from predictive models for anticipating user payment projections using machine learning. They can obtain historical payment information, make sure the information is accurate, organized, and representative of the intended audience, create relevant features that may influence payment behavior, deal with missing data, and outliers, and scale or normalize the data as required [4–7]. To evaluate the model, divide the data into training, validation, and testing sets. Select the most suitable algorithms and techniques for your issue. Train the chosen models using the proper hyperparameters on the training data. Models should be regularized to avoid overfitting. During learning, keep track of and log metrics for performance. When performing regression analyses, evaluate the effectiveness of the model using metrics like Accuracy, Precision, etc. To enhance the accuracy of models, optimize hyperparameters using methods such as grid search, random search, or Bayesian optimization. Deliver the model that was developed to a production setting so that users can benefit from real-time or batch predictions as shown in Fig. 3 [2, 5].

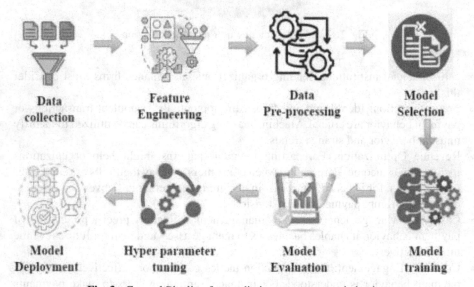

Fig. 3. General Pipeline for predicting user payment behavior.

1.3 Data Sources

Utilizing machine learning to predict user payment behavior necessitates having access to pertinent data sources that can reveal information about user behavior and payment trends. Here are some sources of pertinent data to take into account:

- Historical Payment Data: The most significant information resource is this one. It comprises transaction histories, amounts, time frames, and supplementary information.

    For successful training of deep learning models, one requires a rich dataset that covers a long enough time frame [5–7].
- Customer Profile Data: Data on your users can be really useful. Gather demographic statistics (such as age, gender, and geography), segment client data, and any additional

pertinent data that might assist you in comprehending the interests and behavior of your consumers.

- Website/App Analytics: Information about user actions and behavior can be gleaned from your web page or mobile application data. Page views, click-through rates, session lengths, and conversion rates are all included in this. This is where tools like Analytics from Google can be useful.
- Customer Support Data: Documentation of user contacts with support staff, such as chat logs and email conversations, might offer hints regarding user concerns, payment related problems, and general user happiness.
- User Engagement Metrics: Indicators that measure user involvement, such as the amount of usage and feature uptake, might be useful predictors of purchasing behavior.
- Market Trends and Competitor Data: In particular, for businesses in fiercely competitive marketplaces, data on market developments, competing offerings, and pricing tactics in their sector can be helpful for anticipating payment behavior.

1.4   Case Studies and Applications

Machine learning is a useful tool for predicting customer payment behavior across a range of businesses, including banking, online shopping, service subscriptions, and more. The case studies and applications listed below demonstrate how data science can be utilized for predicting customer payment behavior [9, 10].

- Credit Risk Assessment: To forecast the possibility of borrowers defaulting on loans, several financial institutions utilize machine learning. In addition to credit scores, income, employment history, and prior loan performance, they also examine previous data on borrowers' payment patterns. Banks and lending platforms can assess applicants' credibility and make better-educated choices about granting loans and interest rates using predictive models.
- Subscription Churn Prediction: Machine learning is used by subscription service businesses like Netflix and Spotify to anticipate when consumers may quit their memberships. They examine user actions, usage trends, and interest indicators. These platforms can take proactive steps, such as providing specific suggestions or incentives, to keep consumers by identifying individuals at risk of leaving.
- E-commerce Payment Fraud Detection: Machine learning is used by online merchants to identify fraudulent payment practices. They examine transactional information such as the frequency of transactions, the Internet Protocol (IP) address, and the user's purchase history. Refunds and other money losses are decreased Through the identification of possibly forged transactions.
- Utility Bill Payment Forecasting: Machine learning is used by utility companies to forecast whether customers will pay their bills on time. They examine past payment information, seasonal variables, and client characteristics. Utility providers can increase collection rates by sending warnings or providing alternative payment arrangements to clients who are likely to miss payments.
- Healthcare Billing Prediction: Machine learning is used by hospitals and other healthcare organizations to forecast patient payment behavior. They consider things like past payments, insurance policies, and medical history. This supports financial planning

and revenue forecasting by assisting medical professionals in estimating how much they can anticipate receiving from people.

2 Literature Survey

From the survey mentioned in Table 1 it has been found that the most preferred model for the late payment predicting date is a Decision tree with good accuracy according to the different datasets used by them. XG Boost has also been one of the most recommended models to try on one's own dataset. The system design of the app is shown in the above figure. Firstly, the raw data given by the company will be pre-processed and data cleaning will take place to remove noise/outliers from the data, due to which the errors occur in the data. Then once the final data is ready the data will go through the training phase in which there are different models which are being tested on the data such as Linear Regression, Decision Tree, XG Boost, and Random Forest and then the best suited model is chosen. The admin works on the web interface and enters the company details, the data then goes through the trained model, after that the performance evaluation is checked and then finally the prediction is done in which the number of days when the invoice is due will be printed [1]. In order to reduce the penalties incurred as a result of bills being paid late, machine learning is used to forecast the payment status of invoices. Therefore, rather of relying on teams to monitor invoice processes or do time-consuming analysis on each invoice, our forecasts can empower the process owners to actively work on flagged bills. Modeling a domain with historical (temporal) information as numerical features and categorical features. By replacing all of the unique values in a category with a few extra columns for each row, this significantly shrinks the feature space. Otherwise, if categorical features were subjected to one hot-encoding or indexing, there would be 1885 features produced [2]. The Pre-delinquency Decision Support System (DSS) assisting an organization's management in making judgments regarding the IPPP resolution. The process of the DSS is based on applying a suitable machine-learning algorithm to previous data. The AI algorithm uses data on appropriate characteristics of regular customer profiles, as well as information on paying a history and credit scores, as input and outputs a probability that the customer will miss a payment by a given deadline [9, 10].

To forecast the most severe non-financial payment circumstances among firms and compare the effectiveness of the decision tree model to the conventional Logistic Regression model for this purpose. The same finalized study dataset served as the foundation for the construction of Decision Tree and Logistic Regression models following an information identification step that included inference, extraction, and transformation to identify possible predictors. When comparing different models using the ROC index and Kolmogorov-Smirnov statistic, the Decision Tree model and the Logistic Regression model both fared favorably [17].

Table 1. Summary of papers reviewed

Year	Abstract	Algorithm used	Evaluation Parameters	Observation
2022 [9, 10]	The system is capable of learning payment receptions during any 3 intervals of regular customer profiles, their previous payment history, and their	Logistic regression, Naïve Bayes classifier, a random forest model, a decision tree model, the k-nearest neighbor technique, and a dense neural network	Accuracy = 79% (decision tree)	Forecasting invoice payment behavior involves information on past accounts, A computational implementation of the DSS was nonetheless able to predict invoice payment behavior with between 79.01 to 82.5%
2021 [6]	There are different pre-processing steps given the main proposed solution is to split the problem into 3 steps according to the number of days the delay has been made	Bagging Random Forest, Balanced Random Forest, AdaBoost, Gradient Boosting, RUSBoost, and XGBoost	Precision = 87% (XG Boost)	It was observed that dividing a problem into sub-problems helped to achieve the solution
2019 [11]	A network of nodes with edges displaying the transactions between companies	Decision Tree, Random Forest, Logistic Regression and Support Vector Machine	Precision = 89% Recall = 82% (Decision Tree)	The model was tested in two separate ways. The First was to predict whether the invoice is paid on time or not, next was to segregate the invoice
2018 [2]	Used a super-vised learning approach for training the classifier	SVM, Logistic Classifier, random forest	F1 score = 95% (Random forest)	It has been noted that seasonality and previous reliance are significant factors in determining if the in-voice will be paid on given time or not
2018 [14]	Reduces the problem of A/R by improving collection strategies	Logistic regression, decision trees, naive Bayes, SVM, and KNN		Proactive action lowers past-due accounts receivable and ensures visibility
2018 [11]	Knowing when every invoice should be paid helps portfolio management	Decision tree, Random forest, Ada-Boost, Logistic Regression, SVM	Accuracy = 81% (Random Forest)	features are created on historical data, they are not available for new customers

3   System Design

The system design of the app has been shown in Fig. 4. Firstly, the raw data given by the company will be pre-processed and data cleaning will take place to remove noise/outliers from the data, due to which the errors occur in the data. Then once the final data is ready the data will go through the training phase in which there are different models which are being tested on the data such as Linear Regression, Decision Tree, XG Boost, Random Forest and then the best suited model is being the final predicted output is as shown in Fig. 6 chosen.

A. Data Acquisition and pre-processing

Some of the features of the dataset are shown in the Fig. 5 in which there are the original available parameters of the dataset on the left side, and then the derived parameters, which are derived from the original parameters after the data pre-processing, are on the right side.

B. Algorithms Used

- Linear Regression: The value of a variable can be predicted using linear regression analysis based on the value of another variable. The dependent variable should be predictable. Using the independent variable, predict the value of the other variable.
- Decision tree: A classification technique known as a" decision tree" makes use of a tree-like representation of decisions and potential outcomes. To forecast whether a consumer will make a payment on time or not, we used a decision tree in our model.
- Random forest is a technique that blends different decision trees to increase the model's accuracy. To forecast whether a consumer will make a payment on time or not, we employed a random forest method in our model.

C. Tools used for implementation

- Programming Languages: Machine learning models can be developed using several programming languages, including Python, R, Java, and Scala. In this Python has been used which is the most popular language for machine learning, and it has several libraries and frameworks for machine learning development, including scikit-learn, Tensor-Flow, XGBoost.

  Data Pre-processing Tools: Data pre-processing is an essential step in machine learning. It involves cleaning, transforming, and normalizing the data to make it suitable for training the machine learning models. Tools such as Pandas, NumPy, and Scikit-learn are used for data pre-processing.
- Machine Learning Algorithms: Machine learning models use several algorithms to learn from the data and make predictions. Algorithms such as Decision Trees, Random Forests, Boosting, and Logistic Regression, are commonly used for late payment prediction.
- Model Evaluation and Validation Tools: It is essential to evaluate and validate the machine learning models to ensure that they are accurate and reliable. Tools such as MSE, R2 square, and precision are used to evaluate and validate the models.

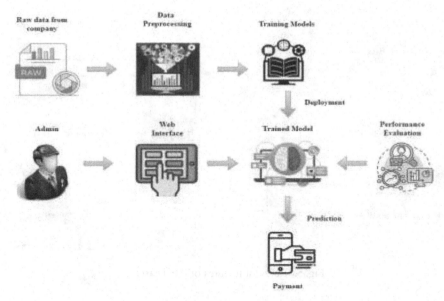

Fig. 4. System architecture of proposed system

D. Evaluation parameters

- Evaluating late payment date prediction using Machine Learning (ML) can be done using various criteria or parameters. The following are some of the suitable criteria or parameters for evaluating late payment date prediction using ML.
- Accuracy: This parameter measures the correctness of the model's prediction compared to the actual payment date. Total number of accurate forecasts divided by the number of predictions is the model's accuracy.
- Precision: This metric calculates the percentage of accurate positive predictions versus all positive forecasts. If the model has a high precision score, it can detect true positive cases with few false positives.
- Recall: This variable counts the number of actual positive cases about the percentage of true positive predictions. A high recall score means that the model can recognize most real positive situations and relatively few false negatives.
- Confusion Matrix: The actual and anticipated values of the model are displayed in the confusion matrix. By comparing the number of true positives, true negatives, false positives, and false negatives, it is used to assess the model's accuracy [4].
- MSE score: This is the average of the square of the errors.
- R2 score. It is also known as coefficient of determination. It is used the amount of variation predicted by the input independent variables of the output dependent variable.

From all these parameters, the two relevant parameters are selected and have been used, which are MSE score and R2 score, and their comparison is as shown in Fig. 6. And comparison of different algorithms based on MSE score and R2 score is shown in Table 2 (Fig. 7).

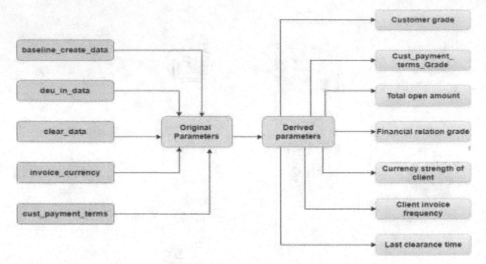

Fig. 5. Relevant features of the dataset

4   Dataset

The dataset of past payment behavior of customers has been used, provided by the company, and is already an existing dataset, along with their demographic and credit information. The dataset contains 50,000 observations and 19 features. The target variable is a binary variable that indicates whether the customer made a payment on time or not. Selected the algorithms used in the model based on the features selected in the dataset. During the literature review, it was found that few common features in this dataset as well as the ones in the previously tested models, so used 3–4 algorithms and then finally selected the most accurate algorithms according to this model, which will give high accuracy and precision value as shown in Fig. 3. The selection of algorithms for testing a late payment prediction model depends on the specific needs of the business, and the resources available for implementing the model. It is important to select algorithms that are well-suited to the specific problem being addressed, and that can provide the required level of accuracy. Additionally, it is important to compare the performance of different algorithms to determine which one is the most effective for predicting late payments.

5   Results

This model's performance has been assessed using several criteria, including accuracy, precision, recall, and F1-score used a 70:30 split between the model's training and testing as shown in Fig. 4. The outcomes demonstrate that the XG boost algorithm performed better than the competition with a 95% accuracy rate. The XG boost algorithm's precision and recall were 0.91 and 0.93, respectively. The decision tree algorithm had an F1-score of 0.90 and a 91.5% accuracy rate. The decision tree algorithm had precision and recall of 0.89 and 0.91, respectively. The comparison of algorithms and data used is mentioned in Tables 2 and 3 respectively. The comparison graphs are shown in Fig. 4.

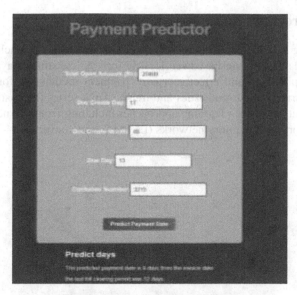

Fig. 6. Output of payment predictor

Table 2. Comparison Values of Different Algorithms Used

Algorithm	MSE Score	R2 Score
Linear Regression	3.20	0.32
Decision tree	2.33	0.50
Random Forest	1.10	0.76
XG Boost	9.9	0.78

Table 3. Data Used In This Study

Account used	Invoice data (given by organization)
Dimension	50,000 x 19
Dimension after pre-processing	50,000 x 8
Features present	cust_number, business_code clear_date, name_customer business_year, doc_id, posting_date, document_create_date, document_create_date.1, due_in_date, invoice_currency, document type, posting_id, area_business, total_open_amount, baseline_create_date, cust_payment_terms, invoice_id, isOpen
Features present after pre-preocessing	total_open_amount, document_create_date, document create month, isOpen, clear date, due day, cust number, doc_id,
Train dataset	35988 rows
Test dataset	9681 rows
Output	Delay (no of days)

6 Future Directions and Recent Challenges

Machine learning is being used extensively in a number of sectors, including finance, e-commerce, and subscription-based services, to forecast consumer payment patterns. To increase the precision and effectiveness of payment models for forecasting, it is crucial to be informed of current issues and trends. Time-series forecasting challenges have shown potential for deep learning approaches including recurrent neural networks (RNNs), long short-term memory networks (LSTMs), and converters.

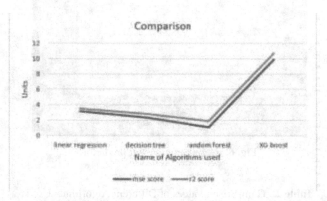

Fig. 7. Comparison graph of MSE score and R2 score

The development of more complex deep learning architectures specifically suited to payment forecasting may be the main focus of future studies. There is an increasing need for model interpretation that can offer insights into the elements driving payment behavior as machine learning models get more complicated. The need for research into developing comprehensible AI models will never diminish. The accuracy of predictions may frequently be increased by creating ensembles from many machine-learning models. Future studies may focus on creating innovative ensemble techniques created expressly for situations involving payment forecasting. For a precise prediction of payments, relevant information from user data must be extracted. Improved feature design approaches and domain-specific feature selection strategies will continue to be investigated by investigators [11, 13, 14, 16].

The processing of customer payment information while adhering to privacy laws is a key difficulty given the growing concern for data privacy and tougher regulations like GDPR and CCPA. Transaction datasets frequently have a class imbalance since most users make their dues on time [15]. It is essential to deal with this discrepancy in order to avoid modeling bias. The nature of payments is subject to shifting as time passes, making it difficult to create reliable models. A significant problem is adjusting to data with irregular patterns. AI models must be comprehensible, particularly in finance where openness is crucial. Complex frameworks continue to pose a difficulty when it comes to explaining the causes of predictions made by models [19–21]. The technological difficulty of scaling up payment forecasting techniques to manage big user bases and high numbers of transactions calls for efficient systems and techniques as shown in Fig. 8 [18].

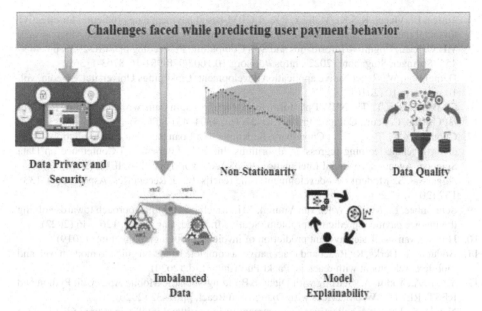

Fig. 8. Challenges faced while predicting user payment behavior.

7 Conclusion

The payment prediction model is a piece of software that makes predictions about upcoming payments based on past data using machine learning techniques. These models are essential for businesses like banks, credit card firms, and other financial institutions that rely on clients' recurrent payments. The proposed system takes input in raw form, and then the noise is removed from the data. The algorithms used for training the input data are Linear Regression, Decision Tree, XG Boost, and Random Forest. The trained model is fed with the company details using the web interface to predict the number of days of late payment, and along with that, performance is evaluated. The comparison of all the algorithms is carried out using performance metrics such as MSE and R2 Score, and from that, we can conclude that XH Boost shows good performance that other algorithms used for predicting late payments.

References

1. Banks, A., Porcello, E.: Learning React: Functional Web Development with React and Redux. O'Reilly Media, Inc. (2017)
2. Tater, T., Dechu, S., Mani, S., Maurya, C.: Prediction of invoice payment status in account payable business process. In: Pahl, C., Vukovic, M., Yin, J., Yu, Qi. (eds.) ICSOC 2018. LNCS, vol. 11236, pp. 165–180. Springer, Cham (2018). https://doi.org/10.1007/978-3-030-03596-9_11
3. Ghimire, D.: Comparative study on Python web frameworks: Flask and Django (2020)

4. Tutica, L., Vineel, K.S.K., Mallick, P.K.: LGBM-based payment date prediction for effective financial statement management. In: Mallick, P.K., Bhoi, A.K., Barsocchi, P., de Albuquerque, V.H.C. (eds.) Cognitive Informatics and Soft Computing: Proceeding of CISC 2021, pp. 445–455. Springer, Singapore (2022). https://doi.org/10.1007/978-981-16-8763-1_36
5. Danielsson, W.: React Native application development. Linköpings Universitet, Swedia, vol. 10, no. 4, p. 10 (2016)
6. Cholia, S., Sun, T.: The NEWT platform: an extensible plugin framework for creating ReSTful HPC APIs. Concurr. Comput. Pract. Exp. **27**(16), 4304–4317 (2015)
7. Choudhary, S., Tyagi, C.S., Choudhary, S., Kumar, A.: Loan payment date prediction model using machine learning regression algorithms. In: 2022 International Conference on Data Science, Agents & Artificial Intelligence (ICDSAAI), vol. 1, pp. 1–6. IEEE (2022)
8. Aggarwal, S.: Modern web-development using reactjs. Int. J. Recent Res. Aspects **5**(1), 133–137 (2018)
9. Schoonbee, L., Moore, W.R., van Vuuren, J.H.: Machine-learning approach towards solving the invoice payment prediction problem. South Afr. J. Ind. Eng. **33**(4), 126–146 (2022)
10. Hovanesyan, A.: Late payment prediction of invoices through graph features (2019)
11. Boduch, A., Derks, R.: React and react native: a complete hands-on guide to modern web and mobile development with react. js. Packt Publishing Ltd. (2020)
12. Yudin, A., Yudin, A.: Starting with Django. Building Versatile Mobile Apps with Python and REST: RESTful Web Services with Django and React, pp. 1–32 (2020)
13. Nanda, S.: Proactive collections management: using artificial intelligence to predict invoice payment dates. Credit Res Found 1Q Credit Finan Manag Rev (2018)
14. Rebelo, S.L.D.C.: Predicting Account Receivables Outcomes with Machine-Learning. Doctoral dissertation (2022)
15. George, N.: Mastering Django: Core. Packt Publishing Ltd. (2016)
16. Rudd, M.P.H., GStat, J.M., Priestley, J.L.: A comparison of decision tree with logistic regression model for prediction of worst non-financial payment status in commercial credit (2017)
17. Vipul, A.M., Sonpatki, P.: ReactJS by Example-Building Modern Web Applications with React. Packt Publishing Ltd. (2016)
18. Thebe, L.: Community parenting platform: development and deployment using the Django framework (2016)
19. Wilson, N., Summers, B., Hope, R.: Using payment behaviour data for credit risk modelling. Int. J. Econ. Bus. **7**(3), 333–346 (2000)
20. Gackenheimer, C.: Introduction to React. Apress (2015)
21. Singh, N.: Stock prediction using machine learning a review paper. Int. J. Comput. Appl. **163**(5), 36–43 (2017). https://doi.org/10.5120/ijca2017913453
22. Khanvilkar, G., Vora, D.: Sentiment analysis for product recommendation using random forest. Int. J. Eng. Technol. **7**(3), 87–89 (2018). https://doi.org/10.14419/ijet.v7i3.3.14492

An Efficient Image Dehazing Technique Using DSRGAN and VGG19

Bhrugesh Jadav(iD), Sashikala Mishra(iD), Pooja Bagane(iD),
and Ranjeet Vasant Bidwe$^{(\boxtimes)}$ (iD)

Symbiosis Institute of Technology, Pune, Symbiosis International (Deemed University), Lavale,
Pune, Maharashtra, India
bhrugeshsetu2000@gmail.com, {sashikala.mishra,
pooja.bagane}@sitpune.edu.in, ranjeetbidwe@hotmail.com

Abstract. Haze and clouds can cause the weather to affect the clarity and contrast of photos that are taken by cameras, air quality, and other reasons. To address the issue of haze, image dehazing has become an area of significant importance. However, many current techniques for unsupervised picture dehazing rely on simplified atmospheric scattering models and a priori knowledge, which can result in inaccuracies and poor dehazing performance. The study of image-dehazing techniques has shown promise Generative Adversarial Networks (GANs) were developed. Unfortunately, because haze is so complicated, the bi-directional mappings domain translation techniques currently used in unsupervised GANs are not suitable for dehazing image work. With haze-free photos, the image may become distorted, lose image details, or retain image features poorly as a result. The paper makes recommendations for an end-to-end unsupervised image-dehazing system that is used to address these problems. Deep Super-Resolution Generative Adversarial Network (DSRGAN) that uses VGG19 for feature extraction. The problem addressed in this project is to create a novel picture dehazing method that uses the DSRGAN and VGG19 models to successfully remove haze from photographs. The specific objectives of this project are to implement the DSRGAN and VGG19 models, modify them for image dehazing, acquire a dataset of hazy images, preprocess the dataset to remove any anomalies, train the models on the dataset to learn the features and characteristics of hazy images and assess the performance of the models using both qualitative and quantitative metrics. The proposed method showed an improvement in both PSNR and SSIM metrics with 24.06 and 0.912. The proposed system achieves negligible generator loss and discriminator loss, offering a promising solution to the challenge of image dehazing in complex and dynamic environments.

Keywords: Generative Adversarial Network · Image Dehazing · DSRGAN · VGG19

1 Introduction

HAZE is a frequent atmospheric condition that can damage the clarity of images taken by external vision systems, like as those used in driverless cars [1, 2], unmanned aerial vehicles (UAVs) [3] in an unpredictable manner, traffic monitoring [4], surveillance [5].

M. A. Jabbar et al. (Eds.): AMLDA 2023, CCIS 2047, pp. 81–96, 2024.
https://doi.org/10.1007/978-3-031-55486-5_7

Even modern methods for object recognition, classification, and tracking can experience significant accuracy losses in the presence of haze. Therefore, Image dehazing is an essential step for enhancing image quality and making complex visual tasks easier. Image dehazing aims to recover crystal-clear images from murky sources. Nowadays, prior-based and learning-based methodologies can be used to categorize picture dehazing techniques. Both techniques can increase visibility, however, there are still several challenging problems that need to be addressed. First, Convolutional neural networks (CNNs) or paired data are used in learning-based methodologies. Additionally, neural networks can repair damaged, blurry images [6]. Unfortunately, it is challenging to collect such matched data in the actual world, and generating synthetic pairs using atmospheric scattering equations can degrade the network's ability to handle believable situations. Second, neural networks have the potential to overfit both artificial and real fog images, particularly with little training data, which can result in further distortions like loss of features, low contrasts, and halos. Lastly, to get the best results from traditional prior-based approaches, users must manually modify a number of parameters which can be a laborious and time-consuming process, and there is no guarantee of achieving optimal results automatically.

A technique for super-resolving images based on deep learning is called Super-Resolution Generative Adversarial Network (SRGAN). SRGAN's primary goal is for high-quality output, enhanced resolution images [7] from low-resolution inputs, a process commonly referred to as super-resolution. The SRGAN model uses a discriminator and a generator, 2 deep neural networks, comprising the architecture of a GAN. A discriminator assesses the output image's quality while the generator network transforms a poor-quality picture into an excellent-quality image and feeds that information back to the producing network. Mapping between low and high images must be learned. SRGAN [8] is training on large-scale image datasets. The network also incorporates perceptual loss and adversarial loss, which help generate realistic and sharp images with high-frequency details. SRGAN has shown significant improvements over traditional image super-resolution techniques and has been applied to various Applications for image processing including video processing, satellite imaging, and medical imaging. It has also been used in the entertainment industry to enhance the resolution of low-quality videos and images.

2   Related Works

This section provides an overview of image dehazing and GANs with a particular emphasis on research on image dehazing using GANs.

2.1   Dehazing of Images

The current classification of image-dehazing algorithms includes deep learning, physical modeling, and image enhancement-based techniques. While each type has shown some success, they still have certain limitations that ultimately lead to unsatisfactory dehazing outcomes. Dehazing is accomplished by increasing the image's contrast and saturation via image enhancement-based techniques such as histogram equalization [9], Retinex, and wavelet modification [10]. Due to these techniques, the haze-free image has issued such Halo aberrations, color distortions, and overly aggressive local area enhancement despite their simplicity in theory and low computational complexity. These problems include halo artifacts, color distortion, and excessive local area enhancement. On the other hand, dehazing algorithms that are based on physical models heavily rely on the atmospheric effects model. We have seen and compiled a large number of haze and haze-free photos. These algorithms obtain mapping relationships that enable them to restore clear images by using the technique by which hazy pictures are created in reverse [11].

Deep learning-based dehazing methods can build a neural network model using training data to comprehend the relationship between photos with and without haze. By overcoming the difficulties involved in physically stimulating haze, this method produces better outcomes. Dehazing algorithms based on deep learning frequently belong to one of two groups. In order to achieve picture dehazing, the first method forecasts the atmospheric scattering parameters models using a model of a neural network. In order to learn the mapping between haze and transmittance, Cai et al. [12] presented the DehazeNet method, which makes use of convolutional neural networks. Afterwards, a haze-free image is produced using the parameters derived from the atmospheric scattering model. The haze-free picture is subsequently retrieved utilizing the atmospheric scattering model. The second type of technique creates a visibility estimate utilizing the blurred picture as its input. The clarity of a restored haze-free picture is improved using a unique nonlinear activation function.

2.2　Prior Information-Based Methods for Dehazing

By using statistical information from haze photos to characterize the creation of haze, the method based on prior knowledge is primarily focused on calculating the medium transmittance and atmospheric light intensity. By solving the air scattering model, the final clear picture is produced. This approach was frequently utilized in early picture dehazing studies. Tan presented a dehazing method to maximize local contrasts on the basis that clear pictures have more contrast than foggy ones. Fattal [13] used reflectivity analysis on the notion that surfaces' shadows and medium transparency are not spatially connected. Additionally, The darkness channels prior (DCP) were created by He et al. [14] and is based on the empirical conclusion that, with the exception of the sky, at least one channel in most local image blocks displays very low-intensity values at certain pixels that even approach zero. With this knowledge in hand, a blurry image can be transformed back into a clear one. In their study, Berman et al. [15] discovered that several hundred different colors can be used to simulate an image without haze. They then presented the non-local color previous (NCP) as an image dehazing method.

2.3　Methods for Dehazing Based on Deep Learning

Despite achieving varying degrees of success, the adopted assumptions or the accuracy of the previous information for the target object limit haze removal techniques based on past knowledge inherently [16]. Moreover, differing selections of past knowledge could lead to a lack of haze removal or color distortions. Deep learning has recently significantly outperformed prior-based techniques tasks requiring poor eyesight, such as image dehazing. This is due to its triumphs in high-level machine vision tasks such as image classification and recognition. Cai et al., [12] introduced DehazeNet, a complete network that is trainable for image dehazing that utilizes deep learning to estimate the medium transmittance. In order to calculate the medium permeability, neural networks are used. DehazeNet achieves greater accuracy compared to traditional methods. AOD-Net, Li et al. presented an integrative dehazing network [17]. AOD-Net uses In contrast to earlier systems that evaluated the medium transmittance map and ambient light independently, a lightweight convolutional neural network can instantaneously provide a haze-free image. When applied to hazy images, this ground-breaking technique makes it straightforward to involve AOD-Net in a variety of models (like Faster R-CNN), improving the performance of difficult computer vision tasks.

He et al. (2019) suggested medium transmittance, ambient light, and dehazing simultaneously using pyramid dehazing networks with dense links (DCPDN) [18]. The network performs direct learning from beginning to conclusion incorporating the air scattering models through the network. In order to estimate medium transmission, the authors created a new edge-preserving dense links encoder-decoder structure, drawing inspiration from DenseNet [19], while U-Net [20] was used to determine ambient light. The GAN [21] framework was employed by DCPDN to optimize and propose a joint discriminator that took into account the mutual understanding of their structures; two datasets anticipated a map of medium transmissivity and dehazing findings. By examining the linked dehazing image's credibility and the expected transmission map, this combined discriminator enhances the details.

2.4 Generative Adversarial Network (GAN)

A two-player game between a discriminator and a generator are symbolized by the letters G and D, respectively the basic idea behind GANs. Denoted as D, to achieve optimal generation performance. G takes in random noise to produce a synthetic image, while D distinguishes the authenticity of the input image by comparing it to real images [22]. During training, G generates images to deceive D, while D aims to distinguish real from synthetic images through adversarial competition. The optimization process terminates when D can no longer differentiate between the two types of images. The effectiveness of this method is often evaluated using the GAN loss function.

$$min_G \, max_D V(D, G) = Ex \sim Pdata(x)[logD(x)] + Ez \sim pz(z)[log \, log(1 - D(G(z)))] \tag{1}$$

where $z \sim Pz(z)$ signifies the a priori input noise distribution and $x \sim Pdata(x)$ denotes the data distribution obeying the haze-free image. Although GANs theoretically can fit the distributions of the chosen picture domain, they are vulnerable to a solution in order to collapse issues that occur during training and cause inconsistent training procedures and poor-quality output images. To address this issue, several studies have proposed different solutions. For example, Arjovsky et al. [23] introduced the Wasserstein distance in WGAN to steady the learning process and offer a gauge to show development. SNGAN is a method that Miyato et al. [24] suggested to stabilize the training procedure without adding computational complexity. The least-squares loss function is used by LSGAN, which was developed by Mao et al. [25], to enhance the images taken' quality and maintain the training process. In their study, Qu et al. [26] introduced an innovative GAN-based dehazing network known as EPDN, along with a carefully crafted refiner that does not rely on any physical model. However, similar to other learning-based approaches, these methods necessitate paired data during training, resulting in limited efficacy when it comes to real-world hazy images.

2.5 Outcome from the Related Work

Based on the literature survey conducted, it appears that three basic groups of image dehazing algorithms are those that rely on image enhancement, physical models, and deep learning. Although these algorithms have had some successes, they have some flaws that lead to subpar dehazing results. Previous research in image dehazing has heavily relied on prior information-based methods. However, these methods are constrained by the veracity of prior knowledge about the target scene or by their presumptions.

The following objectives Have been taken care of from the above literature survey as the objective of the proposed model.

DHQ database is the largest of its kind and includes various haze densities, it only uses seven representative DHAs. There is a need for a more extensive and systematic evaluation of DHAs to find their effectiveness and limitations. The end-to-end gated context aggregation network restores the haze-free image, which surpasses previous state-of-the-art methods. However, the generalization of this method to other image restoration tasks requires further investigation. While Ranks GAN proposes to achieve state-of-the-art performance in perceptual metrics, there is a need to evaluate its performance on a wider range of image resolutions and datasets. These are all the objectives successfully implemented in Our Proposed Model for GAN. Deep learning research has recently made significant strides, with promising outcomes in simple vision tasks such as image dehazing. Several methods based on deep learning, including DehazeNet, AOD-Net, and DCPDN, have been proposed and these have achieved greater accuracy compared to traditional methods by estimating medium transmittance using deep learning. In addition, in their studies on image dehazing, researchers have employed GANs. A generator and a converter help the generation perform better discriminator engage in a two-player game.

In conclusion, the literature survey provides an overview of image dehazing and GANs, with a focus on research related to image dehazing using GANs. The survey highlights the limitations of current algorithms for image dehazing and the possibility of deep learning-based techniques to enhance dehazing results. It also introduces the concept of GANs and their potential for image dehazing research.

3 Methodologies

3.1 Importance of GAN

GANs have great capability to produce accurate synthetic data, It is feasible to create new data using GANs that are comparable to the original data but different enough to be distinct and varied. By supplementing training data with artificial images, GANs have also been used to enhance the performance and accuracy of other machine learning models, such as object identification. GANs have also been used for image-to-image translation, which allows an input image to be changed into a new image, and style transfer, which allows the style of one image to be transferred to another. GANs are crucial because they can produce synthetic data that may be utilized for a range of tasks, including enhancing training data, enhancing the performance of other machine learning models, and producing fresh and original visual material.

3.2 GAN

Image Dehazing using DSRGAN, a technique that employs GANs for generative modeling, has gained significant attention in the recent past. GANs are made up of the discriminator and the generator, two neural networks that are conditioned against one another [27]. The g $\prod_{k=1}^{n} A_k$ Generator networks create fresh data samples that resemble training data from random noise as input. The bias network can tell true data from fake data. Many different industries, including the creation of images and videos, and text generation. In the context of Image Dehazing, DSRGAN utilizes GANs to generate realistic and clear images from hazy or foggy scenes.

3.3 Deep Super-Resolution GAN (DSRGAN)

Enhancing Image Resolution using DSRGAN is an Approach for Generating High-Quality Images with Preserved Content and Details. DSRGANs utilize a generator network that transforms Hazing images into clear image counterparts through a combination of content and antagonistic losses. Additionally, a perceptual loss term based on neural networks that have already been trained is also included to further raise the quality of the images that are produced. The excellent outcome produced by DSRGANs has found numerous uses in industries like surveillance, video compression, and medical image analysis. Moreover, DSRGANs have been expanded to support video super-resolution, which uses the same method for raising the resolution of low-quality video frames.

3.4 Generator

A deep learning algorithm called the Deep Super-resolution generation is used to increase the resolution of poor-quality photographs. The model's generator section employs several convolutional and up-sampling layers to transform an image with low resolution and can be output as one with high resolution.

The discriminator finds it to be impossible to discriminate between high-resolution images made by the generator and real high-resolution photos. The generator's loss function is described [28] as follows:

$$L_G = L_2(y_{true} - y_{pred}) + \lambda L_{adv}(y_{pred} - y_{true}) \qquad (2)$$

where L2 denotes the y_{pred} is the created high-resolution picture, y_{true} is the high-resolution image of the grounded truth, L_{adv} is the adversarial loss and is a hyperparameter that regulates how significant the MSE and adversarial losses are in relation to one another. The adversarial loss uses a deep convolutional neural network characterized by the binary cross-entropy loss and has multiple convolutional and up-sampling layers to measure the generator (see Fig. 1). Each layer executes a convolution operation, then a rectified linear unit-style activation function (ReLU). To generate an image with pixel values ranging from −1 to 1, the final layer of the generator commonly adopts a tanh activation function. For up-sampling, either bilinear interpolation or nearest neighbor interpolation is often employed. Moreover, skip connections can be utilized to connect earlier layers to later ones and help maintain low-level image features.

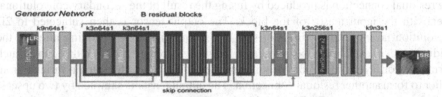

Fig. 1. Architecture of the Generator

To Adam, a stochastic gradient descent (SGD) approach is to instruct the generator. The gradients of the generator loss in regard to its parameters are calculated via backpropagation over the network, and the weights are modified to lessen the loss. The generator and discriminator are typically trained using an incremental min-max game until convergence is attained.

Table 1. Python snippet shows the Generator model

```
"def create_gen(gen_ip, num_res_block):
        layers = Conv2D(64, (9,9), padding="same")(gen_ip)
        layers=PReLU(shared_axes=[1,2])(layer)
        temp = layers
        for i in range(num_res_block):
                layers = res_block(layers)
        layers = Conv2D(64, (3,3), padding="same")(layers)
        layers = BatchNormalization
                        (momentum=0.5)(layers)
    layers = add([layers,temp])
    layers = upscale_block(layers)
    layers = upscale_block(layers)
    op = Conv2D(3, (9,9), padding="same")(layers)
    return Model(inputs=gen_ip, outputs=op)"
```

Table 1 is a Python snippet that shows the Generator model. A generator model for Deep super-resolution image generation can be created by using this Python function, which requires two input arguments: gen_ip and num_res_block.

The gen_ip argument represents the input tensor for the generator model, while num_res_block specifies how many residual blocks should be used in the model. To begin with, the operation involves utilizing a 2D convolutional layer on the input tensor, with a filter bank consisting of 64 filters that have dimensions of 9 × 9. To keep the output at the same size as the inputs, the padding parameter is set to "same". Subsequently, the resulting output is subjected to a Parametric ReLU activation function (PReLU), whereby the shared axes are set to [1, 2]. Finally, the output of this layer is saved in a temporary variable. The execution of num_res_block iterations involves calling the res_block function to incorporate a residual block into the model during each iteration. The res_block function incorporates two 2D convolutional layers with 64 filters each and "same" padding, and then a batch normalization layer with a momentum of 0.5 follows. The residual connection is produced by fusing the result of the secondary convolutional layer with the input tensor of the block. The output tensor is then subjected to 2D convolution layers with 64 filters of size 3 × 3 and "identical" padding after all the residual blocks have already been inserted. This layer's output is passed through a Batch Normalization layer with 0.5 momentum and then combined with the temp variable from earlier to form another residual connection. The output tensor is sampled by two upscale block functions sequentially. The first block performs upsampling by a 2D convolutional layer with 256 filters measuring 3 × 3, followed by an upsampling layer doubling the input tensor's height and width through nearest-neighbor interpolation. The output of the layer that performs the upsampling is then subjected to a shared-axis PReLU activation function. The ultimate output picture is created by the second block by using a 2D convolutional layer with three 9x9 filters. Keras Model object takes the input tensor gen_ip and produces the output tensor op.

3.5 Discriminator

The architecture of the discriminator is designed to facilitate a standard GAN process. Figure 2 illustrates how the generator and discriminator interact in a competitive manner each improving their performance concurrently. The discriminator's objective is to spot fake images, and the generator's goal is to create convincing visuals that will trick the discriminator. The same idea holds true for DSRGANs, where the generating model G [29] attempts to deceive a differentiable specifically taught to distinguish between genuine images and super-resolved images, discriminator D. The structure of the determiner, as shown in the graphic below, successfully differentiates between the genuine photos and super-resolution images. The adversarial min-max issue is intended to be addressed by the discriminator model that has been built. The following general principle can be used to interpret the phrasing of this equation [30]:

$$min\_\theta_G \; max\_\theta_D$$
$$E_I^{HR} \sim ptrain\left(I^{HR}\right)\left\lceil logD\_\theta_D\left(I^{HR}\right)\right\rceil + E_I^{LR} \sim p_G\left(I^{HR}\right)\left\lceil log\left(1 - D\_\theta_D\left(G\_\theta_G\left(I^{LR}\right)\right)\right)\right\rceil \tag{3}$$

The discriminator architecture in this study aims to be easy to understand. It is composed of the early convolutional layer and a 0.2 alpha Leaky ReLU activation function. Using dense layers, batch normalizing with Leaky ReLU activating and sigmoid activation are used to classify the data. After two blocks, the convolutional size scales up to 512 × 512, increasing by a factor of 2 from the initial convolutional size of 64 × 64.

This approach effectively distinguishes between actual and bogus data, which enhances the generator's learning. It can be used for additional picture-generating tasks because of its simple design and performance. Tables 2 and 3 are Python snippets that define the functions used to create a discriminator block and a discriminator model in popular frameworks for deep learning like TensorFlow or Keras. With a GAN, the discriminator model's main goal is to discriminate between authentic and fraudulent images (GAN). The three input arguments for the discriminator block function are the input layer ("ip"), the convolutional layer's stride size, the number of filters (or "filters"), and the convolution ("strides"). Utilizing batch normalization, a 0.2 slope leaky ReLU activation function, and this function includes non-linearity and has a 3 × 3 kernel size convolutional layer. The function "create disc" requires an argument, "disc_ip," which represents the discriminator model's input layer.

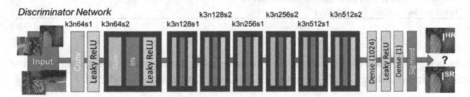

Fig. 2. Architecture of the Discriminator

This function initializes the variable "df" to 64 and builds the discriminator model by stacking multiple discriminator blocks defined by the "discriminator block" function. The discriminator model includes convolutional and dense layers, with the outputs of each discriminator block (d1 to d8) representing the output of each respective layer.

Table 2. Python snippet to create a discriminator block

```
"def discriminator_block(ip, filters, strides=1):
    disc_model = Conv2D(filters, (3,3), strides = strides, padding="same")(ip)
    disc_model = BatchNormalization( momentum=0.8)
        (disc_model)
    disc_model = LeakyReLU( alpha=0.2)(disc_model)
    return disc_model"
```

The output of the final discriminator block, d8, is flattened using the "Flatten()" function and fed into a dense layer d9 with a size of df multiplied by 16, d10, a leaky ReLU activation function, comes next. The output is then processed through a dense layer dubbed "validity," which produces a probability score showing whether the input is real or fraudulent. This layer has a single output and a sigmoid activation function. Together, these functions define a discriminator model that can be trained with a generator model in a GAN to create images that are realistic. The discriminator model determines if a picture is real or fake, whereas the generator model seeks so causing the discriminator

Table 3. Python snippet shows the Discriminator model

```
"def create_disc(disc_ip):
    df = 64
    d1 = discriminator_block(disc_ip, df)
    d2 = discriminator_block(d1, df, strides=2)
    d3 = discriminator_block(d2, df*2)
    d4 = discriminator_block(d3, df*2, strides=2)
    d5 = discriminator_block(d4, df*4)
    d6 = discriminator_block(d5, df*4, strides=2)
    d7 = discriminator_block(d6, df*8)
    d8 = discriminator_block(d7, df*8, strides=2)
d8_5 = Flatten()(d8)
d9 = Dense(df*16)(d8_5)
d10 = LeakyReLU(alpha=0.2)(d9)
validity = Dense(1,activation='sigmoid')(d10)
return Model(disc_ip, validity)"
```

network to misclassify them as real. The weights of both models are changed during training in order to gradually improve the clarity of the images produced.

3.6   VGG19

Table 4. Python snippet shows the VGG19 Model

```
"def build_vgg(gt_shape):
    vgg=VGG19(weights="imagenet",
            include_top=False, input_shape=gt_shape)
    return Model(inputs=vgg.inputs, outputs=vgg.layers[10].output)"
```

Table 4 is a Python snippet defines a function called build_vgg that produces a VGG19, a CNN model [31] that has already been trained with the possibility to alter it. A deep neural network called VGG19 has already been trained to classify images using the ImageNet dataset. The build_vgg function takes in parameters such as weights and top to customize the trained model beforehand. With the previously trained weights, set the weights option to "imagenet". To exclude the fully connected layers that classify photos, the top option is set to False. The input shape parameter sets the expected input image shape for the network. The function returns the final fully connected layers deleted from a modified version of the pre-trained VGG19 network that includes all layers up to layer 10.

The Model function in Keras is then used to create a new model object that takes the input and output pre-trained VGG19 model. The inputs parameter is set to vgg.inputs, which represents the input layer, and the outputs parameter is set to vgg.layers [13].output, which represents the output of layer 10. The modified model can be utilized for removing characteristics from input photographs for other purposes, such as training a separate model for image classification or object detection. This is possible because the modified model has retained the VGG19 model's previously trained features, which can be useful for other image-related tasks.

In summary, the build_vgg function provides a convenient way to modify Feature extraction from input photos done using a pre-trained VGG19 model. The modified model can be used for tasks beyond image classification, and the retained features can be useful for other image-related tasks.

3.7 Model

In this project work the DSRGAN model is used for dehazing images. A specific kind of GAN called DSRGAN is made for jobs involving image super-resolution or turning low-resolution photos into high-resolution ones. However, in this case, it is used to dehaze images, which involves removing the hazy effect and restoring the original clarity and detail of the image. The DSRGAN paradigm includes a discriminator network as well as a generator network as its two main components. The generator network transforms a murky input image into an output image with original clarity. The generator network typically consists of several layers of CNNs and up-sampling layers that help increase the clarity and quality of the output image.

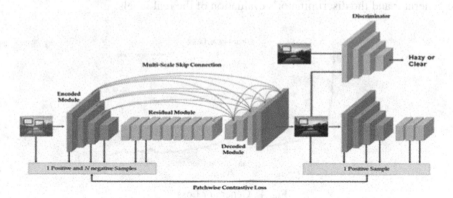

Fig. 3. Proposed Model Of DSRGAN

The discriminator network, on the other hand, is responsible for distinguishing between the original clarity output image produced by the ground-truth image and the generator network. The network discriminator consists of several layers of CNNs that learn to classify pictures as either false or authentic [32]. The generator network tries to create unique clarity pictures during training, causing the discriminator network to misclassify them as real. The discriminator network attempts to accurately categorize the real-world photographs and the ones that were generated as real or false, while the generator network attempts to provide original clarity and outputs images that can trick the discriminator network.

In summary, the DSRGAN model uses a discriminator network and a generator network to perform image super-resolution tasks, and it can be used for various applications, including dehazing. Throughout the training, the model discovers how to produce authentic clarity pictures that are identical to real photos, and during inference, it can produce original clarity images from hazy image inputs [33]. Figure 3 shows the overall structure of the described model.

4   Result Analysis

4.1   Dataset

Realistic Single Image DEhazing (RESIDE), a thorough benchmark that includes both simulated and actual hazy photographs, can be used to conduct a thorough investigation and evaluation of a single picture dehazing algorithm currently in use. The five subsets of RESIDE, which highlight various data sources and image contents and are each used for a distinct type of training or evaluation, are highlighted [34].

4.2   Generator Loss

Generator loss is a measure of how well the generator has the ability to produce data that resembles actual data. It is typically identified as a disparity between the output of the generator and the discriminator's evaluation of the real labels.

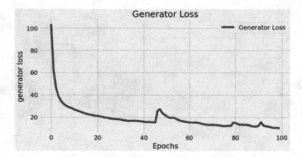

Fig. 4. Generator Loss

In this case, we have trained the generator for 100 epochs. The generator loss would have decreased over time as the image generator gained the ability to produce higher-quality, more realistic images (see Fig. 4).

4.3   Discriminator Loss

The discriminator's loss is an indicator of how well it can discriminate between created samples and actual samples. When the discriminator is fed both actual and produced samples, it calculates the difference between the genuine labels and the output. In this case, we have trained the discriminator for 100 epochs. The discriminator loss would also have decreased over time as the discriminator improved its ability to discriminate between produced and actual photos (see Fig. 5).

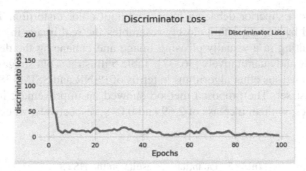

Fig. 5. Discriminator Loss

4.4 Result Analysis

The outcomes of different techniques used to eliminate haze from a picture are shown in Fig. 6. For dehazing high-brightness areas, the DCP method produced a hazy image with significant color distortion and excessive brightness. The total brightness of the picture was slightly diminished as a result of the AOD-Net algorithm's reduction of the haze but not the residue it left behind.

Fig. 6. Results in visual form for the SOTS dataset: **a**. hazy images **b**. corresponding haze-free images **c**. DCP **d**. AOD-Net **e**. GCANet **f**. EPDN **g**. YOLY **h**. DSRGAN

The GCANet algorithm successfully eliminated the haze; however, it did so at the expense of lost image information. While the YOLY algorithm [35] partially generated color distortion in the final image, the EPDN method obscured some characteristics of the hazy picture. The color and texture of the image were preserved while our suggested approach created a superior dehazing impact without color distortion. The haze-free image generated by our algorithm closely resembles the real image in terms of color and details, resulting in a visually pleasing image and enhancing the dehazing effect both qualitatively and quantitatively [36, 37]. Table 5 illustrates our suggested approach outperformed numerous other algorithms in terms of PSNR and SSIM [38] metrics just on the HSTS test set. The proposed method showed an improvement in both PSNR and SSIM metrics, with an increase of 2.69 and 0.038, respectively, when compared to GCANet.

Table 5. Quantitative results on the HSTS.

Algorithm	DCP	AOD-Net	GCANet	EPDN	YOLY	**Proposed Model**
PSNR	17.01	19.68	21.37	20.37	21.02	24.06
SSIM	0.803	0.835	0.874	0.877	0.905	0.912

5 Conclusion

Haze and mist can significantly impact image clarity and contrast, making image dehazing an important area of research for various applications. While current unsupervised techniques for image dehazing suffer from inaccuracies and poor performance, GANs show promise. However, bi-directional mapping domain translation techniques are unsuitable for image dehazing because haze is complicated in the real world. This work suggests an end-to-end unsupervised image dehazing method to overcome these issues using a DSRGAN with VGG19 for feature extraction. The proposed method outperforms numerous other algorithms in terms of PSNR and SSIM metrics, with an increase of 2.69 and 0.038, respectively, when compared to GCANet, just on the HSTS test set. These outcomes show how well the suggested method for image dehazing performs in complicated and dynamic contexts.

References

1. Negru, M., Nedevschi, S., Peter, R.I.: Exponential contrast restoration in fog conditions for driving assistance. IEEE Trans. Intell. Transp. Syst. 16(4), 2257–2268 (2015)
2. Min, X., Zhai, G., Gu, K., Yang, X., Guan, X.: Objective quality evaluation of dehazed images. IEEE Trans. Intell. Transp. Syst. 20(8), 2879–2892 (2019)
3. Peters, J.R., Surana, A., Taylor, G.S., Turpin, T.S., Bullo, F.: UAV surveillance under visibility and dwell-time constraints: a sampling based approach (2019). arXiv:1908.05347
4. Choi, D.-Y., Choi, J.-H., Choi, J., Song, B.C.: Sharpness enhancement and super-resolution of around-view monitor images. IEEE Trans. Intell. Transp. Syst. 19(8), 2650–2662 (2018)
5. Nasir, M., Muhammad, K., Lloret, J., Sangaiah, A.K., Sajjad, M.: Fog computing enabled cost-effective distributed summarization of surveillance videos for smart cities. J. Parallel Distrib. Comput. 126, 161–170 (2019)

6. Makwana, Y., Iyer, S.S., Tiwari, S.: The food recognition and nutrition assessment from images using artificial intelligence: a survey. ECS Trans. **107**(1), 3547 (2022)
7. Zhao, S., Fang, Y., Qiu, L.: Deep learning-based channel estimation with SRGAN in OFDM systems. In: 2021 IEEE Wireless Communications and Networking Conference (WCNC), China, pp. 1–6 (2021). https://doi.org/10.1109/WCNC49053.2021.9417242
8. Kim, J., Lee, J.K., Lee, K.M.: Accurate image super-resolution using very deep convolutional networks. In: Proceedings of the IEEE Conference on Computer Vision and Pattern Recognition, pp. 1646–1654 (2016)
9. Xu, Z., Liu, X., Chen, X.: Fog removal from video sequences using contrast limited adaptive histogram equalization. In: Proceedings of the 2009 International Conference on Computational Intelligence and Software Engineering, Washington, DC, USA, 11–14 December 2009, pp. 1–4 (2009)
10. Nayar, S.K., Narasimhan, S.G.: Vision in bad weather. In: Proceedings of the Proceedings of the Seventh IEEE International Conference on Computer Vision, Corfu, Greece, 20–27 September 1999, vol. 2, pp. 820–827 (1999)
11. Khan, H., et al.: Localization of radiance transformation for image dehazing in wavelet domain. Neurocomputing **381**, 141–151 (2020)
12. Cai, B., Xu, X., Jia, K., Qing, C., Tao, D.: Dehazenet: an end-to-end system for single image haze removal. IEEE Trans. Image Process. **25**, 5187–5198 (2016)
13. Tan, R.T.: Visibility in bad weather from a single image. In: Proceedings of the IEEE Conference on Computer Vision and Pattern Recognition, Anchorage, AK, USA, 23–28 June 2008; IEEE: Piscataway, NJ, USA, 2008; pp. 1–8 (2008)
14. He, K., Sun, J., Tang, X.: Single image haze removal using dark channel prior. IEEE Trans. Pattern Anal. Mach. Intell. **33**, 2341–2353 (2010)
15. Berman, D., Treibitz, T., Avidan, S.: Non-local image dehazing. In: Proceedings of IEEE Conference on Computer Vision and Pattern Recognition (CVPR), June 2016, pp. 1674–1682 (2016)
16. Liu, X., Ma, Y., Shi, Z., Chen, J.: Griddehazenet: attention-based multi-scale network for image Dehazing. In: Proceedings of the IEEE/CVF International Conference on Computer Vision, Seoul, Republic of Korea, 27 October–2 November 2019; IEEE/CVF: Piscataway, NJ, USA, pp. 7314–7323 (2019)
17. Li, B., Peng, X., Wang, Z., Xu, J., Feng, D.: Aod-net: all-in-one Dehazing network. In: Proceedings of the IEEE International Conference on Computer Vision, Venice, Italy, 22–29 October 2017; IEEE: Piscataway, NJ, USA, pp. 4770–4778 (2017)
18. Zhang, H., Patel, V.M.: Densely connected pyramid Dehazing network. In: Proceedings of the IEEE Conference on Computer Vision and Pattern Recognition, Salt Lake City, UT, USA, 18–23 June 2018; IEEE: Piscataway, NJ, USA, pp. 3194–3203 (2018)
19. Huang, G., Liu, Z., Van Der Maaten, L., Weinberger, K.Q.: Densely connected convolutional networks. In: Proceedings of the IEEE Conference on Computer Vision and Pattern Recognition, Honolulu, HI, USA, 21–26 July 2017; IEEE: Piscataway, NJ, USA, pp. 4700–4708 (2017)
20. Ronneberger, O., Fischer, P., Brox, T.: U-Net: convolutional networks for biomedical image segmentation. In: Navab, N., Hornegger, J., Wells, W.M., Frangi, A.F. (eds.) MICCAI 2015. LNCS, vol. 9351, pp. 234–241. Springer, Cham (2015). https://doi.org/10.1007/978-3-319-24574-4_28
21. Goodfellow, I., et al.: Generative adversarial nets. In: Proceedings of the Twenty-Eighth Conference on Neural Information Processing Systems, Montreal, QC, Canada, 8–13 December 2014, pp. 2672–2680 (2014)
22. Wang, K., Gou, C., Duan, Y., Lin, Y., Zheng, X., Wang, F.-Y.: Generative adversarial networks: introduction and outlook. IEEE/CAA J. Autom. Sinica **4**(4), 588598 (2017). https://doi.org/10.1109/jas.2017.751058310.1109/JAS.2017.7510583

23. Arjovsky, M., Chintala, S., Bottou, L.: Wasserstein generative adversarial networks. In: Proceedings of the International Conference on Machine Learning, PMLR: Sydney, Australia, 6–11 August 2017, pp. 214–223 (2017)

24. Miyato, T., Kataoka, T., Koyama, M., Yoshida, Y.: Spectral Normalization for Generative Adversarial Networks. arXiv arXiv:1802.05957 (2018)

25. Mao, X., Li, Q., Xie, H., Lau, R.Y., Wang, Z., Paul Smolley, S.: Least squares generative adversarial networks. In: Proceedings of the IEEE International Conference on Computer Vision, Venice, Italy, 22–29 October 2017, pp. 2794–2802 (2017)

26. Qu, Y., Chen, Y., Huang, J., Xie, Y.: Enhanced pix2pix dehazing network. In: Proceedings of IEEE/CVF Conference on Computer Vision and Pattern Recognition (CVPR), June 2019, pp. 8160–8168 (2019)

27. Creswell, A., et al.: Generative adversarial networks: an overview. IEEE Signal Process. Mag. **35**(1), 53–65 (2018)

28. Ledig, C., et al.: Photo-realistic single image super-resolution using a generative adversarial network. In: Proceedings of the IEEE Conference on Computer Vision and Pattern Recognition (2017)

29. Goodfellow, I., et al.: Generative adversarial networks. In: Advances in Neural Information Processing Systems, pp. 2672–2680 (2014)

30. Lv, B., Liu, Y., Zhang, S., Zeng, H., Zhu, G.: Super Resolution with Generative Adversarial Networks (2018)

31. Tanwar, R., Phukan, O.C., Singh, G., Tiwari, S.: CNN-LSTM Based Stress Recognition Using Wearables (2022)

32. Nalwar, S., et al.: EffResUNet: encoder decoder architecture for cloud-type segmentation. Big Data Cogn. Comput. **6**(4), 150 (2022)

33. Mane, D., Shah, K., Solapure, R., Bidwe, R., Shah, S.: Image-based plant seedling classification using ensemble learning. In: Pati, B., Panigrahi, C.R., Mohapatra, P., Li, K.C. (eds.) ICACIE 2021, pp. 433–447. Springer, Cham (2022). https://doi.org/10.1007/978-981-19-2225-1_39

34. https://www.kaggle.com/datasets/balraj98/indoor-training-set-its-residestandard

35. Hotkar, O., Radhakrishnan, P., Singh, A., Jhamnani, N., Bidwe, R.V.: U-net and YOLO: AIML models for lane and object detection in real-time. In: Proceedings of the 2023 Fifteenth International Conference on Contemporary Computing, pp. 467–473 (2023)

36. Agrawal, G., Jha, U., Bidwe, R.: Automatic facial expression recognition using advanced transfer learning. In: Proceedings of the 2023 Fifteenth International Conference on Contemporary Computing, pp. 450–458 (2023)

37. Bidwe, R.V., Mishra, S., Bajaj, S.: Performance evaluation of transfer learning models for ASD prediction using non-clinical analysis. In: Proceedings of the 2023 Fifteenth International Conference on Contemporary Computing, pp. 474–483 (2023)

38. Bidwe, R.V., et al.: Deep learning approaches for video compression: a bibliometric analysis. Big Data Cogn. Comput. **6**(2), 44 (2022)

Benchmarking ML and DL Models for Mango Leaf Disease Detection: A Comparative Analysis

Hritwik Ghosh[1], Irfan Sadiq Rahat[1(✉)], Rasmita Lenka[2], Sachi Nandan Mohanty[1], and Deepak Chauhan[3]

[1] School of Computer Science and Engineering (SCOPE), VIT-AP University, Amaravati, Andhra Pradesh, India
me.rahat2020@gmail.com
[2] School of Electronics, KIIT Deemed to be University, Bhubaneswar, Odisha, India
rasmitafet@kiit.ac.in
[3] School of Computing, Graphic Era Hill University, Dehradun, R/S, Graphic Era Deemed to be University, Dehradun 248002, India
dchauhan@gehu.ac.in

Abstract. Mango leaf diseases can have detrimental effects on the productivity and health of mango trees, leading to significant economic losses. Early and accurate detection of these diseases is crucial for enabling timely interventions and enhancing crop management strategies. In this study, we conduct a comprehensive comparison of various ML and DL models to effectively detect and classify common mango leaf diseases, as well as to differentiate between healthy and diseased leaves, using a custom dataset of mango leaf images. Our investigation encompasses traditional ML models, such as RandomForestClassifier and k-Nearest Neighbors, in addition to advanced DL models, including AlexNet, EfficientNet-B0, DenseNet121, and ResNet50. The primary objective of this comparative study is to highlight the advantages and limitations of each model, pinpoint the optimal model for mango leaf disease detection and classification, and evaluate the influence of data preprocessing, feature extraction, and hyperparameter optimization on model performance. By systematically comparing a diverse range of ML and DL models, our research aims to contribute to the development of efficient, reliable, and robust methodologies for the early detection and accurate classification of mango leaf diseases. The results of this study have the potential to assist farmers and agricultural experts in making well-informed decisions pertaining to crop management and disease control, thereby promoting sustainable and productive mango cultivation practices.

Keywords: Mango leaf diseases · productivity · economic losses · early detection · machine learning · deep learning

1 Introduction

Mango (Mangifera indica L.), a widely cultivated tropical fruit, is highly sought after for its rich nutritional content, delightful flavor, and economic importance. Regrettably, the production and quality of mango crops are often hindered by a variety of diseases that

M. A. Jabbar et al. (Eds.): AMLDA 2023, CCIS 2047, pp. 97–110, 2024.
https://doi.org/10.1007/978-3-031-55486-5_8

afflict the leaves, leading to significant declines in yield and income. Prompt detection and precise diagnosis of these diseases are vital for enabling early interventions, refining crop management techniques, and mitigating the negative impact on mango farming. Lately, machine learning and deep learning methodologies have garnered substantial interest within the agricultural domain, primarily for their potential to transform disease detection and classification in crops. These computational approaches have exhibited remarkable results across diverse applications, such as image classification, natural language understanding, and speech interpretation. Regarding plant disease identification, ML and DL models present the benefits of swift and accurate recognition, diminished dependence on human specialists, and the ability to process extensive datasets containing intricate patterns. The main aim of this study is to undertake an in-depth comparison of various ML and DL models to effectively detect and categorize prevalent mango leaf diseases, while also distinguishing between healthy and afflicted leaves, utilizing a custom dataset of mango leaf images. Our examination covers conventional machine learning models like RandomForestClassifier and k-Nearest Neighbors, alongside advanced deep learning models such as AlexNet, EfficientNet-B0, DenseNet121, and ResNet50. We assess the performance of each model using established evaluation metrics, including accuracy, precision, recall, and F1-score.This paper is structured as follows: Section 2 offers a review of relevant literature on plant disease detection and classification employing ML and DL techniques. Section 3 and 4 outlines the methodology, encompassing data acquisition, preprocessing, feature extraction, and the execution of various models. Section 5 delivers the results and discussion, emphasizing the advantages and limitations of each model and their suitability for mango leaf disease identification. Lastly, Sect. 6 presents the conclusion and potential avenues for future research. Through a systematic comparison of a diverse array of ML and DL models, our research aspires to contribute to the evolution of effective, dependable, and robust techniques for the early detection and accurate categorization of mango leaf diseases. The insights gained from this study hold the potential to support farmers and agricultural experts in making well-informed decisions concerning crop management and disease mitigation, thus fostering sustainable and fruitful mango cultivation practices.

2 Literature Review

The potential of Convolutional Neural Networks (CNN) for classifying plant diseases using leaf pictures is highlighted by Maheshwari [1]. The study uses the Plant Village database to diagnose illnesses of soybean plants, including healthy leaves, using the Le-Net architecture. Results show that new techniques perform better, especially for classes with small training sample sizes. A neural network ensemble (NNE) is presented by Mia et al. [2] for the detection of mango leaf diseases. By contrasting fresh leaf photos with a training dataset, the system use machine learning to identify disease symptoms. This automated method detects diseases with an average accuracy of 80% and provides a quicker method than manual identification by agriculturists. By facilitating prompt illness treatment, the method seeks to increase mango output and satisfy market demands internationally. The rapid development of machine learning in predictive data analysis and its applications in agriculture is covered in SivaramKrishnan et al. [3]. Automation, weather forecasts, and share market predictions all improve agricultural outcomes.

In addition to highlighting how machine learning can adapt to various environmental circumstances while minimising human involvement, the essay emphasises the significance of agriculture in countries with dense populations. In order to establish which algorithms are best for agricultural applications, the study also investigates a variety of them. According to Tulshan & Raul [4], plant leaf diseases still account for 42% of productivity losses in agriculture, despite technological developments. Their research develops a method for visualising plant leaf diseases. The technique starts with image pre-processing, segmentation, and feature extraction, then moves on to classification using K Nearest Neighbour (KNN). The suggested method offers information on the affected area, the disease name, sensitivity, and processing time and boasts a disease prediction accuracy of 98.56%.While microbial illnesses pose a serious danger to food security, Sanath Rao et al. [5] emphasise that agriculture supports 50% of India's population. Infrastructure limitations make it difficult to use traditional identifying procedures. Using deep learning and transfer learning, the paper presents a solution for AI-based automatic identification of grape and mango leaf diseases. By utilising the pre-trained AlexNet architecture, a deep convolutional neural network (CNN) is trained using a dataset of 8,438 photos. The MATLAB-created algorithm claims to have an accuracy rate of 99% for grape leaves and 89% for mango leaves. For Android smartphones, the "JIT CROPFIX" app is also developed. India dominates the mango industry, producing half of the world's supply, as shown by Deep Learning for Image Based Mango Leaf Disease Detection [6]. The research introduces a deep learning-based picture identification method for efficiently identifying mango illnesses. They train a Convolutional Neural Network (CNN) utilising transfer learning by examining a dataset from the Konkan region of India, and they achieve 91% accuracy. The study emphasises the requirement for cutting-edge methodologies to address the difficulties faced by mango farmers. The difficulties in manual identification of mango leaf illnesses are discussed by Selvakumar & Balasundaram [7], who draw attention to problems including the lack of experts and expensive prices. They suggest an automated approach that makes use of contrast amplification, segmentation with enhanced fuzzy C Means, and feature selection with the Deviation-based Updated..Due to the high demand for mango fruit, Saleem et al. [8] emphasise the significance of prompt disease prevention for mango plants. They draw attention to the difficulties in manually identifying diseases and present a cutting-edge segmentation method that relies on the vein structure of the leaf to identify diseases. Canonical correlation analysis (CCA) is used to extract features and fuse them after segmenting using the "leaf vein-seg" method. With an amazing accuracy of 95.5%, the final identification uses a cubic support vector machine (SVM), providing a useful tool for mango growers. Hemanth & Smys [9] discuss the difficulty of visually diagnosing plant leaf diseases and emphasise how these diseases affect output and product quality. For the purpose of identifying and categorising diseased mango leaf patches, they present an image processing technique. Their suggested approach applies k-means for segmentation and Multiclass SVM for illness classification. The efficiency of their strategy for identifying sick mango leaves has been proven by experimental results. Due to the increased demand for mangoes, Saleem et al. [10] stress the need of tackling mango disease. They draw attention to the difficulties in segmenting and identifying leaf diseases automatically, particularly in light of the wide range of symptoms. The scientists present a CNN-based Fully-convolutional-network (FrCNnet) model for segmenting sick mango leaf portions, reaching an astounding 99.2% segmentation accuracy. According to their research, the FrCNnet offers improved feature learning that improves segmentation and disease identification, which is advantageous to pathologists and mango growers. Ghosh et al. [11] embarked on a comprehensive study to assess water quality through predictive machine learning. Their research underscored the potential of machine learning models in effectively assessing and classifying water quality. The dataset used for this purpose included parameters like pH, dissolved oxygen, BOD, and TDS. Among the various models they employed, the Random Forest model emerged as the most accurate, achieving a commendable accuracy rate of 78.96%. In contrast, the SVM model lagged behind, registering the lowest accuracy of 68.29%1. The difficulties posed by several mango diseases and insect pests in production are discussed by Xie et al. [12]. They stress the significance of identifying particular spores to forecast disease scenarios in the future, assisting in prevention and control. The research offers a deep learning method for identifying and segmenting three types of spores from microscopic photos using the Mask Scoring R-CNN network. When this model is included into a web-based system, it enables real-time spore detection and counting, improving the usefulness of intelligent detection and assisting in the prevention of mango disease. The effects of the fungus disease Anthracnose on mango trees, notably the fruits and leaves, are highlighted by Singh et al. [13]. The purpose of this study is to develop, using computer vision and deep learning, an efficient approach for the early and economical identification of this condition. For categorising mango leaves damaged by Anthracnose, they present a multilayer convolutional neural network (MCNN). The model performs better in terms of classification accuracy than other cutting-edge methods when evaluated on a dataset of 1070 photos from Shri Mata Vaishno Devi University in India. Pham et al.'s [16] discussion of the difficulty of seeing early-stage diseases on plant leaves, particularly those with small disease blobs, highlights the need for high-resolution imaging. Farmers typically visually analyse leaves, although these techniques are prone to inaccuracy. This study uses an artificial neural network (ANN) method rather than convolutional neural networks (CNNs), which have been widely employed for the purpose. The sick blobs are processed and segmented before a hybrid metaheuristic-based feature selection technique is applied. With an accuracy rate of 89.41%, the ANN outperforms well-known CNN models like AlexNet, VGG16, and ResNet-50.

3   Description of the Data Set

The dataset for this inquiry is composed of a wide range of mango leaf photos. Each image is 240 × 320 pixels in size and is stored in the JPG file format. A total of 5,000 photos make up the collection, of which 2,000 have unusual leaves. The remaining photos, which provide additional viewpoints and magnifications, were created by rotating and zooming the original leaves. Eight different categories make up the dataset's organisation. Seven of the categories are diseases that afflict mango leaves, including Anthracnose, Bacterial Canker, Cutting Weevil, Die Back, Gall Midge, Dusty Mildew, and Sooty Mould. One category represents healthy mango leaves. Each category has 500 photos to guarantee an even distribution of instances. This large and diverse dataset is an essential tool for evaluating the performance of various DL and ML models in identifying and categorising mango leaf diseases. The dataset's diversity makes it easier to assess how well the models can identify and respond to a variety of disease presentations, ultimately assisting in the development of more precise and effective disease detection systems.

3.1 Data Augmentation

Data augmentation is an essential technique used to increase the diversity and size of a dataset, particularly in the context of image data. With the mango leaf dataset, data augmentation helps to create additional images that represent various perspectives, scales, and orientations, ultimately improving the generalization capabilities of ML and DL models. To perform data augmentation on the mango leaf dataset, several image transformations are applied to the original 240×320 JPG images. These transformations include rotation, zooming, flipping, and changing brightness levels. By rotating the images at various angles, we create new instances that capture different orientations of the leaves. Zooming in or out of the images produces different scales, which help the models recognize diseases at various magnifications. Flipping the images horizontally and vertically adds more variations, ensuring the models can identify diseases regardless of the leaf's position in the image. Lastly, adjusting the brightness levels simulates different lighting conditions that may be encountered in real-world scenarios. The augmented dataset, consisting of 5,000 images, includes approximately 2,000 unique leaves and an additional 3,000 images generated through data augmentation techniques. This expanded dataset contributes to more robust and accurate ML and DL models, capable of detecting and classifying the diverse range of diseases present in mango leaves under various conditions.

3.2 Splitting the Data Set

The process of dividing the dataset into separate portions is crucial for effectively training and evaluating ML and DL models. In the case of the 5,000-image mango leaf dataset, encompassing eight distinct categories, the data needs to be partitioned into training, validation, and testing subsets. To accomplish this, we adopt a stratified sampling technique that maintains proportional representation of the eight classes (healthy leaves and the seven disease types) in the training, validation, and testing subsets. This approach ensures a consistent distribution of instances throughout the subsets, facilitating a fair assessment of the models' capabilities. A standard partition ratio for datasets is often 70% for training, 15% for validation, and 15% for testing. Applying these proportions to the mango leaf dataset yields 3,500 images for the training set, 750 images for the validation set, and 750 images for the testing set. The training set is employed to instruct the ML and DL models, while the validation set aids in refining the models and determining optimal hyperparameters. The testing set provides an impartial evaluation of the models' performance, offering a trustworthy measure of their effectiveness in identifying and categorizing diseases in mango leaves in real-world situations. Through the careful partitioning of the dataset into separate training, validation, and testing subsets, we can rigorously evaluate the ML and DL models, ultimately leading to the creation of more precise and dependable disease detection systems.

4 Image Resizing

Image resizing is a vital preprocessing step when working with datasets containing images, as it ensures that all input images have the same dimensions, allowing machine learning and deep learning models to process them effectively. For the 5,000-image mango leaf dataset with eight distinct categories, image resizing involves adjusting the dimensions of each image to a uniform size, such as 240 × 320 pixels, before feeding them into the models. There are several methods for resizing images, one of which is interpolation. Common interpolation techniques include nearest-neighbor, bilinear, and bicubic interpolation. These methods adjust the size of an image while minimizing the loss of visual information, preserving essential features for accurate classification. In the case of the mango leaf dataset, resizing images to 240 × 320 pixels allows the models to focus on the most relevant features, such as color, texture, and shape characteristics of the leaves and the associated diseases. This uniformity in size simplifies the input for the ML and DL models, enabling them to perform more efficiently and accurately. Moreover, resizing images can help reduce computational complexity and memory requirements, which is especially important when working with large datasets or resource-intensive models. By ensuring that all images in the mango leaf dataset have consistent dimensions, we can streamline the process of training and evaluating the models, leading to a more reliable and accurate disease detection and classification system.

4.1 Image Masking

Image masking is a crucial preprocessing technique used to extract specific regions of interest and eliminate unwanted elements or background noise from images. In the context of the mango leaf dataset, consisting of 5,000 images across eight categories, image masking involves isolating the relevant parts, such as the mango leaves, while removing any non-essential information. To achieve image masking on the mango leaf dataset, various algorithms and methods can be employed. One commonly used approach is thresholding, where a predefined threshold value is applied to the pixel intensities to separate the foreground (mango leaves) from the background. This process generates a binary mask where the desired regions are represented by white pixels, while the background is depicted as black pixels. Another technique used for image masking is edge detection. Algorithms like the Canny edge detection algorithm can be utilized to identify and accentuate the edges of the mango leaves, resulting in a mask that highlights the leaf boundaries. By applying image masking techniques to the mango leaf dataset, we can extract and emphasize the key features of interest, such as the mango leaves themselves. This preprocessing step helps to enhance the accuracy and performance of ML and DL models when detecting and classifying diseases. By isolating the relevant regions and eliminating irrelevant elements or noise, the models can focus on the critical characteristics of the mango leaves, including texture, shape, and disease-specific patterns, leading to more precise and reliable disease identification and classification.

4.2 Description of All the Algorithm

Here is a brief description of each algorithm used in your study:

- **Random Forest Classifier:** The mango leaf dataset was examined for disease diagnosis using the random forest classifier technique. The model's performance in effectively categorising and detecting illnesses in mango leaves was demonstrated by an accuracy rating of 84.375% on the validation set. The RandomForestClassifier, unlike deep learning models, does not depend on a gradient-based optimisation procedure, hence it is significant to highlight that it lacks a loss metric. An ensemble learning technique called the Random Forest Classifier mixes various decision trees to produce predictions. It offers reliable performance and is well suited to processing complicated datasets. The Random Forest Classifier achieved a respectable accuracy of 84.375% in the setting of the mango leaf dataset, displaying its capacity to accurately distinguish among leaf health and various disease types. The accuracy of the model suggests that it can make a substantial contribution to the creation of a trustworthy disease identification system for mangoes crops.

- **AlexNet:** The mango leaf dataset was examined for disease identification using the AlexNet architecture. The model correctly classified and identified illnesses in mango leaves, as evidenced by its test accuracy of 95.125%. For the dataset, the test's loss value for the AlexNet model was 0.1701262891292572. Deep convolutional network design AlexNet rose to fame as a result of its accomplishments in the Image Net Large-Scale Visual Recognition Challenge. To avoid overfitting, it includes numerous layers of convolution, max-pooling layers, fully linked layers, and dropout regularisation. The architecture's depth and design make it possible for it to successfully learn intricate details from photographs. In the case of the mango leaf dataset, the AlexNet model demonstrated a high accuracy of 95.125%, suggesting its capability to accurately classify mango leaves and identify different diseases. The relatively low test loss value of 0.1701262891292572 further signifies the model's ability to make confident predictions. The successful performance of AlexNet on the mango leaf dataset highlights the potential of DL models for disease detection in agricultural applications. The architecture's ability to learn intricate patterns and features from images makes it a valuable tool in accurately identifying and classifying diseases affecting mango leaves (Table 1).

- **DenseNet121:** The DenseNet121 architecture was applied to the mango leaf dataset for disease detection, achieving a test accuracy of 86.4%. The test loss value for the DenseNet121 model on the dataset was 0.380. DenseNet121 is a deep convolutional neural network architecture known for its densely connected layers. It combines the features learned from earlier layers with subsequent layers, promoting feature reuse and enhancing gradient flow throughout the network. This design enables the model to effectively capture intricate patterns and relationships in the data. In the context of the mango leaf dataset, the DenseNet121 model demonstrated a solid test accuracy of 86.4%, indicating its ability to accurately classify and detect diseases in mango leaves. The relatively low test loss value of 0.380 further signifies the model's capability to make confident predictions. The successful performance of DenseNet121 on the mango leaf dataset underscores the effectiveness of deep learning models in disease

Table 1. Different Values of AleXNet

	Precision	Recall	F1-Score	Support
Anthracnose	0.97	0,97	0.96	92
Bacterial Canker	0.97	0.99	0.98	106
Cutting Weevil	0.97	1.00	0.99	105
Die Back	1.00	0.92	0.96	107
Gall Midge	1.00	0.78	0.88	93
Healthy	0.97	1.00	0.98	96
Powdery Mildew	0.85	0.99	0.92	98
Sooty Mould	0.85	0.88	0.87	103
accuracy			0.94	800
Macro avg	0.95	0.94	0.94	800
Weighted avg	0.95	0.94	0.94	800

detection for agricultural applications. The architecture's ability to capture complex patterns and leverage feature reuse contributes to accurate disease identification and classification in mango leaves (Fig. 1, Table 2).

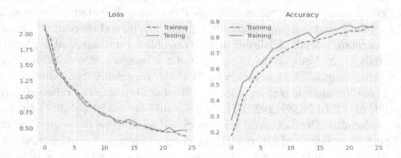

Fig. 1. Training and Validation Loss and Accuracy of DenseNet121

- **ResNet50:** The ResNet50 architecture was employed to analyze the mango leaf dataset for disease detection, achieving a training accuracy of 97.12% and a validation accuracy of 92.12%. The training loss for the ResNet50 model was 0.2006, while the validation loss was 0.9131. ResNet50 is a deep convolutional neural network architecture known for its residual connections, which facilitate the training of very deep networks. By utilizing skip connections, ResNet50 addresses the vanishing gradient problem, enabling the model to effectively learn complex patterns and features from the data. In the case of the mango leaf dataset, the ResNet50 model demonstrated impressive training accuracy of 97.12% and validation accuracy of 92.12%. This indicates the model's ability to accurately classify and detect diseases in mango leaves. The relatively low training loss of 0.2006 and validation loss of 0.9131 further demonstrate the model's capability to make confident predictions and generalize well

Table 2. Different Values of DenseNet121

	Precision	Recall	F1-Score	Support
Powdery Mildew	0.95	0.79	0.87	102
Cutting Weevil	0.85	0.97	0.91	100
Anthracnose	0.93	0.90	0.92	104
Bacterial Canker	0.85	0.98	0.91	98
Sooty Mould	0.77	0.60	0.67	89
Gall Midge	0.67	0.73	0.70	106
Healthy	0.75	0.87	0.80	104
Die Back	0.96	0.82	0.89	97
accuracy			0.83	800
Macro avg	0.84	0.83	0.83	800
Weighted avg	0.84	0.83	0.83	800

to unseen data. The successful performance of ResNet50 on the mango leaf dataset highlights the power of deep learning models in disease detection tasks for agricultural applications. The architecture's ability to capture intricate patterns and leverage residual connections enables accurate identification and classification of diseases in mango leaves (Fig. 2).

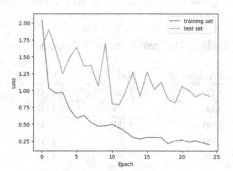

Fig. 2. Epoch and Loss of ResNet50

- **EfficientNet-B0:** EfficientNet-B0 was utilized to analyze the mango leaf dataset for disease detection. The first model achieved a test accuracy of 94.4% and a test loss of 0.863, while the second model achieved a test accuracy of 99.91% and a test loss of 0.3002. EfficientNet is a family of convolutional neural network architectures designed to maximize model efficiency and accuracy by balancing model depth, width, and resolution. EfficientNet-B0 is the smallest and least complex of the EfficientNet models. In the case of the mango leaf dataset, the first EfficientNet-B0 model achieved a test accuracy of 94.4% and a test loss of 0.863, indicating its ability to accurately classify and detect diseases in mango leaves. The second EfficientNet-B0 model achieved an impressive test accuracy of 99.91% and a test loss of 0.3002, highlighting its efficacy in accurately classifying mango leaves and differentiating between healthy and diseased leaves. The successful performance of EfficientNet-B0 on the mango leaf dataset emphasizes the potential of efficient deep learning models for agricultural applications. The architecture's ability to balance model depth, width, and resolution contributes to accurate disease identification and classification in mango leaves (Fig. 3, Table 3).

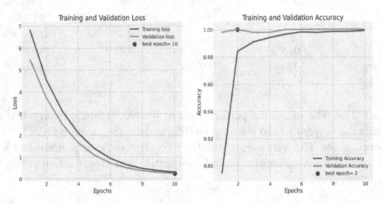

Fig. 3. Training and Validation Loss and Accuracy of EfficientNet-B0

Table 3. Different Values of EfficientNet-B0

	Precision	Recall	F1-Score	Support
Anthracnose	1.00	1.00	1.00	43
Bacterial Canker	1.00	1.00	1.00	37
Cutting Weevil	1.00	1.00	1.00	42
Die Back	1.00	1.00	1.00	46
Gall Midge	1.00	1.00	1.00	36
Healthy	1.00	1.00	1.00	43
Powdery Mildew	1.00	1.00	1.00	30
Sooty Mould	1.00	1.00	1.00	43
accuracy			1.00	320
Macro avg	1.00	1.00	1.00	320
Weighted avg	1.00	1.00	1.00	320

- **KNN:** The application of the k-nearest neighbors (KNN) algorithm to the mango leaf dataset for disease detection resulted in a validation accuracy of 53.125%. KNN, a non-parametric algorithm, classifies instances by determining the majority vote of their k nearest neighbors. In the context of the mango leaf dataset, the KNN algorithm calculates the distances between a test instance and all training instances to identify the k nearest neighbors. The class label of the test instance is then determined based on the majority class among its neighbors. The achieved validation accuracy of 53.125% signifies a moderate level of success for the KNN algorithm in accurately classifying and detecting diseases in mango leaves. However, it is crucial to consider that the performance of KNN can be influenced by various factors, such as the choice of the k value (number of neighbors) and the distance metric used to measure similarity. Although the accuracy achieved by the KNN model may be comparatively lower than that of other models used in the analysis, it remains a valuable algorithm in certain scenarios. KNN is appreciated for its simplicity, computational efficiency, and straightforward implementation. It does not require a training phase and can be particularly suitable for smaller datasets. However, to enhance the accuracy and robustness of the KNN model for mango leaf disease detection in future studies, further optimizations and experimentation may be necessary

4.3 Confusion Matrix

A confusion matrix can be used to assess the effectiveness of a classification model for mango leaf diseases. It depicts the link between the expected and actual disease classes visually. The matrix is a grid with each row representing the actual class and each column representing the expected class. The cells in the matrix represent the number or percentage of cases that fall into a certain combination of actual and anticipated classifications. You can obtain insights into the model's accuracy, precision, and recall by analysing the numbers in the confusion matrix, as well as discover any misclassifications or biases in the prediction results (Fig. 4).

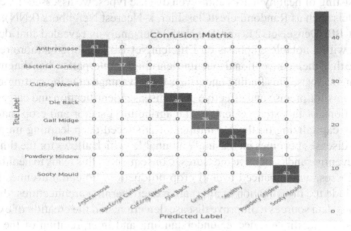

Fig. 4. Confusion Matrix

5 Result

In this analysis, we performed a comparison of ML and DL methods to diagnose diseases affecting mango leaves. We used a dataset containing 240 × 320 JPG images, representing eight distinct classes, including healthy leaves and seven types of diseases. The models analyzed were RandomForestClassifier, k-Nearest Neighbors (kNN), AlexNet, EfficientNet-B0, DenseNet121, and ResNet50.Our findings revealed noticeable differences in performance among the various models. RandomForestClassifier recorded a validation accuracy of 84.375%, while kNN showed a significantly lower validation accuracy of 53.125%. Turning to deep learning models, AlexNet demonstrated a test accuracy of 95.125%, EfficientNet-B0 Model 1 achieved a testing accuracy of 99.9%, and EfficientNet-B0 Model 2 reached a remarkable validation accuracy of 100%. DenseNet121 and ResNet50 displayed testing accuracies of 86.4% and 92.12%, respectively. These results suggest that deep learning models, with EfficientNet-B0 being a prime example, outpace their traditional machine learning counterparts in detecting mango leaf diseases. The study highlights the importance of harnessing state-of-the-art DL models for accurate and efficient plant disease identification and classification. By leveraging these advanced models, disease detection can be improved, enabling better prevention and management strategies for maintaining healthy crops.

6 Conclusion

In summary, this research provided an in-depth comparison between machine learning and deep learning methodologies for identifying and categorizing diseases in mango leaves. By analyzing a dataset of 240 × 320 JPG images, representing eight unique classes consisting of healthy leaves and seven disease types, we assessed the efficacy of diverse models such as RandomForestClassifier, k-Nearest Neighbors (kNN), AlexNet, EfficientNet-B0, DenseNet121, and ResNet50.Our analysis revealed that deep learning models, with a notable emphasis on EfficientNet-B0, exhibited a more remarkable performance than their conventional machine learning counterparts when diagnosing diseases in mango leaves. This finding underlines the advantage of using cutting-edge deep learning models for precise and effective plant disease identification and categorization. The implications of this study extend to the agricultural sector and crop management practices. By capitalizing on the capabilities of advanced deep learning models, early detection of diseases becomes increasingly attainable, which allows for the timely application of preventive and corrective measures. Consequently, this leads to healthier crops, minimized losses, and enhanced overall crop production. Potential avenues for future research include the investigation of alternative deep learning architectures, the integration of various data sources to improve disease detection, and the creation of explainable AI techniques to facilitate a deeper understanding and interpretation of the detection outcomes. Advancements in plant disease detection contribute to the protection of our food resources and support the pursuit of a sustainable future.

References

1. Maheshwari, K.: Performance analysis of mango leaf disease using machine learning technique. Int. J. Res. Appl. Sci. Eng. Technol. **9**(1), 856–862 (2021). https://doi.org/10.22214/ijraset.2021.32926
2. Mia, M.R., Roy, S., Das, S.K., Rahman, M.A.: Mango leaf disease recognition using neural network and support vector machine. Iran J. Comput. Sci. (Online) **3**(3), 185–193 (2020). https://doi.org/10.1007/s42044-020-00057-z
3. SivaramKrishnan, M., et al.: Leaf disease identification using machine learning models. AIP Conf. Proc. **2519**(1) (2022). https://doi.org/10.1063/5.0109675
4. Tulshan, A.S., Raul, N.: Plant leaf disease detection using machine learning. In: 2019 10th International Conference on Computing, Communication and Networking Technologies (ICCCNT), pp. 1–6 (2019). https://doi.org/10.1109/ICCCNT45670.2019.8944556
5. Sanath Rao, U., et al.: Deep learning precision farming: grapes and mango leaf disease detection by transfer learning. Global Trans. Proc. **2**(2), 535–544 (2021). https://doi.org/10.1016/j.gltp.2021.08.002
6. Deep learning for image based mango leaf disease detection. Int. J. Recent Technol. Eng. **8**(3S3), 54–56 (2019). https://doi.org/10.35940/ijrte.C1030.1183S319
7. Selvakumar, A., Balasundaram, A.: Automated mango leaf infection classification using weighted and deep features with optimized recurrent neural network concept. Imaging Sci. J. ahead-of-print (ahead-of-print), 1–19 (2023). https://doi.org/10.1080/13682199.2023.2204036
8. Saleem, R., Shah, J.H., Sharif, M., Yasmin, M., Yong, H.-S., Cha, J.: Mango leaf disease recognition and classification using novel segmentation and vein pattern technique. Appl. Sci. **11**(24), 11901 (2021). https://doi.org/10.3390/app112411901
9. Srunitha, K., Bharathi, D.: Mango leaf unhealthy region detection and classification. In: Hemanth, D.J., Smys, S. (eds.) Computational Vision and Bio Inspired Computing. LNCVB, vol. 28, pp. 422–436. Springer, Cham (2018). https://doi.org/10.1007/978-3-319-71767-8_35
10. Saleem, R., Shah, J.H., Sharif, M., Ansari, G.J.: Mango leaf disease identification using fully resolution convolutional network. Comput. Mater. Continua **69**(3), 3581 (2021). https://doi.org/10.32604/cmc.2021.017700
11. Ghosh, H., Tusher, M.A., Rahat, I.S., Khasim, S., Mohanty, S.N.: Water quality assessment through predictive machine learning. In: Balas, V.E., Semwal, V.B., Khandare, A. (eds.) Intelligent Computing and Networking. IC-ICN 2023. LNNS, vol. 699, pp. 77–88. Springer, Singapore (2023). https://doi.org/10.1007/978-981-99-3177-4_6
12. Xie, X., Wang, J., Hu, Z., Zhao, Y.: Intelligent detection of mango disease spores based on mask scoring R-CNN. In: 2021 5th Asian Conference on Artificial Intelligence Technology (ACAIT), pp. 768–774 (2021). https://doi.org/10.1109/ACAIT53529.2021.9731325
13. Singh, U.P., Chouhan, S.S., Jain, S., Jain, S.: Multilayer convolution neural network for the classification of mango leaves infected by anthracnose disease. IEEE Access **7**, 43721–43729 (2019). https://doi.org/10.1109/ACCESS.2019.2907383
14. Pham, T.N., Tran, L.V., Dao, S.V.T.: Early disease classification of mango leaves using feedforward neural network and hybrid metaheuristic feature selection. IEEE Access **8**, 189960–189973 (2020). https://doi.org/10.1109/ACCESS.2020.3031914
15. Manoharan, N., Thomas, V.J., Anto Sahaya Dhas, D.: Identification of mango leaf disease using deep learning. In: 2021 Asian Conference on Innovation in Technology (ASIANCON), pp. 1–8 (2021). https://doi.org/10.1109/ASIANCON51346.2021.9544689
16. Pruvost, O., Savelon, C., Boyer, C., Chiroleu, F., Gagnevin, L., Jacques, M.-A.: Populations of Xanthomonas citri pv. mangiferaeindicae from asymptomatic mango leaves are primarily endophytic. Microbial. Ecol. **58**(1), 170–178 (2009). https://doi.org/10.1007/s00248-008-9480-x

17. Baeza-Montanez, L., Gomez-Cabrera, R., Garcia-Pedrajas, M.: First report of verticillium wilt caused by verticillium Dahliae on mango trees (Mangifera indica) in Southern Spain. Plant Dis. **94**(3), 380 (2010). https://doi.org/10.1094/PDIS-94-3-0380C
18. Augustyn, W.A., Regnier, T., Combrinck, S., Botha, B.M.: Metabolic profiling of mango cultivars to identify biomarkers for resistance against Fusarium infection. Phytochem. Lett. **10**, civ–cx (2014). https://doi.org/10.1016/j.phytol.2014.05.014

Cassava Syndrome Scan a Pioneering Deep Learning System for Accurate Cassava Leaf Disease Classification

Irfan Sadiq Rahat[1], Hritwik Ghosh[1(✉)], Janjhyam Venkata Naga Ramesh[2], Ajmeera Kiran[3], and Poonam Verma[4]

[1] School of Computer Science and Engineering (SCOPE), VIT-AP University, Amaravati, Andhra Pradesh, India
me.hritwikghosh@gmail.com

[2] Department of Computer Science and Engineering, Koneru Lakshmaiah Education Foundation, Vaddeswaram, Guntur 522502, Andhra Pradesh, India

[3] Department of Computer Science and Engineering, MLR Institute of Technology, Dundigal, Hyderabad 500043, Telangana, India

[4] School of Computing, Graphic Era Hill University, Dehradun R/S, Graphic Era Deemed to be University, Dehradun 248002, India
pverma@gehu.ac.in

Abstract. Cassava serves as a crucial source of carbohydrates for a vast population globally, playing a significant role in food security. The crop, however, faces threats from a variety of leaf diseases, leading to substantial reduction in yield. Prompt and precise identification of these diseases is essential for implementing effective countermeasures and maintaining adequate food supply. Recently, deep learning methodologies have demonstrated remarkable capabilities in image-based recognition and classification, including the diagnosis of plant diseases. The objective of this research is to construct a dependable cassava leaf disease identification system utilizing deep learning approaches, with an emphasis on achieving exceptional accuracy and dependability. We assess the performance of multiple cutting-edge deep learning architectures, such as ResNet50, DenseNet121, EfficientNet-B0, NasNetLarge, and EfficientNet-V2, in the context of cassava leaf disease classification. The dataset is comprised of nearly 15,000 test images, accompanied by image_id and label data in train.csv and sample_submission.csv files. Data preprocessing, including resizing, normalization, and augmentation, is conducted before partitioning the data into training, validation, and test sets. Our findings indicate that the EfficientNet-V2 model surpasses its counterparts in performance, attaining the highest validation accuracy of 0.7480 and a comparatively low validation loss of 0.7488. We further explore several strategies to enhance model performance, such as optimizing hyperparameters, employing data augmentation, utilizing early stopping, implementing learning rate scheduling, applying transfer learning, and adopting ensemble techniques. The resulting classifier offers potential benefits to farmers and agricultural specialists in making informed decisions regarding cassava leaf disease management, ultimately leading to improved crop yields and food security.

© The Author(s), under exclusive license to Springer Nature Switzerland AG 2024
M. A. Jabbar et al. (Eds.): AMLDA 2023, CCIS 2047, pp. 111–123, 2024.
https://doi.org/10.1007/978-3-031-55486-5_9

Keywords: Food security · leaf diseases · reduction in yield · identification · countermeasures

1 Introduction

Cassava (Manihot esculenta), a critical food source for millions of people, is a vital agricultural crop grown in regions such as sub-Saharan Africa, Asia, and Latin America. Its resilience to challenging conditions, such as droughts and nutrient-deficient soils, makes it a crucial contributor to food security in these areas. However, cassava crops are susceptible to numerous leaf diseases, including Cassava Mosaic Disease (CMD), Cassava Brown Streak Disease (CBSD), and Cassava Bacterial Blight (CBB). These diseases can cause significant yield reductions, endangering food security for millions of people. To protect cassava production, it is vital to develop effective tools for the timely and accurate identification of these diseases. Traditionally, detecting cassava leaf diseases has relied on manual inspection and the expertise of agricultural professionals. This approach, while valuable, can be time-consuming, labor-intensive, and prone to inaccuracies. The emergence of artificial intelligence, specifically DL techniques, offers a promising alternative for diagnosing plant diseases. Deep learning algorithms have demonstrated remarkable capabilities in a wide range of image recognition and classification applications across diverse fields, such as healthcare, autonomous vehicles, and agriculture. In agriculture, DL-driven techniques have been employed to detect plant diseases, forecast crop output, and optimize agricultural practices. By leveraging deep learning methodologies for cassava leaf disease classification, it may be possible to significantly enhance the accuracy and efficiency of disease detection. This advancement would provide valuable information to farmers and agricultural experts, enabling them to make informed decisions in managing these diseases and ultimately contributing to increased crop yields and food security. The primary goal of this research is to develop a reliable and accurate cassava leaf disease detection system using deep learning methodologies.

2 Literature Review

DL approaches were investigated by Anitha and Saranya [1] for the identification and detection of Cassava leaf diseases. Their work made clear the value of AI in contemporary agriculture, particularly for jobs like identifying plant diseases and monitoring crop health. Convolutional Neural Networks (CNN) were emphasised as being superior to other neural network techniques for classification and prediction. In this study, they used real-time and Kaggle dataset photos to show how well CNN classified leaf illnesses in Cassava plants, with accuracy serving as the major performance parameter. The importance of cassava as a significant carbohydrate source was emphasised by Ramcharan et al. [4], but they also emphasised how susceptible it is to viral infections, particularly in sub-Saharan Africa. They investigated the possibility of picture recognition, in particular deep learning models, for mobile device-based disease diagnosis to solve this. They used transfer learning to train a deep convolutional neural network using a dataset of photos from Tanzania that were captured on-site during the cassava disease outbreak. The model shown exceptional accuracy, correctly classifying illnesses and pest damage up to 98% of the time. Their results demonstrated the effectiveness of transfer learning in digital plant disease diagnosis and offered a workable, affordable solution. The significance of cassava as a key source of carbohydrates and starch was underlined by Dhasan et al. in 2022 [5]. However, leaf diseases reduce the plant's yield, which directly affects farmers. They presented a Deep Convolutional Neural Network (DCNN) model to identify various disorders in order to address this. The need of early disease symptom detection to stop widespread contamination is emphasised by this automatic detection that helps in monitoring large crop fields. The system first distinguishes between healthy and damaged leaves, then uses Deep Learning (DL) to extract statistical information from the diseased leaf regions, classifying them based on a pre-trained dataset, and finally identifying the exact ailment. The difficulties of data collecting for machine learning in agriculture, particularly with low-quality photos, were highlighted by Abayomi-Alli et al. [6]. With the intention of improving the accuracy of deep learning models on such images, they presented a novel method for creating synthetic images using image colour histogram manipulation. They were able to recognise cassava leaf disease even on lower-quality photographs by altering the MobileNetV2 neural network and employing data augmentation. It was highlighted by Arulkumaran et al. [7] that the yield of cassava is susceptible to leaf diseases. For the purpose of classifying diseases, they introduced a Deep Convolutional Neural Network (DCNN). Deep learning is used by the algorithm to extract characteristics from diseased areas, initially differentiating between healthy and infected leaves. The individual disease is then classified using a pre-trained database of different cassava diseases. The serious issue of plant diseases generating large agricultural losses, particularly in the US, was addressed by Ahmed & Reddy [8]. Convolutional Neural Networks (CNN) were used to categorise 38 different disease categories, and they were introduced as a machine learning-powered mobile solution that automates plant leaf disease diagnostics. The technology, provided as an Android app, enables farmers to take pictures of leaves and get a disease diagnosis using a dataset of 96,206 photographs. The system, which aims to improve agricultural health monitoring, has a 94% accuracy rate for 38 different disease classes in 14 different crops. The significance of cassava in developing nations and the danger presented by Cassava Mosaic Disease (CMD) were highlighted by Oyewola et al. in 2021 [9]. They developed a brand-new deep residual convolution neural network (DRNN) for cassava leaf pictures to identify CMD. They corrected dataset imbalances by using different block processing and improved image quality by applying gamma correction and decorrelation stretching. Their research showed that a balanced dataset increases classification accuracy, with the DRNN model outperforming the PCNN on a Kaggle dataset by 9.25%. A Kaggle competition involving the detection of cassava diseases using a dataset of 10,000 labelled photos from Uganda served as the inspiration for Sambasivam & Opiyo [10]. Traditional detection techniques, which entail physical examinations by farmers or agricultural workers, are time-consuming and labor-intensive. The modest size and notable class imbalance of the given dataset, particularly with regard to CMD and CBB disorders, presented a hurdle when utilising it to train Convolutional Neural Networks (CNNs).

They used methods including class weight, SMOTE, and focus loss to address the frequently ignored problem of class imbalance in multi-class picture datasets, discovering underrepresented classes with over 93% accuracy. Ghosh et al. [11, 12] embarked on a comprehensive study to assess water quality through predictive machine learning. Their research underscored the potential of machine learning models in effectively assessing and classifying water quality. The dataset used for this purpose included parameters like pH, dissolved oxygen, BOD, and TDS. Among the various models they employed, the Random Forest model emerged as the most accurate, achieving a commendable accuracy rate of 78.96%. In contrast, the SVM model lagged behind, registering the lowest accuracy of 68.29%. The issue of viral infections reducing cassava yields in Africa was addressed by Thaiyalnayaki et al. in 2022 [13]. To increase yields, they sought to track different illness types using computer vision. In this study, 1000 labelled photos were used to train a recognition system utilising CNN and data augmentation to identify Cassava Mosaic Disease (CMD). Using a six-layer CNN model, they were able to reach a 92.4% accuracy despite the limited dataset. The classification accuracy for CMD and CGM illnesses using transfer learning was 88.1%.In order to identify plant diseases, image recognition is crucial in the agricultural industry, according to Y et al. [14]. They concentrated on cassava, a crucial source of carbohydrates in Africa that is prone to a number of illnesses. The CBB, CBSD, CMD, and CGM disorders were the focus of the investigation. For early disease diagnosis, they introduced the EfficientNet-B0 model, which performed more accurately and effectively than conventional CNNs. With a remarkable accuracy of 92.6%, this model assists in early disease identification without the need for specialist assistance. Cassava is an important source of carbohydrates for more than 500 million people, according to Methil et al. [15], despite its susceptibility to illnesses like Cassava Mosaic Disease. They presented a deep learning approach utilising a "One-vs-All" methodology with Convolutional Neural Networks to handle early disease diagnosis. Using the Efficient Net B4 model, they trained five binary classifiers for the four main cassava illnesses and healthy leaves. On skewed test data, this strategy has an accuracy of 85.64 percent. They also made the model accessible by making it available on Android platforms. Plant diseases are a threat to the security of the world's food supply, according to Yadav et al. [16], who also emphasised the importance of early and efficient diagnosis. For the purpose of detecting cassava illness, they introduced a convolutional neural network that uses transfer learning. After improving image contrast, they used oversampling and data augmentation to resolve dataset imbalances. Their method increased model accuracy by 4.3% by taking into account the problem of unbalanced data in the real world. Their methods attained a noteworthy accuracy of 94.02% when combining data augmentation with oversampling. Cassava anthracnose disease (CAD), a serious fungal illness that has a negative influence on cassava crops, particularly in Africa and Thailand, was discussed by Kunkeaw et al. [17]. They developed a quick method for identifying CAD-resistant cassava cultivars using a detached leaf assay. They placed the fungus' mycelia to three types of Thai cassava and watched the progression of lesions. Results showed that Hanatee was most sensitive whereas Huay Bong 60 had the best resistance. This rapid screening technique assists in locating CAD-resistant cassava varieties without contaminating the environment. Whiteflies, the main disease-carrying vector for cassava in tropical areas, were emphasised by Tusubira et al. [18]. Current whitefly counting techniques rely on time-consuming manual visual checks. The authors presented a computer vision-based automated counting technique. They used Haar Cascade and Deep Learning approaches to train detectors by gathering photos of infected cassava leaves. These methods were used to locate and count the pests in photos. The suggested method showed great accuracy when counting whiteflies and has potential for similar item detection tasks with minor adjustments.

3 Data Description

In our research, we employed an extensive dataset containing cassava leaf images to train and evaluate multiple DL models for cassava leaf disease classification. The dataset features a wide variety of images, each marked with the relevant disease, offering valuable information for the deep learning algorithms. The dataset is organized into several components, which include training and testing image files, a train.csv file that contains image IDs alongside their corresponding disease labels, and a sample_submission.csv file illustrating the appropriate submission format. The complete set of test images, which comprises roughly 15,000 images, is accessible only upon submitting the notebook for scoring. The dataset also provides images in tfrecord format and a JSON file presenting the mapping between each disease code and the actual disease name.

3.1 Preprocessing of the Dataset

To ensure the optimal performance of the deep learning models for cassava leaf disease classification, we conducted several pre-processing steps on the dataset containing cassava leaf images. These pre-processing steps aimed to prepare the data for efficient and effective training of the models. The data pre-processing included the following:

- **Image Resizing:** To maintain consistency across the dataset and to accommodate the input size requirements of various deep learning architectures, all images were resized to a uniform dimension. This step ensured that each image had the same height and width, enabling the models to process the images effectively.
- **Data Normalization:** The image pixel values were normalised to a standard range to allow faster convergence during training and to decrease the potential of vanishing or exploding gradients. This was accomplished by scaling the pixel values to a range of [0, 1], ensuring that the models got consistent and standardised input data.
- **Train-Validation Split:** To evaluate the performance of the deep learning models during training, the dataset was divided into training and validation sets. This allowed for the continuous monitoring of model performance on unseen data, enabling the early detection of overfitting and guiding the selection of the best-performing models.

By implementing these data pre-processing steps, we prepared the cassava leaf image dataset for efficient training and validation of the deep learning models, ultimately leading to the development of a reliable and accurate cassava leaf disease classification system.

4 Image Classification

In our study on cassava leaf disease classification, we employed deep learning models to perform image classification tasks. Image classification involves assigning a specific class or label to an input image based on the content or features present in the image. In our research, the primary goal was to classify cassava leaf images into various disease categories or healthy leaves, thereby assisting in disease diagnosis and management. Using the extensive dataset containing cassava leaf images, we trained and evaluated multiple deep learning models, including ResNet50, DenseNet121, EfficientNet-B0, NasNetLarge, and EfficientNet-V2. These models were designed to automatically learn and extract meaningful features from the images, facilitating accurate classification of cassava leaf diseases. To prepare the image data for efficient and effective training, we implemented several preprocessing steps, such as image resizing, data normalization, data augmentation, and train-validation split. These steps helped ensure that the models received consistent and standardized input data, which allowed them to effectively learn from the dataset and achieve accurate disease classification. During the training process, the deep learning models learned to recognize relevant features and patterns in the images that were essential for accurate cassava leaf disease classification. The models' performance was continuously evaluated on a validation set to monitor their ability to generalize to unseen data and to detect potential overfitting. Upon completion of the training process, the deep learning models demonstrated varying levels of performance in cassava leaf disease classification. By selecting the best-performing models and fine-tuning their hyperparameters, we developed a robust and accurate system for cassava leaf disease diagnosis and management.

4.1 Description of All the Algorithm and Performance

Here is a brief description of each algorithm and their performance used in your study:

– **NASNetLarge Algorithm and Performance:** NASNetLarge emerges from the realm of Neural Architecture Search (NAS), an automated approach that shapes the structure of artificial neural networks via machine learning. This recurrent network-driven method generates model descriptions of neural networks and steers the search towards architectures that deliver superior results using reinforcement learning. As a variant of the NASNet models, NASNetLarge is built to offer superior performance for image classification tasks. Its unique design comprises intricate cell structures, including normal cells for preserving the dimensions of the feature map, and reduction cells responsible for reducing the width and height while simultaneously doubling the number of filters. In our cassava leaf disease classification experiment, NASNetLarge showcased robust performance. It achieved an impressive accuracy rate of 91.90%, reflecting its adeptness at correctly identifying a vast majority of cassava leaf disease images. The model's mean squared error, reflecting the prediction error, was a mere 0.0238, suggesting that the model's predictions were largely congruent with the actual values. When it came to the validation set, the model displayed an accuracy rate of 86.28% and a slightly increased mean squared error of 0.0420. Despite this, the model's performance can still be considered commendable given the task's complexity. The validation loss, indicative of the model's ability to generalize to unseen data, was 0.1614, indicating reasonable generalization. In sum, the NASNetLarge model, with its architecture rooted in NAS, has demonstrated its potential as an effective tool for cassava leaf disease classification. The high degree of accuracy and low loss rates underscore its ability to navigate complex image classification tasks while maintaining superior predictive accuracy. This performance underscores its potential as a valuable asset in the domain of plant disease detection and management.

– **ResNet50 Algorithm and Performance:** The ResNet50 model is a variant of the Residual Network (ResNet) family, which revolutionized the field of deep learning. It's a convolutional neural network that consists of 50 layers, hence the name "ResNet50". Its defining feature is the inclusion of "skip" or "shortcut" connections that circumvent one or more layers. This novel approach mitigates the problem of vanishing or exploding gradients, which is common in deep neural networks, enabling efficient training of deeper networks. Applying the ResNet50 model to the task of cassava leaf disease classification in our research yielded promising outcomes. The model demonstrated a training loss of 0.761, signifying its adeptness at learning from the training data. This measure of the model's performance, referred to as the loss, is a quantification of the discrepancy between the model's predictions and the actual data. Lower loss values correspond to better performance. In terms of validation, the ResNet50 model showcased a loss of 0.5585, suggesting effective generalization to data unseen during training. Precision and recall, metrics indicating the model's ability to accurately classify positive instances and to capture all positive instances, respectively, were recorded at 0.825 and 0.8875. Furthermore, the F1-score, a harmonic mean of precision and recall, stood at 0.830952380952381, indicating a balanced high performance in both precision and recall. In summary, the innovative design of ResNet50, with its implementation of shortcut connections, has proven effective in the classification of cassava leaf diseases. The high precision, recall, and F1-score, together with low loss rates during both training and validation, underscore

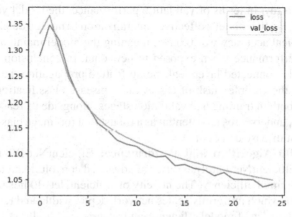

Fig. 1. Loss and val of ResNet50

its robustness and reliability as a tool for image classification tasks, including those in the agricultural domain, such as plant disease identification (Fig. 1, 2).

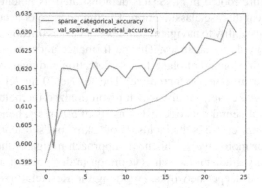

Fig. 2. Sparse and val categorical accuracy of ResNet50

- **DenseNet121 Algorithm and Performance:** The DenseNet121 algorithm, belonging to the Dense Convolutional Network (DenseNet) family, is a deep learning model that sets itself apart with its unique architecture. DenseNet121 contains 121 layers, hence the name. The innovation lies in its dense connectivity, where each layer is directly connected to all others in a feed-forward manner, enhancing feature propagation and reducing the number of parameters, which can lead to more compact models. In the study of cassava leaf disease classification, DenseNet121 showcased substantial performance. The model reached a loss of 1.0411 during training, which indicates the difference between the model's predictions and the actual data. The lower the loss, the better the model has learned from the training data. Alongside this, the model achieved a sparse categorical accuracy of 0.6300. Sparse categorical accuracy is a metric suitable for multiclass classification where the predictions are an integer array. In terms of validation performance, the model yielded a loss of 1.0494, signifying the model's effective generalization to unseen data. The validation sparse categorical accuracy was 0.6245, meaning the model maintained a comparable level of performance when exposed to new data. In conclusion, DenseNet121, with its densely connected layers enhancing feature propagation, has demonstrated its strength in the complex task of cassava leaf disease classification. The model's performance, both in training and validation stages, alongside its reasonable loss and accuracy rates, underscores its potential as a robust tool for image classification tasks, including plant disease detection.
- **EfficientNet-B0 Algorithm and Performance:** EfficientNet-B0 is the baseline model of the EfficientNet family, a series of advanced convolutional neural networks designed for optimal efficiency. The novelty of EfficientNet-B0 lies in its compound scaling method, which uniformly scales network depth, width, and resolution, resulting in a better balance of model efficiency and accuracy. This allows EfficientNet-B0

to achieve comparable or superior performance while using a fraction of the computational resources typically required by other models. In our study on cassava leaf disease classification, EfficientNet-B0 yielded noteworthy results. The model recorded a training loss of 0.8007216453552246, suggesting that the model learned effectively from the training data. The loss function value serves as an indicator of how far the model's predictions deviate from the actual data, with a lower value indicating better performance. Concurrently, the model achieved perfect training accuracy, highlighting its capability to classify the training images correctly. In the validation phase, EfficientNet-B0 continued to demonstrate robust performance. The model achieved a validation loss of 1.5468380451202393, suggesting that the model's ability to generalize to unseen data was fairly effective, despite the increase in loss compared to the training phase. The validation accuracy was 0.7448598146438599, demonstrating that the model maintained a high level of performance when confronted with new data.

In summary, EfficientNet-B0, with its unique scaling method, has proven to be a promising model for cassava leaf disease classification. Its relatively low loss and high accuracy rates, both during training and validation, highlight its capacity to handle complex image classification tasks, positioning it as a valuable tool in the field of plant disease identification (Fig. 3).

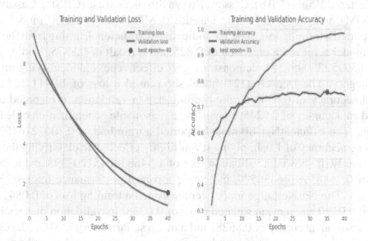

Fig. 3. EfficientNet-V2 Algorithm and Performance

– **EfficientNet-V2 Algorithm and Performance:** EfficientNet-V2 represents an evolution in the EfficientNet family of convolutional neural networks, characterized by its unique approach to model scaling and training. The key innovation in EfficientNet-V2 is the implementation of Progressive Learning. This strategy begins the training process with smaller, less complex images, gradually introducing larger and more intricate images as the model learns, which leads to efficiency in training time and enhanced performance. When applied to our cassava leaf disease classification task,

EfficientNet-V2 demonstrated substantial performance. The model posted a training loss of 0.7313, a measure of how well the model's predictions aligned with the actual data during the learning process. The lower the loss, the better the model is at learning from the training data. Furthermore, the model achieved a training accuracy of 0.7245, reflecting the proportion of correct classifications made by the model on the training set. On the validation front, EfficientNet-V2 exhibited a loss of 0.7488, indicative of the model's ability to generalize its learning to new, unseen data. The validation accuracy of the model was recorded at 0.7480, suggesting the model maintained a high level of performance when introduced to new data. To summarize, EfficientNet-V2, with its distinct progressive learning strategy and efficient scaling, has shown promise in the complex task of cassava leaf disease classification. Its relatively low loss values and high accuracy rates during both the training and validation stages underscore its potential as a reliable tool for image classification tasks, including the detection of plant diseases.

5 Result

The study utilized five deep learning models: ResNet50, DenseNet121, EfficientNet-B0, NasNetLarge, and EfficientNet-V2 for the classification of cassava leaf diseases using a dataset of leaf images. The models classified these images into five categories: Healthy, Cassava Bacterial Blight (CBB), Cassava Brown Streak Disease (CBSD), Cassava Green Mottle (CGM), and Cassava Mosaic Disease (CMD).The ResNet50 model, after 10 epochs, reported a training loss of 0.761, indicating an efficient learning from the training data. The model achieved a precision of 0.825 and a recall of 0.8875, leading to an F-score of 0.830952380952381, demonstrating its effectiveness in identifying the correct disease category. The DenseNet121 model showcased a loss of 1.0411 and a sparse categorical accuracy of 0.6300 during training. Upon validation, it recorded a loss of 1.0494 and an accuracy of 0.6245, suggesting a reasonable generalization of learning to unseen data. The EfficientNet-B0 model reported a train loss of 0.8007216453552246 and a training accuracy of 1.0, implying it was highly effective in classifying the training images correctly. It showed a validation loss of 1.5468380451202393 and a validation accuracy of 0.7448598146438599, indicating a robust performance in classifying the validation set. The NasNetLarge model demonstrated a training loss of 0.0842 with an accuracy of 0.9190 and a mean squared error of 0.0238. Its validation metrics included a loss of 0.1614, an accuracy of 0.8628, and a mean squared error of 0.0420, suggesting a strong performance in terms of both learning from the training data and generalizing this learning to unseen data. Lastly, the EfficientNet-V2 model had a training loss of 0.7313 and a training accuracy of 0.7245. It also showed a validation loss of 0.7488 and a validation accuracy of 0.7480, denoting its effectiveness in classifying the validation data correctly. Overall, these results suggest that all models, to varying extents, were successful in the classification of cassava leaf diseases, with high accuracy and relatively low loss values (Fig. 4, 5, 6).

Fig. 4. Cassava Green Mottle (CGM)   **Fig. 5.** Cassava Mosaic Disease (CMD)

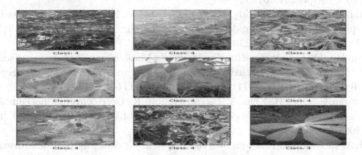

Fig. 6. Healthy

6   Conclusion

Our study aimed to build a robust classifier for the identification and classification of Cassava Leaf Diseases, namely Cassava Bacterial Blight (CBB), Cassava Green Mottle (CGM), and Cassava Mosaic Disease (CMD). For this purpose, we utilized DL models such as ResNet50, DenseNet121, EfficientNet-B0, NasNetLarge, and EfficientNet-V2.These models were trained and tested on a dataset of cassava leaf images, and they demonstrated varying degrees of effectiveness in classifying the diseases correctly. While all models showed promising results, it was evident that certain models excelled more than others. For instance, the ResNet50 model reported a high F-score, suggesting a good balance between precision and recall. On the other hand, EfficientNet-B0 demonstrated an excellent training accuracy, indicating its effectiveness in classifying the training images correctly. The study underlines the potential of deep learning in revolutionizing plant disease diagnosis, providing a promising solution for the rapid and accurate detection of diseases like CBSD, CGM, CMD, and CBB. Future research could focus on optimizing these models further and exploring their application in real-world settings to aid farmers and agronomists in early disease detection and management. It is hoped that the results of this research will contribute to more sustainable cassava production and enhanced food security in regions heavily reliant on this vital crop.

References

1. Anitha, J., Saranya, N.: Cassava leaf disease identification and detection using deep learning approach. Int. J. Comput. Commun. Control **17**(2) (2022). https://doi.org/10.15837/ijccc.2022.2.4356
2. Manick, Srivastava, J.: Cassava leaf disease detection using deep learning. In: 2022 IEEE International IOT, Electronics and Mechatronics Conference (IEMTRONICS), pp. 1–7 (2022). https://doi.org/10.1109/IEMTRONICS55184.2022.9795751
3. Ayu, H.R., Surtono, A., Apriyanto, D.K.: Deep learning for detection cassava leaf disease. J. Phys. Conf. Ser. **1751**(1), 12072 (2021). https://doi.org/10.1088/1742-6596/1751/1/012072
4. Ramcharan, A., Baranowski, K., McCloskey, P., Ahmed, B., Legg, J., Hughes, D.P.: Deep learning for image-based cassava disease detection. Front. Plant Sci. **8**, 1852 (2017). https://doi.org/10.3389/fpls.2017.01852
5. Dhasan, D.B., Karthik, K., Reddy, M.L., Yadav, M.G.S.: Identification and classification of cassava plant leaf disease using deep learning technique. AIP Conf. Proc. **2519**(1) (2022). https://doi.org/10.1063/5.0110238
6. Abayomi-Alli, O.O., Damaševičius, R., Misra, S., Maskeliūnas, R.: Cassava disease recognition from low-quality images using enhanced data augmentation model and deep learning. Expert Syst. **38**(7), n/a–n/a (2021). https://doi.org/10.1111/exsy.12746
7. Arulkumaran, G., Gopi, B., Khan, V., Parameshwaran, R.: Deep convolutional neural network-based cassava plant leaf disease classification. AIP Conf. Proc. **2519**(1) (2022). https://doi.org/10.1063/5.0110659
8. Ahmed, A.A., Reddy, G.H.: A mobile-based system for detecting plant leaf diseases using deep learning. AgriEngineering **3**(3), 478–493 (2021). https://doi.org/10.3390/agriengineering3030032
9. Oyewola, D.O., Dada, E.G., Misra, S., Damasevicius, R.: Detecting cassava mosaic disease using a deep residual convolutional neural network with distinct block processing. PeerJ. Comput. Sci. **7**, e352–e352 (2021). https://doi.org/10.7717/peerj-cs.352
10. Sambasivam, G., Opiyo, G.D.: A predictive machine learning application in agriculture: Cassava disease detection and classification with imbalanced dataset using convolutional neural networks. Egypt. Inform. J. **22**(1), 27–34 (2021). https://doi.org/10.1016/j.eij.2020.02.007
11. Ghosh, H., Tusher, M.A., Rahat, I.S., Khasim, S., Mohanty, S.N.: Water quality assessment through predictive machine learning. In: Balas, V.E., Semwal, V.B., Khandare, A. (eds.) Intelligent Computing and Networking. IC-ICN 2023. LNNS, vol. 699, pp. 77–88. Springer, Singapore (2023). https://doi.org/10.1007/978-981-99-3177-4_6
12. Thaiyalnayaki, K., Raghul, S., Kumar, U.K., Ramachandran, S.: Automatic classification of cassava using data augmentation and CNN. AIP Conf. Proc. **2405**(1) (2022). https://doi.org/10.1063/5.0072729
13. Vijayalata, Y., Billakanti, N., Veeravalli, K., Deepa, A., Kota, L.: early detection of casava plant leaf diseases using EfficientNet-B0. In: 2022 IEEE Delhi Section Conference (DELCON), pp. 1–5 (2022). https://doi.org/10.1109/DELCON54057.2022.9753210
14. Methil, A., Agrawal, H., Kaushik, V.: One-vs-all methodology based cassava leaf disease detection. In: 2021 12th International Conference on Computing Communication and Networking Technologies (ICCCNT), pp. 1–7 (2021). https://doi.org/10.1109/ICCCNT51525.2021.9579920

15. Yadav, R., Pandey, M., Sahu, S.K.: Cassava plant disease detection with imbalanced dataset using transfer learning. In: 2022 IEEE World Conference on Applied Intelligence and Computing (AIC), pp. 220–225 (2022). https://doi.org/10.1109/AIC55036.2022.9848882

16. Kunkeaw, S., Worapong, J., Smith, D.R., Triwitayakorn, K.: In vitro detached leaf assay for pre-screening resistance to anthracnose disease in cassava (Manihot esculenta Crantz). Australas. Plant Pathol. **39**(6), 547–550 (2010). https://doi.org/10.1071/AP10024

17. Tusubira, J.F., et al.: Improving in-field cassava whitefly pest surveillance with machine learning. In: 2020 IEEE/CVF Conference on Computer Vision and Pattern Recognition Workshops (CVPRW), pp. 303–309 (2020). https://doi.org/10.1109/CVPRW50498.2020.00042

18. Mathulaprangsan, S., Lanthong, K.: Cassava leaf disease recognition using convolutional neural networks. In: 2021 9th International Conference on Orange Technology (ICOT), pp. 1–5 (2021). https://doi.org/10.1109/ICOT54518.2021.9680655

19. Nuwamanya, E., et al.: Cassava brown streak disease effects on leaf metabolites and pigment accumulation. Afr. Crop Sci. J. **25**(1), 33 (2017). https://doi.org/10.4314/acsj.v25i1.3

20. Liu, M., Liang, H., Hou, M.: Research on cassava disease classification using the multi-scale fusion model based on EfficientNet and attention mechanism. Front. Plant Sci. **13**, 1088531 (2022). https://doi.org/10.3389/fpls.2022.1088531

21. Julião, E.C., et al.: Reduction of brown leaf spot and changes in the chlorophyll a content induced by fungicides in cassava plants. Eur. J. Plant Pathol. **157**(2), 433–439 (2020). https://doi.org/10.1007/s10658-020-02001-0

22. Hillocks, R., et al.: Disparity between leaf and root symptoms and crop losses associated with cassava brown streak disease in four countries in Eastern Africa. J. Phytopathol. **164**(2), 86–93 (2016). https://doi.org/10.1111/jph.12430

Aspect-Based Sentiment Classification of Online Product Reviews Using Hybrid Lexicon-Machine Learning Approach

Daniel Asuquo[1,2]([✉]) [ID], Kingsley Attai[3] [ID], Patience Usip[1,2] [ID], Uduak George[1], and Francis Osang[4]

[1] Department of Computer Science, Faculty of Science, University of Uyo, Uyo, Nigeria
danielasuquo@uniuyo.edu.ng
[2] TETFund Center of Excellence in Computational Intelligence Research, UNIUYO, Uyo, Nigeria
[3] Department of Mathematics and Computer Science, Ritman University, IkotEkpene, Ikot Ekpene, Nigeria
[4] Department of Computer Science, National Open University of Nigeria, Abuja, Nigeria

Abstract. Nowadays, a good number of customers express their experience with online products. These reviews have an important role in customers' purchase decision process. There may be hundreds or thousands of unstructured and heterogeneous reviews for a popular product. Traditional text processing techniques have limited capability in extracting opinions on customers' product reviews from huge data over the Internet. Although lexical approaches aim to map words to sentiments by building a lexicon, the process of developing a lexicon with sentiment scores for phrases and sentences becomes tedious and time consuming as data volume increases. Currently, text sentiment analysis requires fast and accurate techniques to decode and quantify the emotion in tweets. This paper presents a hybrid framework based on lexicon and machine learning (ML) algorithms to train previously seen tweets in order to predict the sentiments of some new input tweets into positive, negative, and neutral polarities. Tweepy library was used to extract tweets on Laptop reviews to identify some aspects and classify sentiments towards them into specific polarity. After data pre-processing, the implementation in Python used Natural Language Processing package called TextBlob to assign subjectivity and polarity scores to text. The scores were used by the ML algorithms to analyze and classify sentiments. A dataset of 2226 tweets was used for training and testing Support Vector Machine, Random Forest, and Naïve Bayes classifiers. Results indicate that Random Forest classifier outperforms others in the task of classifying sentiments on Laptop reviews with the highest accuracy (96%), precision (97%), and F1-score (96%).

Keywords: Sentiment Analysis · Aspect Level · Online Reviews · Lexicon · Machine Learning · Python

M. A. Jabbar et al. (Eds.): AMLDA 2023, CCIS 2047, pp. 124–143, 2024.
https://doi.org/10.1007/978-3-031-55486-5_10

1 Introduction

Web-based purchases have seen a significant increase in recent years. The increasing number of online comments on product features is due to the advancements in e-commerce [1]. New product categories are constantly emerging and customer preferences are constantly changing. It is difficult to keep up with the trend and manually identify the features of each newly created category and the needs of new customers. Online reviews have the potential of boosting confidence in purchasing decisions by helping to reduce risk and uncertainty thereby making online shopping more effective. Although many microblogging and social networking platforms exist, massive instant messages called tweets are posted daily on Twitter, making it one of the most popular sources of online reviews [2]. Tweets have a limited number of characters (a maximum of 280 characters for each tweet) and the use of hashtags between words facilitates information search, retrieval, and processing [3, 4].

Nowadays, customers purchase goods and services from online retailers using computers and other handheld devices like smartphones, tablets, and iPads. The opinions or emotions of customers referred to as online reviews, reflect their perception of the product over a period of time. The ability to gather such huge unstructured, heterogeneous data and process the textual information to determine expressed sentiments about a product can aid new customers in making useful purchase decisions while manufacturers can include innovative preferences during production for higher sales rates. According to Kumar and Zymbler [5], sentiment analysis is the process of using natural language processing techniques, textual analysis, and computer language to systematically identify, extract and manipulate relevant information about product reviews. The result is a classification expressed opinions into positive, negative, or neutral polarity. The disclosure of sentiment expressed in product reviews is essential to both consumers and manufacturers. According to Ligthart et al. [6], each of them could take necessary actions on the product based on the extracted information. Such an outcome can help manufacturers gain insight into the needs and expectations of their customers while helping customers to make purchase decisions about a product and maintain brand loyalty with improved satisfaction. Ideally, negative sentiments signify that the product feature should be improved, while positive sentiments indicate that the product feature should be maintained.

The work in [1] reports that the ability to find the sentiments of specific product features is vital to emotional product design and development. During this process, the sentiment polarity of a sentence can be discovered and properly classified. Summarizing such opinions based on certain aspects or features of the product is called aspect-based sentiment analysis [7]. The task of extracting information from product reviews using traditional lexicon-based approaches is tedious, cumbersome, and inherent with uncertainty. The author in [8] reports that the approach is limited in its capability to identify sentiment feature words and opinion words in textual information. Nevertheless, automatically identifying product features is challenging. Semantic web technology seeks to enable machine understandability with the use of ontology [9, 10]. ML techniques have recently received a widespread application in diverse problem domains due to their learning and predictive capability with high accuracy and precision [3, 7, 11], when classifying items into different labels or categories. These methods focus on the use of data and algorithms to simulate human learning, gradually improving accuracy and interpretability performance for timely decision-making. Thus, they can improve accuracy in identifying product features and opinion words. Furthermore, hybrid approaches cooperatively exhibit the accuracy of the ML approach and the speed of the lexical approach in sentiment classification [12].

Most sentiment analysis studies focus on movie, tourism, hotel, or restaurant reviews [12–16], neglecting Laptop reviews, and opinions on its specific aspects. Most studies also focus on classifying sentiments into positive and negative, neglecting neutral sentiment polarity. Notable advancements in computing and data analytics, communication technology, internet, and web applications have made it possible for people of diverse careers to choose to work anytime, anywhere with the help of Laptop computers. This daily dependence on laptop use for work at home, office, café, or school makes it important to review sentiments expressed by potential customers on specific aspects of the product for informed decision-making by both prospective customers and manufacturers. This study aims at developing a hybrid lexicon-ML predictive framework to analyze reviews on specific aspects of Laptops in order to determine the sentiments (neutral, positive, and negative) towards the product.

The rest of the paper is organized as follows. Section 2 reviews related works on the concept and levels of sentiment analysis, phases of aspect-based sentiment analysis as well as limitations and strengths of approaches to aspect-based sentiment analysis. Section 3 describes the methodology deployed for this study, the experimental setup and framework of the proposed hybrid lexicon-ML approach as well as a description of the ML algorithms and performance metrics used. Section 4 presents the results and compares the prediction accuracy of the classifiers, indicating their ability to effectively classify sentiments into neutral, positive, and negative polarity. Section 5 presents the concluding remarks with direction for future works.

2   Related Works

Many studies on sentiment analysis have been reported with a focus on a range of domains such as movie reviews, product reviews, restaurant reviews, and news and blogs [1, 3, 8, 17–19]. The authors in [20] noted that the huge volume of data from reviews has captured the interest of researchers and companies in many domains. Numerous studies have shown that a large amount of information about users' needs and preferences can be extracted from online reviews [21–23]. This type of information can be used by prospective customers to make purchase decisions or by manufacturers during production to meet customers' needs for innovative products in a competitive market economy. In [24], it was observed that collecting online reviews is much easier as such data are open to everyone where the web crawling process allows for automatic download. The reviews are relatively anonymous, available to multiple individuals for an indefinite period of time, and accessible to companies interested in learning about consumer feedback. The application of computational analysis to people's feelings and opinions for an entity is called sentiment analysis or opinion mining. The work in [3] describes sentiment analysis as the application of computing techniques in analyzing people's emotions, expressions, ideas, and opinions about a particular product or service.

Normally, the online review texts are unstructured in nature with heterogeneous expressions displayed in the hypertext markup language (HTML) document. Most online markets sort these reviews in order of helpfulness or relevance. Consumers are not able to easily process the details from thousands of reviews to fully understand the strengths and weaknesses of each product. Firms are also not able to easily gather understanding from the contents of informal reviews of their products to determine market trends and discover hidden knowledge to stay competitive with higher market sales. Hence, the need to adopt an appropriate computational intelligent approach to analyze sentiments contained in reviews about specific aspects or features of a product.

2.1 Aspect Level Sentiment Analysis

Sentiment analysis can take place at the document level, sentence level, or aspect level [25]. At the document level, it aims to classify the opinion about the whole document into negative, positive, or neutral polarity. At the sentence level, the process aims to establish whether each opinion text expresses negative, positive, or neutral polarity. These two levels of sentiment analysis lack the ability to establish what aspects of a product people like or dislike as expressed in the review texts. Aspect-level sentiment analysis handles this limitation as it focuses on classifying opinions from textual reviews to certain product features. Such classification results can help manufacturers identify consumers' emotions about specific aspects of a product thereby utilizing such discovered hidden knowledge in emotional product development. According to [1], aspect identification, opinion extraction, and polarity detection are the three phases of an aspect-based sentiment analysis task. The work of [26] describes an opinion by a quadruple (g, s, h, t). The author denotes g as the target of the sentiment, s signifies the opinion sentiment with respect to the target, h is the opinionholder, and t denotes the time when the opinion is expressed by the opinion holder. Essentially, the sentiment target of an opinion can be the whole, a part, or aspects of an entity, upon which an opinion holder expresses his/her sentiment. The entity refers to a product, service, person, organization, topic, issue, or event. The aspect refers to a feature, an attribute or a part of the entity. Questions that must be solved when handling sentiment analysis at aspect level include:

 (i) How can one identify aspects automatically with reduced cost and improved flexibility?
 (ii) How can one better capture the semantic relationship among keywords to construct aspects?
(iii) Does the hierarchical structure among aspects exist, and can the hierarchical structure improve the understanding of identified aspects?

Some studies have proposed various methods to automatically identify and structure meaningful words and expressions from online reviews using Natural Language Processing (NLP) technique [12, 13, 27–29], in order to summarize the main idea of the review text. The authors in [30] first proposed a feature-based opinion mining method to analyze the polarity of the reviewer's subjective opinions towards a set of product features. Product feature words and subjective opinion words were targeted based on the following assumptions: the product feature words are the nouns and noun phrases that appear frequently in the review text; the opinion words are the adjectives associated with the product feature words. The polarity of the opinion words was determined with the help of existing sentiment lexicon like SentiWordNet. Finally, for each product feature, the number of positive opinion words and the number of negative opinion words are counted. More positive opinion words mean that reviewers are satisfied with the product feature. More negative opinion words mean that reviewers are unsatisfied with the product feature.

Aspect extraction can be done explicitly by using traditional frequency-based analysis method that finds frequently used nouns or compound nouns [31], or implicitly by syntax-based method that identifies aspects through syntactic relations where they are preceded by a modifying adjective in the sentiment word [6] or by supervised, unsupervised, and semi-supervised ML techniques [1, 15, 32]. For Laptop reviews, aspects may include 'battery', 'processor', 'screen', 'memory', 'design', 'storage', 'resolution', etc. The work in [28] used Chi Square test to identify and select the best features in tweets extracted with Twitter application programming interface (API) while Naïve Bayes algorithm was used to classify the sentiment polarity of the tweets as positive and negative for effective decision making. The implementation was done in Python programming language. In [12], a novel Latent Dirichlet Allocation- Conditional Random Field (LDA–CRF) hybrid model was developed to extract aspect-specific sentiment expression and aspect rating prediction simultaneously for each aspect in reviews. They used a dataset of hotel and restaurant reviews from TripAdvisor.com where experimental results show that both task potentially reinforce each other and joint modeling outperformed state-of-the-art baselines for each individual task.

Opinions are words that modify the aspects such as 'faster' 'slow', 'good', 'bad', 'long-lasting' 'short', 'superior' 'inferior', 'low', 'high', which can precisely express a sentiment. Basically, there are two approaches to extracting opinions concerning the identified aspects. They are the relation-based approach and the ML approach. The relation-based method uses the associations between aspects and opinions to extract opinion words of aspects. Ideally, the distance, syntactic dependency, and co-occurrence among them are always utilized to extract the opinion words of an aspect. While the distance-based technique extracts opinion words based on a certain distance from a specific aspect [33], the dependency technique uses a dependency parsing algorithm to extract opinion words modifying aspects [13, 34–36]. Lastly, the co-occurrence technique extracts opinion words of specific aspects using the co-occurrence relationship between aspects and opinions [37]. The ML approach adopts traditional ML and deep learning (DL) techniques including their ensemble. However, commonly used traditional ML models for opinion extraction include Probabilistic Latent Semantic Analysis (PLSA), Latent Dirichlet Allocation (LDA), Hidden Markov Model (HMM), and Conditional Random Field (CRF) [38]. On the other hand, commonly used DL models for opinion extraction include Long Short-Term Memory (LSTM), Gated Recurrent Units (GRU), and Recurrent Neural Network (RNN) [39, 40].

2.2 Techniques for Analyzing Sentiments

Techniques for sentiment analysis have been categorized into lexicon-based approach, ML approach, and hybrid approach. The following sections briefly describe these approaches.

Lexicon-Based Approach. The lexicon-based approaches require a knowledge base in terms of a predefined list of words, which associates the opinion words to their corresponding semantic orientations as positive, negative, or neutral words [41]. It simply builds a 'dictionary of sentiments'. The orientation of each aspect is usually derived by aggregating the semantic orientations of all opinion words [32]. Thus, this approach can be implemented by either a dictionary-based or corpus-based method [42, 43], as depicted in Fig. 1. A dictionary or corpus database contains words with a polarity label or number indicating $+1$, -1, or 0 expressing each word's polarity. The polarity label can be assigned to a sentence based on the many marks obtained on a trained set. The procedure for analyzing sentiments based on the lexicon approach is shown in Algorithm 1. Nevertheless, this method is less accurate and may not be operational due to dependence on the dictionary. If the words where the polarity needs analysis are not found in the dictionary, then the sentence will remain blank. There are suggestions that a dictionary-based approach is wrong especially where humor or sarcasm seems to be one thing but means something else.

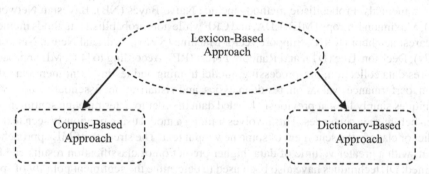

Fig. 1. Lexicon-based approaches to sentiment classification

Algorithm 1. Sentiments Classification based on Lexicon Approach
Step 1: Tokenization. Split the given input text into smaller tokens, which can be a word, phrases or whole sentence.
Step 2: Bag of Words. Count each word in the document by number and the resulting value is called the bag of words.
Step 3: Subjectivity. Look at the polarity of each word from the existing lexicon available in the database, consisting of the emotional values for words that are pre-recorded by the analysts.
   Step 4: Compute the sentiment of the input text

VADER (Valence Aware Dictionary for sEntiment Reasoning) is an example of a lexical method. VADER model is a lexicon and rule-based model for sentiment analysis. It can be used to classify sentiments into polarities. Lexical features for contextual communications affect sentiment. These are colloquialisms such as slang like 'meh', emoticons like ':-)', and acronyms like 'LOL', that get mapped to intensity values. Apart from that, other contextual elements, like punctuation, capitalization, and modifiers also impart emotion. The result generated by VADER is a dictionary of four keys *neg*, *neu*, *pos* and *compound* where, *neg*, *neu*, and *pos* represent negative, neutral, and positive respectively. Their sum should be equal to 1 or close to it with float operation. On the other hand, *compound* corresponds to the sum of the valence score of each word in the lexicon and determines the degree of the sentiment rather than the actual value. Its value is between −1 (most extreme negative sentiment) and +1 (most extreme positive sentiment). Using the *compound* score, the underlying sentiment of a text can be determined as follows:

$$\text{sentiment of a text} = \begin{cases} positive, \ if \ compound \geq 0.05 \\ negative, \ if \ compound \leq -0.05 \\ neutral, \ if \ -0.05 < compound < 0.05 \end{cases} \quad (1)$$

Machine Learning Approach. The ML approach works better to get emotion compared to the dictionary-based approach. This approach uses techniques that could be unsupervised, supervised, or reinforcement learning algorithms [44–46], as depicted in Fig. 2. Mostly supervised learning algorithms have been applied for sentiment classification as shown in Fig. 3.They are split into probabilistic and non-probabilistic classification methods. Probabilistic methods include Naïve Bayes (NB), Bayesian Network (BN), Maximum Entropy (ME), LDA, and CRF while non-probabilistic methods include K-nearest neighbor (KNN), Support Vector Machine (SVM), Artificial Neural Network (ANN), Decision Tree (DT), and Random Forest (RF). According to [11], ML approach requires data collection, pre-processing, model training and testing, sentiment classification, performance evaluation, result analytics, and visualization. Essentially, most ML techniques simply look at previously labeled data in order to determine the sentiment of never-before-seen sentences. This involves training a model using previously seen text to predict or classify the sentiment of some new input text. The strength of ML approaches is that, with a greater volume of data, higher prediction or classification results can be obtained. DL techniques have also been used to determine the sentiment polarity of specific aspects of a product, including the ones based on Multiple Attention Mechanism Network (MAMN) [47], Convolution Neural Network (CNN) [48, 49], RNN [50], and LSTM [51–53], GRU [54].

Moreover, [4] proposed an ensemble ML approach for Twitter sentiment analysis. Several ML algorithms including raw RF, gradient boosting RF, SVM, Multilayer Perceptron (MLP), RNN, and CNN were used in classifying emotional expressions. Results indicate that the best RNN achieved an accuracy of 83.0%, while the best CNN yielded 83.34%. Also, the convolutional model with the SVM classifier showed better performance than the single CNN. In general, the proposed ensemble method based on receiving the most votes according to the five best models' predictions yielded an accuracy of 85.71%, demonstrating its effectiveness in real life.

Hybrid Approach. Hybrid approach cooperatively exhibits the accuracy of a ML approach and the speed of lexical approach. Figure 4 shows the description of the hybrid approach to sentiment analysis. The work in [55] used two-word lexicons and an unlabeled data, where the two-word lexicons were divided in two discrete classes, negative and positive. The cosine similarity amongst pseudo documents and the unlabeled documents were computed and the documents were classified into positive or negative sentiment. This training dataset was then fed to a Naïve Bayes classifier for training and

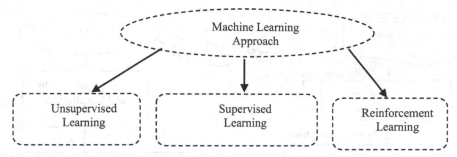

Fig. 2. ML techniques for sentiment classification

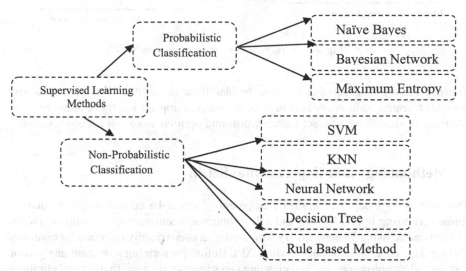

Fig. 3. Supervised ML methods for sentiment classification

result evaluation. Also, [56] derived a "unified framework" using background lexical information as word class associations. With available datasets or training examples from Twitter data, they proposed a multinomial Naïve Bayes classifier where manually labeled data was incorporated for training task with a performance accuracy of 84%.

Pang and Lee [19] were the first to apply for patented machines in feature-based concept mining. They used NB, ME and SVM to identify and distinguish emotions in online movie reviews. While [57] reported that SVM can be effectively used to categorize emotional expressions; [17] used SVM to identify the emotional power and words of a product feature. The authors in [18] used NB and SVM classifiers to analyze feelings or opinions from restaurant reviews written in Cantonese. Advances in computing, communication technology, internet and web applications have endeared more people to the use of Laptop computers for their daily tasks at home, office, and school. A lot of literatures abound for feature-based opinion mining on movie reviews and hotel reviews [58, 59], while studies on laptop reviews are scarce. Previous studies indicate that some non-feature nouns (or noun phrases) and non-opinion words could also be extracted.

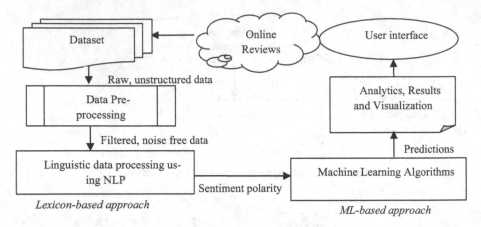

Fig. 4. Hybrid sentiment analysis approach

These words are considered as *noise* in the identification results. Therefore, sentiment analysis research community is in need of data-driven approaches that can improve the accuracy in identifying product feature words and opinion words on Laptop reviews.

3 Methodology and Experimental Setup

The methodology deployed in the development of aspect-based text sentiment analysis framework using hybrid lexicon and ML techniques is summarized as follows. Tweets were extracted using Tweepy library which offers a user-friendly interface for obtaining Twitter data, accessible through Twitter API. Before performing sentiment analysis on text data, data pre-processing and cleaning tasks were performed to filter and eliminate noisy data. This helps transform unstructured data into understandable format. The process comprises removing special characters such as @, #, $, *, ", unwanted blanks, punctuations, uniform resource locators (URLs), and hypertext markup language (HTML) tags from the tweet text, converting text to lowercase, removing stopwords (common words like "the," "is," "as", "be", "are", etc.) that do not contribute much to sentiment analysis, tokenizing the text into individual words or tokens, lemmatizing or stemming the tokens to reduce them to their base form such as reduces the words chocolates, choco, chocolately to the word "chocolate". The entire process generates processed data in a format suitable for utilization as input for sentiment analysis task.

Later, TextBlob, a Python NLP package that offers a variety of features for sentiment analysis was deployed. TextBlob is a popular Python library for text processing and sentiment analysis. It provides a simple API for performing sentiment analysis on textual data by simply assigning polarity and subjectivity scores to text. Polarity represents the sentiment (positive or negative) or emotion conveyed in a text and is quantified on a scale from -1 to $+1$, with -1 denoting a negative emotion, 0 denoting a neutral emotion, and 1 denoting a positive emotion. Subjectivity represents the degree of objectivity or subjectivity in the text. The degree of subjective or objective content in a text is quantified instead by subjectivity, which is similarly measured on a scale from 0 to 1, with 0 denoting an objective statement and 1 denoting a subjective statement.

TextBlob calculates polarity and subjectivity using the Pattern Analyzer or NB method. In the first method, TextBlob uses the Pattern library to analyze patterns for sentiment. To determine the sentiment polarity of each word in a text, the Pattern library consults a lexicon of adjectives and their hand-tagged scores. TextBlob calculates the overall polarity of the text by averaging the polarity scores of all the words in the passage. Alternatively, TextBlob applies a learned classifier that was trained on a dataset when using the NB analyzer. With consideration for the context and patterns observed in the reviews, this classifier calculates sentiment scores based on the words and phrases discovered in the text.

Hence, the subjectivity and polarity scores were used as inputs while generated sentiment was the output in the labeled dataset for the ML algorithms. The dataset of 2226 tweets was split in the ratio of 8:2 for model training and testing respectively. Specific aspects considered in this work are 'Battery', 'Processor', 'Screen', 'Storage', and 'Design'. Figure 5 presents the architecture of the proposed hybrid lexicon-ML framework for aspect-based sentiment analysis.

The ML algorithms used for the sentiment classification task include Support Vector Machines (SVM), Random Forest (RF), and Naïve Bayes (NB). NB is a probabilistic classifier that excels at sentiment analysis and other text classification applications [60]. It can handle text data effectively even with a small amount of training data, making it especially well-suited for sentiment analysis [61, 62]. is an ensemble technique that merges multiple decision trees to make predictions and it is robust and works well with both unstructured and structured data, including text [63–65]. SVM are excellent for sentiment analysis because they can handle high-dimensional data well, which is typical in text analysis when there are many features such as words or phrases [66, 67]. The performance of these classifiers was evaluated using accuracy, precision, recall, and F1-score to determine the best classifier for classifying sentiments into negative, positive, and neutral.

3.1 Performance Evaluation

The performance of the ML classifiers was evaluated based on some metrics including accuracy, precision, recall, and F1-score as represented in the confusion matrix. These metrics are represented in Eqs. (2)–(5). While True Positive (TP) represents reviews that are observed as positive and also predicted as positive, True Negative (TN) represents reviews observed to be negative and also predicted as negative. False Positive (FP) represents reviews observed to be negative but predicted as positive while False Negative (FN) represents reviews observed to be positive but predicted as negative by the classifiers.

$$Accuracy = \frac{TP + TN}{TP + TN + FP + FN} \tag{2}$$

$$Precision = \frac{TP}{TP + FP} \tag{3}$$

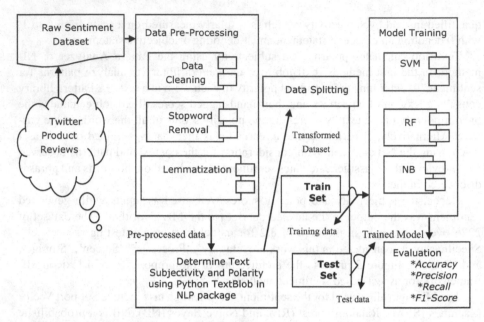

Fig. 5. Proposed hybrid lexicon-ML framework for aspect-based sentiment classification

$$Recall = \frac{TP}{TP + FN} \tag{4}$$

$$F1 - score = \frac{2 \times (Precision \times Recall)}{Precision + Recall} \tag{5}$$

4   Results and Discussion

Figure 6 shows the class distribution of positive, negative, and neutral sentiments from the NLP processing package in TextBlob. TextBlob presents subjectivity, polarity, and sentiments (positive, negative, and neutral). It indicates that 48% of the tweets belong to neutral sentiment while 40% were in the positive sentiment polarity. However, only 12% of the tweets were categorized as negative sentiment. This reveals that majority of the opinions expressed on Laptop reviews did not clearly provide information to aid purchase-decision by prospective buyers. The sample code in Python for the Laptop sentiment analysis can be obtained from GitHub.com [68]. The sample tweets collected along with TextBlob subjectivity and polarity scores including sentiment polarity is presented in Fig. 7. The sentiments were then encoded for easy classification by ML algorithms as follows: (Neutral Sentiment = 0, Negative sentiment = 1, Positive sentiment = 2).

Figure 8 shows the transformed sentiment dataset for predictive modeling of sentiment classes. The parameters of the multi-class classification algorithms are given as follows:

X(Input Variable) = Subjectivity, Polarity.

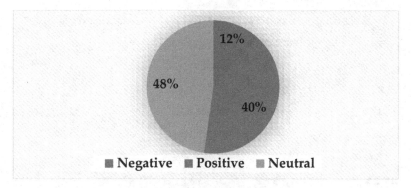

Fig. 6. Class distribution of the tweets

1	Tweets	Subjectivi	Polarity	Sentiment
	3M Privacy Filter for HP EliteBook 840 G1 / G2 Laptop (PFNHP001) UHMM6QN			
2	https://t.co/wiJ29IldSR https://t.co/zEwgwAbvQt	0	0	Neutral
	HP 2022 Newest 17z Laptop, 17 3" HD+ Touchscreen, AMD Ryzen 5 5500U Processor, Bluetooth, Wi-Fi 6, Webcam, HDMI, Windows 11 8LEAGHN			
3	https://t.co/hchhqTgtJ3 https://t.co/ThyrovEAut	0	0	Neutral
4	RT @vimalkumar_ice: After send time service laptop is w	0.5	0	Neutral
5	HP Chromebook x360 Intel Celeron N4120 14 inch(35.6 cm	0	0	Neutral
	Dc Power Adapter Converter 5.5*2.5mm Female to USB Type C Jack Converter for Macbook Lenovo Dell Hp Asus Laptop Charger $3.92 click>>https://t.co/GtpSHoDR6Y			
6	#amazon #aliexpress #rt https://t.co/68vc4DUIWq	0.166667	0	Neutral
	2022 HP Pavilion Laptop, 14-inch HD Touchscreen, AMD 3000 Series Processor, 16GB RAM, 576GB Storage, Long Battery Life, Webca EA9THKA			
7	https://t.co/RIoP5Ii1DH https://t.co/2GFEX4pJ5T	0.4	-0.05	Negative
8	RT @IntelIndia: Get ready to meet a laptop that's evolved	0.7	0.45	Positive
	Choose HP Wireless Keyboard and Mouse CS10, for smooth and stress-free typing. Order Now: https://t.co/U3tbLSPGYb #costtocost #uae #shopping #dubai #hp #keyboard #mouse #keyboardmouse #hpkeyboard #pc #laptop #keyboardsetup #dsf #difc #wirlessKeyboard			
9	#wirlessMouse https://t.co/z41qHXMdMh	0.5	0.4	Positive
10	RT @world94321: Open Box(Just Like New) OMEN X 2S by 300pcs M2-M2.5-M3 Laptop Notebook Computer Screws	0.477273	0.068182	Positive

Fig. 7. Sample collected tweets

Y(Classes) = Sentiments (0, 1, 2).

Tables 1, 2 and 3 show the predictive performance of SVM, RF and NB classifiers. Table 1 indicates that SVM yields a prediction accuracy of 94% with precision (95%, 86%, 95%), recall (95%, 84%, 96%) and F1-score (95%, 85%, 95%) for neutral, negative, and positive sentiments respectively.Similarly, Table 2 shows that the RF classifier has an average accuracy of 96% along with precision (96%, 92%, 97%), recall (96%, 92%, 96%) and F1-score (96%, 92%, 96%) for neutral, negative, and positive sentiments respectively. Finally, Table 3 shows that the NB classifier has an average accuracy of 84% along with precision (77%, 67%, 96%), recall (95%, 24%, 87%) and F1-score (85%, 35%, 91%) for neutral, negative, and positive sentiments respectively. In general, results indicate that RF classifier demonstrates superior performance compared to others

	Subjectivity	Polarity	Sentiment
0	0.000000	0.000000	0
1	0.000000	0.000000	0
2	0.500000	0.000000	0
3	0.000000	0.000000	0
4	0.166667	0.000000	0
...	...	...	...
2221	0.426190	0.332778	2
2222	0.000000	0.000000	0
2223	0.400000	0.300000	2
2224	0.000000	0.000000	0
2225	0.266667	0.200000	2

2226 rows × 3 columns

Fig. 8. Transformed sentiment dataset

in the task of classifying sentiments on Laptop review into neutral, negative, and positive polarities.

Table 1. SVM performance on considered metrics

Sentiment Polarity	Precision	Recall	F1-score	Support
0	0.95	0.95	0.95	213
1	0.86	0.84	0.85	51
2	0.95	0.96	0.95	182
Accuracy	0.94			446
Macro avg	0.92	0.92	0.92	446
Weighted avg	0.94	0.94	0.94	446

While Fig. 9 shows the pictorial representation of the prediction accuracy of the classifiers, the overall performance of the classifiers with respect to the precision, recall and F1-score for neutral, negative and positive sentiments are represented in Figs. 10, 11 and 12.

Table 2. RF performance on considered metrics

Sentiment Polarity	Precision	Recall	F1-score	Support
0	0.96	0.96	0.96	213
1	0.92	0.92	0.92	51
2	0.97	0.96	0.96	182
Accuracy	0.96			446
Macro avg	0.95	0.95	0.95	446
Weighted avg	0.96	0.96	0.96	446

Table 3. NB performance on considered metrics

Sentiment Polarity	Precision	Recall	F1-score	Support
0	0.77	0.95	0.85	213
1	0.67	0.24	0.35	51
2	0.96	0.87	0.91	182
Accuracy	0.84			446
Macro avg	0.90	0.69	0.71	446
Weighted avg	0.84	0.84	0.82	446

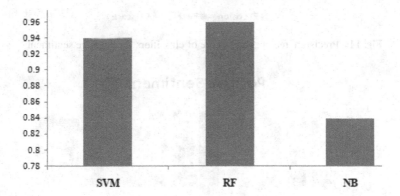

Fig. 9. Prediction accuracy of the classifiers

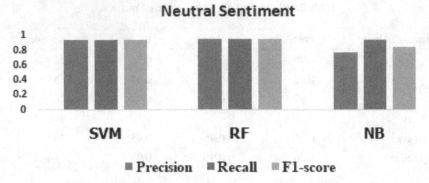

Fig. 10. Precision, recall and f1-score of classifiers for neutral sentiment

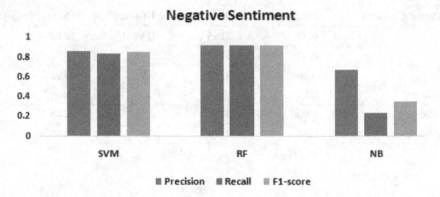

Fig. 11. Precision, recall and f1-score of classifiers for negative sentiment

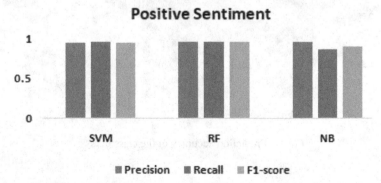

Fig. 12. Precision, recall and f1-score for positive sentiment

5 Conclusion

This paper presents a hybrid framework for classification of sentiments from Laptop reviews comprising 2226 tweets. Twitter API named Tweepy was used for tweets extraction while data pre-processing was performed to make the textual data fit for ML modeling. Later, TextBlob, a Python NLP package was used to calculate the polarity and subjectivity of words in a text by consulting a lexicon and then calculates the overall polarity of the text by averaging the polarity scores of all the words in the passage.

The multi-class classification of sentiments was done into three polarities namely; positive, negative and neutral. Two non-probabilistic (SVM, RF), and one probabilistic (NB) ML models were trained to determine the best classifier with the highest prediction accuracy. Results indicate that RF classifier demonstrates best performance with the highest accuracy (96%), precision (97%) and F1-score (96%), followed by SVM and NB. This shows that ML algorithms can be used to classify huge unstructured data from online reviews. Furthermore, the drawbacks of lexicon-based sentiment analysis can be overcome and the sentiment of never-before-seen sentences can be determined with acceptable results. Future works may consider additional Laptop features, a larger-sized dataset and other ML algorithms.

Acknowledgments. The authors are grateful to TETFund for supporting this research through the TETFund Centre of Excellence in Computational Intelligence Research and the University of Uyo Management for creating a conducive environment for research.

References

1. Yan, H.-B., Li, Z.: Review of sentiment analysis: an emotional product development view. Front. Eng. Manag. **9**(4), 592–609 (2022). https://doi.org/10.1007/s42524-022-0227-z
2. Alayba, A., Palade, V., England, M., Iqbal, R.: Arabic language sentiment analysis on health services. In: Proceedings of the 1st International Workshop on Arabic Script Analysis and Recognition (ASAR), Nancy, France, pp. 114–118. IEEE Computer Society (2017). https://doi.org/10.1109/ASAR.2017.8067771
3. Madni, H.A., et al.: Improving sentiment prediction of textual tweets using feature fusion and deep machine ensemble model. Electronics **12**(6) (2023). https://doi.org/10.3390/electronics12061302
4. Radiuk, P., Pavlova, O., Hrypynska, N.: An ensemble machine learning approach for twitter sentiment analysis. In: Proceedings of the 6th International Conference on Computational Linguistics and Intelligent Systems, Gliwice, Poland (2022)
5. Kumar, S., Zymbler, M.: A machine learning approach to analyze customer satisfaction from airline tweets. J. Big Data **6**(62) (2019). https://doi.org/10.1186/s40537-019-0224-1
6. Ligthart, A., Catal, C., Tekinerdogan, B.: Systematic reviews in sentiment analysis: a tertiary study. Artif. Intell. Rev. **54**, 4997–5053 (2021). https://doi.org/10.1007/s10462-021-09973-3
7. AlBadani, B., Shi, R., Dong, J.: A novel machine learning approach for sentiment analysis on twitter incorporating the universal language model fine-tuning and SVM. Appl. Syst. Innov. **5**(1) (2022). https://doi.org/10.3390/asi5010013
8. Birjali, M., Kasri, M., Beni-Hssane, A.: A comprehensive survey on sentiment analysis: approaches, challenges and trends. Knowl.-Based Syst. **226** (2021). https://doi.org/10.1016/j.knosys.2021.107134

9. Usip, P.U., Ntekop, M.M.: The use of ontologies as efficient and intelligent knowledge management tool. In: Proceedings of Future Technologies Conference 2016, San Francisco, United States, 6–7 December 2016 (2016)

10. Usip, P.U., Ekpenyong, M.E., Ijebu, F.F., Usang, K.J.: Integrated context-aware ontology for MNCH decision support. In: Tiwari, S., Rodriguez, F.O., Jabbar, M.A. (eds.) Intelligent Data-Centric Systems, Semantic Models in IoT and eHealth Applications, pp. 227–243. Academic Press (2022). https://doi.org/10.1016/B978-0-32-391773-5.00017-0

11. Asuquo, D.E., Umoh, U.A., Osang, F.B., Okokon, E.W.: Performance evaluation of c4.5, random forest and naïve bayes classifiers in employee performance and promotion prediction, Afr. J. Manage. Inf. Syst. 2(4), 41–55 (2020a)

12. Laddha, A., Mukherjee, A.: Aspect opinion expression and rating prediction via LDA–CRF hybrid. Nat. Lang. Eng. 24(4), 611–639 (2018). https://doi.org/10.1017/S135132491800013X

13. Afzaal, M., Usman, M., Fong, A.: Tourism mobile app with aspect-based sentiment classification framework for tourist reviews. IEEE Trans. Consum. Electron. 65(2), 233–242 (2019)

14. Sharif, O., Hoque, M.M., Hossain, E.: Sentiment analysis of Bengali texts on online restaurant reviews using multinomial naïve bayes. In: Proceedings of the 1st International Conference on Advances in Science, Engineering and Robotics Technology. IEEE (2019). https://doi.org/10.1109/ICASERT.2019.8934655

15. Perera, I., Caldera, H.: Aspect-based opinion mining on restaurant reviews. In: Proceedings of the 2nd International Conference on Computational Intelligence and Applications, pp. 542–546. IEEE (2017). https://doi.org/10.1109/CIAPP.2017.8167276

16. Marrese-Taylor, E., VelÃasquez, J., Bravo-Marquez, F., Matsuo, Y.: Identifying customer preferences about tourism products using an aspect-based opinion mining approach. Procedia Comput. Sci. 22, 182–191 (2013). https://doi.org/10.1016/j.procs.2013.09.094

17. Saleh, M.R., Martín-Valdivia, M.T., Montejo-Ráez, A., Ureña-López, L.A.: Experiments with SVM to classify opinions in different domains. Expert Syst. Appl. 38(12), 14799–14804 (2011). https://doi.org/10.1016/j.eswa.2011.05.070

18. Zhang, L., Liu, B.: Identifying noun product features that imply opinions. In: Proceedings of the 49th Annual Meeting of the Association for Computational Linguistics: Human Language Technologies, Portland, Oregon, USA, pp. 575–580. Association for Computational Linguistics (2011)

19. Pang, B., Lee, L.: Opinion mining and sentiment analysis. Found Trends InfRetr 2(1–2), 1–135 (2008)

20. Hussain, A., Cambria, E.: Semi-supervised learning for big social data analysis. Neurocomputing 275, 1662–1673 (2018). https://doi.org/10.1016/j.neucom.2017.10.010

21. Alsaeedi, A., Khan, M.Z.: A study on sentiment analysis techniques of twitter data. Int. J. Adv. Comput. Sci. Appl. 10(2): 361–374 (2019). https://doi.org/10.14569/IJACSA.2019.0100248

22. Min, H., Junghwan, Y., Geum, Y.: Analyzing dynamic change in customer requirements: an approach using review-based kano analysis. Sustainability 10(3) (2018). https://doi.org/10.3390/su10030746

23. Bakar, N.H., Kasirun, Z.M., Salleh, N., Jalab, H.A.: Extracting features from online software reviews to aid requirements reuse. Appl. Soft Comput. 49, 1297–1315 (2016). https://doi.org/10.1016/j.asoc.2016.07.048

24. van der Vegte, W.F.: Taking advantage of data generated by products: trends, opportunities and challenges. In: Proceedings of the ASME-CIE 2016 International Design Engineering Technical Conferences and Computers and Information in Engineering Conference, Charlotte, NC. American Society of Mechanical Engineers (2016). https://doi.org/10.1115/DETC2016-59177

25. Tan, L.K.-W., Na, J.-C., Theng, Y.-L., Chang, K.: Sentence-level sentiment polarity classification using a linguistic approach. In: Xing, C., Crestani, F., Rauber, A. (eds.) ICADL 2011. LNCS, vol. 7008, pp. 77–87. Springer, Heidelberg (2011). https://doi.org/10.1007/978-3-642-24826-9_13

26. Liu, B.: Sentiment analysis: mining opinions, sentiments and emotions 1, 1–386 (2015). https://doi.org/10.1017/CBO9781139084789

27. Jiao, Y.R., Qu, Q.X.: A proposal for Kansei knowledge extraction method based on natural language processing technology and online product reviews. Comput. Ind. 108, 1–11 (2019). https://doi.org/10.1016/j.compind.2019.02.011

28. Vadivukarassi, M., Puviarasan, N., Aruna, P.: Sentimental analysis of tweets using naïve bayes algorithm. World Appl. Sci. J. 35(1), 54–59 (2017). https://doi.org/10.5829/idosi.wasj.2017.54.59

29. Usip, P.U., Ekpenyong, M.E., Ijebu, F.F., Usang, K.J., Udo, I.J.: PeNLP Parser: an extraction and visualization tool for precise maternal, neonatal and child healthcare geo-locations from unstructured data. In: Deep Learning in Biomedical and Health Informatics, pp. 157–181. CRC Press (2021)

30. Hu, M., Liu, B.: Mining and summarizing customer reviews. In: Proceedings of the 10th ACM SIGKDD International Conference on Knowledge Discovery and Data Mining, pp. 168–177 (2004)

31. Schouten, K., Frasincar, F.: Survey on aspect-level sentiment analysis. IEEE Trans. Knowl. Data Eng. 28(3), 813–830 (2016). https://doi.org/10.1109/TKDE.2015.2485209

32. Jiménez-Zafra, S.M., Martín-Valdivia, M.T., Martínez-Cámara, E., Ureña-López, L.A.: Combining resources to improve unsupervised sentiment analysis at aspect-level. J. Inf. Sci. 42(2), 213–229 (2016). https://doi.org/10.1177/0165551515593686

33. Yadav, M.L., Roychoudhury, B.: Effectiveness of domain-based lexicons vis-a-vis general lexicon for aspect-level sentiment analysis: a comparative analysis. J. Inf. Knowl. Manage. 18(3), 1950033 (2019). https://doi.org/10.1142/S0219649219500333

34. Wang, Y.Y., Chen, Q., Ahmed, M., Li, Z.H., Pan, W., Liu, H.L.: Joint inference for aspect-level sentiment analysis by deep neural networks and linguistic hints. IEEE Trans. Knowl. Data Eng. 99, 1–14 (2019). https://doi.org/10.1109/TKDE.2019.2947587

35. Wang, W., Tan, G., Wang, H.: Cross-domain comparison of algorithm performance in extracting aspect-based opinions from Chinese online reviews. Int. J. Mach. Learn. Cybern. 8(3), 1053–1070 (2016). https://doi.org/10.1007/s13042-016-0596-x

36. Xu, K., Liao, S.S., Li, J., Song, Y.: Mining comparative opinions from customer reviews for competitive intelligence. Decision Support Syst. 50(4), 743–754 (2011)

37. Fu, X., Guo, Y., Guo, W., Wang, Z.: Aspect and sentiment extraction based on information-theoretic co-clustering. In: Wang, J., Yen, G.G., Polycarpou, M.M. (eds.) ISNN 2012. LNCS, vol. 7368, pp. 326–335. Springer, Heidelberg (2012). https://doi.org/10.1007/978-3-642-31362-2_37

38. Miao, Y.L., Cheng, W.F., Ji, Y.C., Zhang, S., Kong, Y.L.: Aspect-based sentiment analysis in Chinese based on mobile reviews for BiLSTM-CRF. J. Intell. Fuzzy Syst. 40(7), 1–11 (2021). https://doi.org/10.3233/JIFS-192078

39. Aydin, C.R., Gungor, T.: Combination of recursive and recurrent neural networks for aspect-based sentiment analysis using inter-aspect relations. IEEE Access 8, 77820–77832 (2020). https://doi.org/10.1109/ACCESS.2020.2990306

40. Yu, J.F., Jiang, J., Xia, R.: Global inference for aspect and opinion terms co-extraction based on multi-task neural networks. IEEE/ACM Trans. Audio Speech Lang. Process. 27(1), 168–177 (2019). https://doi.org/10.1109/TASLP.2018.2875170

41. Jurek-Loughrey, A., Mulvenna, M., Bi, Y.: Improved lexicon-based sentiment analysis for social media analytics. Secur. Inform. 4(1) (2015). https://doi.org/10.1186/s13388-015-0024-x

42. Wilson, T., Wiebe, J., Hoffmann, P.: Recognizing contextual polarity in phrase-level sentiment analysis In: Proceedings of the Conference on Human Language Technology and Empirical Methods in Natural Language Processing, Vancouver, Canada, pp. 347–354. Association for Computational Linguistics (2005)

43. Wiebe, J.: Learning subjective adjectives from corpora. In: Proceedings of the 17th National Conference on Artificial Intelligence and 12th Conference on Innovative Applications of Artificial Intelligence, pp. 735–740. AAAI Press/The MIT Press (2000)

44. Asuquo, D.E., Ekpenyong, M.E., Udoh, S.S., Robinson, S.A., Attai, K.F.: Optimized channel allocation in emerging mobile cellular networks. J. Soft Comput. (2020). https://doi.org/10.1007/s00500-020-04947-z

45. Asuquo, D.E., Umoren, I., Osang, F., Attai, K.: A machine learning framework for length of stay minimization in healthcare emergency department. Stud. Eng. Technol. J. **10**(1), 1–17 (2023). https://doi.org/10.11114/set.v10i1.6372

46. Ekpenyong, M.E., Asuquo, D.E., Udo, I.J., Robinson, S.A., Ijebu, F.F.: IPv6 routing protocol enhancements over low-power and lossy networks for IoT applications: a systematic review. New Rev. Inf. Netw. **27**(1), 30–68 (2022). https://doi.org/10.1080/13614576.2022.2078396

47. Wang, X., Tang, M., Yang, T., Wang, Z.: A novel network with multiple attention mechanisms for aspect-level sentiment analysis. Knowl.-Based Syst. **227**, 107196 (2021). https://doi.org/10.1016/j.knosys.2021.107196

48. Wu, C., et al.: Residual attention and other aspects module for aspect-based sentiment analysis. Neurocomputing **435**(1–2), 42–52 (2021). https://doi.org/10.1016/j.neucom.2021.01.019

49. Ye, X.X., Xu, Y., Luo, M.S.: ALBERTC-CNN based aspect level sentiment analysis. IEEE Access **9**, 94748–94755 (2021). https://doi.org/10.1109/ACCESS.2021.3094026

50. Chen, P., Sun, Z., Bing, L., Yang, W.: Recurrent attention network on memory for aspect sentiment analysis. In: Proceedings of the Conference on Empirical Methods in Natural Language Processing, Copenhagen, Denmark, pp. 452–461. Association for Computational Linguistics (2017)

51. Song, M., Park, H., Shin, K.S.: Attention-based long short-term memory network using sentiment lexicon embedding for aspect level sentiment analysis in Korean. Inf. Process. Manage. **56**(3), 637–653 (2019). https://doi.org/10.1016/j.ipm.2018.12.005

52. Liu, M.Z., Zhou, F.Y., Chen, K., Zhao, Y.: Co-attention networks based on aspect and context for aspect-level sentiment analysis. Knowl.-Based Syst. **217**(2), 106810 (2021). https://doi.org/10.1016/j.knosys.2021.106810

53. Lv, Y.X., et al.: Aspect-level sentiment analysis using context and aspect memory network. Neurocomputing **428**, 195–205 (2021). https://doi.org/10.1016/j.neucom.2020.11.049

54. Ali, W., Yang, Y.W., Qiu, X.L., Ke, Y.Q., Wang, Y.Y.: Aspect-level sentiment analysis based on bidirectional-GRU in SIoT. IEEE Access **9**, 69938–69950 (2021). https://doi.org/10.1109/ACCESS.2021.3078114

55. Pak, A., Paroubek, P.: Twitter as a corpus for sentiment analysis and opinion mining. In: Proceedings of the 7th International Conference on Language Resources and Evaluation, pp. 1320–1326. European Languages Resources Association, Valletta (2010)

56. Liu, B., Li, X., Lee, W.S., Yu, P.S.: Text classification by labeling words. In: Proceedings of the 19th National Conference on Artificial Intelligence, 16th Conference on Innovative Applications of Artificial Intelligence, San Jose, California, USA (2004)

57. Dang, N.C., Moreno-García, M.N., De la Prieta, F.: Sentiment analysis based on deep learning: a comparative study. Electronics **9**(3), 483 (2020)

58. Kang, Y., Zhou, L.N.: RubE: rule-based methods for extracting product features from online consumer reviews. Inf. Manage. **54**(2), 166–176 (2017). https://doi.org/10.1016/j.im.2016.05.007

59. Liu, B.: Sentiment analysis and opinion mining. Synth. Lect. Hum. Lang. Technol. **5**(1), 1–167 (2012). https://doi.org/10.2200/S00416ED1V01Y201204HLT016

60. Ressan, M.B., Hassan, R.F.: Naive-bayes family for sentiment analysis during COVID-19 pandemic and classification tweets. Indones. J. Electr. Eng. Comput. Sci. **28**(1), 375–383 (2022). https://doi.org/10.11591/ijeecs.v28.i1.pp375-383
61. Anwar, M.K., Yusoff, M., Kassim, M.: Decision tree and naïve bayes for sentiment analysis in smoking perception. In: Proceedings of the 12th Symposium on Computer Applications and Industrial Electronics, pp. 294–299. IEEE (2022)
62. Gaur, P., Vashistha, S., Jha, P.: Twitter sentiment analysis using naive bayes-based machine learning technique. In: Shakya, S., Du, KL., Ntalianis, K. (eds.) Proceedings of the International Conference on Sentiment Analysis and Deep Learning. AISC, vol. 1432, pp. 367–376. Springer, Singapore (2023). https://doi.org/10.1007/978-981-19-5443-6_27
63. Mardjo, A., Choksuchat, C.: HyVADRF: hybrid VADER–random forest and GWO for bitcoin tweet sentiment analysis. IEEE Access **10**, 101889–101897 (2022). https://doi.org/10.1109/ACCESS.2022.3209662
64. Kanimozhi, T., Belina, V.J., Sara, S.: Classification of tweet on disaster management using random forest. In: Rajagopal, S., Faruki, P., Popat, K. (eds.) ASCIS 2022. CCIS, vol. 1759, pp. 180–193. Springer, Cham (2022). https://doi.org/10.1007/978-3-031-23092-9_15
65. Dewi, M.P.K., Setiawan, E.B.: Feature expansion using word2vec for hate speech detection on Indonesian twitter with classification using SVM and random forest. Jurnal Media InformatikaBudidarma **6**(2), 979–988 (2022)
66. Nurkholis, A., Alita, D., Munandar, A.: Comparison of kernel support vector machine multi-class in PPKM sentiment analysis on twitter. Jurnal RESTI (RekayasaSistem Dan TeknologiInformasi) **6**(2), 227–233 (2022)
67. Styawati, S., Nurkholis, A., Aldino, A.A., Samsugi, S., Suryati, E., Cahyono, R.P.: Sentiment analysis on online transportation reviews using word2Vec text embedding model feature extraction and support vector machine algorithm. In: Proceedings of the 2021 International Seminar on Machine Learning, Optimization, and Data Science, pp. 163–167. IEEE (2022). https://doi.org/10.1109/ISMODE53584.2022.9742906
68. https://github.com/kingattai/Sentiment-Analysis.git

DESI: Diversification of E-Commerce Recommendations Using Semantic Intelligence

Gerard Deepak[1]([⊠]) and Harshada Vinay Anavkar[2]

[1] Department of Computer Science and Engineering, Manipal Institute of Technology
Bengaluru, Manipal Academy of Higher Education, Manipal, India
gerard.deepak.christuni@gmail.com
[2] Department of Mechanical Engineering, Indian Institute of Technology, Kharagpur, India

Abstract. Due to the dynamism in the Web 3.0 there is need for semantically driven framework for ecommerce based recommendations. This paper proposes the DESI framework, which is a query-driven, semantically oriented, Web 3.0 conforming ecommerce recommendation framework. The pre-process query was enriched using the Latent Semantic Indexing. Ontologies are generated from the ecommerce product dataset. The classification of the metadata takes place using the LSTM classifier. The relevance computation is staged and is achieved using Lin similarity, Adaptive Pointwise Mutual Information measure. The semantics oriented reasoning on the basis of semantic similarity measures yield the matching products and Frog Leap algorithm. The normalized point wise mutual information measure is used to compute the intermediate results and probability algorithm ensures optimality computation from the initial feasible solution set. An overall precision accuracy measure of so and so on with the lowest value of False Discovery Rate has been achieved with a proposed framework.

Keywords: Latent Semantic Indexing · Adaptive Pointwise Mutual Information · NPMI · LSTM · Frog Leap Algorithm

1 Introduction

Product recommendation systems play a crucial role in the digital landscape of the present day. Using algorithms and user data, these systems analyse customer preferences and behaviour in order to recommend personalised products. Using approaches such as collaborative filtering, filtering based on content, or combined methods, recommendation systems enhance the user experience by providing personalised recommendations, thereby boosting customer engagement and sales conversions. There's a need for diversification of recommendations in the present day times because a recommendation system cannot cater to the needs of every specific user. Although personalization can be achieved by imbibing some amount of user historical data, the exact current need of the user cannot be identified as the search term is quite new and he has no history regarding the same in the web usage data. So personalizing the recommended results yielded can work wonders for already existed search but for a new search query or a search topic, it will not

M. A. Jabbar et al. (Eds.): AMLDA 2023, CCIS 2047, pp. 144–155, 2024.
https://doi.org/10.1007/978-3-031-55486-5_11

work out. So thereby it is always necessary that diversified recommendations that is, a full cover of all possible entities should and must be recommended to the user, such that every possibility for the specific query with diversified instances is required and has to take place specifically for ecommerce recommendations, because ecommerce products are quite diversified and when relevant distractions allow the recommendations, then it is also a targeted marketing strategy which can work well. These systems are essential for online platforms because they allow businesses to implement targeted marketing, cross-selling, and upselling strategies. With the ability to comprehend individual preferences and discover new products, recommendation systems enhance customer satisfaction, increase customer loyalty, and ultimately contribute to business growth in the highly competitive e-commerce environment. Therefore the diversified web search is the need of the hour and specifically for ecommerce applications. Web 3.0 compliant, semantically driven, knowledge centric model has to be present for recommending instances from ecommerce websites. It is the need in the present day era.

Motivation: The dynamic nature of the Web 3.0 and its continuous changing structure mandates a need for a semantically driven, semantically web compliant, inferential learning driven model for web e-commerce product recommendation from the world wide web. There is a strong need for a model that amalgamates learning with inferencing by not just mandating learning as that would result in a lot of underfitted results.

Contribution: This paper proposes the DESI framework, E-commerce product recommendation framework. The novel contributions include the application of leading semantic indexing for topic modeling from the query end. Relevance computation is achieved using the APMI measure to yield the matching instances and ontologies are generated from the dataset. Jaccard and Lin similarity are used to anchor the ontologies with the enriched query words to yield matching entities. LSTM is subjected on the meta-data for classification and handling of metadata which is in turn, atomized using frog leap algorithm under the normalized pointwise mutual information measure. Precision and F-measure are elevated in comparison with the models used as a baseline.

Organization: This paper is structured as follows. Section 2 provides a summary of the Related Works. Section 3 presents the Proposed System Architecture. Implementation, Results and Performance Evaluation are discussed in Sect. 4. This paper is concluded in Sect. 5.

2 Related Works

Hyunwoo Hwangbo et al., [1], presents a model named K-RecSys which is an extension on the existing collaborative filtering algorithm. It presents a preference decay function which shows a decrease in preferences over time. Shakila Shaikh et al., [2] describes the different algorithms used in e commerce recommendation systems which include content-based, collaborative, and hybrid recommendation approaches. She also empha-sises on the lack of semantics in the current approaches. Jai Prakash Verma et al., [3] presents the analysis of big data using the Hadoop framework which is an open source framework. Liaoliang Jiang et al., [4] describes a model to get better ecommerce rec-ommendations by encompassing slope one algorithm along with trusted data and user similarity.

Yan Guo et al., [5] proposes a better data mining approach. An improved algorithm called the Apriori algorithm is introduced to better the ecommerce recommendations. Arodh Lal Karn et al., [6] puts forth approach by adding sentiment analysis in recommendation systems. It is based on hybrid recommendation model(HRM) and hybrid sentiment analysis. Harsh Khatter et al., [7] produces an approach which combines collaborative filtering along with clustering textual analysis of product description. J. Ben Schafer et al., [8] introduces meta recommenders which give access to user to a single recommendation list from combining multiple information sources and recommendation techniques.

Duraisamy Deenadayalan et al., [9] proposes a model which include collaborative filtering and web usage mining. Random forest and XG Boost are the classifiers and uses frog leap algorithm for finding the nearest neighbors. Korab Rrmoku et al., [10] displays a model which comprises of Naïve Bayes algorithm to increase compilation time. Feng, L et al., [11] uses collaborative filtering for o2o ecommerce recommendation systems. Nguyen Ngoc Chan et al., [12] puts forth an approach to better the web services results using vector space model and latent semantic indexing. The framework in [13] emphasizes on Big Data Models for facilitating recommendations from e-commerce sites and [14] puts the emphasis on hierarchical recommendations on the basis of user reviews for products on e-commerce websites. In [15–25] several semantic models for inclusive recommendations have been put forth where the focus is on knowledge based modeling and recommendations through facts on the basis of semantics oriented reasoning using benchmark knowledge is discussed.

3 Proposed System Architecture

Figure 1 depicts the e-commerce recommendation framework's proposed system architecture. Pre-processing is applied to the user query that is entered. This framework is query-driven, but it is knowledge-centric. Tokenization, lemmatization, stop-word elimination, and the identification of names as entities are all components of pre-processing. The individual query words are obtained at the conclusion of the pre-processing stage. These search terms are in their original base form and do not contain any stop words. These query words are then subjected to topic modelling, which is accomplished through the use of Latent Semantic Indexing (LSI). LSI is used to identify and extract similarities and underlying links between words and data in a large document. In this case, the LSI aids in the transformation of high-dimensional sparse data into low-dimensional dense representation of data. This is achieved by singular value decomposition which helps in clustering words which don't show direct relationships through wordings but can be grouped under a column. By leveraging the semantic relationships captured by LSI, these tasks can benefit from a deeper understanding of the textual content, leading to improved performance and more nuanced analyses.

The World Wide Web's current layout serves as a reference corpus for topic modelling. The dataset, which is an e-commerce dataset, is subjected to category extraction, in which the dataset's categories are extracted. Ontologies are created based on these categories. Ontologies are highly compact, structured, linked, and hierarchical knowledge description models. The ontology is a knowledge descriptor model in which knowledge

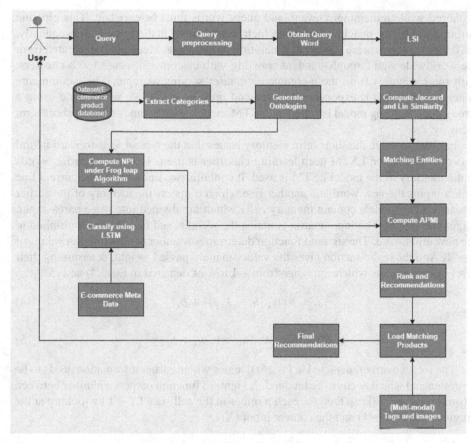

Fig. 1. Architecture Design of DESI model

is represented as an ontology and the ontology is generated using OntoCollab, a standard tool.

Ontology is achieved by using the dataset's categories as input. These ontologies are standard knowledge models subjected to semantic similarity computation with LSI enriched query words using the Jaccard Similarity as depicted in Eq. (1) and Lin similarity as Eq. (2), the two distinct frameworks for semantic similarity. Equation (3) depicts the Information Content of (X) for computing the Lin Similarity.

$$J(X, Y) = \frac{|X \cap Y|}{|X \cup Y|} = \frac{|X \cap Y|}{|X| + |Y| - |X \cap Y|} \tag{1}$$

$$\text{LinSimilarity} = 2 \times \frac{\text{ResnikSimilarity}(X, Y)}{\text{IC}(X) + \text{IC}(Y)} \tag{2}$$

$$IC(X) = -\log\left(\frac{freq(X)}{maxFreq}\right) \tag{3}$$

The Jaccard similarity threshold is set to 0.75, and the Lin similarity threshold is set to 0.5. The reason for using a variational threshold is that more instances must be anchored while remaining relevant, and query words must be enriched. This pipeline output provides the matching entities, which are then used in the process. Subsequently, the dataset categories are subject to generation of metadata. Metadata is generated from the worldwide web through standard crawling with customised focused web crawlers, with the categories from the e-commerce dataset serving as input. The e-commerce generated metadata is exponentially large and must be classified, which done using a strong deep learning model is called the LSTM model, which stands for long short-term memory.

In order to solve the short-term memory issues that the typical feed-forward neural networks encounter, LSTM deep learning classifier is used. To keep the earlier words in the memory of the model LSTM is used. It contains two lines, one is the current line which inputs the new word and another line which transfers the memory of the earlier words. LSTM models contain memory cells which are divided into three parts- input, forget and output. The input matrix contains the weights and biases to be multiplied to the new input word. The sigmoid function determines whether to pass through values of 0 or 1. And the tanh function gives the values that are passed weight, determining their level of importance, which can range from -1 to 1 as depicted in Eqs. (4) and (5).

$$i_t = \sigma(W_i.[h_t - 1, x_t] + b_i) \tag{4}$$

$$C_t = \tanh(W_c.[h_t - 1, x_t] + b_c) \tag{5}$$

The forget matrix f_t depicted in Eq. (6) decides which earlier information needs to be forgotten and which needs to be retained. A sigmoid function outputs a number between 0 (omit this) and 1 (keep this) for each number in the cell state $Ct - 1$ by looking at the previous state ($ht - 1$) and the content input (Xt).

$$f_t = \sigma\left(W_f.[h_t - 1, x_t] + b_f\right) \tag{6}$$

In EquaThe output matrix decides what needs to be passed to the next time step. The block's input and memory are used to determine its output. Sigmoid function determines which 0 or 1 values are permitted to pass. And the tanh function determines which values are permitted to pass 0, 1. And the tanh function assigns weights to the passed values, determining their relative importance on a scale from -1 to 1 and multiplying the result with a sigmoid output as depicted in Eqs. (7) and (8).

$$O_t = \sigma(W_o[h_t - 1, x_t] + b_o) \tag{7}$$

$$h_t = o_t * \tanh(C_t) \tag{8}$$

Because of the large volume of e-commerce metadata, the LSTM is preferred. The LSTM is a deep learning classifier that classifies e-commerce metadata using auto hand-crafted feature selection. The classified metadata produced by the LSTM and the generated ontologies are then subjected to the computation of NPMI, or normalised pointwise mutual information, with a threshold of 0.5, and a median threshold determined by considering the positive values of NPMI depicted as Eq. (9) between 0 and 1. Equation (10) depicts the PMI value.

$$NPMI = \frac{pmi(x, y)}{\log(p(x, y))} \tag{9}$$

$$pmi = \log\left(\frac{p(x, y)}{p(x)p(y)}\right) \tag{10}$$

This is accomplished by the frog leap algorithm. The frog Leap Algorithm is used considering the large quantity of e-commerce metadata and the large quantity of classified metadata using the LSTM. The frog leap algorithm is based on how frogs jump when they are looking for food. It is a metaheuristic optimisation algorithm that is widely used to address challenging optimisation issues. A random population of frogs with random positions within the search space are first created by the algorithm. A fitness function then assesses each person's success in addressing the optimisation challenge.

The computer then separates the frog population into various subpopulations according on their fitness scores. The most physically fit people are placed in the subpopulations with the highest fitness values, while the rest are put in the subpopulations with the lowest fitness values. The leader of each subpopulation is then determined by the algorithm, which also calculates the average position of all leaders. The term "global greatest position" is used to describe this position.

The model then uses the three operator's local search, frog leaping, and crossover to create a new population of amphibians. By looking at each subpopulation's local neighborhoods, the local search operator is employed to improve the individuals inside each subpopulation. The frog bounding operator imitates frog action by jumping to a new spot. It involves adding a random value to the current position to create a new position for the worst members of each subpopulation. The crossover operator creates new persons by combining the coordinates of two individuals.

The best fit individuals are then picked to make up the following population once the new population has been evaluated using the fitness function. These phases are repeated until a termination requirement is satisfied, such as a predetermined number of iterations or a minimum fitness value. By integrating local search, frog leaping, and crossover, the frog leap algorithm may efficiently traverse the search space and provide excellent answers to challenging optimisation issues.

The semantic similarity computation happens using the normalized pointwise mutual information measure. The initial solution set requires a large number of entities. The frog leap algorithm is used as a meta-heuristic optimisation algorithm to achieve the most optimal solution set from a set of initial solutions, where NPMI itself is used as an objective function with the same threshold of 0.5, and the most optimal solution sets are obtained.

This optimal solution set, which includes the best knowledge from metadata and ontologies, is matched with the best entities from the enriched query words with ontology applied.

The Adaptive Pointwise Mutual Information (APMI) measure depicted as Eq. (11), is computed on this. At this point, the APMI is set to 0.05 because the frog leap algorithm is already being used to compute the relevant entities, with the NPMI and the Jaccard and Lin similarity at the two extreme ends.

$$APMI(x, y) = \frac{pmi(x, y)}{p(m)(n)} + \frac{1 + \log p(x, y)}{p(y) \log p(x) - p(x) \log p(y)} \quad (11)$$

The APMI is computed at this stage, but the threshold for APMI is increased to 0.75 because the most relevant among the relevant entities must be computed. The threshold is primarily less than 0.5 because the threshold is only computed among the relevant entities. The entities that emerge from the APMI are ranked and recommended as the best query relevant viable facets in increasing order of the APMI measure. Based on the user's click on the subject facets, e-commerce product recommendations are generated from the generated assets for all of these facets. If the user satisfies the search hauls, the user clicks on the facets. This process is repeated until the user is content or no further clicks are recorded.

4 Performance Evaluation and Results

To conduct the experiments for the proposed framework, three distinct ecommerce datasets were used which are: the ecommerce dataset with 30k products from kaggle, product catalog from Ecommerce ETL site newchick.com dataset and a product catalog from Ecommerce retail site nutrition.com. So these two datasets are independent datasets and are merged together by populating the categories using customized annotation tools. And based on the categories and annotations, they are prioritized in a specific order by ensuring that the most similar categories stay adjacent to each other and the experimentation is conducted on the single large dataset. Documents as well as images for these particular terms are extracted from the web image and the web 3.0 and a multimodal dataset is prepared.

The recommendations are conducted on this dataset not only for this particular proposed work but even to evaluate the baseline models. The experimentation were conducted with the same datasets for the exact configurations as for the proposed framework. Python 3 was used for the implementation, and Google Collaborator was used as the IDE. The NLP tasks were carried out using the using the Python NLTK framework. For Lin similarity and APMI standard formulations were used. For LSI the agent based configuration was set up by using JADE.

The performance of the proposed Diversified Ecommerce Precision recall accuracy and F measure percentages are used as prospective measures to assess the semantically inclined recommendation architecture. In order to measure the inaccuracy, the false discovery rate (FDR) is also utilised as a standard statistic. Because they assess the importance of data, precision recall accuracy F measure percentages are chosen as a standard metric. The amount or rate of error contained in the framework is quantified by the false discovery rate. So going forward, it will also serve as a useful indicator of model error.

The RDSE, TCFA, Comma PRSE, and HRSE models, respectively, serve as the basis for evaluating the performance of the suggested conceptual framework. The proposed desi framework has provided the maximum precision of 96.29%, average recall percentage of 98.2, average accuracy percentage of 97.155, average F measure percentage of 97.147, and the lowest value of FDR of 0.4, according to Table 1.

Table 1. Performance comparison of the proposed DESI with other baseline methods

Model	Average Precision %	Average Recall %	Average Accuracy %	Average F-Measure %	FDR
RDSE [1]	84.07	87.85	85.96	85.92	0.16
TCFA [4]	88.39	91.04	89.715	89.695	0.12
PRSE [13]	91.22	92.69	91.955	91.95	0.09
HRSE [14]	92.39	94.47	93.43	93.418	0.08
Proposed DESI	96.29	98.02	97.155	97.147	0.04

Table 1 shows that the RDSE model, which is utilised to compare the performance of the suggested DESI model, has produced an average measure FDR of 0.16, 84.7% of average precision, and 87.85% average recall percentage accuracy. The other baseline models, namely the TCFA and PRSE has furnished 88.39% average precision and 91.2% of average precision, respectively, 91.4% average recall and 92.69% average recall, respectively. The TCFA furnishes 89.715% of average accuracy percentage 89.695% with an average F measure and a 0.12 FDR. The PRSE provided average accuracy of 91.955%, average F measure of 91.955%, and FDR of 0.09 for this test. The HRSE produced average precision of 92.39% and average recall percentage of 94.47%. Average accuracy of 92.43% with an FDR of 0.08, the average F measurement was 93.418%.

The proposed DESI has produced the highest precision accuracy and F measure percentages as well as the lowest value of FDR, according to Table 1. This is mostly caused by the fact that it is first semantically motivated and inclined. Moreover, it is knowledge centric which uses knowledge instances in the form of ontologies which are generated from the categories extracted from the ecommerce product dataset. In addition, the query terms are enriched when the topic model, Latent Semantic Indexing, is applied, which is a strategic topic model which discovers topics from the external Web 3.0 corpora and to which the generated ontologies are further enhanced and integrated using the Jaccard and the Lin similarity, which are strong relevant computation mechanisms. And the entity's aggregation takes place, which means the intensification of knowledge density happens. Subsequently, the model uses a classification technique, namely the LSTM model which is a powerful deep learning classifier where the ecommerce metadata which is crawled which is classified owing to its large and voluminous size. LSTM is preferred because of its versatility and also because feature selection is auto handcrafted and most importantly the usage of the computation of APMI measure.

Moreover, the NPMI is used as the objective function of the Frog Leap algorithm to strategically compute the most feasible solution set from the ecommerce metadata, which is categorised, and the ontology created from the dataset changes the original solution set into the most practical solution set. The Frog Leap algorithm is a meta-heuristic optimisation method that improves the relevance of the intermediate outputs in relation to the dataset. For all of these reasons, the suggested DESI framework performs better than all of the baseline models. As it has a very strong optimization model, it has a very strong classifier. The LSTM classifier has strong knowledge density in the model in terms of latent semantic indexing as a topic model, in terms of ontologies generated from the categories of the dataset and in terms of ecommerce metadata, which increases the amount of knowledge seven fold and exponentially into the model. Computation of APMI, Lin similarity, Jaccard Similarity and NPMI in the model ensures strong relevance, computation mechanisms and presence of Frog Leap algorithms, serves as an optimization algorithm and helps to refine the intermediate solutions and achieve convergence to optimality much at a much quicker rate.

Despite being a recommendation system for fashion retail, the RDSE model does not perform as predicted when compared to the recommended framework because it uses item based collaborative filtering.Buyers give some specific ratings or characteristics, but in terms of a rating matrix, every entity on the World Wide Web cannot be rated, and specifically, ecommerce products are rated upon a lot of buyers. So this is not the best fit model. Apart from this, the choice of the collaborative filtering along with the click data and the sale data weighted is not the right combination in order to recommend products or items from an ecommerce perspective. Moreover, this model has no strong relevance, computation mechanisms and auxiliary knowledge is absolutely nil. Therefore, RDSE framework does not perform as expected.

When compared to the proposed model, the TCFA model underperforms as anticipated because, although being a trust-based model, its fundamental algorithm uses collaborative filtering, which necessitates ratings that can be biassed. It is not based on user or content interests. Rather the slope one algorithm is proposed which intensifies the collaborative filtering and aggregates with some scope of trust and a weighting factor with similarity which is also formalized in this model. The relevant computation mechanisms although it is present in the form of a weighting similarity algorithm, is not strong. Depending on collaborative filtering, which requires rating of the items is not concrete and absence of strong machine learning or deep learning models into the model and absence of knowledge into the model provides weak semantics and henceforth model lags when you compare to the DESI model.

Although it is a personalised ecommerce recommendation model, the PRSE model uses text matching, where some amount of semantics is attained, which is why it also doesn't work as predicted. The use of big data analytics is also included. The big data tools are incorporated, but they cannot provide a strong ecosystem like that of the learning algorithms. Similarity with big data models is not as efficacious and efficient when compared to knowledge centric models which involve some amount of partial learning. So going forward, this PRSE model likewise lags behind the suggested model.

When compared to the suggested model, the HRSE model similarly does not perform as anticipated although it is a hierarchical recommendation systems which uses reviews and embedding, vectors are generated into the model. It uses bi directional encoder text representations and, attention based sequential recommendation model is incorporated, still it strategically lags. Where there is sparsity of knowledge, there is excessive data. This can be replaced or this can be overridden by algorithms. Learning model with large amount of knowledge for inferencing can overcome this. Therefore, when compared to DESI, the HRSE model similarly doesn't perform as expected.

Due to the deficiency of baseline models and the efficacy of relevance computation mechanisms, the presence of optimisation algorithm in terms of shuffled frog leap

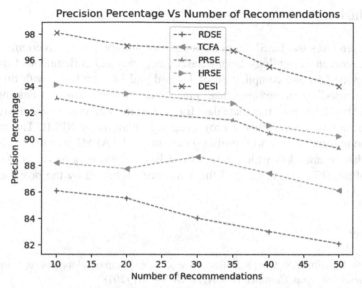

Fig. 2. Recall % vs Number of recommendations of the proposed DESI and other baseline models

algorithm and the presence of, Jaccard similarity, Lin similarity, NPMI, and APMI measures for element computation mechanisms are deemed necessary. The incorporation of ontologies and ecommerce metadata into the model distinguishes the proposed DESI model from all other models as the finest model in its category.

A distribution curve depicting the relationship between percentage of precision and number of recommendations is depicted in Fig. 2. The Fig. 2 indicates that the proposed DESI occupies the topmost position in the hierarchy. The position at the bottom of the hierarchy is held by the RDSE model. PRSE occupies the middle position in the hierarchy, while TCFA occupies the bottom position and HRSE occupies the second-to-last position from the summit.

The RDSE and TCFA models majorly underperform than the rest of the models is because of their base algorithm being collaborative filtering which is based on user ratings which are biased. This isn't a strong machine learning or deep learning model which reduces the precision percentage of RDSE and TCFA. Though PRSE performs better than RDSE and TCFA because of the integration of text matching, it still lacks a strong learning algorithm. The big data tools use partial learning but don't come close to the LSTM model of DESI, making PRSE fall significantly short. HRSE shows the best performance compared to RDSE, TCFA and PRSE. The use of hierarchical recommendation systems which take reviews and embedding into consideration help to bridge the gap between the precision percentage between HRSE and DESI but again aren't successful due to the lack of knowledge of the learning model. Considering all the shortcomings of the other models, the proposed framework works on solving all the problematic areas. The strong deep learning model LSTM is used along with NPMI for the frog leap algorithm, APMI and LSI for increasing the precision accuracy by approximately 12% in comparison with RDSE.

5 Conclusion

This paper proposes the DESI framework for Ecommerce product recommendation, strategic generation of ontology from dataset categories and enrichment of the query words using the LSI and computation of Jaccard and Lin similarity with differential threshold and subdivision measures takes place to ease the matching entities and subsequently the classification of metadata data fraud from the web is achieved using LSTM and optimization is achieved using Frog Leap algorithm under NPMI. The relevance computation in form of semantic similarity measure is the APMI measure to yield rank recommendations and okay which in turn furnishes the matching products. An overall precision of 96.29%, lowest value of the 5 has been achieved by the proposed DESI model.

References

1. Hwangbo, H., Kim, Y.S., Cha, K.J.: Recommendation system development for fashion retail e-commerce. Electron. Commer. Res. Appl. **28**, 94–101 (2018)
2. Shaikh, S., Rathi, S., Janrao, P.: Recommendation system in E-commerce websites: a graph based approached. In: 2017 IEEE 7th International Advance Computing Conference (IACC), Hyderabad, India, pp. 931–934 (2017). https://doi.org/10.1109/IACC.2017.0189
3. Verma, J.P., Patel, B., Patel, A.: Big data analysis: recommendation system with Hadoop framework. In: 2015 IEEE International Conference on Computational Intelligence & Communication Technology, pp. 92–97. IEEE, February 2015
4. Jiang, L., Cheng, Y., Yang, L., et al.: A trust-based collaborative filtering algorithm for E-commerce recommendation system. J. Ambient Intell. Hum. Comput. **10**, 3023–3034 (2019). https://doi.org/10.1007/s12652-018-0928-7
5. Guo, Y., Wang, M., Li, X.: Application of an improved Apriori algorithm in a mobile e-commerce recommendation system. Ind. Manag. Data Syst. **117**(2), 287–303 (2017)
6. Karn, A.L., et al.: Customer centric hybrid recommendation system for E-commerce applications by integrating hybrid sentiment analysis. Electron. Commer. Res. **23**(1), 279–314 (2023)
7. Khatter, H., Arif, S., Singh, U., Mathur, S., Jain, S.: Product recommendation system for E-commerce using collaborative filtering and textual clustering. In: 2021 Third International Conference on Inventive Research in Computing Applications (ICIRCA), pp. 612–618. IEEE, September 2021
8. Schafer, J.B., Konstan, J.A., Riedl, J.: Meta-recommendation systems: user-controlled integration of diverse recommendations. In: Proceedings of the Eleventh International Conference on Information and Knowledge Management, pp. 43–51, November 2002
9. Deenadayalan, D., Kangaiammal, A.: User feature similarity supported collaborative filtering for page recommendation using hybrid shuffled frog leaping algorithm. Int. J. Intell. Eng. Syst. **16**(1) (2023)
10. Rrmoku, K., Selimi, B., Ahmedi, L.: Application of trust in recommender systems—utilizing naive Bayes classifier. Computation **10**(1), 6 (2022)
11. Feng, L.: E-commerce recommendation technology based on collaborative filtering algorithm and mobile cloud computing. Wirel. Commun. Mob. Comput. (2022)
12. Chan, N.N., Gaaloul, W., Tata, S.: A web service recommender system using vector space model and latent semantic indexing. In: 2011 IEEE International Conference on Advanced Information Networking and Applications, pp. 602–609. IEEE, March 2011

13. Chen, H.: Personalized recommendation system of e-commerce based on big data analysis. J. Interdisc. Math. **21**(5), 1243–1247 (2018)
14. Islek, I., Oguducu, S.G.: A hierarchical recommendation system for E-commerce using online user reviews. Electron. Commer. Res. Appl. **52**, 101131 (2022)
15. Deepak, G., Santhanavijayan, A.: OntoBestFit: a best-fit occurrence estimation strategy for RDF driven faceted semantic search. Comput. Commun. **160**, 284–298 (2020)
16. Deepak, G., Priyadarshini, J.S.: Personalized and enhanced hybridized semantic algorithm for web image retrieval incorporating ontology classification, strategic query expansion, and content-based analysis. Comput. Electr. Eng. **72**, 14–25 (2018)
17. Tiwari, S., Rodriguez, F.O., Abbes, S.B., Usip, P.U., Hantach, R. (eds.): Semantic AI in Knowledge Graphs. CRC Press (2023)
18. Mihindukulasooriya, N., Tiwari, S., Enguix, C.F., Lata, K.: Text2KGBench: A Benchmark for Ontology-Driven Knowledge Graph Generation from Text. arXiv preprint (2023)
19. Dogan, O., Tiwari, S., Jabbar, M.A., Guggari, S.: A systematic review on AI/ML approaches against COVID-19 outbreak. Complex Intell. Syst. **7**, 2655–2678 (2021)
20. Rai, C., Sivastava, A., Tiwari, S., Abhishek, K.: Towards a conceptual modelling of ontologies. In: Emerging Technologies in Data Mining and Information Security: Proceedings of IEMIS 2020, vol. 1, p. 1286, 39 (2021)
21. Amara, F.Z., Djezzar, M., Hemam, M., Tiwari, S., Hafidi, M.M.: Unlocking the power of semantic interoperability in industry 4.0: a comprehensive overview. In: Ortiz-Rodriguez, F., Villazón-Terrazas, B., Tiwari, S., Bobed, C. (eds.) Iberoamerican Knowledge Graphs and Semantic Web Conference, vol. 14382, pp. 82–96. Springer, Cham (2023). https://doi.org/10.1007/978-3-031-47745-4_7
22. Yadav, S., Powers, M., Vakaj, E., Tiwari, S., Ortiz-Rodriguez, F.: Semantic carbon footprint of food supply chain management. In: Tiwari, S., Ortiz-Rodríguez, F., Mishra, S., Vakaj, E., Kotecha, K. (eds.) International Conference on Artificial Intelligence: Towards Sustainable Intelligence, vol. 1907, pp. 202–216. Springer, Cham (2023). https://doi.org/10.1007/978-3-031-47997-7_16
23. Deepak, G., Ahmed, A., Skanda, B.: An intelligent inventive system for personalised webpage recommendation based on ontology semantics. Int. J. Intell. Syst. Technol. Appl. **18**(1–2), 115–132 (2019)
24. Khorashadizadeh, H., Mihindukulasooriya, N., Tiwari, S., Groppe, J., Groppe, S.: Exploring in-context learning capabilities of foundation models for generating knowledge graphs from text (2023). arXiv preprint arXiv:2305.08804
25. Gulzar, Z., Leema, A.A., Deepak, G.: PCRS: personalized course recommender system based on hybrid approach. Procedia Comput. Sci. **125**, 518–524 (2018)

Adaptive Neuro Fuzzy-Based Depression Detection Model for Students in Tertiary Education

Samuel S. Udoh[1,2](✉) ⓘ, Patience U. Usip[1,2](✉) ⓘ, Uduak D. George[1], and Imeobong E. Akpan[1]

[1] Department of Computer Science, Faculty of Science, University of Uyo, Uyo, Nigeria
{samueludoh,patienceusip}@uniuyo.edu.ng
[2] TETFund Center of Excellence in Computational Intelligence Research, University of Uyo, Uyo, Nigeria

Abstract. Depression is a severe mental disorder with characteristic symptoms such as sadness, feeling of emptiness, anger, anxiety and sleep disturbance as well as general loss of initiative and interest in activities. The effects of late diagnosis of depression have culminated in many students dropping out of school, becoming unfulfilled in life and thereby posing a threat to human and environmental stability. Linear models for depression detection lack the intelligence to decode the non-linear interactions and imprecision proliferated in depression data. This work is aimed at utilizing Adaptive Neuro Fuzzy Inference (ANFIS) model furnished with intelligence for handling imprecision and non-linear modelling for diagnosis of depression. ANFIS model for depression detection was designed to provide a means of handling imprecision that characterizes depression detection attributes. Data collected from questionnaires administered to students in University of Uyo were analyzed. MATLAB programming tools were deployed for implementation of the model. The proposed fuzzy model identified and classified depression cases with 94.21% accuracy. The system would assist in early detection of depression in students studying in tertiary institutions and would guide health workers in administration of therapy to depressed students.

Keywords: Depression detection · Adaptive Neuro Fuzzy · machine learning · decision support systems

1 Introduction

Depression is a disorder that affects mood, thoughts and quality of life. It is usually accompanied by physical discomfort. It affects a person's eating habits, sleeping pattern, and self-perception. Depression is a mental state whose symptoms in primary care are controversial, vague, imprecise and ambiguous [1]. Depression symptoms range from everyday feelings of sadness, loss of interest or pleasure to suicidal ideations normally lasting a cycle of at least two weeks [2]. Although many other symptoms occur in varying proportions, the disease is a comorbid factor in many chronic health conditions such as

M. A. Jabbar et al. (Eds.): AMLDA 2023, CCIS 2047, pp. 156–167, 2024.
https://doi.org/10.1007/978-3-031-55486-5_12

diabetes, cardiovascular diseases (CVD), human immune deficiency (HIV), cancer, renal dysfunctions, alcohol abuse and drug addiction [3–6]. The disease has a relapsing course that adds to the morbidity resulting in higher costs to healthcare systems [7, 8]. Based on psychiatric morbidity surveys, one in six persons in Nigeria would be diagnosed as having depression or chronic anxiety disorder, which means that one family in twenty-five, is likely to be affected [9, 10].

Students seem to experience depressive symptoms at some point during their studies as they deal with stressful situations such as stress of separation from family, stress of coursework and assessment, repetition of a particular course, management of their interpersonal relationships and their social environment thereby heralding interpersonal tension and conflicts as well as constantly seeking for confirmation self-worth [11]. University students have been found struggling with emotions such as hopelessness and despair, that keep them unstable and down trodden. A normal part of life includes feelings of sadness and grief but when these feelings become continuous, it could result in depression [12]. Many authors have disputed the exact cause of depression disorder, some argue that genetic links to the disorder is closely related, while others attribute the disease with an imbalance of chemicals in the brain and hormonal deficiencies. It is however generally accepted that in some cases it could be set off by certain conditions, such as sleep deprivation, environmental factors, childhood precursors, adverse life event or experiences such as loss of a loved one or job, hypothyroidism, and the use of antidepressant medications [13, 14]. Chattopadhyay et al. [15] observed that the onset and course of the disease is capricious, highly fluctuating and often shows resistance to treatment. The debilitating effect of the disease reduces the quality of life of individuals hence there is much emphasis on early and correct diagnosis of the disease.

In the study of depression, the response to treatment, recurrence or disease-free is subjective. Statistical methods are commonly used in the analysis of depression data following the guidelines in Diagnostic and Statistical Manual of Mental Disorders [16, 17]. Recent research efforts have considered soft computing (SC) techniques as alternative methods of proffering approximate solutions to real world problems poised with various kinds of inaccuracies and uncertainties [18–24]. The underlying paradigms of SC are Artificial Neural Networks (ANNs), Fuzzy logic (FL), and Genetic Algorithms (GA). Early SC models in medicine emerged to model expert's behavior by utilizing their knowledge and representing it in a symbolic form. This approach has been accepted by clinicians for its ability to produce high-quality results and demonstrate improvements upon previous techniques used [25–27].

Obot and Udoh [28] buttressed the importance of fuzzy logic and its usage when the data available is uncertain or imprecise to warrant the use of numbers or exact values and also when imprecision can be tolerated. Fuzzy logic due to its ability to handle imprecision and uncertainty has found its application in numerous fields of study. The application of fuzzy logic in detecting depression in students gives effective and attainable solutions as the knowledge of fuzzy logic is suitably required when human evaluation is needed. Furthermore, researches show that fuzzy logic is a more essential technique to handle imprecision and uncertainty given that evaluating the prior knowledge or past achievements of students with the aim of discovering the risk of students' depression involves dealing with uncertain and imprecise data. A combination of neural networks and fuzzy logic to learn from previous knowledge and handle imprecise data in proffering solution to detection, forecasting and prediction problems improved performance in previous works [29, 30].

Therefore, this work aims at developing adaptive neuro-fuzzy inference system (ANFIS) based depression assessment system for depression detection in students studying in tertiary institutions. This work would assist decision making by educating stakeholders and health workers on depressed students. In the remainder of this work. Related works on depression diagnosis are reviewed in Sect. 2. ANFIS design for depression detection is presented in Sect. 3 while Sects. 4 and 5 deal with results and conclusions respectively.

2 Review of Related Literature

Depression is a common mood disorder that is characterized by sadness, loss of interest, feelings of guilt or low self-worth, and poor concentration [1]. It can be long-lasting or recurrent, and can have a significant impact on individuals and their families, and even on society as a whole [31]. According to Bayram and Bilgel [32], depression is one of the most common forms of mental disorder in the general population. It is associated with substantial morbidity and mortality, and imposes a substantial burden in developing and developed countries. Depression is among the leading causes of disability in industrialized countries. It is characterized by a combination of feelings of sadness, loneliness, irritability, worthlessness, hopelessness, guilt, and/or agitation accompanied by an array of physical symptoms lasting at least two weeks. Depression is closely associated symptomatically not only with normal intense sadness, but also with culpability and guilt, feeling stressed at work, excessive fatigue, deep sorrow, general lassitude, and diffuse unhappiness. Because of its medical nature, depression has a chance to get socially accepted as an excuse for impaired role functioning. Common co-occurring problems for depressed children and adolescents are academic underachievement, school attendance problems, and school failure [33–36].

Although it is often presumed that the co-occurring problems are consequences of depression in youths, academic problems can precede the onset of depressive symptoms for some children. It is generally recognized that cognitive components of depressive syndromes make it exceedingly difficult for children, adolescents, and adults to fully maintain their normal level of academic and vocational functioning. Young persons with depression often experience problems with decreasing levels of subjective interest in academic progress, difficulty concentrating and paying attention in class and during homework periods, and loss of the necessary energy and motivation levels that are required for academic achievement, making premorbid levels of school functioning increasingly difficult to maintain. At times, some individuals become so impaired that they may abandon their hopes of attaining any academic achievement or success and even withdraw entirely from attending school, making clinical depression one of the more common psychiatric diagnoses identifiable in populations of school refusers [9, 12–14].

Symptoms of depression represent a significant health problem for adolescents [3]. Increasingly, evidence points to greater risk for depression among adolescents from racial and ethnic minority groups [19]. Given that this evidence comes from studies that focus on different populations, of different ages, and use different measures, it is a major challenge to draw any firm conclusions about how great this differential risk actually is, or how this risk might vary for different sociodemographic groups [9]. The need to meet this challenge is urgent, given that high rates of depressive symptoms in adolescence create a considerable risk for depression in later life. Feeling excessively tired (fatigue)is a very common symptom of depression. Although everyone feels tired from time to time, people who have severe or persistent tiredness—especially if it accompanies other symptoms—may have hidden depression [19]. Many researchers have satisfactorily deployed qualitative and quantitative models in the task of finding solution to real life problems [37–39]. Ekong et al. [9] carried out an experimental study of an intelligent system on predicting depression risk levels using a neuro-fuzzy approach. This work described research result in the development of a system driven by fuzzy logic to determine the risk levels of depressed patients in primary care settings. 54 instances were obtained, 40 were trained using a feed-forward back-propagation neural network algorithm and 14 were used for testing purpose. This work was implemented and simulated using an Adaptive Neuro-Fuzzy Inference System (ANFIS) which handled fuzzy rules used in the diagnostic decision making. The result of the system was found consistent with an expert specialist's opinion on evaluating the performance of the system. Though the level of accuracy was high, the data set was small to generalize the accuracy. Ashish et al. (2018) in a study, developed a genetic-neuro-fuzzy system for grading depression. This study aimed to help general physicians for first hand applications. Key symptoms for depression were identified. Data from patients through physicians were collected. Two approaches were utilized and optimized in the performance of the mode. The back-propagation algorithm with the Genetic Algorithm were considered and used in this model. The model was trained with seventy-eight data and validated with ten. In terms of diagnostic accuracy, the genetic algorithm superseded back-propagation algorithm. It was therefore concluded that the soft computing-based diagnostic models could assist the doctors to make informed decisions. The limitation of this study is that the training data set was small. Ding et al., [41] carried out an experimental study on depression recognition method from college students. This study aimed to analyze the user's social network data to detect the user's depression. A text-level mining approach was used to detect depression among college students. Deep integrated support vector machine (DISVM) algorithm was introduced to classify the input data, and realize the recognition of depression.

3 Design of Adaptive Neuro-Fuzzy-Based Depression Detection System

In this Section, design of a Adaptive neuro-fuzzy model for detection of depression is presented in Fig. 1. The major components of the model are Fuzzification of Depression Input Data, Fuzzy Inference Engine, User Interface, Defuzzification, Depression Detection Output.

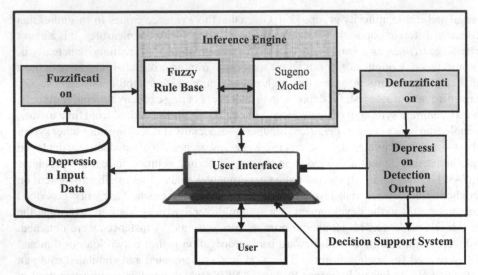

Fig. 1. Architectural Design of ANFIS-Based Depression Detection System

3.1 User Interface

The user interface describes the flow of the interfaces in the software from the user login page through the end of the user's operations. It is a graphical representation that allows users to communicate with the software system. The user interface accepts the user's identification (ID) and symptoms as input. The user interface outputs diagnosis and prescription in a form that can be understood by the user.

3.2 Fuzzification of Depression Input Data

Fuzzification is the process of converting the crisp input values into fuzzy values Membership Function (MF). The triangular MF as shown in Eq. 1 is deployed in this work. The triangular MF is specified by a vector, x, which depends on three scalar parameters a, b and c. The parameters a and c locate the "feet" of the triangle and the parameter b locates the peak.

$$\mu_{triangle}(x;\ a, b, c) = \begin{cases} 0, & x \leq a \\ \frac{x-a}{b-a}, & a \leq x \leq b \\ \frac{c-x}{c-b}, & b \leq x \leq c \\ 0, & c \leq x \end{cases}$$
$$= \max(\min(\tfrac{x-a}{b-a}, \tfrac{c-x}{c-b}), 0) \tag{1}$$

The following attributes of depression were fuzzified: Trouble in Relationship (TR), Hopelessness (HS), Sadness (SS), Lack of Concentration (LC), Low self-esteem (LS), Forced Happiness (FH), Problem making decisions (MD), and depression level. In choosing the triangular MF for the input variables. At the fuzzification interface, the input variables TR, HS, SS, LC, LS, FH, and MD ranges from 0 to 10 were fuzzified into three linguistic variables: **'Near absent, 'Slightly present'** and **'Present** as shown in Eq. 2. The output linguistic variables are defined in Eq. 3.

$$\mu(x) = \begin{cases} \text{Near absent} & \text{if } x \text{ is } < 0.25 \\ \text{Slightly present} & \text{if } 0.25 \leq x < 0.45 \\ \text{Present} & \text{if } 0.45 \leq x \leq 1 \end{cases} \qquad (2)$$

$$\mu(x) = \begin{cases} \text{Near absent} & \text{if } x \text{ is } < 0.25 \\ \text{Minimal} & \text{if } 0.25 \leq x < 0.45 \\ \text{Moderate} & \text{if } 0.45 \leq x < 0.65 \\ \text{Severe} & \text{if } 0.65 \leq x < 0.85 \\ \text{Very Severe} & \text{if } 0.85 \leq x \leq 1.00 \end{cases} \qquad (3)$$

3.3 Inference Engine

The domain knowledge is represented by a set of facts about the current state of a patient. The inference engine compares each rule stored in the knowledge base with facts contained in the database. When the IF (condition) part of the rule matches a fact, the rule is fired and its THEN (action) part is executed. The inference engine uses a system of rules to make decisions through the fuzzy 'AND' operator and generates a single truth value that determines the outcome of the rules. This way, they emulate human cognitive process and decision making ability and finally they represent knowledge in a structured homogenous and modular way. Some of the fuzzy rules deployed in the system are presented as follows:

Rule 1:   If (TR is ABSENT) and (HS is ABSENT) and (SS is ABSENT) and (LC is ABSENT) then (**DL is NEAR_ABSENT**)

Rule 2:   If (TR is ABSENT) and (HS is ABSENT) and (SS is ABSENT) and (LC is SLIGHTLY_PRESENT) then (**DL is NEAR_ABSENT**)

Rule 3:   If (TR is ABSENT) and (HS is ABSENT) and (SS is ABSENT) and (LC is PRESENT) then (**DL is NEAR_ABSENT**)

Rule 4:   If (TR is ABSENT) and (HS is ABSENT) and (SS is SLIGHTLY_PRESENT) and (LC is ABSENT) then (DL is **NEAR_ABSENT**)

Rule 5:   If (TR is ABSENT) and (HS is ABSENT) and (SS is SLIGHTLY_PRESENT) and (LC is SLIGHTLY_PRESENT) then (**DL is MINIMAL**)

Rule 6:   If (TR is ABSENT) and (HS is ABSENT) and (SS is SLIGHTLY_PRESENT) and (LC is PRESENT) then (**DL is MINIMAL**)

Rule 7:   If (TR is ABSENT) and (HS is ABSENT) and (SS is PRESENT) and (LC is PRESENT) then (**DL is MODERATE**)

Rule 8:   If (TR is ABSENT) and (HS is SLIGHTLY_PRESENT) and (SS is SLIGHTLY_PRESENT) and (LC is PRESENT) then (**DL is MODERATE**)

Rule 80: If (TR is PRESENT) and (HS is PRESENT) and (SS is PRESENT) and (LC is SLIGHTLY_PRESENT) then (**DL is SEVERE**)

Rule 81: If (TR is PRESENT) and (HS is PRESENT) and (SS is PRESENT) and (LC is PRESENT) then (**DL is VERY_SEVERE**)

3.4 Defuzzification

Defuzzification is the process of converting the final output of a fuzzy system to a crisp value. For decision making purposes, the output fuzzy sets must be defuzzified to crisp value in the real-life domain. The most commonly used defuzzification method is the center of area method (COA), also commonly referred to as the centroid method. This method determines the center of area of fuzzy set and returns the corresponding crisp value. COA defuzzification method finds a point representing the center of area of the fuzzy set and is given in Eq. 4.

$$z = \frac{\sum_{i=1}^{n} \mu ai(x) yi}{\sum_{i=1}^{n} \mu ai(x)} \qquad (4)$$

where z is the crisp value that represents the severity level used for decision making, μ_{ai} (x) is the degree of membership of the likelihood of the jth rule, y_i is the consequent of each rule.

3.5 Depression Detection Output

Depression detection output presents the depression level (DL) which determines the level of severity of depression risk given the input variables. A multiple input single output (MISO) fuzzy system is used to obtain severity level which is the only output variable of the system. The output linguistic variables are defined in Eq. 3. The fuzzy system provides an objective process for obtaining the depression risk level.

4   Results and Discussion

Data totaling 5530 data samples was collected from students in, University of Uyo Nigeria. The data was spitted in the ratio of 8:1:1 for training, validation and testing of the model. This translated into 4424 training data sample, 553 validation data set and 553 testing data sample. The Data were collected through a questionnaire comprising twenty-three (23) questions specifically designed to obtained depression information. The setting of questions and assignment of weights to answers in the questionnaire were carried out via the help of human psychology and sociology. Answers to questions that could test depression level such as: 'Not at all' was assigned 0, 'Several days' was assigned 1, 'More than half the days' was assigned 2, and 'Nearly every day' was assigned 3. The scoring had a range from 0–70, where ≤ 14 signified 'Near absent Depression', 15–28 signified 'Minimal Depression', 29–42 signified 'Moderate Depression', 43–56 signified 'Severe Depression' and >=57 signified 'Very Severe Depression'. From the data obtained, 23 variables were considered for measuring depression level. In the choice of parameters for the purpose of this work, Principal Component Analysis (PCA) was used to reduce the number of variables by making use of the correlation values. The data was captured into International Business Machines (IBM) statistical package. Three correlation models namely: Pearson, Kendall and Spearman were used for the correlation computation and the Mean was obtained. Table 1 shows the correlation summary for the 23 variables.

Table 1. Attribute Correlations for Depression Diagnosis

SN	Attribute Description	Code	Pearson	Kendall	Spearman	Mean Correlation
1	Trouble in Relationships	TR	0.604	0.473	0.587	0.555
2	Hopelessness	HS	0.613	0.453	0.554	0.540
3	Sadness	SS	0.584	0.457	0.564	0.535
4	Lack of concentration	LC	0.584	0.449	0.558	0.530
5	Low self-esteem	LS	0.581	0.450	0.557	0.529
6	Forced Happiness	FH	0.569	0.436	0.547	0.517
7	Problem making decisions	MD	0.526	0.440	0.562	0.509
8	Anger	AG	0.559	0.427	0.528	0.505
9	Loss of Interest	LI	0.558	0.407	0.508	0.491
10	Feeling Guilty	FG	0.540	0.401	0.501	0.481
11	Restlessness	RS	0.535	0.390	0.489	0.472
12	Trust Issues	TI	0.513	0.394	0.500	0.469
13	No Success Feeling	NS	0.541	0.388	0.472	0.467
14	Suicidal Thoughts	ST	0.530	0.386	0.469	0.462
15	Past Failure	PF	0.519	0.365	0.454	0.446
16	Lack of concentration	LC	0.473	0.355	0.441	0.423
17	Feeling Detached	FD	0.473	0.351	0.437	0.420
18	Insomnia	IM	0.451	0.348	0.435	0.411
19	Feeling of no Future	FF	0.466	0.320	0.386	0.391
20	Tiredness	TS	0.402	0.287	0.365	0.351
21	Weight Loss	WL	0.348	0.297	0.372	0.339
22	Poor Appetite	PA	0.321	0.282	0.351	0.318
23	Hypersomnia	HP	0.327	0.180	0.226	0.244

Result from the data gathered showed that TR is the major cause of depression. The variables were sorted in descending order and the best four (4) were selected for further investigation thus: TR, HS, SS, and LC. The selected attributes served as inputs to the ANFIS model whose training plot is depicted in Fig. 2. The training error as shown in Fig. 2a is decreasing with increase in the number of epochs. The decreasing training error values together with the high validation error value observed in Fig. 2b indicate

(a)   **(b)**

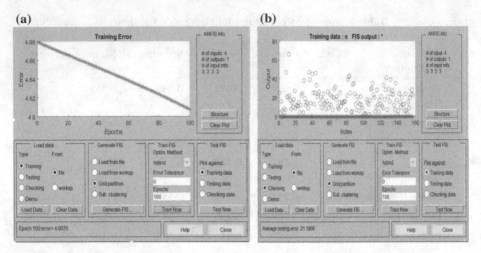

Fig. 2. a: Plot for training data set. b: Plot for validation data set

that the model needs more training for optimal results. The adaptation of depression level to changes in depression variables is depicted in the Rule Viewer in Fig. 3.

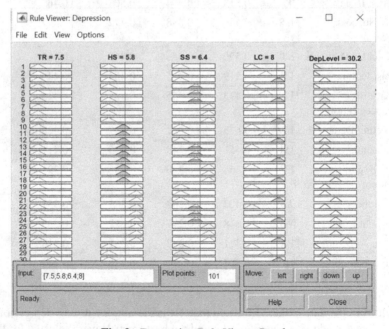

Fig. 3. Depression Rule Viewer Panel

Values of 7.5, 5.8. 6.4 and 8 from the test data were entered for TR, HS, SC and LC depressions variables respectively. The depression level value of 30.2 was observed.

Based on the Depression level which falls within the output range of 29 42. The model inferred that the diagnosis of depression level for the student is Moderate. Out of the 553 data samples in the test data set 521 cases produced correct diagnosis while 32 cases produced wrong diagnosis. This translates to 94.21% accuracy of the model on the tested data.

5 Conclusion

This research has reviewed some depression diagnosis models. The work has deployed Adaptive Neuro Fuzzy Inference mechanism for prediction of depression level with 94.21% accuracy. The system would be helpful in the early diagnosis of depression in tertiary institutions to thwart the deteriorating condition of victims. The work would help medical doctors and health workers proffer solutions to victims based on detected level of depression. Further research would deploy larger training and testing data sets as well as implement different training models with varying parameters to improve depression detection precision and accuracy.

Acknowledgements. The authors are grateful to TETFund for supporting this research through the TETFund Centre of Excellence in Computational Intelligence Research and the University of Uyo Management for creating a conducive environment for conducting the research.

References

1. Abela, J.R.Z., Hankin, B.L.: Cognitive vulnerability to depression in children and adolescents: a developmental psychopathology perspective. In: Abela, J.R.Z., Hankin, B.L. (eds.) Handbook of Depression in Children and Adolescents, pp. 35–78. The Guilford Press (2008)
2. Mila, K., Kielan, K., Michalak, K.: A fuzzy semiotic framework for modeling imprecision in the assessment of depression. In: IFSA_EUSFLAT2009, pp. 1717–1722 (2009). ISBN: 978-989-950-79-6-8
3. Cohen, S.D., Norris, L., Acquaviva, K., Peterson, R.A., Kummel, P.L.: Screening, diagnosis and treatment of depression in patients with end stage renal disease. Clin. J. Am. Soc. Nephrol. **2**(6), 1332–1342 (2007). http://cjasn.asnjournals.org/content/archive/. Accessed Aug 2010
4. Udoh, S.S., Umoh, U.A., Umoh, M.E., Udo, M.E.: Diagnosis of prostate cancer using soft computing paradigms. Glob. J. Comput. Sci. Technol. Neural Artif. Intell. **19**(2), 19–26 (2019)
5. Umoh, U., Udoh, S., Abayomi, A., Abdulzeez, A.: Interval type 2 fuzzy logic system for remote vital signs monitoring and shock level prediction. J. Fuzzy Extension Appl. **2**(1), 41–68 (2021)
6. Obot, O., et al.: Modelling differential diagnosis of febrile diseases with fuzzy cognitive map. J. Trop. Med. Infect. Dis. **8**, 352 (2023). https://doi.org/10.3390/tropicalmed807035
7. Maja, H., Meifania, C., Tharam, S.D.: Towards mental health ontology. In: Proceedings of IEEE International Conference on Bioinformatics and Biomedicine, p. 284 (2008). https://doi.org/10.1109/BIBM.2008.59. ISBN: 978-7695-3452-7
8. Markus, N.: Artificial intelligence diagnostics in psychological medicine. Ph.D. thesis, Department of Computer Science and Engineering, Malardalen University, Sweden (2004). http://www.idt.mdh.se/ai. Accessed 12 Sept 2010

9. Ekong, V.E., Onibere, E.A., Uwadiae, E.: A model of depression diagnosis using a neuro-fuzzy approach. World J. Appl. Sci. Technol. **5**(1), 63–70 (2013)
10. Ewhrudjakpor, C.: Socio-demographics, life event stressors and psychosomatic disorders among public servants in the Niger Delta region of Nigeria. Int. J. Sociol. Anthropol. **1**(3), 55–61 (2009)
11. Arnett, J.J.: Emerging adulthood: a theory of development from the late teens through the twenties. Am. Psychol. **55**, 469–480 (2000)
12. Yalemwork, G.: Depression among Addis Ababa University students Sidist Kilo Campus: prevalence, gender, difference and other associated factors. Master's thesis on the internet. Addis Ababa University (2015)
13. Nunes, L.C., Pinheiro, P.R., Pequeno, T.C., Pinheiro, M.C.D.: Support tool in the diagnosis of major depressive disorder. In: Lytras, M.D., Ordonez de Pablos, P., Ziderman, A., Roulstone, A., Maurer, H., Imber, J.B. (eds.) Organizational, Business, and Technological Aspects of the Knowledge Society. CCIS, vol. 112, pp. 136–145. Springer, Heidelberg (2010). https://doi.org/10.1007/978-3-642-16324-1_15
14. Olawale, O.O., Francis, A.O., Abasiubong, F., Adebayo R.E.: Detection of mental disorders with the patient health questionnaire in primary care settings in Nigeria. J. Ment. Illn. **2**(1) (2010)
15. Chattopadhyay, S., Kaur, P., Rabhi, F., Acharya, R.: An automated system to diagnose the severity of adult depression. In: Proceedings of 2nd IEEE International Conference on Emerging Applications of Information Technology, pp. 121–124 (2012). https://doi.org/10.1109/EAIT.2011.17
16. Klinsman, M.S.: The role of algorithms in the detection and treatment of depression in primary care. J. Clin. Psychiatry **64**(2), 19–24 (2003)
17. Jabar, H.Y.: Classification of mental disorders figures based on soft computing methods. Int. J. Comput. Appl. **117**(2), 5–11 (2015)
18. Fayaz, A., Manaj, D., Risji, A.: Different approaches of soft computing techniques (inference system) which are used in clinical decision support system for risk based prioritization. Asian J. Comput. Inf. Syst. **3**(1), 28–47 (2015)
19. Dinga, R., et al.: Predicting the naturalistic course of depression from a wide range of clinical, psychological, and biological data: a machine learning approach (2018)
20. Udoh, S.S., Asuquo, D.E., Inyang, U.G.: Adaptive neuro-fuzzy model for oil pipelines monitoring in a cluster-based sensor network environment. World J. Appl. Sci. Technol. (WOJAST) **10**(1B), 184–190 (2018)
21. Ekpenyong, M.E., et al.: Hybrid collaborative model for evidence-based healthcare. In: Association for Computing Machinery Digital Library, New York United States, pp. 90–97 (2020). https://doi.org/10.1145/3418094.3418105
22. Zadeh, L.A.: Fuzzy logic, neural networks, and soft computing **37**, 77–84 (1994)
23. Obot, O.U., Akinyokun, O.C., Udoh, S.S.: Application of neuro-fuzzy expert system for diagnosis of hypertension. J. Nigeria Comput. Soc. (NCS) **15**(2), 131–147 (2008)
24. Obot, O.U., Udo, I.I., Udoh, S.S.: Differential diagnosis of eye diseases based on fuzzy cognitive map. J. Nurs. Health Sci. (IOSR-JNHS) **7**(6), 42–52 (2018)
25. Olugbenga, O., Esther, A., Fatumo, S.: Building a computer-based expert system for malaria environmental diagnosis: an alternative malaria control strategy. Egypt. Comput. Sci. J. **33**(1), 55–69 (2009)
26. Nazmy, T.M., Messiry, H.E., Bokhity, B.A.: Classification of cardiac Arrhythmia based on hybrid adaptive neuro-fuzzy inference system. Egypt. Comput. Sci. J. **34**(3), 55–69 (2010)
27. Asuquo, D., Ekpenyong, M., Udoh, S., Robinson, S., Attai, K.: Optimized channel allocation in emerging mobile cellular networks. J. Soft Comput. Fusion Found. Methodol. Appl. **24**(21), 16361–16382 (2020). https://doi.org/10.1007/s00500-020-04947-z

28. Udoh, S.S., George, U.D., Etuk, U.R.: Cassava yield forecasting using artificial neural network. In: Ayandele, I.A., (eds.) Contemporary Discourse on Nigeria's Economic Profile, A Festschrift in Honour of Professor Prof Ndaudoh Ukpabio Ndaeyo, pp. 667–679. Publication of University of Uyo, Uyo, Akwa Ibom State (2023)

29. Obot, O.U., Uzoka, F.-M.E., John, A.E., Udoh, S.S.: Soft-computing method for settling land disputes cases based on text similarity. Int. J. Bus. Inf. Syst. Inderscience 43(3), 369–393 (2023)

30. Udoh, S.S., George, U.D., Obot, O.U., Tom, I.S.: Investigation of similarity paradigms for electronic document query and retrieval. Int. J. Sci. Eng. Res. 13(3), 946–959 (2022)

31. Angold, A., Costello, E.J.: The epidemiology of depression in children and adolescents. In: Goodyer, I.M. (ed.) The Depressed Child and Adolescent, pp. 143–178. Cambridge University Press, UK (2001)

32. Bayram, N., Bilgel, N.: The prevalence and socio-demographic correlations of depression, anxiety and stress among a group of university students. Soc. Psychiatry Psychiatr. Epidemiol. 43(8), 667–672 (2008)

33. Penninx, B.W.: Two-year course of depressive and anxiety disorders: results from the Netherlands study of depression and anxiety (NESDA). J. Affect. Disord. 133, 76–85 (2011)

34. Sharp, L.E., Lipsky, M.S.: Screening for depression across the lifespan: a review of measures for use in primary care settings. Am. Fam. Physician 66, 1001–1008 (2002)

35. Hammen, C., Rudolph, K., Weisz, J., et al.: The context of depression in clinic-referred youth: neglected areas in treatment. J. Am. Acad. Child Adolesc. Psychiatry 38, 64–71 (1999)

36. Heilman, R.N., Kallay, E., Miclea, M.: The role of computer-based psychotherapy in the treatment of anxiety disorders. Cogn. Brain Behav. Interdisc. J. 14(3), 209–230 (2010)

37. Bassey, P.C., Akinkunmi, B.O.: Introducing the spatial qualification problem and its qualitative model. Afr. J. Comp. ICTs 6(1), 190–196 (2013)

38. Usip, P.U., Akinkunmi, B.O.: A semi-decidable qualitative spatial qualification logic. Benin J. Adv. Comput. Sci. 5(1), 10–29 (2020)

39. Usip, P.U., Inyang, U.G., Asuquo, D.E., Umoren, E.M.: An evaluation model for a probability weighted ontology of temporal complexities. In: 2017 2nd International Conference on Computational Systems and Information Technology for Sustainable Solution (CSITSS), pp. 1–5 (2017)

40. Ashish, K., Dasari, A., Chattopadyay, S., Hui, N.B.: Genetic-neurofuzzy system for grading depression. Appl. Comput. Inform. 14(1), 08–105 (2018)

41. Ding, Y., Chen, X., Fu, Q., Zhong, S.: A depression recognition method for college students using deep integrated support vector algorithm. IEEE Access 8, 75616–75629 (2020)

Optimizing Portfolio for Highly Funded Industries Within Budget Constraints for the Period of 2023–2024

Preethi Nanjundan[1]([✉]), Jossy P. George[1], Abhijeet Birari[1],
Pamidimukkala Sai Geetha[2], and Manka Manwali[3]

[1] CHRIST(Deemed to be University), Bengaluru, India
{preethi.n,frjossy,abhijeet.birari}@christuniversity.in
[2] Koneru Lakshmaiah Education Foundation, Vijayawada, Andhra Pradesh, India
[3] Graphic Era Hill University, Dehradun, India
mmanwal@gehu.ac.in

Abstract. This research paper aims to analyze and optimize portfolios for the top funded industries based on the budget'23. The study uses a data-driven app-roach to identify the best investment opportunities within these industries. The methodology involves collecting financial data, conducting market analysis, and using optimization techniques to create an optimal portfolio. The results of the study show that the top funded industries have a high potential for growth, and the optimized portfolios can maximize returns while minimizing risk. The findings can provide valuable insights for investors and fund managers who are seeking to make informed investment decisions in these industries. The study also highlights the importance of considering the budget constraints while optimizing portfolios.

Keywords: Portfolio Optimization · Budget 2023 · Time Series Analysis

1 Introduction

The Budget is an executive outline of the Government's economic vision as well as the key measures in the thrust areas of the economy for growth and welfare. A bird's eye perspective of the most important budget proposals for the fiscal year 2022–2023 is provided together with significant accomplishments in fiscal consolidation and man-agement of the government finances. Here comes the need for portfolio optimization to achieve a stable, minimized risk, loss-free proposal portfolio. The risk tolerance, invest-ment horizon, and investment goals of the investor are a few variables that can affect the optimization of a portfolio. Overall, the objective of portfolio optimization is to assist investors in making defensible choices regarding the distribution of their assets to meet their financial objectives while reducing the risk of capital loss. Of all the sectors, share performance is considered for selection. The composition of the portfolio and the amount of cash to be invested in risky financial assets may be significantly changed by small adjustments to the calculation of return and risk characteristics. This paper is an attempt to do portfolio optimization while keeping an eye on the budget, as every penny

M. A. Jabbar et al. (Eds.): AMLDA 2023, CCIS 2047, pp. 168–179, 2024.
https://doi.org/10.1007/978-3-031-55486-5_13

is equally responsible for the movement of stocks. Monte Carlo Simulation technique for optimization is used to optimize the processes that are too complex for too many variables in an analytical approach (Table 1).

Table 1. List of Sectors and Chosen Companies for Portfolio Optimization

Sector	Company 1	Company 2	Company 3	Company 4	Company 5
Manufacturing	TATA Steel	Reliance Industries	JSW Steel	Lupin Limited	GMR Infrastructure Limited
Fintech	Bajaj Finserv	Kotak Mahindra	OnMobile Global Limited	Intellect Design Arena Limited	Tanla Platforms Limited
Healthcare	Sun Pharma	Apollo Hospital Enterprise Limited	Dr Reddy's Laboratories	Divis Pharmaceuticals	Cipla Limited
Tourism	Taj Hotel and Resort	EI Hotel Limited	Thomas Cook Limited	BLS International	The Indian Hotel Company

2 Related Work

There are different asset classes already making people either rich or even more rich. Here comes the need for portfolio optimization to achieve a stable, minimized risk, loss-free proposal portfolio. [1] The use of deep learning in portfolio optimization is a rapidly evolving field, with ongoing research and experimentation to improve its effectiveness. [2] The stock market is complex and influenced by a multitude of factors, and there is always a risk of loss involved. [3] combination of the above two approaches to create a framework for selecting an optimal stock portfolio over time. The main idea is to use time series prediction to forecast the future behavior of individual assets or the market, and then use multi-objective optimization to select a portfolio that maximizes the desired objectives while considering the predicted values and their uncertainties. [4] Additionally, the use of a decoder component in the model enables it to generate multiple steps ahead forecasts, making it suitable for a wide range of forecasting applications. [5] It is observed that LSTM performs significantly better than GARCH in terms of both (Mean Absolute Error) MAE and (Mean Square Error) MSE. [6] The optimization problem is formulated as a quadratic program, which can be solved using various numerical optimization techniques.[7].The accuracy of the stock price prediction models can significantly impact the performance of the portfolio optimization process. Therefore, it is important to choose an appropriate machine learning algorithm and train it on a diverse set of historical data. [8] Threshold autoregressive (TAR) models are a type of time series model that incorporate nonlinearity by allowing for different regression coefficients in different regions of the data. [9] Portfolio selection based on value and risk involves the use of mathematical models and data-driven techniques to construct an investment portfolio that maximizes return while minimizing risk. Value and risk are important factors to consider when selecting an investment portfolio. [10] Ensemble methods, such as bagging and boosting, can be used to improve the accuracy and stability of stock return predictions. Interpretability of deep learning models is a challenge, and techniques such as SHAP values and attention mechanisms can be used to gain insight into the factors driving stock returns. [11] Monte Carlo simulation can be used to model and evaluate the performance of different portfolio management strategies, including CPPI, under various market conditions. [12] VaR is a useful tool for portfolio optimization, as it provides a clear measure of downside risk that can help investors make informed decisions about asset allocation and risk management. [13]. This paper will talk about generating an optimized portfolio for the potential investors based on budget announcement of 2023. The sectors are chosen based on the fundings that the sectors have been allocated by the Government of India [14].

3   Methodology

The paper is focused on generating an optimized portfolio for potential investors who aims to earn rewards by diversifying the level of risk that comes along. It can be done by allocating your funds in a diversified manner and understanding the pros and cons of investing in a certain company. Hence, understanding of the company is not enough, an investor should investigate the same through various aspects, e.g., Volume, Sector Analysis, Volatility etc. The Budget 2023 allocated funds to Fintech, Tourism, and Healthcare sectors to drive economic growth and development in the coming year. These sectors were chosen strategically due to their potential to increase GDP and contribute to long-term growth.

Description of the Dataset

The data is collected from Yahoo Finance to analyze stock prices of seven companies from five sectors heavily funded by the Indian government in the Budget 2023. The data was collected over five years from February 2018 to February 2023, allowing for a comprehensive analysis of stock market trends. Companies were selected based on their significance and influence in their respective industries. The data will be used to examine the relationships between the selected industries and the stock market, as well as the performance of individual companies. This data provides valuable insights into the dynamics of the stock market in the selected industries and their respective companies.

4   Model Description

BETA: Beta is a widely used financial metric that measures the sensitivity of a stock's returns to changes in the overall market which is directly related to volatility of the stock.

The beta coefficient (β) is calculated as the covariance between the stock's returns and the market's returns divided by the variance of the market's returns.

$$\beta = \text{Covariance (r, rm) / Variance (rm)} \tag{1}$$

- Covariance (r, rm) is the covariance between the stock's returns (r) and the market's returns (rm)
- Variance (rm) is the variance of the market's return.

CAGR: Compound Annual Growth Rate (CAGR) is a financial metric used to measure the rate of return of an investment over a specified period. It represents the average annual growth rate of an investment assuming that the investment has been compounding over that period.

$$CAGR = (\text{EndingValue/BeginningValue})^{(1/n)} - 1 \tag{2}$$

- Ending Value is the value of the investment at the end of the period
- Beginning Value is the value of the investment at the beginning of the period.
- n is the number of years in the investment period

Covariance: Covariance is a statistical measure that shows how much the values in a dataset vary from their mean. It indicates the degree to which two variables move together or apart from each other. When it comes to asset prices, higher variance means higher risk and potential returns. The covariance matrix is a widely used risk model that helps to understand how different assets relate to each other and how their prices move in tandem or independently.

$$\text{cov}(X, Y) = \Sigma[(Xi - X\_mean) * (Yi - Y\_mean)] / (n - 1) \tag{5}$$

Xi is the i-th value of the variable X
X_mean is the mean of X
Yi is the i-th value of the variable Y
Y_mean is the mean of Y
n is the number of observations in X and Y

5 Experiments and Results

The analysis of time series stock price data is crucial for any investor or analyst to make informed decisions. In this regard, analysing the stock prices for each sector together can provide valuable insights. The data for seven companies have been merged and separated using their ticker identifiers. First, exploratory data analysis has been performed on all the five companies. This includes checking the data types, identifying null values, and changing data types where necessary. Additionally, pulling out the best five stocks has been done based on the volume of trade over the last five years. This analysis provides information on which stocks are traded the most and can guide investors in their investment decisions (Fig. 1).

The research paper provides a detailed time series analysis of five companies from each sector, focusing on the volatility of stocks, annual return provided, Liquidity of the

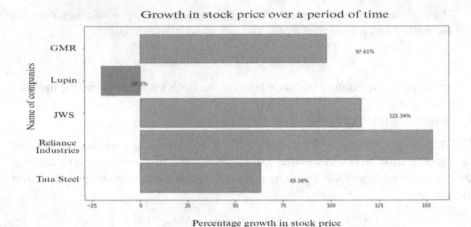

Fig. 1. 5 year growth rate for Manufacturing Industry

stocks and compounded annual growth. The study begins by analysing the fluctuations in the stock prices of each company over time and plotting their closing prices to visualize the movement of the stock in the market. The aim is to provide insights into the behaviour of stocks in different sectors, which can be useful for investors in making informed decisions about their investment portfolio (Fig. 2, 3 and 4).

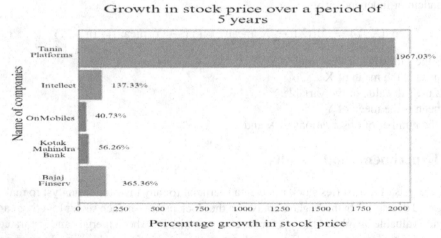

Fig. 2. 5 year growth rate for Fintech Industry

The beta values provide insights into the risk associated with each stock, with higher beta values indicating higher volatility and risk (Table 2).

The given values for the healthcare companies range from 0.42 to 0.82, with Sun-Pharma having the highest beta value of 0.72. In comparison, the beta values for the tourism companies range from 0.81 to 1.04, with Indian Hotel having the highest beta

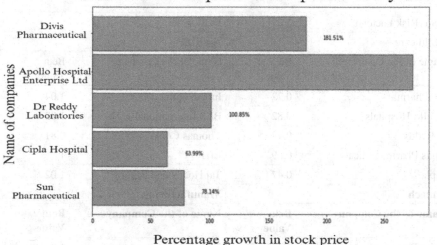

Fig. 3. 5 year growth rate for Healthcare Industry

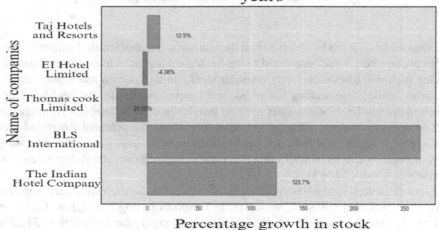

Fig. 4. 5 year growth rate for Tourism Industryls

value of 1.04. The beta values for the fintech companies range from 0.8 to 1.42, with Bajaj Finserv having the highest beta value of 1.42. Finally, the beta values for the manufacturing companies range from 0.57 to 1.36, with JSW Steel having the highest beta value of 1.36.

Table 2. Risk Comparison of stocks under different industries

Beta (Risk Factor)			
Healthcare		Tourism	
Name of the Company	Beta Value	Name of the Company	Beta Value
SunPharma	0.72	Indian Hotel	1.04
Apollo Hospitals	0.82	BLS International	1.02
DrReddy	0.42	Thomas Cook	0.81
Divis Pharmaceuticals	0.69	EIH	1
Cipla	0.47	Taj Hotels and Resorts	1.02
Fintech		**Manufacturing**	
Name of the Company	**Beta Value**	**Name of the Company**	**Beta Value**
Bajaj Finserv	1.42	Tata Steel	1.2
Kotak	1.03	Lupin	0.57
OnMobile	1.02	GMR Infrastructure	1.17
Intellect	1.11	JSW Steel	1.36
Tanla	0.8	Reliance Industries	1.09

From the table, it can be observed that the tourism and manufacturing industries have higher average beta values compared to the healthcare and fintech industries. Investors seeking high-risk investments may consider stocks in the tourism and manufacturing industries, while those seeking lower-risk investments may prefer the healthcare and fintech industries. The CAGR values provide insights into the historical performance of each company and sector, allowing investors to evaluate the potential returns of their investments. A high CAGR indicates that the investment has grown at a faster rate, while a low or negative CAGR indicates that the investment has grown at a slower rate or has experienced losses (Table 3).

From the table, it can be observed that the CAGR values for the healthcare companies range from 10.79% to 30.48%, with Apollo Hospitals having the highest CAGR of 30.48%. The tourism companies have CAGR values ranging from −6.47% to 31.28%, with BLS International having the highest CAGR of 31.28%. The fintech companies have CAGR values ranging from 9.36% to 84.33%, with Tanla having the highest CAGR of 84.33%. Finally, the manufacturing companies have CAGR values ranging from −3.86% to 32.74%, with Tata Steel having the highest CAGR of 32.74%.

The liquidity of a stock represents how easily it can be bought or sold in the market without affecting its price. It is an important factor to consider while making investment decisions, as high liquidity stocks offer better opportunities for trading and are less risky (Table 4).

Table 3. CAGR of stocks under different industries

CAGR for given sectors			
Healthcare		Tourism	
Name of the Company	CAGR	Name of the Company	CAGR
SunPharma	13.41	Indian Hotel	17.81
Apollo Hospitals	30.48	BLS International	31.28
DrReddy	10.79	Thomas Cook	−6.47
Divis Pharmaceuticals	23.61	EIH	−0.19
Cipla	10.9	Taj Hotels and Resorts	2.27
Fintech		**Manufacturing**	
Name of the Company	**CAGR**	**Name of the Company**	**CAGR**
Bajaj Finserv	21.42	Tata Steel	32.74
Kotak	9.39	Lupin	−3.86
OnMobile	9.36	GMR Infrastructure	14.9
Intellect	18.83	JSW Steel	20.85
Tanla	84.33	Reliance	20.81

Table 4. Liquidity of stocks under Fintech Industry

Liquidity Of Given Companies			
Healthcare		Tourism	
Name of the Company	Liquidity	Name of the Company	Liquidity
SunPharma	6705409.99	Indian Hotel	3645224
Apollo Hospitals	836715.117	BLS International	1535135
DrReddy	211155.29	Thomas Cook	778295.9
Divis Pharaceuticals	746349.138	EIH	589360.8
Cipla	3615510.77	Taj Hotels and Resorts	178428.9
Fintech		**Manufacturing**	
Name of the Company	**Liquidity**	**Name of the Company**	**Liquidity**
Bajaj Finserv	4088395.69	Tata Steel	1.17E + 08
Kotak	3529461.8	Lupin	2160923
OnMobile	683453.153	GMR Infrastructure	20094387
Intellect	448839.1	JSW Steel	6901180
Tanla	357559.466	Reliance	9962274

For the healthcare and tourism industry, SunPharma has the highest liquidity value of 6705409.99, followed by Cipla with a liquidity value of 3615510.77. Among the tourism industry stocks, Indian Hotel has a liquidity value of 3645224, and Taj Hotels and Resorts have the lowest liquidity value of 178428.9.

In the fintech and manufacturing industry, Tata Steel has the highest liquidity value of 1.17E + 08, followed by Reliance with a liquidity value of 9962274. Among the fintech stocks, Bajaj Finserv has a liquidity value of 4088395.69, and OnMobile has the lowest liquidity value of 683453.153.

Portfolio Optimization

The research methodology for portfolio optimization involves a multi-step process. The stocks are selected based on specific filters, including short-term and long-term returns, risk, liquidity, volume traded, and growth in the last five years. The theory employed for this research is the Modern Portfolio Theory, which seeks to maximize the expected return of a portfolio for a given level of risk by diversifying investments among different assets. The expected return of the portfolio is calculated by weighting the individual assets' returns. The portfolio's risk is determined by the proportion invested in each security, their individual risks, and their correlation or covariance. To represent all possible portfolio combinations, an efficient frontier is generated, which depicts the best possible risk-return tradeoff for a given set of stocks (Figs. 5 and 6).

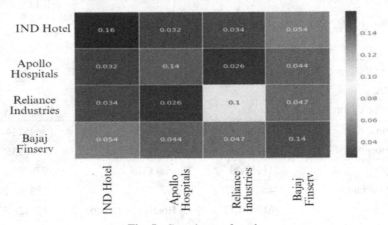

Fig. 5. Covariance of stock

Covariance is used to understand the reduction of risk by avoiding uncorrelated or non-related bets in the stock market. The graph shows the covariance or correlation between the stocks of all companies. There is a positive relationship between the companies, indicating that they tend to move in the same direction. However, there is no high correlation between any of the companies, suggesting that they are not highly dependent on each other. This is a good sign as it allows an investor to diversify their funds based on the risk and return of each stock, as the stocks are not affecting each other significantly.

By investing in a portfolio that includes stocks from these companies, we can potentially reduce the overall risk of our investment without sacrificing returns. This helps to

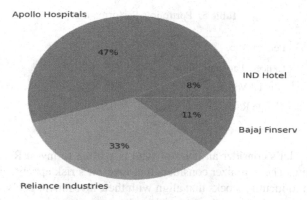

Fig. 6. Fund Allocation in Portfolio

minimize the risk of losing money in the market and provides a safer investment option. This approach can help to maximize returns while minimizing risk, providing a better chance of achieving investment goals over the long term.

The allocation of funds is represented by the optimizer based on the given parameters. The highest weightage is given to Apollo Hospitals, suggesting that it is perceived as having lower risk and a good market position compared to the other companies in the portfolio. The allocation in the graph only shows the percentage of funds allocated to each company based on the risk and return factors.

The graph also indicates the allocation percentages for the other companies in the portfolio, which are relatively lower compared to Apollo Hospitals. This suggests that the optimizer may have identified higher levels of risk associated with these companies or lower potential for returns. The expected annual return of 25.5% for a portfolio is quite high and suggests that the portfolio has the potential to generate significant returns for investors. However, the annual volatility of 25.9% indicates that the portfolio carries a relatively high level of risk. The Sharpe ratio of 0.91 is a measure of risk-adjusted return, which indicates the excess return earned by the portfolio for each unit of risk taken. A Sharpe ratio of 0.91 is relatively good, as it indicates that the portfolio is generating returns that are higher than the risk-free rate for each unit of risk taken. The high expected annual return of the portfolio is attractive, but the high annual volatility suggests that the portfolio may not be suitable for all investors. The Sharpe ratio of 0.98 indicates that the portfolio is generating returns that are higher than the risk-free rate for each unit of risk taken, which is a positive sign. However, investors should consider their own risk tolerance and investment goals when evaluating the suitability of this portfolio for their own needs.

The optimizer helps an investor to make better investment decisions. It takes input from the investor on the funds they want to invest and uses this information to allocate their funds across a range of stocks. The optimizer considers various factors, such as the risk and reward of the stocks provided, current market conditions, and the current market price, to allocate the funds in a manner that minimizes risk and maximizes returns (Table 5).

Table 5. Portfolio's Performance

Performance	
Expected annual return	25.50%
Annual Volatility	25.90%
Sharpe Ratio	0.91

For example, let's consider an investor who is willing to invest Rs. 50,000 with a good risk appetite. The optimizer considers that investor's risk appetite is high and use this information to identify stocks that align with their investment goals. The optimizer algorithm determines the best allocation of funds across these stocks. The optimizer's output would be an allocation plan that shows how the investor's funds should be invested across a range of stocks. The allocation plan would provide information on the amount of funds allocated to each stock, based on the investor's risk appetite and the optimizer's assessment of the stock's potential risk and reward (Table 6).

Table 6. Dummy Portfolio Plan

Amount	50000
Stock	**Number of Stocks to Buy**
The Indian Hotel Company	13
Apollo Hospital Enterprise Limited	5
Reliance Industries	7
Bajaj Finserv	5

6 Conclusion

In conclusion, this research paper has highlighted a data-driven approach for analyzing and optimizing portfolios for the top funded industries based on the budget'23. The study has utilized specific filters such as short-term and long-term returns, risk, liquidity, volume traded, and growth in the last five years, based on the Modern Portfolio Theory, to identify the best investment opportunities. The results indicate that the optimized portfolios can maximize returns while minimizing risk, providing valuable insights for investors and fund managers. The study also emphasizes the importance of considering the budget constraints while optimizing portfolios. The use of an optimizer is an effective tool for making informed investment decisions that minimize risk and maximize returns. The study concludes that investing in portfolios comprising of stocks from diverse industries with low correlation could potentially reduce overall investment risk without sacrificing returns. Nonetheless, investors should assess their risk tolerance and investment goals before making any investment decisions.

References

1. India Budget | Ministry of Finance | Government of India. (n.d.). https://www.indiabudget.gov.in/
2. Zhang, Z., et al.: Deep learning for portfolio optimization. J. Finan. Data Sci. **2**(4), 8–20 (2020). https://doi.org/10.3905/jfds.2020.1.042. Accessed 1 May 2021
3. Mahendra Reddy, D., et al.: Stock market analysis using LSTM in deep learning. Int. J. Eng. Res. **V9**(04), (2020). https://doi.org/10.17577/ijertv9is040649
4. The application of monte carlo simulation and mean-variance in portfolio selection. BCP Bus. Manage. **26**, 1216–1221 (2022). https://doi.org/10.54691/bcpbm.v26i.2089. Accessed 13 Oct. 2022
5. Zandi, G., et al.: Research on stock portfolio based on time series prediction and multi-objective optimization. Adv. Math. Sci. J. **10**(3), 1509–1528 (2021). https://doi.org/10.37418/amsj.10.3.37. Accessed 18 Oct 2021
6. Huang, Y., Abdul, B.: Application of predictive data analytics to model time series forecasting of petroleum production. SSRN Electron. J. (2022). https://doi.org/10.2139/ssrn.4007905. Accessed 14 Mar. 2022
7. Kim, H.Y., Chang, H.W.: Forecasting the volatility of stock price index: a hybrid model integrating LSTM with multiple GARCH-type models. Expert Syst. Appl. **103**, 25–37 (2018). www.sciencedirect.com/science/article/pii/S0957417418301416, https://doi.org/10.1016/j.eswa.2018.03.002
8. Shinzato, T.: Minimal investment risk of a portfolio optimization problem with budget and investment concentration constraints. J. Stat. Mech. Theor. Exp. **2017**(2), 023301 (2017), https://doi.org/10.1088/1742-5468/aa56a0. Accessed 19 July 2020
9. Chen, W., et al.: Mean–variance portfolio optimization using machine learning-based stock price prediction. Appl. Soft Comput. **100**, 106943 (2021). https://doi.org/10.1016/j.asoc.2020.106943
10. Maciel, L.: Financial interval time series modelling and forecasting using threshold autoregressive models. Int. J. Bus. Innov. Res. (2019). www.semanticscholar.org/paper/0e63a679b5ae37ec7574ffd44bd171ed08fc534e. Accessed 6 Mar 2023
11. Wei, H., et al.: Model and data-driven system portfolio selection based on value and risk. Appl. Sci. **9**(8), 1657 (2019). https://doi.org/10.3390/app9081657. Accessed 6 Mar. 2023
12. Arora, N., Parimala, M.: Financial analysis: stock market prediction using deep learning algorithms. SSRN Electron. J. (2019). https://doi.org/10.2139/ssrn.3358252. Accessed 20 Apr. 2019
13. Li, Q., Wenyue, Z.: The application of monte carlo simulation and mean-variance in portfolio selection. BCP Bus. Manage. 26, 1216–1221 (2022). https://doi.org/10.54691/bcpbm.v26i.2089. Accessed 13 Oct 2022
14. Opartpunyasarn, R.: International portfolio optimisation under nonlinear dependence of asset returns. SSRN Electron. J. (2022). https://doi.org/10.2139/ssrn.4249665. Accessed 6 Mar 2023

AI Insights: Unleashing Financial Distress Signals

Devraj Deshmukh[✉], Nishant Mishra, Kshitij Tripathi, Rohan Menon,
and Amit Aylani

Vidyalankar Institute of Technology, Mumbai, India
{devraj.deshmukh,nishant.mishra,kshitij.tripathi,
rohan.menon}@vit.edu.in

Abstract. Bankruptcy prediction is an important problem in finance since successful predictions would allow stakeholders to take early actions to limit their economic losses. In recent years, many studies have explored the application of machine learning models to bankruptcy prediction with financial ratios as predictors. Bankruptcies can lead to substantial financial losses, and the ability to anticipate such events is of paramount importance. This paper explored different models and techniques for bankruptcy prediction, indicating a diverse range of approaches to tackle the problem. Over the years, researchers have developed various models and techniques to predict bankruptcy based on financial and non-financial indicators. This paper represents a bankruptcy prediction model with a high accuracy rate.

Keywords: Bankruptcy · Financial losses · Sustainability · Machine learning

1 Introduction

Bankruptcy prediction models have become increasingly important in financial research and decision-making, especially since the 2008 monetary crisis. The ability to predict the likelihood of a company's financial distress or bankruptcy allows for proactive management and mitigation of risk, and can help investors, creditors, and regulators make more informed decisions. In recent years, there has been growing interest in the development and evaluation of more accurate and reliable bankruptcy prediction models. This research area has seen significant advancements in machine learning techniques, allowing for the incorporation of larger and more diverse datasets, as well as the creation of more sophisticated algorithms [1].

It has significant consequences for both the debtor and creditors. For debtors, bankruptcy can result in the loss of assets, damage to credit, and potentially the inability to obtain credit in the future. For creditors, bankruptcy can result in the loss of funds owed, and potentially the inability to recover debts in full.

Bankruptcy can be a challenging and emotional process, but it can also be an opportunity for debtors to obtain relief from overwhelming debt and start anew. It is important for debtors and creditors alike to understand the legal and financial implications

M. A. Jabbar et al. (Eds.): AMLDA 2023, CCIS 2047, pp. 180–198, 2024.
https://doi.org/10.1007/978-3-031-55486-5_14

of bankruptcy and to seek professional advice before making any decisions related to the bankruptcy process. It can be caused by a variety of factors, including economic downturns, mismanagement, high debt levels, and unexpected expenses.

In some cases, bankruptcy can be avoided by taking proactive measures to manage debt, such as reducing expenses, negotiating with creditors, or seeking professional financial advice. For individuals and companies considering bankruptcy, it is important to understand the legal and financial implications and to seek professional advice to make informed decisions [2].

The Silicon Valley Bank, flush with cash, had bought enormous amounts of bonds more than a year ago. Like other banks, it kept a small amount of the deposits on hand and invested the rest with the hope of earning a return. However, it didn't last long as the Federal Reserve kept on raising interest rates to taper down inflation since last year.

And at the same time, a start-up funding freeze put pressure on the bank's clients, who then began to withdraw their money.

To pay those requests, SVB was forced to sell off some of its investments at a time when their value had declined. In its surprise disclosure on Wednesday, the bank said it had lost nearly $2 billion. Apart from that, SVB's deposit inflows became as outflows as its clients burned cash and stopped getting new funds from public offerings or fundraisings. Getting new deposits also became far more expensive, as the deposit rates were rising with the Fed's hikes. As a result, deposits fell from nearly $200 billion at the end of March 2022 to $173 billion at year-end 2022 [3].

This research paper aims to explore the different approaches and methodologies used in bankruptcy prediction modeling, including traditional statistical methods, machine learning techniques, and hybrid models. Additionally, the study will examine the effectiveness and reliability of these models in predicting financial distress and bankruptcy, as well as identify any limitations and challenges in the development and evaluation of such models. The insights gained from this research can provide valuable guidance to investors, creditors, and regulators in making informed decisions about managing financial risk.

2 Literature Review

When the first econometric indicators were put forth to describe the predictive capabilities of business failure (Fitzpatrick, 1932; Merwin, 1942; Winakor & Smith, 1935) [4], the first formal attempts at bankruptcy prediction were made. In the study of the early detection of business failure symptoms, the 1960s marked a turning point in history. First off, Beaver's work from 1966 was the first to apply statistical models to bankruptcy prediction. Following this line of reasoning, others (Altman & Loris, 1976; Blum, 1974; Deakin, 1972; Edmister, 1972; Ketz, 1978; Koh & Killough, 1990; Laitinen, 1991; Libby, 1975; Meyer & Pifer, 1970; Pettway & Sinkey, 1980; Rujoub, Cook, & Hay, 1992) proposed using multidimensional analysis to predict corporate bankruptcy.

In parallel, a great interest was paid to the generalized linear models that can be used in both decision making and providing certainty of the prediction (Aziz, Emanuel, & Lawson, 1988; Grice & Dugan, 2003; Hopwood, McKeown, & Mutchler, 1994; Koh, 1991; Li & Miu, 2010; Ohlson, 1980; Platt & Platt, 1990; Platt, Platt, & Pedersen, 1994;

Zavgren, 1983; Zmijewski, 1984) [5]. Furthermore, the estimated weights of the model's linear combination of economic indicators are of particular interest because they can be used to further assess the significance of the economic indicators. In the bankruptcy prediction field, artificial intelligence and machine learning have grown significantly since the 1990s. The linear models turned out to be more effective in the era of growing data volumes. Furthermore, the estimated weights of the linear models, which indicate the significance of the metrics, are rather unreliable.

Decision rules expressed in terms of first-order logic were induced using various techniques, to name just a few, such as rough sets (Dimitras, Slowinski, Susmaga, & Zopounidis, 1999) [6] or evolutionary programming, in order to obtain understandable models with an understandable knowledge representation. More precise methods were used to predict bankruptcy because the classification accuracy of the decision rules is often insufficient. Support vector machines (SVM) was one of the best models. The kernel function of SVM must be carefully hand-tuned, and it is impossible to produce a model that is understandable.

A different strategy aims to automatically combine non-linear econometric indicators from data, which solves the problem of deciding a specific kernel function in the context of SVM. This approach applies neural networks to the bankruptcy prediction (Bell, Ribar, & Verchio, 1990; Cadden, 1991; Coats & Fant, 1991; Geng, Bose, & Chen, 2015; Koster, Sondak, & Bourbia, 1991; Salchenberger, Cinar, & Lash, 1992; Serrano- Cinca, 1996; Tam, 1991; Tam & Kiang, 1992; Wilson & Sharda, 1994; Zhang, Hu, Patuwo, & Indro, 1999) [7]. The main issue with neural networks is that multimodal data can cause them to malfunction. To ensure that all features are of the same size, the econometric metrics must typically be normalized or standardized.

Shetty et al. (2022) In this study, advanced machine learning techniques were employed, encompassing the utilization of extreme gradient boosting (XGBoost), support vector machine (SVM), and a deep neural network, to forecast bankruptcy utilizing readily available financial data of 3728 Belgian Small and Medium Enterprises (SMEs) over the span of 2002–2012. The focus of the investigation was on achieving predictive accuracy through the application of these sophisticated machine learning models. Notably, the outcomes demonstrated a global accuracy ranging between 82–83%, an impressive feat considering the exclusive reliance on merely three easily obtainable financial ratios. This research highlights the potential of leveraging cutting-edge machine learning methodologies for robust bankruptcy prediction models, emphasizing the efficiency and effectiveness of these techniques in the financial domain [8].

3   Methodology

We presented a formal problem statement for bankruptcy prediction in the preceding section. We describe the method we used to obtain benchmark results for this problem in this section. To begin, we will introduce the Taiwan bankruptcy dataset that we used for our analysis. We describe the dataset in detail, including its features, instances, and data organization.

These steps aim to enhance the quality, consistency, and reliability of the data, enabling more accurate and meaningful analysis. The following professional data preprocessing techniques were applied to the dataset, which was sourced as a sample from

Kaggle It allows users to find and publish data sets, explore, and build models in a web-based data-science environment which are largely present in Public Domain. Following with the data preprocessing, classification models that considered for analysis. Also explain how to use these models to train data and supply insights into their strengths and limitations. At last, assess these models' performance using various metrics such as accuracy and precision.

3.1 Data

The data were collected from the Taiwan Economic Journal for the years 1999 to 2009. Company bankruptcy was defined based on the business regulations of the Taiwan Stock Exchange from Kaggle.

1. The number of company bankruptcies in Taiwan steadily declined over this period. In 1999, there were 8,195 company bankruptcies, compared to only 3,195 in 2009 - a 61% decline. This decline coincided with Taiwan's economic recovery and growth during this period.
2. Most bankruptcies were among small and medium enterprises (SMEs). For example, in 2009, SMEs accounted for 98.8% of bankruptcies. This highlights the greater vulnerability of SMEs during economic downturns.
3. The manufacturing sector accounted for the largest number of bankruptcies. For example, in 2009, manufacturing companies made up 30.7% of all bankruptcies. The wholesale and retail trade sector came second, accounting for 14.8% of bankruptcies. These sectors were most affected by the Asian Financial Crisis of the late 1990s and early 2000s recession.
4. Taipei City and Kaohsiung City had the highest numbers of company bankruptcies. For example, in 2009, Taipei City and Kaohsiung City accounted for 22.9% and 12.5% of bankruptcies, respectively. This is not surprising given these cities have the largest business concentrations.
5. The Variables Used for this Analysis.
    1. Y - Bankrupt?: Class label
    2. X1 - ROA(C) before interest and depreciation before interest: Return On Total Assets(C)
    3. X2 - ROA(A) before interest and % after tax: Return On Total Assets(A)
    4. X3 - ROA(B) before interest and depreciation after tax: Return On Total Assets(B)
    5. X4 - Operating Gross Margin: Gross Profit/Net Sales
    6. X5 - Realized Sales Gross Margin: Realized Gross Profit/Net Sales
    7. X6 - Operating Profit Rate: Operating Income/Net Sales
    8. X7 - Pre-tax net Interest Rate: Pre-Tax Income/Net Sales
    9. X8 - After-tax net Interest Rate: Net Income/Net Sales
    10. X9 - Non-industry income and expenditure/revenue: Net Non-operating Income Ratio
    11. X10 - Continuous interest rate (after tax): Net Income-Exclude Disposal Gain or Loss/Net Sales
    12. X11 - Operating Expense Rate: Operating Expenses/Net Sales
    13. X12 - Research and development expense rate: (Research and Development Expenses)/Net Sales

14. X13 - Cash flow rate: Cash Flow from Operating/Current Liabilities
15. X14 - Interest-bearing debt interest rate: Interest-bearing Debt/Equity
16. X15 - Tax rate (A): Effective Tax Rate
17. X16 - Net Value Per Share (B): Book Value Per Share(B)
18. X17 - Net Value Per Share (A): Book Value Per Share(A)
19. X18 - Net Value Per Share (C): Book Value Per Share(C)
20. X19 - Persistent EPS in the Last Four Seasons: EPS-Net Income
21. X20 - Cash Flow Per Share
22. X21 - Revenue Per Share (Yuan ¥): Sales Per Share
23. X22 - Operating Profit Per Share (Yuan ¥): Operating Income Per Share
24. X23 - Per Share Net profit before tax (Yuan ¥): Pretax Income Per Share
25. X24 - Realized Sales Gross Profit Growth Rate
26. X25 - Operating Profit Growth Rate: Operating Income Growth
27. X26 - After-tax Net Profit Growth Rate: Net Income Growth
28. X27 - Regular Net Profit Growth Rate: Continuing Operating Income after Tax Growth
29. X28 - Continuous Net Profit Growth Rate: Net Income-Excluding Disposal Gain or Loss Growth
30. X29 - Total Asset Growth Rate: Total Asset Growth
31. X30 - Net Value Growth Rate: Total Equity Growth
32. X31 - Total Asset Return Growth Rate Ratio: Return on Total Asset Growth
33. X32 - Cash Reinvestment %: Cash Reinvestment Ratio
34. X33 - Current Ratio
35. X34 - Quick Ratio: Acid Test
36. X35 - Interest Expense Ratio: Interest Expenses/Total Revenue
37. X36 - Total debt/Total net worth: Total Liability/Equity Ratio
38. X37 - Debt ratio %: Liability/Total Assets
39. X38 - Net worth/Assets: Equity/Total Assets
40. X39 - Long-term fund suitability ratio (A): (Long-term Liability + Equity)/Fixed Assets
41. X40 - Borrowing dependency: Cost of Interest-bearing Debt
42. X41 - Contingent liabilities/Net worth: Contingent Liability/Equity
43. X42 - Operating profit/Paid-in capital: Operating Income/Capital
44. X43 - Net profit before tax/Paid-in capital: Pretax Income/Capital
45. X44 - Inventory and accounts receivable/Net value:(Inventory + Accounts Receivables)/Equity
46. X45 - Total Asset Turnover
47. X46 - Accounts Receivable Turnover
48. X47 - Average Collection Days: Days Receivable Outstanding
49. X48 - Inventory Turnover Rate (times)
50. X49 - Fixed Assets Turnover Frequency
51. X50 - Net Worth Turnover Rate (times): Equity Turnover
52. X51 - Revenue per person: Sales Per Employee
53. X52 - Operating profit per person: Operation Income Per Employee
54. X53 - Allocation rate per person: Fixed Assets Per Employee

55. X54 - Working Capital to Total Assets
56. X55 - Quick Assets/Total Assets
57. X56 - Current Assets/Total Assets
58. X57 - Cash/Total Assets
59. X58 - Quick Assets/Current Liability
60. X59 - Cash/Current Liability
61. X60 - Current Liability to Assets
62. X61 - Operating Funds to Liability
63. X62 - Inventory/Working Capital
64. X63 - Inventory/Current Liability
65. X64 - Current Liabilities/Liability
66. X65 - Working Capital/Equity
67. X66 - Current Liabilities/Equity
68. X67 - Long-term Liability to Current Assets
69. X68 - Retained Earnings to Total Assets
70. X69 - Total income/Total expense
71. X70 - Total expense/Assets
72. X71 - Current Asset Turnover Rate: Current Assets to Sales
73. X72 - Quick Asset Turnover Rate: Quick Assets to Sales
74. X73 - Working capitcal Turnover Rate: Working Capital to Sales
75. X74 - Cash Turnover Rate: Cash to Sales
76. X75 - Cash Flow to Sales
77. X76 - Fixed Assets to Assets
78. X77 - Current Liability to Liability
79. X78 - Current Liability to Equity
80. X79 - Equity to Long-term Liability
81. X80 - Cash Flow to Total Assets
82. X81 - Cash Flow to Liability
83. X82 - CFO to Assets
84. X83 - Cash Flow to Equity
85. X84 - Current Liability to Current Assets
86. X85 - Liability-Assets Flag: 1 if Total Liability exceeds Total Assets, 0 otherwise
87. X86 - Net Income to Total Assets
88. X87 - Total assets to GNP price
89. X88 - No-credit Interval
90. X89 - Gross Profit to Sales
91. X90 - Net Income to Stockholder's Equity
92. X91 - Liability to Equity
93. X92 - Degree of Financial Leverage (DFL)
94. X93 - Interest Coverage Ratio (Interest expense to EBIT)
95. X94 - Net Income Flag: 1 if Net Income is Negative for the last two years, 0 otherwise
96. X95 - Equity to Liability.

The reason of selecting this dataset over other dataset was mainly the large number of attributes that are available. However, SMEs and certain sectors like manufacturing remained vulnerable. Geographically, most bankruptcies were concentrated in the largest cities. Common causes of bankruptcies pointed to weak profitability, poor management, and high debt levels [9].

3.2 Data Cleaning

Data cleaning involves identifying and correcting errors and inconsistencies in the data. This may involve removing duplicate records, correcting spelling errors, and resolving inconsistencies in data values. Data cleaning is critical to ensuring that the data is correct and reliable, which is essential for making informed decisions based on the data.

When collecting and cleaning data for bankruptcy prediction, it is critical to keep privacy and data security in mind. The data collected should only include information relevant to the study's purpose and should be obtained with informed consent from the sources if necessary. The data should be protected during the handling process to prevent unauthorized access or leaks.

3.3 Data Preprocessing

Data preprocessing involves transforming the raw data into a format that is suitable for analysis. This process includes removing errors, inconsistencies, and missing values from the data, as well as transforming the data into a more structured and organized format. This includes data normalization, feature scaling, and feature selection. Data normalization involves scaling the data to a common range of values, which is important for ensuring that all features contribute equally to the analysis. Feature scaling involves adjusting the scale of individual features to reduce the influence of outliers and improve the accuracy of the analysis. Feature selection involves selecting the most relevant features for analysis and removing irrelevant or redundant features.

Overall, data preprocessing and cleaning are critical steps in the data analysis process, as they ensure that the data is correct, reliable, and suitable for analysis. By performing these steps, analysts can obtain insights from the data that can inform decision-making and drive business success. Considering the proposed approach, we have learnt about normalization, feature scaling, and feature selection. However, the data-model which we used was pre-processed and clean. The model was taken as a reference from a web-based data-science environment which is largely present in Public Domain by Kaggle.

4 Proposed Approach

Synthetic Minority Oversampling Technique (SMOTE) is a widely used oversampling technique. To illustrate how this technique works consider some training data which has S samples, and f features in the feature space of the data. For simplicity, assume the features are continuous. As an example, let us consider a dataset of birds for clarity. The feature space for the minority class for which we want to oversample could be beak length, wingspan, and weight. To oversample, take a sample from the dataset, and consider its k nearest neighbors in the feature space. To create a synthetic data point, take the vector between one of those k neighbors, and the current data point. Multiply this vector by a random number x which lies between 0, and 1. Adding this to the current data point will create a new synthetic data point. SMOTE was implemented from the imbalanced learn library (Fig. 1).

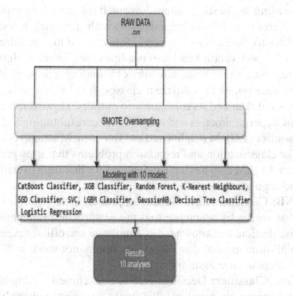

Fig. 1. System Architecture

In this section, we will look at the various classification models that we considered for training on the Taiwanese bankruptcy datasets to create a predictive model that can accurately predict the bankruptcy status of a given (unseen) company. We considered the nine models listed below:

A. **CatBoost Classifier:** CatBoost is a machine learning algorithm for classification and regression problems that uses gradient boosting on decision trees. Efficient handling of categorical variables commonly found in bankruptcy datasets, such as industry classification codes and corporate governance indicators. It also has built-in features for handling overfitting, such as early stopping and regularization.

B. **XGB Classifier:** XGBoost (Extreme Gradient Boosting) is a popular machine learning algorithm for classification and regression problems that uses gradient boosting on decision trees. Extreme gradient boosting is known for its execution speed and model performance. It is widely used in industry and has won numerous machine learning competitions.

C. **Random Forest:** Random Forest is a machine learning algorithm for classification and regression problems that uses an ensemble of decision trees. It minimizes overfitting, a common problem in decision tree models, by generating a multitude of decision trees during training and creating an average prediction class of each individual tree.

D. **K-Nearest Neighbors:** K-Nearest Neighbors is a non-parametric algorithm for classification and regression problems that works by finding the k-nearest neighbors to a given data point and using their labels to make a prediction. The market dynamics that impact bankruptcy predictions are often complex, interconnected, and nonlinear, which the K-NN algorithm can effectively learn from [11]

E. **SGD Classifier:** The SGD Classifier is a linear classifier that works by minimizing a loss function using stochastic gradient descent. It is known for its speed and efficiency, as well as its ability to handle large datasets with high dimensionality. However, it can be sensitive to the choice of hyperparameters and may require careful tuning.

F. **SVC:** SVC (Support Vector Machine) is a linear or nonlinear algorithm for classification and regression problems that works by finding a hyperplane that maximally separates the data points into different classes. It is known for its ability to handle high-dimensional data and its robustness to outliers. However, it can be sensitive to the choice of hyperparameters and may require careful tuning.[12]

G. **LGBM Classifier:** LGBM (Light Gradient Boosting Machine) is a machine learning algorithm for classification and regression problems that uses gradient boosting on decision trees. LGBM also has built-in features for handling overfitting, such as early stopping and regularization.

H. **Gaussian NB:** Gaussian Naive Bayes is a probabilistic algorithm for classification problems that works by assuming that the features are independent and follow a Gaussian distribution. It is known for its simplicity and efficiency, as well as its ability to handle high-dimensional data. However, it may not work well with datasets that violate the independence assumption.

I. **Decision Tree Classifier:** Decision Tree is a machine learning algorithm for classification and regression problems that works by recursively splitting the data into subsets based on the most informative feature. However, it can be sensitive to the choice of hyperparameters and may suffer from overfitting.

J. **Logistic Regression:** Logistic regression is a supervised machine learning algorithm mainly used for classification tasks where the goal is to predict the probability that an instance of belonging to a given class. The difference between linear regression and logistic regression is that linear regression output is the continuous value that can be anything while logistic regression predicts the probability that an instance belongs to a given class or not [13].

5   Result

The following are the results after implementation of various models. The number of exact and inaccurate predictions made by the model for each class is displayed in the confusion matrix. The actual negative class is represented by the first row in this instance, and the actual positive class is represented by the second row. The predicted negative class is represented by the first column, and the predicted positive class is represented by the second column.

5.1   CatBoost Classifier

The model's accuracy of 95.97% shows that it correctly predicted bankruptcy in nearly 96% of all cases. While this suggests that the model is effective, there are more metrics to consider in order to gain a better understanding of the model's performance.

The recall of 52.5% shows that the model correctly identified 52.5% of all actual positive instances. When discussing a bankruptcy prediction model, recall is critical because it is critical to identify as many actual bankruptcy cases as possible to mitigate financial risks. A lower recall could result in many bankruptcies going unnoticed, implying that the model is overly cautious. It is so careful to avoid false positives (predicting a bankruptcy that does not occur) that it is missing a considerable number of actual bankruptcies.

The figure of 36.84% writes down that the model was correct in 36.84% of the cases where it predicted bankruptcy. This could imply that, while the model's overall accuracy is high, its false positive rate is higher. This may result in unnecessary preventive measures or missed investment opportunities in the context of bankruptcy prediction.

The F1 score combines both precision and recall into a single metric, seeking a balance between both. An F1 score of 43.3% might suggest that the model is not doing well in supporting this balance and that there may be room for improvement (Fig. 2).

```
CatBoost Classifier
Confusion Matrix:
[[1288    36]
 [  19    21]]
Accuracy :  95.96774193548387
Recall :  52.5
Precision :  36.84210526315789
F1 :  43.29896907216495
```

Fig. 2. Accuracy score of CatBoost

5.2 XGB

The model's performance metrics supply significant insights into its effectiveness. With an accuracy of 96.04%, the model correctly classified a high percentage of instances, indicating that its overall ability to predict both positive and negative outcomes is quite impressive. However, to delve deeper into its precision in predicting positive instances, we must look at recall and precision.

The model's recall rate is 50.0%, which means it correctly identifies only half of all actual positive instances, resulting in a notable number of false negatives – cases where the model mistakenly predicts a negative outcome for situations that are actually positive.

On the precision front, the model's score is 37.04%, suggesting some over- prediction with several cases being wrongly identified as positive (false positives).

The F1 score, which combines precision and recall, is 42.55%, emphasizing the need for improvement in the model's capacity to correctly identify positive cases while simultaneously reducing both false positives and false negatives.

These metrics reveal potential areas for improvement in the model's ability to correctly identify positive instances, a critical aspect in fields such as healthcare, spam detection, and fraud prediction.

Understanding these dynamics empowers us to further refine the model and reduce the likelihood of incorrect positive predictions, ultimately leading us towards more dependable and precise outcomes (Fig. 3).

```
XGB Classifier
Confusion Matrix:
[[1290    34]
 [  20    20]]
Accuracy :   96.04105571847508
Recall :   50.0
Precision :   37.03703703703704
F1 :   42.5531914893617
```

Fig. 3. Accuracy score using XGB.

5.3   Random Forest

The Random Forest model's effectiveness can be measured through various metrics. With an accuracy of 95.60%, the model is exhibiting high proficiency in correctly distinguishing between positive and negative instances overall.

However, considering the full picture with the other metrics can provide a more nuanced understanding.

Contrasting the high accuracy, recall stands at 55.00%. This indicates a moderate rate, suggesting that the model only accurately detected a little over half of all actual positive instances. The model's recall is 55.00%, indicating it correctly detects just over half of actual positive instances, leading to notable false negatives. Precision is at 34.38%, signifying a struggle to precisely identify positives, resulting in considerable false positives.

Despite high accuracy, the model's recall is at 55.00%, suggesting room for improvement in correctly identifying positive instances. Precision, at 34.38%, indicates challenges in precise positive identification. The F1 score of 42.31% highlights the need to strike a better balance between minimizing false positives and false negatives in the model.

Despite a relatively high accuracy rate, the model's performance in pinpointing positive instances accurately requires enhancements. The imbalance between the model's accuracy and its recall, precision and F1 score suggests that although it's generally good at predicting, it struggles in correctly identifying positive instances. To elevate the effectiveness of the Random Forest model, a focus on improving its recall and precision and, by extension, the F1 score, is recommended (Fig. 4).

```
Random Forest
Confusion Matrix:
[[1282    42]
 [  18    22]]
Accuracy :  95.60117302052787
Recall :  55.00000000000001
Precision :  34.375
F1 :  42.307692307692314
```

Fig. 4. Accuracy score using Random Forest

5.4 K-Nearest Neighbours

The K-Nearest Neighbours algorithm's performance metrics present a mixed scenario. The accuracy being at 89.52% demonstrates the model's capability to correctly classify instances overall. It means that when asked to predict whether instances were upcoming or negative, the model got it right approximately nine out of ten times. While the accuracy appears promising, a deeper analysis via other metrics offers additional details on the model's abilities.

Recall for this model is 67.5%, which can be seen as a relatively strong level. This suggests that when faced with a set of actual positive instances, the model could successfully identify around two-thirds of them, showcasing respectable sensitivity. However, this also implies that around 32.5% of positive cases went unnoticed, which were incorrectly classified as negative - these are known as false negatives.

On the downside, the precision stands at a lower 17.20%. With precision assessing the proportion of correctly predicted positive instances out of all instances that the model labeled as positive, the low precision score suggests that the model has predicted a substantial number of instances incorrectly as positive - these are false positives. In other words, out of every 100 instances that the model predicts as positive, only approximately 17 are actually accurate.

The F1 score, as an aggregated measure of precision and recall, is only at 27.41%. Considering that the F1 score ideally should be close to 1, this suggests there's a considerable imbalance between precision and recall in the model. The low F1 score hints at a leaning towards a larger volume of false positives, reflected in the lower precision rate, and this disrupts the balance needed for a higher F1 score (Fig. 5).

5.5 SGD Classifier

Classifier provides a mixed performance that can be understood more clearly when we look beyond the accuracy metric. The reported accuracy of 88.86% reveals that the model correctly finds a high percentage of instances, whether they are positive or negative.

Diving into other performance metrics, the model's recall is strong at 77.5%, correctly identifying about three-quarters of actual positive instances. However, it misses approximately 22.5% of positive instances, which are incorrectly classified as negative, indicating room for improvement.

```
K-Nearest Neighbours
Confusion Matrix:
[[1194  130]
 [  13   27]]
Accuracy :  89.51612903225806
Recall :  67.5
Precision :  17.197452229299362
F1 :  27.411167512690355
```

Fig. 5. Accuracy score using K-Nearest Neighbors

On the precision side, it's less promising, with a score of 17.82%, indicating a high rate of false positives – instances incorrectly predicted as positive when they are actually negative. The model tends to be overly optimistic in predicting positives, with only around 18 out of every 100 of these predictions being correct.

The F1 score, the harmonic mean of precision and recall, is 28.97%, suggesting a skewed balance between precision and recall. The lower F1 score reflects a tendency of the model towards falsely identifying negative instances as positive, as suggested by the low precision.

In conclusion, the SGD Classifier, while having a reasonably high accuracy and recall rate, struggles with precision, leading to a low F1 score. Reducing the number of false positives is key to improving model performance (Fig. 6).

```
SGD Classifier
Confusion Matrix:
[[1181  143]
 [   9   31]]
Accuracy :  88.85630498533725
Recall :  77.5
Precision :  17.81609195402299
F1 :  28.971962616822427
```

Fig. 6. Accuracy score using SGD

5.6 SVC

The performance of the SVC (Support Vector Classification) model shines through its accuracy of 92.96%, indicating it correctly classified a majority of instances. Yet, understanding this model's effectiveness requires more than just the surface-level insights provided by accuracy.

The SVC model exhibits a recall of 62.5%, which means it successfully captures a substantial portion of actual positive instances, reflecting its ability to detect relevant information. However, there is still a room for enhancement since approximately 37.5% of positive instances remain undetected, leading to false negatives.

Precision, on the other hand, stands at 23.58%, indicating a relatively high number of false positive predictions. This scenario could pose challenges in practical applications where resources might be wasted on erroneously identified positives.

The F1 score, combining recall and precision, is 34.25%, suggesting a need for further refinement of the model to strike a better balance between identifying more actual positives (higher recall) and minimizing false positive predictions (higher precision).

By incorporating the interpretation of these metrics into our evaluation, we have an expanded view of the performance of the SVC model (Fig. 7).

```
SVC
Confusion Matrix:
[[1243    81]
 [  15    25]]
Accuracy :  92.96187683284457
Recall :  62.5
Precision :  23.58490566037736
F1 :  34.24657534246575
```

Fig. 7. Accuracy score using SVC.

5.7 LGBM

Algorithm is a powerful tool for classification and regression tasks. With an impressive accuracy of 96.70%, the model has an excellent ability to identify the correct class of each instance, irrespective of their positive or negative value.

Analyzing further, the recall rate of the model is 55.00%, implying that the model identifies an outsize proportion of positive instances correctly. However, there might still be room for improvement since almost half of the actual positive instances could be overlooked.

However, the model's precision stands high at 44.90%, indicating a lower rate of false positives, only about 1 in every 2 instances predicted as positive is expected to be accurate.

The F1 score of the model, which combines precision and recall, is an encouraging 49.44%, indicating a reasonable balance between minimizing false positives and addressing missed positive instances.

In summary, the LGBM algorithm appears to be a robust and reliable model for classification tasks as seen by its high accuracy, precision, recall, and F1 score. While there is negligible room for improvement regarding false positives, there is a possibility for better identification of actual positive cases by the model (Fig. 8).

5.8 GaussianNB

The Gaussian Naive Bayes algorithm presents a challenging case, as the accuracy is quite low at 24.34%. Lacking insightful adjustments, this low figure indicates most of

```
LGBM Classifier
Confusion Matrix:
[[1297    27]
 [  18    22]]
Accuracy :   96.7008797653959
Recall :   55.00000000000001
Precision :   44.89795918367347
F1 :    49.43820224719101
```

Fig. 8. Accuracy score using LGBM

the instances are misclassified. However, understanding the recall metric for this model is important, which sits at an encouragingly high 90.0%. Given this, the model can accurately predict most actual positive instances, suggesting that it's potentially useful for identifying any potential positive cases within the data.

Nonetheless, the precision performance is quite poor, standing at just 3.38%. This scenario suggests that the model is highly prone to producing false positives, inaccurately identifying instances as positive that are actually negative. This will lead to wasted resources if used as a classifier. This further presents itself in the low F1 score of 6.52%, which indicates the simultaneous lack of effectiveness for both precision and recall to this model for this use case.

To address these challenges and raise the efficacy of the Gaussian Naive Bayes algorithm, more work needs to be done on its performance in model training and feature selection. That should involve identifying the most relevant features to yield higher accuracy in model calibration. Furthermore, finding better ways to balance precision and recall could enable better performance.

Thus, while the recall for this model is high, the precision's low value has inhibited the model's accuracy in identifying positive instances accurately. With low accuracy and F1 score, there remains ample room for improvement in the effectiveness of the Gaussian Naive Bayes (Fig. 9).

```
GaussianNB
Confusion Matrix:
[[ 296 1028]
 [   4   36]]
Accuracy :   24.34017595307918
Recall :   90.0
Precision :   3.3834586466165413
F1 :   6.521739130434782
```

Fig. 9. Accuracy score using GaussianNB.

5.9 Decision Tree Classifier

The Decision Tree Classifier algorithm offers a robust approach for dealing with classification and regression problems. The accuracy score of this model is notable at 93.77%, indicating that it has an ability to efficiently classify most of the instances in its dataset.

However, one downside of the model is the relatively low recall of 42.5%, indicating that the model was not able to accurately identify a significant portion of actual positive instances, potentially leading to missing potential positive profit streams.

Another shortcoming is its precision, which is at a low 21.52%. This means that the model produces a high rate of false positives, predicting positive instances that are, in reality, negative.

Lastly, F1 score, a measure of precision and recall, is at 28.57%, which translates to a less-productive balance between reducing false positives and improving chances of detecting positive instances.

Overall, while the Decision Tree algorithm displays high accuracy rate, its recognition and false positive detection of actual positives remain relatively low on the recall and precision metrics, respectively, leading to low overall F1 score (Fig. 10).

```
Decision Tree Classifier
Confusion Matrix:
[[1262   62]
 [  23   17]]
Accuracy :  93.76832844574781
Recall :  42.5
Precision :  21.518987341772153
F1 :  28.571428571428577
```

Fig. 10. Accuracy score using Decision tress

5.10 Logistic Regression Algorithm

The linear logistic regression algorithm is a useful tool for solving classification problems through fitting linear relationships between input features and output labels. The model's accuracy of 88.93% suggests a relatively robust predictive performance, as it indicates the model can correctly classify instances in most circumstances.

However, a key metric in investigating the model's overall effectiveness is recall, which sits at a relatively high of 67.5%. This suggests that the model can accurately identify a sizable portion of actual positive instances. But still, there appears to be room for improvement since about 32.5% of actual positives are not identified by the model.

Challenges, however, arise when considering precision, which performs poorly at just 16.36%. This indicates a high rate of false positives, suggesting that a considerable number of instances classified as positive may be negative. Additionally, the F1 score of 26.34%, combining precision and recall, confirms the limitation in performance of the model in correctly identifying positive instances while reducing false positives effectively.

Therefore, addressing the different metrics recorded would aid to improve the performance of the linear logistic regression algorithm [14] (Fig. 11).

```
Logistic Regression
Confusion Matrix:
[[1186  138]
 [  13   27]]
Accuracy :  88.92961876832844
Recall :  67.5
Precision :  16.363636363636363
F1 :  26.34146341463415
```

Fig. 11. Accuracy score using Logistic Regression

6 Result Analysis

In the result analysis comparing different classifiers based on the accuracy and precision score. It allows to visually assess and compare their performance. The graph may have the classifiers plotted on the x-axis, while the y-axis represents the values of accuracy, precision, F1 score. This analysis will help to determine which models perform better in terms of overall correctness or precision or accuracy in positive predictions (Figs. 12 and Table 1).

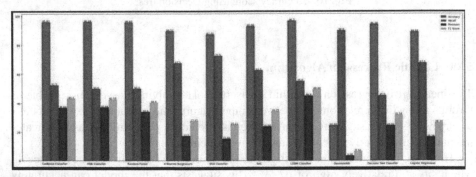

Fig. 12. Output Comparison for all Classifiers

Table 1. Comparison table of all classifiers

Classifiers	Accuracy	Recall	Precision	F1
CatBoost	95.96774193548387	52.5	36.84210526315789	43.29896907216495
XGB	96.04105571847508	50.0	37.03703703703704	42.5531914893617
Random Forest	95.60117302052787	55.0	34.375	42.307692307692314
K-Nearest Neighbours	89.51612903225806	67.5	17.197452229299362	27.411167512690355
SGD Classifier	88.85630498533725	77.5	17.81609195402299	28.971962616822427
SVC	92.96187683284457	62.5	23.58490566037736	34.24657534246575
LGBM	96.7008797653959	55.00	44.89795918367347	49.43820224719101
GaussianNB	24.34017595307918	90.0	3.3834586466165413	6.521739130434782
Decision Tree	93.76832844574781	42.5	21.518987341772153	28.571428571428577
Logistic Regression	88.92961876832844	67.5	16.363636363636363	26.34146341463415

7 Conclusion

Finally, our findings show that the LGBM Classifier outperforms other models in predicting bankruptcy, with an impressive accuracy of 96.7%. This high accuracy demonstrates the model's ability to make overall correct predictions. Furthermore, with an accuracy of 44.9%, the LGBM model has a low misleading positive rate, indicating a lower likelihood of incorrectly predicting company failure when it is not actually at risk. The K-Nearest Neighbours model and the SGD Classifier, on the other hand, have significantly lower precision values of 17.2% and 17.8%, respectively, indicating a higher chance of false positive predictions. The K-Nearest Neighbours model, on the other hand, has a higher recall of 67.5%, indicating a lower rate of false negatives.

Despite having a recall value of 55.0%, indicating a potential higher rate of false negatives, the LGBM model remains a promising choice for bankruptcy prediction. However, it is critical to evaluate the LGBM model's suitability in light of the problem's specific requirements and constraints. Six classification models, including Gaussian Naive Bayes, Logistic Regression, Decision Trees, Random Forests, Extreme Gradient Boosting, and Balanced Bagging, were successfully modelled. We used the Synthetic Minority Oversampling Technique to ensure balanced class labels in the training sets. To handle missing values in the data, we used mean imputation, k-NN, Expectation-Maximization (EM), and Multiple Imputation using Chained Equations (MICE).

Managing incomplete or sparse data was a significant challenge during our research. Because businesses facing bankruptcy do not operate on the same timetables, gathering and organising useful data proved difficult. The factors used to predict bankruptcy are more complex than the financial ratios displayed on the balance sheets of companies, necessitating careful examination and verification. While our research successfully documented the project's best bankruptcy prediction model, it is critical to acknowledge the data's complexity and limitation.

References

1. Kristóf, T., Miklós, V.: A comprehensive review of corporate bankruptcy prediction in Hungary. J. Risk Finan. Manage. **13**(2), 35 (2020)
2. Shetty, S., Musa, M., Brédart, X.: Bankruptcy prediction using machine learning techniques. J. Risk Finan. Manage. **15**(1), 35 (2022)
3. Heskin, D., Jerome, R.C.: How the Coming Global Crash Will Create a Historic Gold Rush. Post Hill Press, New York (2023)
4. Mraihi, F., Kanzari, I.: Failure prediction models: development and comparison between the multivariate discriminant analysis and the support vector machine for Tunisian companies. Int. J. Entrep. Small Bus.Entrep. Small Bus. **43**(3), 411–437 (2021)
5. Wilcox, J.W.: A prediction of business failure using accounting data. J. Account. Res. **11**, 163–179 (1973)
6. Chen, T., He, T.L xgboost: extreme gradient boosting. R package version 0.3–0. Technical Report (2015)
7. Friedman, J.H.: Greedy function approximation: a gradient boosting machine. In: Annals of Statistics, pp. 1189–1232 (2001)
8. Shetty, S., Mohamed, M., Xavier, B.: Bankruptcy prediction using machine learning techniques. J. Risk Financ. Manage. **15**(1), 35 (2022)
9. Wang, H., Liu, X.: Undersampling bankruptcy prediction: Taiwan bankruptcy data. PLoS ONE **16**(7), e0254030 (2021)
10. Friedman, J., Hastie, T., Tibshirani, R.: Additive logistic regression: a statistical view of boosting. Ann. Stat. **28**(2), 337–407 (2000)
11. Kittler, J., Hatef, M., Duin, R.P., Matas, J.: On combining classifiers pattern analysis and machine intelligence. IEEE Trans. **20**, 226–239 (1998)
12. Kitowski, J., Kowal-Pawul, A., Lichota, W.: Identifying symptoms of bankruptcy risk based on bankruptcy prediction models—a case study of Poland in sustainability. MDPI **14**(3), 1416 (2022)
13. Altman, E.I., Hotchkiss, E., Wang, W.: Corporate Financial Distress, Restructuring,and Bankruptcy: Analyze Leveraged Finance, Distressed Debt, and Bankruptcy. Wiley, Hoboken (2019)
14. Medina-Quintero, J.M., Ortiz-Rodriguez, F., Tiwari, S., Saenz, F.I.M.: Trust in electronic banking with the use of cell phones for user satisfaction. In Global Perspectives on the Strategic Role of Marketing Information Systems" IGI Global, pp. 87–106 (2023)
15. Barrera, R.M., Martinez-Rodriguez, J.L., Tiwari, S., Barrera, V.: Political Marketing app based on citizens. In: Global Perspectives on the Strategic Role of Marketing Information Systems" in IGI Global, pp. 118–147 (2023)
16. Puagwatana, S., Gunawardana, K.: Logistic regression model for business failures prediction of technology industry in Thailand. In: SSRN electronic Journal (2012)
17. Nanni, L., Lumini, A.: An experimental comparison of ensemble of classifiers for bankruptcy prediction and credit scoring. Expert Syst. Appl. **36**, 3028–3033 (2009)

Intensity-Chromaticity-Luminance (ICL) Based Technique for Face Spoofing Detection

S. Karthika[✉] 🆔 and G. Padmavathi 🆔

Avinashilingam Institute for Home Science and Higher Education for Women,
Coimbatore 641043, India
karthika.it.avi@gmail.com, padmavathi_cs@avinuty.ac.in

Abstract. The significance of Face Recognition and Face Biometric Authentication systems has grown significantly in diverse security applications; nonetheless, the ability of the facial identification system to withstand an attack remains a significant concern. Research on non-invasive software-centric face spoofing detection systems have primarily focused on analyzing the luminance information present in face images, neglecting other components such as chroma and intensity which has the potential to be quite valuable for discriminating false faces from genuine ones. The proposed research work aims to utilize these components to find the differences or inconsistencies that could indicate the presence of a face spoofing attack. It is done by extracting and analyzing crucial information including energy, color distributions, and brightness of the color channels in an image. First, texture feature is extracted using Gray-Level Co-occurrence Matrix, GLCM. Second, the statistical descriptors features of RGB, HSV, YCbCr, CMYK, YIQ and YUV color channels are extracted to get the color distribution information. Subsequently, the integration of texture and color channel features results in the formation of a refined and enriched feature vector. At last, the feature vector is inputted into CNN architecture to classify the spoofed and genuine face images. The proposed method is assessed on NUAA Photograph Imposter dataset and has obtained a test accuracy of 99.88% in face spoof detection with HTER of 0.01%.

Keywords: Face Spoofing Detection · Presentation Attack Detection · NUAA · Color-Texture · Color channels · GLCM

1 Introduction

The adoption of biometric technologies for individual authentication and verification has witnessed substantial growth, leading to their widespread utilization in various sectors, including personal, governmental, and international security, ensuring heightened levels of safety and protection. Face Biometric Authentication System is one among such biometric systems used in many different fields, including forensics, law enforcement, health, specialized monitoring services, banking systems, some registration systems and smart phone access because of their non-intrusive nature. [1, 2]. Face biometric authentication systems, however, are also vulnerable to a number of security risks, such

© The Author(s), under exclusive license to Springer Nature Switzerland AG 2024
M. A. Jabbar et al. (Eds.): AMLDA 2023, CCIS 2047, pp. 199–214, 2024.
https://doi.org/10.1007/978-3-031-55486-5_15

as an attempt to bypass the authentication process by giving fake biometric information, which put the system into a vulnerable position. Spoofing is one such attempt by a fraudster pretending to be an authentic user to obtain system access by presenting to the biometric sensor, a created artifact that impersonates a genuine user, like a photo or video [3]. The most common method of spoofing is known as photo attack which involves presenting a genuine user's printed or digital photo to the camera. Another type of spoofing is video replay attack, in which the biometric system is shown the screen of a device playing a recorded video of a legitimate user.

The act of donning a genuine user's mask and presenting it to the biometric authentication system is known as a "mask attack" [4]. Spoofing attack is a sensor level attack which is often considered more dangerous compared to other types due to several reasons such as direct exploitation, difficulty of detection, low barrier of entry, potential for mass exploitation, and high success rate of spoofed faces. Moreover, the National Vulnerability Database, a repository preserved by the National Institute of Standards and Technology, included Face spoofing as one of the important vulnerabilities. To improve the security of face authentication systems and reduce their vulnerability to face spoofing, it is crucial to implement effective countermeasures. These measures will help bolster the overall security of the systems and ensure reliable authentication processes. Face liveness detection techniques serve as an optimal solution to tackle the diverse range of spoofing attacks. Both hardware and software based methods are proven efficient in face spoofing detection in literature perspective [48]. Typically, software based methods, often referred to as, Presentation Attack Detection (PAD), depend on extracting unique features like texture, image quality, frequency, motion, and distinctive facial characteristics extracted from face images to classify them as genuine or spoof.

The primary focus and contribution of this work is to extract texture descriptors and statistical descriptors considering Intensity, Chromaticity and Luminance of the presented face images. This research work makes use of statistical-based feature extraction methods from color channels of various color spaces like RGB, YCbCr, HSV, CMYK, YUV, and YIQ, for the purpose of detecting face spoofing attacks. The idea is to carry out a comprehensive texture analysis for capturing diverse texture aspects in the face images by combining the most significant features namely Contrast, Energy, Homogeneity and Correlation. Contrast computes the difference in local intensity variations, energy calculates overall texture uniformity, correlation evaluates linear dependencies between pixel pairs, and homogeneity determines the closeness of pixel values. Since this set comprises diverse features, it concurrently diminishes the potential for redundancy within the feature set. Furthermore, the exploration of statistical features from multiple color spaces provides various aspects such as color intensity, hue, brightness, and chrominance. This holistic analysis of color can potentially enhance the discrimination ability of the face spoofing detection approach using distinct characteristics of each color space. Thus, the fusion of the statistical descriptors of multiple color channels and texture features provides a more comprehensive feature set that summarizes both the structural and chromatic aspects of the facial images. The proposed approach of face anti-spoofing has practical applications in various real-world scenarios such as Airport Security, Online Identity Verification for Financial Transactions, Access Control in Corporate Environments, Mobile Device Authentication and Smart Home Security.

The paper is organized as follows: Sect. 2 presents a summary of current face spoofing attack detection methods that rely on color feature information. Section 3 introduces the proposed anti-spoofing method in detail. Section 4 encompasses the experiments performed, the evaluation process undertaken, and the comparative results obtained. Section 5 analyzes the obtained results on NUAA imposter dataset using the proposed approach. Finally, Sect. 6 concludes the research work done with scope for enhancement.

2 Related Works

In face spoofing detection literature, there are four types of face anti-spoofing approaches namely Texture feature-based, Frequency based, Image Quality Assessment (IQA) based and Deep Learning based approaches. Texture feature-based approaches focus on closely examining the micro-textural patterns visible in facial photos since they are crucial for differentiating and spotting fake artifacts. The authors of [6–8] used Local Binary Pattern, which measures gray-scale texture that relies on the relationship between each pixel and its neighboring pixels. In [9], the authors used rotational invariant LBP along with Gabor filter and Gray-level co-occurrence features. The other variants of LBP texture feature such as Uniform LBP, Extended LBP, Completed LBP, mLBP, dLBP and chromatic co-occurrence LBP (CCoLBP) are also proven as efficient in combating various face spoofing attacks [10, 11].

In [12], the author employed a method for detecting face liveness using Difference of Gaussian with Local Binary Pattern Variance technique. The research work in [13] introduces a novel approach to detection face spoofing attacks by combining entropy-based texture and image quality features with enhanced robustness and impressive accuracy rate of 98.2%. The paper [14] presents a novel detection method which analyzes both the texture cues and the facial movements to detect face spoofing attacks. The method focuses on extracting optical flows from video sequences and then combined with texture cues and could achieve notable accuracy in discerning various types of counterfeit faces when compared to state-of-the-art methods.

Next, in Frequency based approaches, high and low frequency signals are used to extract inherent differences from face images by applying Frequency analysis techniques such as Fourier Transform, Discrete Cosine Transform, Wavelet Transform and Gabor Transform. In [15], the author proposed a technique for real-time face detection that combines facial template matching with energy analysis using the Discrete Cosine Transform (DCT). In [16], a novel method Dynamic High Frequency Descriptor is proposed which examines the high-frequency energy components of facial images, both under varying illumination conditions and without, with the objective of discriminating any distinct changes.

Image Quality Assessment (IQA) based approaches detect the face liveness by analyzing the quality difference between genuine and spoofed face images. IQA techniques evaluate the quality of the face images derived from visual characteristics, including sharpness, contrast, noise level, blur, lighting, colour accuracy, and complexity of the texture. In [17–19], Image Quality Measures (IQM) such as Structural Similarity Index (SSIM), Peak Signal-to-Noise Ratio (PSNR) and Feature Similarity Index (FSIM) are employed to analyze the quality of face images. The author of [20] used distinct image distortions of spoofed images to distinguish from real images and in [21], the statistics of noise distortions such as texture mismatch and unnatural lighting has been used to determine the liveness of a face.

Deep learning based approaches have made a significant advancement in recent years. In [22], the proposed framework encompasses dimensionality reduction and the extraction of salient features from input frames through the utilization of pre-trained weights derived from Convolutional auto encoders. The framework showcases superior performance in both cross-database and intra-database testing scenarios across three benchmark datasets. The work proposed in [23] utilizes client identity information and employs a deep Siamese network trained with image pairs to effectively detect spoofed faces with enhanced performance. The research work [24], a novel video pre-processing technique called Temporal Sequence Sampling is proposed to improve generalization and achieves promising results across multiple public benchmarks. The research work in [25] proposed a two-stream spatial-temporal network which integrates depth information, utilizes a temporal shift module, and employs a Symmetry Loss for auxiliary supervision and finally achieved impressive results across multiple datasets.

In [26–29], the traditional deep learning methods such as CNN, LSTM, LiveNet, ResNet and Patch-based CNN were used to extract highly discriminatory features. Face spoofing detection techniques that combine handcrafted features and deep learning techniques enable a more thorough study of facial images. The accuracy and resilience of the detection system are improved by this hybrid technique, which makes use of the advantages of both methods [30]. Some other research contributions [31, 32] made use of color based features such as color-texture features from RGB, YCbCr, CIE, XYZ and HSV color spaces, color moments and dynamic color texture information. In [33], discrimination of spoofed and real faces are done by extracting the Color Channel Markov feature and Color Channel Difference Markov features [34, 35] made use of deep color features and multi color channel features for spoofing detection. According to [36], the YIQ color space demonstrates the greatest level of distinctiveness between pixels representing skin and non-skin elements across the examined color spaces, based on color features. In [37], the CMYK color space features are used for skin detection which resulted in better accuracy than RGB and HSV color models.

While the current texture-based approaches have demonstrated promising outcomes, they still encounter certain challenges, such as dealing with rotational variance, sensitivity to image resolution and illumination changes. Hence, this research work concentrates on extracting statistical descriptors which are useful to obtain a global summary of the color distribution and intensity values from the color channels. As the statistical properties of color distributions are preserved regardless of the image's rotation and resolution and they focus on the distribution rather than the spatial arrangement of pixels, the approach becomes more robust to facial variances caused by different poses.

3 Proposed Approach

The proposed research work is anticipated to make use of both texture features and statistical features of color channels together to discriminate between the real and spoofed face images. Figure 1 illustrates a block diagram depicting the proposed face anti-spoofing approach. Initially, the texture features, such as contrast, energy, homogeneity, and correlation, are extracted using Gray-Level Co-occurrence Matrix. Next, the statistical descriptors mean, standard deviation and maximum value from the color channels of RGB, YCbCr, HSV, CMYK, YUV, and YIQ images are extracted to understand the face image color distribution. Then, all the extracted features are organized into an efficient feature vector. Finally, a deep learning model is designed and trained with the feature vector to classify the genuine and spoofed face images.

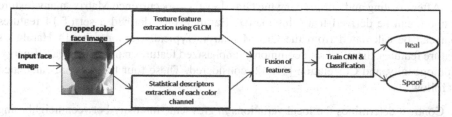

Fig. 1. The proposed approach

3.1 Extracting Texture Features

The examination of facial image texture features involves the utilization of Gray-Level Co-occurrence Matrix function. This GLCM is statistical analysis based descriptor and considered as a powerful method for extracting color based texture information. The advantage of GLCM compared to other texture analysis methods lies in its ability to capture detailed spatial relationships between pixel intensities in an image [38]. The fundamental concept is to calculate texture features by analyzing the relationship between adjacent pixels. A straightforward approach to separate the channels of a color image is by using the grey-level method. This method involves creating separate 2D matrices for each color channel of the image. GLCM is a two-dimensional matrix that captures the joint probabilities of pixel intensity values occurring together at a certain distance *dist* and in a specific direction θ. It provides information about the spatial patterns and texture characteristics present in an image by analyzing the frequency and arrangement of different pixel value combinations [39, 40]. The GLCM features are higher order components in texture analysis.

The texture pattern's scale invariance is determined by normalizing the GLCM in relation to the overall count of pairs of pixels. This normalization process ensures that the computed texture features are independent of the image size or resolution.

$$ P_{dist,\theta} = \frac{P_{dist,\theta}(L1, L2)}{X_{all}} \tag{1} $$

The joint probabilities between pairs of neighboring pixels at a certain distance (*dist*) and direction (θ) are represented by $P_{dist,\theta}$(L1, L2), where L1 and L2 correspond to the luminance values of those pixels. The term X_{all} represents the count of all possible pairs of pixels [41]. Several parameters were carefully configured to ensure meaningful texture feature extraction. The 'distances' parameter was set to 1 pixel to consider immediate neighboring pixels for co-occurrence calculations. The 'angles' parameter was set to [0] to analyze texture patterns along the horizontal direction. 'Levels' was set to 256, reflecting the 8-bit grayscale nature of the face images. A symmetric GLCM is used to consider bidirectional pixel pairs and applied normalization to standardize GLCM values within the [1] range. These parameter choices were made to comprehensively capture texture information while ensuring the invariance of the analysis to changes in image size.

After creating and normalizing the Gray-Level Co-occurrence Matrix, many texture features can be derived from this matrix. Haralick [40] defined a set of 14 features that can be calculated from the GLCM matrix. Typically, among the 14 Haralick's texture features, there are four commonly emphasized features namely Contrast, Energy, Homogeneity, and Correlation [41, 42] considered. These four features are calculated as follow.

- Contrast determines the local variations in grayscale intensity between neighboring pixels

$$\text{Contrast} = \sum_{i=1}^{N} \sum_{j=1}^{N} (i-j)^2 P(i,j) \tag{2}$$

- Energy represents the summation of squared elements in the GLCM and describes the overall texture uniformity

$$\text{Energy} = \sum_{i=1}^{N} \sum_{j=1}^{N} P(i,j)^2 \tag{3}$$

- Homogeneity refers to the proximity of the GLCM (Gray Level Co-occurrence Matrix) values to the diagonal, which serves as an indicator of the texture's local homogeneity.

$$\text{Homogeneity} = \sum_{i=1}^{N} \sum_{j=1}^{N} \frac{P(i,j)}{1 + (i-j)^2} \tag{4}$$

- Correlation calculates the linear dependency between the grayscale values of neighboring pixels within the image

$$\text{Correlation} = \frac{\sum_{i=1}^{N} \sum_{j=1}^{N} (i - \mu_i)(j - \mu_j) P(i,j)}{\sigma_i \sigma_j} \tag{5}$$

These statistics provide insights into the image's texture characteristics. Figure 2. Depicts the GLCMs of both a client face and imposter face from NUAA Photograph Imposter Dataset.

Texture feature based methods are based on complex patterns and variations in color information in a face image. Though the texture features are efficient in discriminating real and spoofed face images, these features alone may not be performed well in other

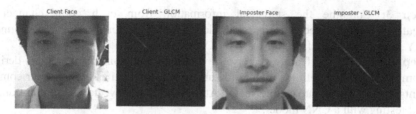

Fig. 2. GLCMs of Client Face and Imposter Face

circumstances such as rotational and illumination variations which can profoundly alter the perceived image structures [43]. Thus, only texture based method alone cannot be a fool-proof one under such circumstances. Hence, the statistical features of color channels are included in the proposed approach to achieve rotational and illumination invariance.

3.2 Extracting Statistical Descriptors of Color Channels

The color channels of RGB, HSV, YCbCr, CMYK, YIQ and YUV are taken into consideration to extract statistical descriptors such as mean, standard deviation and maximum value from the input face image. The main intention of extracting the statistical descriptors is to compute the color distribution information of the input face images. The color distribution can also be computed by color histograms, but histograms lack of spatial information [44]. Hence, the statistical features are used to get the global information of overall color distributions in an image and often referred to as lower order color moments. Mean value measures the average intensity of color channel pixels, the standard deviation measures the dispersion of color channel intensities and Maximum value measures the most intense pixel value in each channel. For computing these features, each color channel is considered as a separate univariate distribution.

The calculation process of the lower order components namely mean, standard deviation and maximum value is as follows:

$$\text{Mean}_i = \frac{1}{N} \sum\nolimits_{j=1}^{N} P_{ij} \tag{6}$$

$$\sigma = \sqrt{\frac{1}{N} \sum\nolimits_{j=1}^{N} \left(P_{ij} - \text{Mean}_i \right)^2} \tag{7}$$

$$\text{Max}_i = \text{Max}\left(P_{ij} \right), \ j = 1, 2, \ldots . N \tag{8}$$

where, N is the total pixels count in the image, P_{ij} is the jth pixel value of the image at the color i^{th} channel, and Max_i is the utmost pixel value achievable in channel i.

The color channel features are calculated as follows:

- **Step 1**: Partition the input face image into its individual color channels. For instance, an YUV image is to be split into Luma(Y), Chroma(U) and Chroma(V) channels and analyzed separately
- **Step 2:** Compute the statistical descriptors mean, standard deviation and maximum pixel value for each channel

- **Step 3:** Combine the statistical information from each color channel to create a feature vector (for example, feature vector for a YUV image $[\mu Y, \sigma Y, XY, \mu U, \sigma U, XU_U, \mu V, \sigma V, XV]$).
- **Step 4:** Combine the feature vector of low order color moments which are derived from previous step with the texture feature vector, referred as higher order components, to form a absolute feature vector. At last, this feature vector is used for training and testing with a CNN model.

Individual color channels of a client face and an imposter face from NUAA Photograph Imposter Dataset is depicted in Fig. 3

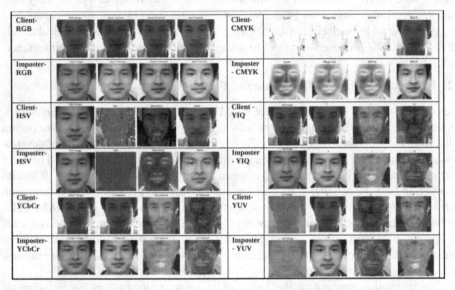

Fig. 3. Color channels of a sample image from NUAA Photograph Imposter dataset

4 Experimental Work

4.1 Dataset

The NUAA Imposter Dataset is a publicly accessible benchmark dataset, developed and released by the China's National University of Defense Technology. For this proposed approach, we conducted training and testing using the NUAA Photograph Imposter Dataset which comprises 15 subjects, featuring a total of 5,105 genuine access images and 7,509 face spoofing attack images. The images were obtained using a standard webcam with a frame rate of 20 fps and a resolution of 640 x 480 pixels. The dataset includes face images captured from three distinct sections, each representing different environments and lighting conditions. To generate the spoofing attack samples, high-resolution photographs were captured using a Canon digital camera. This process involved shooting the subjects with various spoofing methods, such as printed photographs, masks, and other types of presentation attacks. The specification of the dataset is given in Table 1. The dataset exhibits some limitations in representing diverse attack modalities and demographics. The bias in the lighting and environmental may not accurately represent the variations in real world scenarios. The dataset may not adequately cover variations in pose, especially extreme or non-frontal poses. This bias can affect a model's ability to handle pose variations commonly seen in practical applications.

Table 1. NUAA Photograph Imposter Dataset specification

NUAA Photograph Imposter dataset			
Class	Dataset Distribution	Number of instances	Total
Client Face	Training	4084	5105
	Testing	1021	
Imposter Face	Training	6007	7509
	Testing	1502	
Total instances in the NUAA dataset			**12,614**

4.2 Experimental Setup

Evaluation is carried out with a sequential CNN model which has two convolution layers with 64 neurons each and adopts the ReLU activation function. Subsequently, a binary classification process is established by incorporating an output layer consisting of a single neuron with a sigmoid activation function. The model is trained using training data feature vector. For model optimization, the model is compiled with the Adam optimizer, employing binary cross-entropy as the loss function. The output layer has a distinct neuron with a sigmoid activation function to predict the probability of face spoofing. For model optimization, the model is compiled with the Adam optimizer, employing binary cross-entropy as the loss function. Once the model is trained, it is utilized on the test dataset to make predictions regarding the probabilities of face spoofing. A threshold of 0.5 is utilized to convert the probabilities into binary predictions. Subsequently, accuracy of the model is found by comparing the predicted labels with the actual labels present in the test dataset.

4.3 Evaluation Metrics

The primary evaluation metrics used in this research work is accuracy, which evaluates the percentage of correctly classified instances within the test dataset. Other metrics are Precision, Recall, F1-Score, Half Total Error Rate and Equal Error Rate calculated as in Table 2.

Table 2. Evaluation metrics used.

Metrics	Description	Formula
Accuracy	Classification accuracy of distinguishing genuine and spoof faces	$Acc = \frac{TP+TN}{Total\ number\ of\ samples}$
Precision	Accuracy of a model's positive predictions	$Precision = \frac{TP}{(TP+FP)}$ $Precision = \frac{TP}{(TP+FP)}$ $Precision = \frac{TP}{(TP+FP)}$
Recall	Proportion of correctly classified genuine face samples as genuine by the model	$Recall = \frac{TP}{(TP+FN)}$
F1 Score	Harmonic mean of recall and precision	$F1\ Score = 2 * \frac{(Precision*Recall)}{(Precision+Recall)}$
Half Total Error Rate	Average of False Acceptance Rate and False Rejection Rate	$HTER = \frac{(FAR+FRR)}{2}$
Equal Error Rate	The point where error rates are equal	At certain threshold when $FAR = FRR$

5 Result Analysis

Texture features include contrast, energy, homogeneity and correlation are extracted using GLCM from the input face images. These features measure the amount of local intensity variation between pixel pairs in specific directions and distances which are useful in spoofed imaged detection. Particularly, in contrast, genuine faces typically exhibit higher contrast values where as spoofed faces will have lower contrast values as they have variations in pixel intensities. The CNN model is trained and tested on the texture feature vector which provides 95.79% accuracy with the error rate of 4.32%. (Table 3). Furthermore, the color distribution information extracted from statistical features of RGB, HSV, YCbCr, CMYK, YIQ and YUV color channels is used as feature vector to train the deep learning model and the result is listed in Table 3.

Table 4 provides the results acquired by training the deep learning model with the various combinations of features. Texture features is combined with statistical descriptors of all the color channel features and used to classify the genuine and spoofed facial images.

Due to the inherent lack of rotational and luminance variance in texture features, we have chosen to combine the statistical descriptors of the images. The statistical descriptors of RGB, HSV, YCbCr, CMYK, YIQ and YUV color channels are calculated separately. The CNN model is trained with the color features and the result is listed in Table 4. The results obtained by the CNN model when trained with the vector of combined texture and statistical descriptors of color channel features are given in Table 4. The

Table. 3 Results of the texture feature and statistical features in NUAA Photograph Imposter dataset.

Feature	Accuracy	Precision	Recall	F1 Score	HTER (%)	EER (%)
Texture	95.79	95.92	97.07	96.49	4.5	4.32
Statistical descriptors of RGB	98.85	98.16	99.02	98.59	1.15	1.13
Statistical descriptors of HSV	99.40	99.31	99.22	99.27	0.59	0.60
Statistical descriptors of YCbCr	99.60	99.51	99.70	99.61	0.28	0.26
Statistical descriptors of CMYK	98.81	98.34	98.53	98.43	1.27	1.26
Statistical descriptors of YIQ	99.20	99.31	98.73	99.02	0.79	0.80
Statistical descriptors of YUV	99.80	99.22	99.61	99.41	0.36	0.33

Table. 4 Results of the proposed approach in NUAA Photograph Imposter dataset.

Feature	Accuracy	Precision	Recall	F1 Score	HTER (%)	EER (%)
Texture + Statistical descriptors of RGB	99.45	99.60	99.53	99.57	0.56	0.59
Texture + Statistical descriptors of HSV	99.32	99.57	99.20	99.43	0.76	0.78
Texture + Statistical descriptors of YCbCr	**99.88**	100.0	99.80	99.90	0.01	0.09
Texture + Statistical descriptors of CMYK	99.60	99.87	99.47	99.67	0.40	0.39
Texture + Statistical descriptors of YIQ	99.72	99.67	99.87	99.77	0.28	0.29
Texture + Statistical descriptors of YUV	99.84	99.93	99.80	99.86	0.15	0.10

proposed approach demonstrates a significantly lower error rate compared to existing techniques. The comparison of the proposed approach with the State-of-the-Art methods is presented in Table 5 for examination.

It is clearly evident that the luminance-centric color spaces such as HSV, YCbCr, YIQ and YUV exhibit the best performance compared to alternative color spaces. The texture features are combined with the statistical features of color channels to test the efficiency of the final feature vector, and it provides 99.88% accuracy on NUAA Photograph Imposter dataset. Along with accuracy other performance metric also evaluated and listed in Table 4.

Table. 5 A Comparison of the proposed approach with state-of-art techniques

Reference		Features/Architecture	Accuracy/ EER
S. Kumar, S. Singh and J.Kumar	[46]	Blur edges + SegNet	97%
Raghavendra and Kunte	[47]	EDDTCP descriptor	93.04%, 89.83%, 92.22%
Anand, and Vishwakarma	[48]	Deep features + Color Texture	
		Features with Spatial feature fusion	94.31%, 98.15%
Delouse, et al.	[49]	LBPNet (LBP + CNN)	97.60%
Yang, Lei, Liao et al.	[50]	Component-dependent descriptor	97.78%
Tan, Li, Liu et al.	[51]	Texture features with DoG and	
		Sparse Nonlinear Logistic Regression	88.15%
P. P. P. Linn et al.	[52]	Patch-based CNN	98%
G. Thippeswamy et al.	[53]	Ensemble of Texture descriptors + KNN	98.39%
Fu-Mei Chen, et al.	[55]	Color texture + Deep features	EER: 0.5
Xiao Song, et al.	[56]	Template Face Matched Binocular depth	
		with spatial pyramid coding Micro-Texture	99.16%, HTER 0.89
Phoo Pyae Pyae Linn, et al.	[57]	Eye movements +Local features	98%, HTER 2.1
Raghavendra R J, et al.	[58]	Combined HOG and ELTP features	
		and anisotropic smoothing	HTER 2.59
W. Zheng, et al.	[25]	Face depth with temporal information	99.5%
The Proposed approach		GLCM Texture + Color channel features	
		+ CNN	**99.88%**, HTER 0.01

6   Conclusion

In this paper, a face spoofing detection method is proposed which mainly uses luminance, chrominance and intensity values of individual color channels in the images. Luminance predominantly captures the overall brightness, and chromaticity is concerned with distinctions in color, which are less prone to substantial modification in spoofing attacks. The intensity component remains relatively unaffected by changes in illumination, making it a valuable factor in enhancing the robustness of the face spoofing detection method against variations in lighting conditions. The effectiveness of statistical descriptors of RGB, HSV, YCbCr, CMYK, YIQ and YUV color channels is investigated in this work. The results show that color channels which contain ICL components are able to achieve the better accuracy than other color channel features. Nevertheless, printed photo attacks can manipulate the luminance and chromaticity characteristics to mimic real faces, making it difficult to distinguish between the two. Hence, the idea of combining the ICL features with texture feature acquired using GLCM method is proposed. The accuracy of 99.88% with the Half Total Error Rate of 0.01% is achieved by using the combined feature vector on NUAA Photograph Imposter dataset. In future work, the deep learning approaches are to be explored to automatically learn hierarchical features and subtle patterns potentially. In addition, transfer learning and domain adaptation techniques are to be utilized to enhance the generalization of the proposed feature vector across diverse datasets and real-world circumstances.

References

1. Sudeep, S.V.N.V.S., Venkata Kiran, S., Nandan, D., Kumar, S.: An overview of biometrics and face spoofing detection. In: Kumar, A. and Mozar, S., Eds., ICCCE 2020, Springer, Singapore, pp. 871–881 (2021). https://doi.org/10.1007/978-981-15-7961-5_82
2. Ramachandra, R., Busch, C., Biometric, N.: Presentation attack detection methods for face recognition systems: a comprehensive survey. ACM Comput. Surv. 50(1), 37 (2017)
3. Sharma, D., Selwal, A.: A survey on face presentation attack detection mechanisms: hitherto and future perspectives. Multimedia Syst. 29, 1527–1577 (2023). https://doi.org/10.1007/s00530-023-01070-5
4. Jain, A.K., Flynn, P., Ross, A.A.: Handbook of biometrics. Springer Science & Business Media. (2007)
5. Yang, J., Lei, Z., Li, S.Z.: Learn convolutional neural network for face anti-spoofing. arXiv preprint arXiv:1408.5601 (2014)
6. Maatta, J., Hadid, A., Pietikainen, M.: Face spoofing detection from single images using micro-texture analysis. In: Proceedings of IAPR IEEE International Joint Conference on Biometrics (IJCB), Washington DC, USA (2011)
7. Erdogmus, N., Marce, S.: Spoofing face recognition with 3D masks. no. July, (2014). https://doi.org/10.1109/TIFS.2014.2322255
8. Peng, F., Qin, L., Long, M.: Face presentation attack detection using guided scale texture. Multimed Tools Appl 77, 8883–8909 (2018). https://doi.org/10.1007/s11042-017-4780-0
9. Waris, M., Zhang, H., Ahmad, I., Kiranyaz, S., Gabbouj, M.: Analysis of textural features for face biometric anti-spoofing," no. February 2018, (2013)
10. Yu, Z., Li, X., Shi, J., Xia, Z., Zhao, G.: Revisiting pixel-wise supervision for face anti-spoofing. IEEE TBBIS 3(3), 285–295 (2021)
11. Peng, F., Qin, L., Long, M.: CCoLBP : chromatic co - occurrence of local binary pattern for face presentation attack detection (2018)
12. Hasan, R., Mahmud, S.M.H., Li, X.Y.: Face anti-spoofing using texture-based techniques and filtering methods. J. Phys. Conf. Ser. (2019). https://doi.org/10.1088/1742-6596/1229/1/012044
13. Daniel, N., Anith, A.: Texture and quality analysis for face spoofing detection. Comput. Electr. Eng. 94, 107293 (2021)
14. Li, L., Xia, Z., Wu, J., Yang, L., Han, H.: Face presentation attack detection based on optical flow and texture analysis. J. King Saud Univ. Comput. Inf. Sci. 34(4), 1455–1467 (2022). https://doi.org/10.1016/j.jksuci.2022.02.019
15. Teja, M.H.: Real-time live face detection using face template matching and DCT energy analysis. In: International Conference of Soft Computing and Pattern Recognition (SoCPaR), Dalian, China (2011)
16. Peng, J., Chan, P. P. K.: Face liveness detection for combating the spoofing attack in face recognition, pp 13–16 (2014)
17. Galbally, J., Marcel, S., Fierrez, J.: Image quality assessment for fake biometric detection: application to iris, fingerprint, and face recognition. Image Process IEEE Trans. Biometrics Compendium 23, 710–724 (2013)
18. Bhogal, A.P.S., Söllinger, D., Trung, P., Uhl, A.: Non-reference image quality assessment for biometric presentation attack detection. In: 5th International Workshop on Biometrics and Forensics (IWBF), Coventry, United Kingdom (2017)
19. Nikisins, O., Mohammadi, A.: On effectiveness of anomaly detection approaches against unseen presentation attacks in face anti-spoofing (1920)
20. Wen, D., Han, H., Jain, A.K.: Face spoof detection with image distortion analysis. IEEE Trans. Inf. Forens. Secur. XX(X), 1–16 (2015)

21. Nguyen, H.P., Delahaies, A.: Face presentation attack detection based on a statistical model of image noise. IEEE Access **7**, 175429–175442 (2019)

22. Arora, S., Bhatia, M.P.S., Mittal, V.: A robust framework for spoofing detection in faces using deep learning. Vis. Comput. **38**, 2461–2472 (2022). https://doi.org/10.1007/s00371-021-021 23-4

23. Pei, M., Yan, B., Hao, H., Zhao, M.: Person-specific face spoofing detection based on a siamese network. Pattern Recognit. **135**, 109148 (2023). https://doi.org/10.1016/j.patcog. 2022.109148

24. Li, X., Komulainen, J., Zhao, G., Yuen, P., Pietik, M.: Generalized face anti-spoofing by detecting pulse from face videos. In: International Conference Pattern Recognition, December, pp. 4244–4249. (2016). https://doi.org/10.1109/ICPR.2016.7900300

25. Zheng, W., Yue, M., Zhao, S., Liu S.: Attention-based spatial-temporal multi-scale network for face anti-spoofing. IEEE Trans. Biom. Behav. Identity Sci **3**, 296–307 (2021). https://doi. org/10.1109/TBIOM.2021.3066983

26. Yang, X., et al.: Face anti-spoofing: model matters, so does data. In: Proceedings of the IEEE/CVF Conference on Computer Vision and Pattern Recognition, pp. 3507–3516 (2019)

27. Abbas, Y., Rehman, U., Po, L.M., Liu, M.: LiveNet: improving features generalization for face liveness detection using convolution neural networks. Expert Syst. Appl. **108**, 159–169 (2018). https://doi.org/10.1016/j.eswa.2018.05.004

28. Li, L., Xia, Z., Jiang, X., Roli, F., Feng, X.: CompactNet: learning a compact space for face presentation attack detection. Neurocomputing **409**, 191–207 (2020). https://doi.org/10.1016/ j.neucom.2020.05.017

29. Wang, C.Y., Lu, Y.D., Yang, S.T., Lai, S.H.: Patchnet: a simple face anti spoofing framework via fine-grained patch recognition. In: CVPR, pp. 20249–. 20258 (2022)

30. Khammari, M.: Robust face anti-spoofing using CNN with LBP and WLD. IET Image Process. **13**, 1880–1884 (2019)

31. Zhou, J., Shu, K., Liu, P., Xiang, J., Xiong, S.: Face anti-spoofing based on dynamic color texture analysis using local directional number pattern. In: 25th International Conference on Pattern Recognition (ICPR), Milan, Italy (2021)

32. Boulkenafet, Z., Komulainen. J., Hadid, A.: Face anti-spoofing based on color texture analysis. In: Proceedings - International Conference on Image Processing, ICIP, pp. 2636–2640 (2015). https://doi.org/10.1109/ICIP.2015.7351280

33. Zhang, L.B., Peng, F., Qin, L., Long, M.: Face spoofing detection based on color texture Markov feature and support vector machine recursive feature elimination. J. Vis. Commun. Image Represent. **51**, 56–69 (2018). https://doi.org/10.1016/j.jvcir.2018.01.001

34. Larbi, K., Ouarda, W., Drira, H., Amor, B.B., Amar, C.B.: Deep colorfasd: Face anti spoofing solution using a multi channeled color spaces CNN. In: IEEE International Conference on Systems, Man, and Cybernetics (SMC), Miyazaki, Japan (2018)

35. Li, L., Feng, X.: Face anti-spoofing via deep local binary pattern. In: Deep Learning in Object Detection and Recognition, Singapore, pp. 91–111 (2019)

36. Hani, K.A., Mohamad-Saleh, J., Azmin Suandi, S.: Color space selection for human skin detection using color-texture features and neural network. In: International Conference on Computer and Information Sciences (ICCOINS), Kuala Lumpur, Malaysia (2014). https:// doi.org/10.1109/ICCOINS33058.2014

37. Sawicki, D.J., Miziolek, W.: Human colour skin detection in CMYK colour space. IET-IPR(9), 751–757, (2015)

38. Pramestya, R.H., Sulistyaningrum, D.R., Setiyono, B., Mukhlash, I., Firdaus, Z.: Road defect classification using gray level co-occurrence matrix (GLCM) and radial basis function (RBF). In: 2018 10th International Conference on Information Technology and Electrical Engineering (ICITEE), pp. 285–289 (2018). https://doi.org/10.1109/ICITEED.2018.8534769

39. Haralick, R.M., Shanmugam, K., Dinstein, I.H.: Textural features for image classification Systems. Man Cybern. IEEE Trans. **3**, 610–621 (1973)
40. Haralick, R.M.: Statistical and structural approaches to texture. Proc. of the IEEE **67**, 786–804 (1979)
41. Hall-Beyer M.: GLCM texture: a tutorial v. 3.0. (2017) https://prism.ucalgary.ca/handle/1880/51900
42. Gade, A.A., Vyavahare, A.J: Feature extraction using GLCM for dietary assessment application. Int. J. Multimedia Image Process. **8**(2), 409–413 (2018)
43. Cernadas, E., Fernández-Delgado, M., González-Rufino, E., Carrión, P: Influence of normalization and color space to color texture classification. Pattern Recogn. **61**, 120–138 (2017)
44. Zhou, Y.: Building regionally spatial appearance model by topological color histogram. In: 14th IEEE International Conference on Computational Science and Engineering (2011)
45. Tan, X., Li, Y., Liu, J., Jiang, L.: Face liveness detection from a single image with sparse low rank bilinear discriminative model. In: Daniilidis, K., Maragos, P., Paragios, N. (eds.) Computer Vision – ECCV 2010. ECCV 2010. LNCS, vol. 6316, pp. 504–517. Springer, Berlin)2010_. https://doi.org/10.1007/978-3-642-15567-3_37
46. Kumar, S., Singh, S., Kumar, J.: Face spoofing detection using improved SegNet architecture with a blur estimation technique. Int. J. Biomet. **13**(2), 131–149 (2021)
47. Raghavendra, R.J., Kunte, R.S.: A novel feature descriptor for face anti-spoofing using texture based method. Cybern. Inf. Technol. **20**(3), 159–176 (2020)
48. Anand, A., Vishwakarma, D.K.: Face anti-spoofing by spatial fusion of color texture features and deep features. In: 3rd International Conference on Intelligent Sustainable Systems (ICISS'20), pp. 1012–1017. IEEE, Coimbatore, India (2020)
49. Souza, D., Da Silva Santos, D.F., Pires, R.G., Marana, A.N., Papa, J.P.: Deep texture features for robust face spoofing detection. IEEE Trans. Circuits Syst. II Express Briefs **64**(12), 1397–1401 (2017)
50. Yang, J., Lei, Z., Liao, S., Li, S.Z.: Face liveness detection with component dependent descriptor. In: 2013 International Conference on Biometrics (ICB), IEEE (2013)
51. Tan, X., Li, Y., Liu, J., Jiang, L.: Face liveness detection from a single image with sparse low rank bilinear discriminative model. In: Daniilidis, K., Maragos, P., Paragios, N. (eds.) Computer Vision – ECCV 2010. ECCV 2010. LNCS, vol. 6316, pp. 507–517. Springer, Berlin (2010). https://doi.org/10.1007/978-3-642-15567-3_37
52. Linn, P.P.P., Htoon, E.C.: Face anti-spoofing using eyes movement and CNN-based liveness detection. In: International Conference on Advanced Information Technologies (ICAIT), pp. 149–154. IEEE, Yangon, Myanmar (2019). https://doi.org/10.1109/AITC.2019.8921091
53. Thippeswamy, G., Vinutha, H., Dhanapal, R.: A new ensemble of texture descriptors based on local appearance-based methods for face anti-spoofing system. Crit. Rev. **7**(11), 644–649 (2020)
54. Ming, Z., Visani, M., Luqman, M., Burie, J.C.: A survey on anti-spoofing methods for face recognition with RGB cameras of generic consumer devices. J. Imaging **6**(12), 139 (2020)
55. Chen, F., Wen, C., Xie, K., Wen, F., Sheng, G., Tang, X.: Face liveness detection: fusing colour texture feature and deep feature. IET Biometr. (2019). https://doi.org/10.1049/iet-bmt.2018.5235
56. Song, X., Zhao, X., Fang, L., Lin, T.: Discriminative representation combinations for accurate face spoofing detection. Pattern Recogn. **85**, 220–231 (2019)
57. Raghavendra, Kunte, R.S.: Anisotropic smoothing for illumination invariant face anti-spoofing. In: 4th International Conference on Trends in Electronics and Informatics (ICOEI) (48184). IEEE, Tirunelveli, India (2020)

58. Zhuo, W., Zezheng, W., Zitong, Y., Weihong, D., Jiahong, L., Tingting, G., Zhongyuan, W.: Domain generalization via shuffled style assembly for face anti-spoofing. In: Conference on Computer Vision and Pattern Recognition (CVPR), pp. 4113–4123. IEEE/CVF, New Orleans, LA, USA (2022)
59. Wang, Z., Wang, Q., Deng, W., Guo, G.: Learning multi-granularity temporal characteristics for face anti-spoofing. IEEE TIFS 17, 1254–1269 (2022)

Developers' Perspective on Trustworthiness of Code Generated by ChatGPT: Insights from Interviews

Zeinab Sadat Rabani[1]([envelope]), Hanieh Khorashadizadeh[1], Shirin Abdollahzade[2], Sven Groppe[1], and Javad Ghofrani[1]

[1] Universität zu Lübeck, Lübeck, Germany
zeinab.rabani@uni-luebeck.de
[2] University of Guilan, Rasht, Iran

Abstract. The emergence of ChatGPT as a tool for code generation has garnered significant attention from software developers. Nevertheless, the reliability of code produced by Large Language Models (LLMs) like ChatGPT remains insufficiently explored. This article delves into the realm of ChatGPT-generated code, aiming to investigate the perspectives of esteemed programmers and researchers through interviews. The consensus among interviewees highlights that code generated by ChatGPT often lack accuracy, necessitating manual debugging and substantial time investment, particularly when dealing with complex code structures. Through a comprehensive analysis of the interview findings, this article identifies five primary challenges inherent to ChatGPT's code generation process. The core objective of this research is to engage in an exploration of ChatGPT's code generation trustworthiness, drawing insights from interviews with experts. By facilitating insightful discussions, the research aims to pave the way for proposing impactful enhancements that bolster the reliability of ChatGPT's code outputs. To enhance the performance and overall dependability of LLMs, the article presents seven potential solutions tailored to address these challenges.

Keywords: Large Language Model (LLM) · ChatGPT · Trustworthiness · Code Generation

1 Introduction

OpenAI has developed ChatGPT, a chatbot based on a large language model (LLM) tailored for conversational purposes. OpenAI is improving the LLM continuously. It has been started with the first version of this model which is called Generative Pre-trained Transformer(GPT) in 2018 [15]. ChatGPT is using version 3.5 and 4 of GPT while version 5 is going to release in the near future. By leveraging its comprehension of the context and conversation history, ChatGPT is capable of generating responses that closely resemble those of a human [11]. ChatGPT has gained significant global attention and is widely discussed and utilized across various domains and applications [3]–particularly programmers

© The Author(s), under exclusive license to Springer Nature Switzerland AG 2024
M. A. Jabbar et al. (Eds.): AMLDA 2023, CCIS 2047, pp. 215–229, 2024.
https://doi.org/10.1007/978-3-031-55486-5_16

who find it valuable for code generation and error identification purposes [20]. ChatGPT has been utilized for various purposes in code generation, including code writing and debugging, preparing for programming interviews, working on programming-related assignments, and other related tasks [4]. Various other AI-based code generation tools, such as Amazon's CodeWhisper and Google's Bard, are also available. Table 1 presents some of the existing code generation AI tools.

Table 1. Existing Code Generation AI Tools

	Tools
OpenAI	ChatGPT, OpenAI Codex
Google	BARD
Tabnine	Tabnine
CodeT5	Salesforce
GitHub Copilot	GitHub, OpenAI, and Microsoft
Amazon CodeWhisperer	Amazon

Many developers commonly reuse code they find in open-access repositories like GitHub, online forums, and websites such as Stack Overflow. Large Language Models (LLMs) are now being used by software developers to speed up their projects by generating code. However, it's important to be cautious about the quality of code generated by LLMs or other third-party sources, even if it seems to be free from major bugs or vulnerabilities in experimental situations. [11]. Copying code snippets from such sources can introduce security vulnerabilities, compatibility issues, and make project maintenance more challenging. Several studies, tools, and projects have delved into the reliability of reused code from third-party sources and its impact on project development and maintenance. It's worth noting that ChatGPT has its limitations, particularly in terms of the accuracy and trustworthiness of the code it generates. Occasionally, the model may produce responses that sound plausible but are factually incorrect or nonsensical, a phenomenon referred to as "hallucination." [19]. It is also sensitive to input phrasing and can exhibit biases present in the training data. For this reason, reusing the generated code by ChatGPT can cause security or maintenance issues in software projects. If we assume that the generated code is correct and explainable, then there is no guarantee that this code will not cause problems in the future of the project. This issue which is addressed as the trustworthiness of generated code by ChatGPT–as well as other LLM-based models–is overlooked amid the excitement over ChatGPT's capabilities.

In this paper, we address the problem of the trustworthiness of generated code by ChatGPT. In software development, "trustworthiness" refers to the quality of a software system or application in terms of its reliability, security, and overall performance. Trustworthiness encompasses several key aspects such as security, stability, or performance. Achieving trustworthiness often involves rigorous testing, security assessments, adherence to coding standards, and ongoing maintenance and updates to address emerging issues. Our contribution is to provide an overview of challenges and opportunities for starting the research on issues related to this topic. Because the subject is relatively new, there is a limited body of research and resources addressing the challenges associated with reusing the code generated by ChatGPT. As a result, we initiated our investigation of this field by conducting a study based on interviews. We interviewed 20 developers who use ChatGPT for code generation and asked their opinion about trusting the generated code of ChatGPT. We analyzed the results of the interviews with the aim of examining the strengths and weaknesses of ChatGPT in code generation. Drawing from their expertise, we have identified various challenges and provided recommendations to mitigate potential issues regarding the trustworthiness of the generated code of ChatGPT.

The results of our interview-based study can be used as a starting point for further studies and development of methods and tools regarding automated controlling and checking the trust issues in generated code with LLMs. Furthermore, this study fills the gap of knowledge and communication between software developers who are using the development tools and the machine learning experts who are developing tools like ChatGPT.

The rest of this paper is structured as follows. In Sect. 2, we review prior research carried out in this domain. In Sect. 3 we delve into the interviews and the concerns raised by the interviewees. In Sect. 4 we discuss potential approaches that can improve the reliability and authenticity of ChatGPT.

2   Related Work

Within this domain, we delve into two distinct contexts. Firstly, we discuss articles related to LLMs and mostly ChatGPT, highlighting their relevance. Secondly, we explore articles that focus on the verification of reliable coding, providing insights into this particular area.

2.1   ChatGPT

While ChatGPT demonstrates impressive language generation capabilities, it is important to note that it has limitations. The model can sometimes produce responses that may be plausible-sounding but factually incorrect or nonsensical called hallucination [19]. Numerous techniques exist for addressing hallucination within the field of Natural Language Generation (NLG) One strategy involves considering the degree of hallucination as a manageable characteristic and restraining it to a minimum using controlled generation methods like controlled re-sampling and control codes, which can either be manually input or predicted automatically. Another method entails employing metrics to assess the excellence of the produced text, including factors like factual coherence. Additionally, refining pre-trained language models using synthetic data containing automatically integrated hallucinations is proposed as an alternative technique for pinpointing hallucinatory elements in summaries [8].

Sun et al. [18] proposed an evaluation of ChatGPT's performance in code summarization using three metrics: BLEU, METEOR, and ROUGE-L. BLEU measures how much a generated summary is like the provided reference summaries. It looks at the words used and higher scores mean the generated summary is more similar to the references. METEOR also compares the generated summary to the reference summaries, but it looks at many aspects like matching words, and it gives higher scores when the generated summary is more like the references. ROUGE-L checks the longest shared part between the generated summary and the references. Higher scores mean the generated summary and references have more words in common. These metrics gauge the quality of the generated comments in comparison to the ground-truth comments. Among these metrics, ChatGPT's performance is inferior to three state-of-the-art models (NCS, CodeBERT, and CodeT5) in terms of BLEU, METEOR, and ROUGE-L scores. However, it is noteworthy that ChatGPT achieves a higher METEOR score compared to the other models, implying that its generated comments may possess specific linguistic qualities captured by METEOR but not entirely reflected in the other metrics [18]. Despite this, recent studies have revealed limitations in match-based metrics when evaluating code. For example, [16] discovered that BLEU struggles to capture code-specific semantic features and proposed various semantic adjustments to improve the scoring accuracy [1]. As a result recent studies have shifted their focus to prioritize functional correctness. Under this approach, a code sample is deemed correct only when it successfully passes a predefined set of unit tests [1]. In their assessment, Kul [10] utilized the pass@k metric to asses functional correctness. They produced k-code samples for each problem and deemed a problem solved if any of the samples generated passed the unit tests. The reported metric reflects the overall fraction of successfully solved problems using this particular criterion.

Liu et al. [11] state that the effectiveness of ChatGPT in generating code is often influenced by how prompts are designed. Two main factors affect prompt design:

1. Chain-of-Thought (CoT) prompting: This strategy allows an LLM to solve problems by guiding it to produce a sequence of intermediate steps before providing the final answer. CoT prompting has been extensively studied and applied to guide ChatGPT in code generation tasks.
2. Manual Prompt Design: Prompt design and multi-step optimizations are based on human understanding and observations. The knowledge and expertise of the designer can impact the performance of the prompts used. To minimize bias, prompt design, and combination choices should be based on a large and randomized sample size.

To enhance generation performance through prompt design, they propose a two-step approach:

1. Prompt Description: Analyze the requirements of a code generation task and create a basic prompt in a natural manner. Then, present the basic prompt

to ChatGPT and ask for suggestions on how to improve it. Incorporate Chat-GPT's suggestions to refine the prompt further.
2. Multi-Step Optimizations: Evaluate the prompt designed in the first step using samples from the training data of the relevant dataset. Analyze the generation performance by comparing it with the ground-truth results. Continuously optimize the generation results by providing ChatGPT with a series of new prompts.

It is important to acknowledge that the prompt design and combination choices were based on a limited number of tests. Conducting more tests can contribute to further enhancing the effectiveness of the designed prompts and reinforcing the conclusions and findings [11].

Jansen et al. [7] assert that large language models (LLMs) have the potential to tackle certain issues related to survey research, such as question formulation and response bias, by generating responses to survey items. However, LLMs have limitations in terms of addressing sampling and nonresponse bias in survey research. Consequently, it is necessary to combine LLMs with other methods and approaches to maximize the effectiveness of survey research. By adopting careful and nuanced approaches to their development and utilization, LLMs can be employed responsibly and advantageously while mitigating potential risks [7].

Feng et al. [4] introduces a crowdsourcing data-driven framework that integrates multiple social media data sources to assess the code generation performance of ChatGPT, a generative language model. The framework consists of three main components: keyword expansion, data collection, and data analytics. The authors utilized topic modeling and expert knowledge to identify programming-related keywords specifically relevant to ChatGPT, thus expanding its initial seed keyword. With these expanded keywords, they collected 316K tweets and 3.2K Reddit posts discussing ChatGPT's code generation between December 1, 2022, and January 31, 2023. The study discovered that Python was the most widely used programming language in ChatGPT, and users primarily employed it for tasks such as generating code snippets, debugging, and producing code for machine learning models. The study also analyzed the temporal distribution of discussions related to ChatGPT's code generation and found that peak activity occurred in mid-January 2023. Furthermore, the research examined stakeholders' perspectives on ChatGPT's code generation, the quality of the generated code, and the presence of any ethical concerns associated with the generated code [4].

2.2 Trustworthiness

Dener and Batisti [2] discuss the security and ethical considerations surrounding the use of LLMs such as ChatGPT. While artificial intelligence (AI) advancements in natural language processing (NLP) have been remarkable, there is a growing apprehension regarding the potential safety and security risks and ethical implications associated with these models. The article points out that ChatGPT's filters are not completely foolproof and can be circumvented through creative instructions and role-playing. Utilizing large language models like Chat-GPT raises ethical concerns related to privacy, security, fairness, and the possibility of generating inappropriate or harmful content. The paper emphasizes the necessity for further research to address the ethical and security implications of large language models. It also presents a qualitative analysis of ChatGPT's security implications and explores potential strategies to mitigate these risks. The intention of the paper is to provide insights to researchers, policymakers, and industry professionals about the complex security challenges posed by LLMs like ChatGPT. Additionally, the paper includes an empirical study that assesses the effectiveness of ChatGPT's content filters and identifies potential methods to bypass them. The study demonstrates the existence of ethical and security risks in LLMs, even when protective measures are implemented. In summary, the paper underscores the ongoing need for research and development efforts to address the ethical and security implications associated with large language models like ChatGPT [2].

Mylrea and Robinson [13] assert that the AI Trust Framework and Maturity Model (AI-TFMM) is a method aimed at enhancing the measurement of trust in AI technologies used by Autonomous Human Machine Teams & Systems (A-HMT-S). The framework addresses important aspects like security, privacy, explainability, transparency, and other ethical requirements for the development and implementation of AI technologies. The maturity model framework employed in this approach helps quantify trust and associated evaluation metrics while identifying areas that need improvement. It offers a structured assessment of an organization's current trust in AI technologies and provides a roadmap for enhancing that trust. By utilizing the maturity model framework, organizations can track their progress and continually improve trust in AI technologies. Overall, the maturity model framework is an invaluable tool for quantifying trust in AI technologies and ensuring ethical practices in their development and use. The AI-TFMM is also examined in relation to a popular AI technology, ChatGPT, and the article concludes with results and findings from testing the framework. The AI-TFMM serves as a critical framework in addressing key questions about trust in AI technology. Striking the right balance between performance, governance, and ethics is essential, and the AI-TFMM provides a method for measuring trust and associated evaluation metrics. The framework can be utilized to enhance the accuracy, efficacy, application, and methodology of the AI-TFMM. The article also identifies areas for future research to fill gaps and improve the AI-TFMM and its application to AI technology. In summary, the AI Trust Framework and Maturity Model is a valuable tool for enhancing trust in AI technologies and ensuring their ethical development and application [13].

Ghofrani et al. [5] conducted a study focusing on trust-related challenges when reusing open-source software from a human factors perspective. The objective of the study was to gain insights into the concerns of developers that hinder trust and present potential solutions suggested by developers to enhance trust levels. Sixteen software developers with 5 to 10 years of industry experience participated in exploratory interviews for the study. The findings indicate that developers possess a good understanding of the associated risks and have a reasonable level of trust in third-party open-source projects and libraries. However, the proposed solutions generally lack recommendations for utilizing automated tools or systematic methods. Instead, the suggested solutions primarily rely on developers' personal experiences rather than existing frameworks or tools. The study concludes that these limitations are interconnected, and the absence of ongoing support can gradually lead to security vulnerabilities. In turn, a project with numerous vulnerabilities may become prohibitively expensive to maintain, ultimately resulting in abandonment [5].

Wermke et al. [21] explore the advantages and difficulties associated with integrating open-source components (OSCs) into software projects. The research reveals that OSCs have a significant role in numerous software projects, with most projects implementing company policies or best practices for including external code. However, the inclusion of OSCs presents specific security challenges and potential vulnerabilities, such as the use of code contributed by individuals without proper vetting and the obligation to assess and address vulnerabilities in external components. The study also indicates that many developers desire additional resources, dedicated teams, or tools to effectively evaluate the components they include. Additionally, the article outlines the study's approach, which involved conducting 25 detailed, semi-structured interviews with software developers, architects, and engineers involved in various industrial projects. The participants represented a diverse range of projects and backgrounds, spanning from web applications to scientific computing frameworks. Overall, the findings emphasize the importance of thoroughly considering the security implications of incorporating OSCs into software projects and the necessity for companies to establish policies and best practices to mitigate the impact of vulnerabilities in external components [21].

In contrast to above mentioned contributions, we focus on trustworthiness in generated code by LLMs in particular ChatGPT in the practical stage. The focus of the previous studies are mainly on security concerns of code from third parties which are written by a human or generated from Models which are created by human. This kind of code is different than written code by LLM-based tools. Therefore, it is necessary to investigate the measures which may be required for trust in the code generated with new LLM-based tools.

3   Methodology

Because our research topic has not been extensively explored, interview-based studies align effectively with our chosen research methodology. This approach allows us to thoroughly investigate the subject and gather valuable insights due to its suitability for exploring uncharted areas of inquiry. Consequently, among the spectrum of available research methods, interviews are selectively employed to elicit a more comprehensive array of viewpoints pertaining to the research subject, thereby serving as a foundational step for the progression of future investigations in this domain. [12]. In this context, we distributed a set of interview questions to programmers with the aim of collecting their insights and viewpoints regarding the generation of code using ChatGPT. To fulfill this objective, we formulated interview questions specifically tailored for individuals with diverse expertise in this particular. We conducted interviews with 20 individuals, including developers, engineers, students, and researchers, who work in reputable companies with large teams. As stated by Saunders and Townsend [17], the most common sample size in qualitative research typically falls between 15 and 60 participants. To gather their perspectives, we posed a set of 10 questions that delved into their positions, programming expertise, frequency of ChatGPT usage, reliability of the generated code, and suggestions for future improvements. Our Interviews are inspired by a questionnaire from Parnel et al. [14]. Here are the questions:

- What is your expertise?
- What is your current activity?
- How big is your working company?
- Do you employ generative AI models, like ChatGPT, for the purpose of code generation? Furthermore, what is the frequency of utilization for code produced by ChatGPT, and in which typical scenarios does this usage occur?
- Can you recall a point in this situation when you did not trust the generated code by ChatGPT?
- Would you generally tend to trust the generated code by ChatGPT? Please expand on why.
- Do you have any distrust in the generated code by ChatGPT? What is the cause of this distrust? How could it be repaired?
- Would you have any reason not to trust the generated code by ChatGPT in the future?
- For the future, how reliable/dependent do you view the generated code by ChatGPT to be?
- What information/knowledge would you need to trust the generated code by ChatGPT?

Table 2 lists the summary of the various backgrounds and expertise of the interviewees.

Table 2. Overviewing of the interviewees' expertise

Expertise	Count
Frontend Engineer	6
Software Engineer	4
Student	4
Android/iOS Developer	3
Backend Developer	2
Data Scientist	1

The majority of participants reported using ChatGPT on a daily basis, with some utilizing tools like the GitHub Co-pilot plugin and Tabnine. However, all interviewees shared instances where the generated code proved to be unreliable and inaccurate, necessitating manual verification and extensive time investment. Some participants mentioned using ChatGPT-generated code as a starting point, but modifying it extensively to suit their specific use cases. Overall, the consensus among the interviewees was that the generated code should not be blindly trusted or relied upon, and thorough checking and review are essential. Fig. 1 shows one instance provided by interviewees highlighting the unreliability of ChatGPT. He first asked ChatGPT to write code in Python to implement a box plot for a dataframe. The output worked fine, but on the second step, he asked ChatGPT

  I want to have different colors for each quartile

  Certainly! You can achieve this by specifying the `boxprops` parameter in `boxplot` function of `matplotlib`. This allows you to customize various properties of the boxes, including their colors. Here's an example of how to create a box plot with different colors for each quartile using Matplotlib:

```python
import pandas as pd
import matplotlib.pyplot as plt

# Sample DataFrame
data = {
    'A': [10, 15, 20, 25, 30, 35, 40, 45, 50],
    'B': [5, 12, 18, 24, 31, 37, 42, 47, 52],
}

df = pd.DataFrame(data)

# Define colors for each quartile
box_colors = ['skyblue', 'lightgreen', 'lightcoral', 'gold']

# Creating a box plot with custom colors for each quartile
plt.boxplot(df.values, labels=df.columns, boxprops=dict(facecolor=box_colors
plt.title('Box Plot with Custom Quartile Colors')
plt.ylabel('Values')
plt.show()
```

Fig. 1. Asking ChatGPT to provide different colors for each quartile in a box plot

to provide that box plot with different colors for each quartile which is depicted in Fig. 1 where ChatGPT provided some code that resulted in errors. The error states that Line2D.set() got an unexpected keyword argument 'facecolor'. So ChatGPT might hallucinate when it has no idea what to produce as output [9].

It's important to highlight that all interviewees have experience with Chat-GPT 3.5, but it is important to recognize the advancements made in the updated model, ChatGPT 4.0. This newer version has made strides in addressing some of the issues and bugs that were present in the initial release. However, it is pertinent to acknowledge that accessibility to ChatGPT 4.0 is limited, as it is not available for free. This limitation poses a challenge for certain students and programmers who may lack the financial resources to afford the updated version.

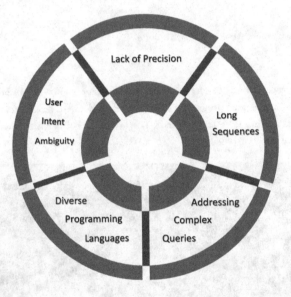

Fig. 2. Main problems of ChatGPT for generating reusable code according to our interviews

After analyzing these questions, we identified five issues that were unanimously agreed upon by all interviewees. These problems undermine the trustworthiness of ChatGPT and its ability to provide accurate answers. Figure 2 illustrates these problems briefly. The full description of each problem is as follows:

1. Lack of Precision: ChatGPT may not generate code that is as precise and efficient as what experienced developers can produce. Code requires strict adherence to syntax, logic, and optimization, which might not always be guaranteed by the model.
2. Long Sequences: ChatGPT has a token limit that can restrict the length and complexity of code generated in a single prompt. This can limit the

model's ability to generate longer or more complex code segments. This might necessitate breaking down the task into smaller parts.

3. User Intent Ambiguity: ChatGPT might misinterpret user intent, leading to code that doesn't accurately address the user's needs.

4. Diverse Programming Languages, Libraries, and Frameworks: The realm of programming encompasses an extensive spectrum of languages tailored to diverse applications, ranging from versatile options like Python, Java, and C++ to specialized alternatives such as R and MATLAB. However, it is imperative to acknowledge that while ChatGPT has been extensively trained on a substantial corpus of internet text, its mastery is not all-encompassing. Its competence across programming languages is not uniform, exhibiting variations, and certain languages may command a more limited familiarity. Additionally, its grasp may be less robust concerning nascent or niche programming languages. Thus, it is advisable to provide contextual specifics when dealing with relatively uncommon or specialized technologies, as ChatGPT's exposure during training might not encompass these facets comprehensively. Also, many projects rely on specific libraries or frameworks. The model might not be up-to-date on these tools, causing it to generate code that doesn't effectively leverage available resources.

5. Addressing Complex Queries: The queries presented to ChatGPT are intricate, spanning from inquiries about solving theoretical mathematical concepts to abstract ideas that even experts might find challenging. It's crucial to recognize that ChatGPT's training and intended purpose are distinct, which limits the range of questions it can adeptly address.

4 Future Research Directions

Considering the issues and shortcomings discussed earlier, we can suggest potential solutions and future research to enhance the performance of ChatGPT and formulate a roadmap and policy for its continuous development and improvement. Figure 3 presents a visual representation of recommendations aimed at enhancing the performance of LLMs in code generation.

1. Fine-Tuning for Code Generation: Tailoring ChatGPT's training on specific programming domains and languages could enhance its code generation accuracy within those areas, addressing challenges related to syntax and semantics.

2. Standardize ChatGPT: To ensure clarity and facilitate effective usage of ChatGPT, it is important to establish and publish documents and standards that outline guidelines for its utilization. Currently, there is a lack of standardized documentation that clearly defines how to use ChatGPT and sets expectations regarding its capabilities and limitations. By creating comprehensive documentation, developers and users would have access to a clear set of instructions, best practices, and recommended approaches for interacting with ChatGPT. This would encompass guidance on various aspects, such as

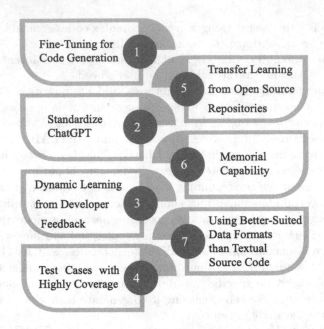

Fig. 3. Suggestion for enriching LLMs for generating code

input format, understanding response types, addressing potential biases, and providing context to optimize the quality of responses. The availability of such documents and standards would promote consistent and informed utilization of ChatGPT, enabling users to leverage its potential effectively and navigate its capabilities with confidence.

3. Dynamic Learning from Developer Feedback: Developing methods for Chat-GPT to learn from developers' corrections and suggestions, allowing the model to continuously improve its code generation abilities.

4. Test Cases with High Coverage: To validate the quality of the generated code, it is imperative to develop exhaustive test cases that achieve high coverage. These test cases play a crucial role in confirming the functionality and accuracy of the code produced by ChatGPT. By formulating test cases that encompass a diverse range of scenarios, including edge cases and potential inputs, we can thoroughly scrutinize the reliability and precision of the generated code. Robust test coverage ensures a comprehensive examination of various code aspects, including corner cases and potential pitfalls. This scrutiny allows us to detect any inconsistencies or errors within the generated code and implement corrective measures as needed. Through meticulous testing, we can establish a high level of confidence in the authenticity and effectiveness of the generated code, thus validating its applicability to real-world contexts

5. Transfer Learning from Open Source Repositories: Exploring the use of open-source code repositories to train the model on real-world coding patterns and practices, improving its understanding of actual coding conventions.
6. Memorial Capability: The suggestion is to enhance the ChatGPT model by enabling it to remember previous searches and provide tailored solutions based on previous questions and the user's skill level. For example, if someone asks multiple programming-related questions involving various libraries and frameworks, the response should include generated code incorporating sophisticated algorithms and a broader perspective.
7. Using Better-Suited Data Formats than Textual Source Code: Contributions like [6] show that textual source code might not be the best choice for the training of machine learning tasks on source code. Actually in the experiments of [6], higher accuracies with less memory consumption are achieved for the same amount of training data when eliminating variable names but still maintaining declaration-usage relations in a graph representation of the source code. Future Large Language Models may be based on these or similar techniques for the purpose of generating better code with less training data.

5   Discussion

The purpose of the interview is to gather valuable insights and opinions of prominent programmers and researchers in relation to the code generated by Chat-GPT. Great care was taken in the selection process to ensure a comprehensive representation of diverse perspectives, avoiding any potential biases towards specific individuals. Although the number of participants in the interviews may not have been extensive, their feedback still provides significant and meaningful information about the current state of LLMs and especially ChatGPT. Through these interviews, various problems and weaknesses of the model have been brought to light, shedding light on areas that require improvement.

Nonetheless, the research conducted through these interviews serves as a significant starting point for initiating discussions within the researchers' community. The aim is to explore the reliability and trustworthiness of ChatGPT and brainstorm potential solutions to enhance the model. By fostering a collaborative environment for knowledge sharing and problem-solving, this research endeavor hopes to contribute to the ongoing efforts to improve LLMs and ensure its effectiveness and usability for a wider range of users.

6   Conclusion

This article delves into a topic that has sparked considerable debate: trustworthiness of the code generated by ChatGPT. By conducting interviews with esteemed programmers and researchers, the authors aim to delve into their perspectives regarding the trustworthiness of the code produced by the model. The consensus emerging from these interviews is that ChatGPT's generated code frequently lacks precision, necessitating manual debugging, and substantial time investment, particularly when handling complex code scenarios. Through a meticulous analysis of the interview data, the article identifies five key challenges inherent to ChatGPT's code generation process. These challenges encompass issues related to the accuracy, code length limitations of a single prompt, interpreting user intent, accommodating diverse programming languages, tools, and methodologies, as well as addressing intricate inquiries. Each challenge is thoroughly scrutinized to provide a comprehensive grasp of the encountered hurdles. To enhance the performance of Large Language Models (LLMs) and elevate precision, the article proposes seven potential solutions. These solutions are meticulously tailored to tackle the identified challenges and enhance the model's overall reliability. The fundamental aim of this research is to cultivate an inclusive environment conducive to evaluating the trustworthiness of ChatGPT's code generation outputs.

Acknowledgments. This work is funded by the Deutsche Forschungsgemeinschaft (DFG, German Research Foundation) - Project-ID 490998901.

References

1. Chen, M., et al.: Evaluating large language models trained on code. arXiv preprint arXiv:2107.03374 (2021)
2. Derner, E., Batistič, K.: Beyond the safeguards: exploring the security risks of ChatGPT. arXiv preprint arXiv:2305.08005 (2023)
3. Dinesh, K., Nathan, S.: Study and analysis of chat GPT and its impact on different fields of study (2023)
4. Feng, Y., Vanam, S., Cherukupally, M., Zheng, W., Qiu, M., Chen, H.: Investigating code generation performance of chat-GPT with crowdsourcing social data. In: Proceedings of the 47th IEEE Computer Software and Applications Conference, pp. 1–10 (2023)
5. Ghofrani, J., Heravi, P., Babaei, K.A., Soora-ti, M.D.: Trust challenges in reusing open source software: an interview-based initial study. In: Proceedings of the 26th ACM International Systems and Software Product Line Conference-Volume B, pp. 110–116 (2022)
6. Groppe, J., Groppe, S., Möller, R.: Variables are a curse in software vulnerability prediction. In: The 34th International Conference on Database and Expert Systems Applications (DEXA), Panang, Malaysia (2023)
7. Jansen, B.J., Jung, S.G., Salminen, J.: Employing large language models in survey research. Nat. Lang. Process. J. **4**, 100020 (2023)
8. Ji, Z., et al.: Survey of hallucination in natural language generation. ACM Comput. Surv. **55**(12), 1–38 (2023)
9. Khorashadizadeh, H., Mihindukulasooriya, N., Tiwari, S., Groppe, J., Groppe, S.: Exploring in-context learning capabilities of foundation models for generating knowledge graphs from text. arXiv preprint arXiv:2305.08804 (2023)
10. Kulal, S., et al.: SPOC: search-based pseudocode to code. In: Advances in Neural Information Processing Systems, vol. 32 (2019)
11. Liu, C., et al.: Improving ChatGPT prompt for code generation. arXiv preprint arXiv:2305.08360 (2023)

12. Magnusson, E., Marecek, J.: Doing Interview-based Qualitative Research: A Learner's Guide. Cambridge University Press, Cambridge (2015)
13. Mylrea, M., Robinson, N.: Ai trust framework and maturity model: improving security, ethics and trust in AI. Cybersecur. Innov. Technol. J. **1**(1), 1–15 (2023)
14. Parnell, K.J., et al.: Trustworthy UAV relationships: applying the schema action world taxonomy to UAVs and UAV swarm operations. Int. J. Hum.-Comput. Interact. **39**, 1–17 (2022)
15. Radford, A., Narasimhan, K., Salimans, T., Sutskever, I., et al.: Improving language understanding by generative pre-training (2018)
16. Ren, S., et al.: Codebleu: a method for automatic evaluation of code synthesis. arXiv preprint arXiv:2009.10297 (2020)
17. Saunders, M.N., Townsend, K.: Reporting and justifying the number of interview participants in organization and workplace research. Br. J. Manag. **27**(4), 836–852 (2016)
18. Sun, W., et al.: Automatic code summarization via ChatGPT: how far are we? arXiv preprint arXiv:2305.12865 (2023)
19. Tao, H., Cao, Q., Chen, H., Xian, Y., Shang, S., Niu, X.: A novel software trustworthiness evaluation strategy via relationships between criteria. Symmetry **14**(11), 2458 (2022)
20. Tao, H., Fu, L., Chen, Y., Han, L., Wang, X.: Improved allocation and reallocation approaches for software trustworthiness based on mathematical programming. Symmetry **14**(3), 628 (2022)
21. Wermke, D., et al.: "Always contribute back": a qualitative study on security challenges of the open source supply chain. In: Proceedings of the 44th IEEE Symposium on Security and Privacy (S&P 2023). IEEE (2023)

Sentiment Analysis of Monkeypox Tweets in Latin America

Josimar Chire-Saire[1] ⓘ, Anabel Pineda-Briseño[2](✉) ⓘ,
and Jimy Oblitas-Cruz[3] ⓘ

[1] University of São Paulo (USP), São Carlos, Brazil
jecs89@usp.br
[2] TecNM/Instituto Tecnológico de Matamoros, H. Matamoros, Mexico
anabel.pb@matamoros.tecnm.mx
[3] Universidad Privada del Norte, Trujillo, Peru
jimy.oblitas@upn.edu.pe

Abstract. Even during the Covid-19 pandemic, a new outbreak of Monkeypox was confirmed in the United Kingdom, and from there it has spread throughout the world. Among the most affected countries are those located in Latin America, one of the most vulnerable regions due to the lack of adequate hospital infrastructure, the shortcomings or deficiencies of health care systems, or populations with a high prevalence of chronic diseases. Social media platforms, such as Twitter, have become valuable sources of real-time information and public sentiment during disease outbreaks. This study presents an analysis of sentiment expressed in tweets related to Monkeypox in Latin America, aiming to understand public perceptions and emotional responses. We collected a dataset of tweets containing keywords associated with Monkeypox, originating from Latin American countries, over a specific time frame (from May 31, 2022, to October 31, 2022). Natural language processing techniques were employed to preprocess and analyze the textual content. Sentiment analysis tools were applied to classify tweets into positive or negative sentiments. Our findings reveal valuable insights into the sentiment dynamics surrounding Monkeypox in Latin America. We observed fluctuations in sentiment over time, closely aligned with the progression of the disease and related events.

Keywords: Sentiment Analysis · Monkeypox · Social Media · Machine Learning

1 Introduction

Monkeypox is a re-emerging zoonotic disease caused by the monkeypox virus (MPXV). MPXV was first detected in monkeys in 1958 [25]. Since its first manifestation in humans, in the Democratic Republic of the Congo in 1970 [8,27], outbreaks have been reported in many countries, where most cases are restricted to endemic areas [5]. Nevertheless, at the beginning of the year 2022, even during the Covid-19 pandemic, a new outbreak of MPXV was confirmed in the

M. A. Jabbar et al. (Eds.): AMLDA 2023, CCIS 2047, pp. 230–245, 2024.
https://doi.org/10.1007/978-3-031-55486-5_17

United Kingdom on May 7, 2022 [41]. Now, due to the rapidly spreading around the world, the MPXV outbreak represents a global health emergency. For this reason, on July 23, 2022, the World Health Organization (WHO) declared the highest level of alert [47].

In another order of ideas, the ubiquity of social media has made them a valuable source of data for public health research in the digital age. Through them, people express their ideas, interests, feelings, opinions, experiences, and events, including information related to both physical and mental health. One of the most used social networks is Twitter, which offers a free service for sharing short-text messages or "tweets". By January 2022, Twitter has around 436 million active users around the world [9]. Thanks to their characteristics and use, Twitter is a promising data source for surveillance because of message volume, frequency, and public availability.

Sentiment analysis in the context of public health is a vital tool for understanding public perceptions and emotions. There are seminal papers about advanced sentiment analysis techniques employed for monitoring of public sentiment through social media, news sources, and online forums, of various types of health conditions such as: cancer [6], diabetes [13], asperger syndrome [12], COVID-19 pandemic [1,10,14,16,21,24,36,42,46], and Monkeypox disease [3,20,49]. Researchers and public health authorities have utilized sentiment analysis to identify and track misinformation and gauge the emotional states of individuals and communities. Emotion detection and multilingual analysis plays key roles in comprehensively assessing public sentiment. Moreover, sentiment analysis when integrating with epidemiological data could help to explore potential correlations between public sentiment, policy interventions, and disease spread.

This research contributes to understanding of public sentiment during disease outbreaks and provides guidance for public health agencies and policymakers in Latin America to tailor their communication strategies effectively.

The rest of this paper is structured as follows. Section 2 presents an overview of the MPXV outbreak around the world, with an emphasis on Latin America. In Sect. 3 the methodology employed in this study is described. In Sect. 3.4 the results of our research are presented. Next, in Sect. 4 final reflections are exposed. Last, Sect. 5 displays the conclusions and future work.

2   Monkeypox Outbreak Global Situation

2.1   Overview

This section is providing a global overview of the MPXV epidemiological situation as reported to WHO as of October 31, 2022. The information used in this section was obtained from [38]. Since January 1, 2022, cases of MPXV have been reported to WHO from 109 member countries across 6 regions (Region of the Americas, European Region, African Region, Western Pacific Region, Eastern Mediterranean Region, and South-East Asia Region) into which the WHO is divided. As of October 31, 2022, a total of 77,300 laboratory-confirmed cases worldwide, including 36 deaths, have been reported to WHO. In each country, an outbreak is considered when there is confirmation of a case of MPXV. With the aforementioned information, we have created a map with the global perspective, which is shown in Fig. 1. In early May 2022, MPVX cases were reported in non-endemic countries such as the UK, Spain, and elsewhere in Europe. In the same way, we have create the Table 1 with the 10 most affected countries globally. It is important to point out that this list is in order to contextualize the general situation of MPXVin the world and does not consider the total population of the countries.

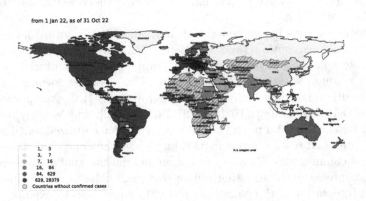

Fig. 1. 2022 Monkeypox Outbreak Global Map.

On the other hand, Fig. 2 shows the number of confirmed cases and deaths weekly from January 1, 2022, to October 31, 2022. The cases and deaths shown in the epidemic curve are aggregated according to international standard weeks, running from Monday to Sunday, based on ISO 8601 [19]. It can be seen in Fig. 2 that the MPVX virus in non-endemic countries started to increase its spreading at week 20 (from May 16 to 22). The first peak of the wave was reached during week 32 (from Aug 8 to 14). After that, the cases reported were decreasing. However, it was not until July 23, 2022, that the WHO declared MPVX an international health emergency [47].

The WHO is continually assessing the level of global risk. According to reports for October 31, 2022, a moderate risk has been globally determined. Nevertheless, according to how contagions have been spreading by regions, for the region of the Americas the risk is high; for African, Eastern Mediterranean, European, and South-East Asia Regions the risk is moderate, and a low risk has been assessed for the Western Pacific Region. As of October 31, 2022, the WHO maintains the status of the MPVX outbreak as an international public health emergency. This was determined in the third meeting of the International

Table 1. The 10 most affected countries globally (MPXV).

#	Flag	Country	Cases - cumulative total (Oct 31)	Deaths - cumulative total (Oct 31)
1		United States of America	28,379	6
2		Brazil	9,183	8
3		Spain	7,317	2
4		France	4,094	0
5		United Kingdom	3,698	0
6		Germany	3,662	0
7		Colombia	3,298	0
8		Peru	3,048	0
9		Mexico	2,654	0
10		Canada	1,437	0

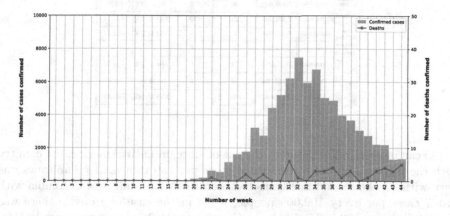

Fig. 2. Map of confirmed cases and deaths of MPXV in the World.

Health Regulations (2005) (IHR) Emergency Committee regarding the multi-country outbreak of MPVX, which was held on Thursday, 20 October 2022 [39].

2.2 Monkeypox Spreading in Latin America

This section introduces the context of MPVX spreading in Latin America from January 1, 2022, to October 31, 2022. Table 2 presents a summary of total confirmed cases and deaths by country in Latin America. In addition, we have included the total number of inhabitants by country, the date on which the first case was registered, and the date on which each country reported the first contagion to the WHO. The datasets used in this section were obtained from [38]. Until October 31, 2022, the total number of cases confirmed was 11,466, while the total number of deaths was 1. This represents 14.83% of confirmed cases and 2.77% of deaths globally, respectively.

Table 2. Information about Latin American countries, population (thousands).

Flag	Country	Population	Cases (cumulative total)	Deaths (cumulative total)	First Case	First case (reported to WHO)
	Argentina	45,479,000	675	0	May 27 [7]	Jun 03
	Bolivia	11,640,000	241	0	Aug 01 [40]	Aug 03
	Chile	18,187,000	1,163	0	Jun 17 [30]	Jun 18
	Colombia	49,085,000	3,298	0	Jun 23 [31]	Jun 25
	Ecuador	16,905,000	243	1	Jul 06 [18]	Jun 14
	Peru	31,915,000	3,048	0	Jun 26 [29]	Jun 28
	Paraguay	7,192,000	3	0	Aug 25 [22]	Aug 26
	Uruguay	3,388,000	13	0	Jul 29 [33]	Jul 31
	Venezuela	2,020,000	10	0	Jun 12 [2]	Jun 12
	Costa Rica	5,098,000	8	0	Jul 20 [32]	Jul 21
	El Salvador	6,481,000	13	0	Aug 30 [23]	Aug 14
	Honduras	9,235,000	7	0	Aug 12 [48]	Aug 14
	Nicaragua	6,203,000	0	0	—	—
	Guatemala	17,153,000	74	0	Aug 03 [34]	Aug 04
	Panama	3,894,000	16	0	Jul 05 [11]	Jul 06
	Mexico	134,829,000	2,654	0	May 28 [45]	Jun 03

As can be seen in Fig. 3 and at the cut-off date, in Latin America, the country with the highest number of confirmed cases per 100 thousand inhabitants was Peru with 10, the second most affected countries were Chile and Colombia with just 7 cases per every 100,000 people, while in the case of Bolivia, there was about 3 for every 100,000 individuals. Countries with 2 or fewer cases per 100,000 settlers were Mexico, Argentina, Ecuador, Venezuela, Paraguay, Honduras, Costa Rica, Guatemala, Uruguay, El Salvador, and Panama. The countries Nicaragua and Belize have not reported cases to the WHO.

The foregoing exposes that Latin America is one of the most vulnerable regions due to the lack of adequate hospital infrastructure, the shortcomings or deficiencies of health care systems, or due to populations with a high prevalence of chronic diseases [26, 50]. Due to confirmed cases and the MPVX spread behaviour in Latin American countries, the WHO has assessed the region of the Americas with a high-risk status [38].

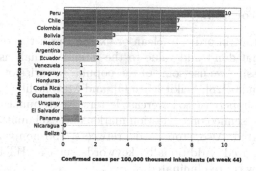

Fig. 3. 2022 MPXV Confirmed Cases in Latin American.

3 Methodology

This section describes data collection, data pre-processing, and data analysis. These are the methods employed to achieve the main objectives of this study, which are summarized in Fig. 4.

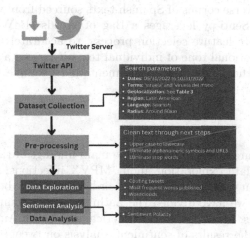

Fig. 4. Summary of the proposed methodology.

3.1 Data Collection

For this work, a total of 55,009 Spanish-language tweets were collected between May 31, 2022, and October 31, 2022. The collection was using the Twitter application programming interface (API). The keywords used for collecting the tweets were "viruela" and "viruela del mono". The search was carried out within a radius of 50 km with the epicenter of each capital city.

3.2 Data Pre-processing

This step is important in order to clean or extract from the text, any symbols, which are words that don't add value to the intended analysis from this work. For data pre-processing we use some of the popular libraries of Python [43] such as NumPy [37], Pandas [28], Scikit-learn [4], and Matplotlib [17]. First, the text was converted from uppercase to lowercase letters. Next, punctuation marks such as commas, periods, semicolons, question marks, and exclamation marks, among others were eliminated. Also, stop words, retweets, and nonprintable characters as emojis were removed. Additionally, keywords such as HTTPS, HTTP, and URL, to name a few, were eliminated.

3.3 Data Analysis

The processed tweets were counted and analyzed using word frequencies of single words (unigrams). Then, they were visualized through word clouds to help to measure public opinion. A heat map was generated with the top 10 words per week of tweets published in Latin America. To complete these tasks we use Python packages Pandas [28], Matplotlib [17], and Wordcloud [35]. Last, a Twitter sentiment analysis was realized using the Senti-py model [15], which was trained on a diverse corpus of Spanish texts sourced from various platforms, including Twitter. Senti-py leverages a Bag of Words (BoW) model, coupled with an intermediate feature selection process, to accurately gauge sentiment. To evaluate the emotional tone of individual texts it is used a scale from 0 to 1, where 0 represents the most negative sentiment, and 1 signifies the most positive sentiment.

3.4 Results

In this section, we are going to present the main findings of this research. First, we will present a data exploration about MPVX infections, tweets published, and most important terms by region. In order to have a better organization of the information, we have divided the Latin American countries into regions, remaining as follows: Mexico, Central America, and South America. Finally, we are going to show the results of sentiment analysis on tweets related to MPVX in Latin America.

Mexico Country. Since the first case of MPVX was reported in Mexico on May 28, 2022, around 2,901 cases have been confirmed by the Mexican Secretariat of Health until October 28, 2022 [44]. The top 5 states from Mexico with a high number of confirmed cases are Ciudad de México, Jalisco, Estado de México, Yucatán and Quintana Roo with 1725, 327, 295, 102 and 85 cases respectively, together representing 87.34% of the total cases diagnosed in the country. The first case was diagnosed in Mexico City [45], which maintains the first position with the highest number of confirmed cases.

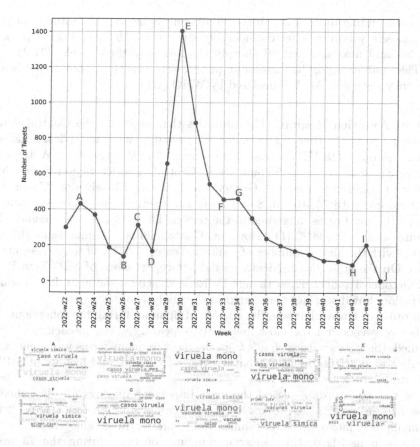

Fig. 5. Published tweets about MPVX and clouds generated from most frequent terms used each week in Mexico.

As shown in Fig. 5, the frequency of tweets was plotted with a weekly granularity from May 31, 2022, to October 31, 2022. When observing the graphic, a specific number of published tweet inflections were labeled during the period analyzed. These labels are A, B, C, D, E, F, G, H, I, and J.

To trace what was the domain of opinion during the inflections, the number of tweets and the most frequently appearing terms in each week are obtained. Next, we generate word clouds from the most frequent terms. In this way, we were able to identify the behavior of the opinions as well as the main concerns about MPVX of Twitter users in Mexico.

The most important findings during the data explored period are described as follows: From week 22 to week 44, the predominate public terms were: "viruela/smallpox", "mono/monkey", "simica/ape", "caso/case", and "casos/cases". As can be seen in Fig. 5, this behavior remains constant during the 23 weeks explored, even when there is variability in the number of tweets published. Unlike the different labeled inflection points (A-D:F-J), the inflection point labeled as

"E" corresponding to week 30, showed a different behavior. The number of published tweets was increasing considerably since week 29, reaching its peak at week 30, and next dropped off sharply the following three weeks (31,32, and 33). The main cause of the increase in publications was the international health emergency regarding MPVX declared by WHO [47].

Central America Region. The countries that make up the Central America region are Costa Rica, El Salvador, Guatemala, Honduras, Nicaragua, and Panama. Around 118 MPVX cases were confirmed in this region by WHO, until October 31, 2022. The top 5 countries in Central America region with a high number of confirmed cases are Guatemala, Panamá, El Salvador, Costa Rica and Honduras with 74, 16, 13, 8 and 7 cases respectively, together representing 100% of the total cases diagnosed in the region. The first case was diagnosed in Panama on July 06, 2022 [11]. However, Guatemala is who maintains the first position with the highest number of confirmed cases, 62.71% of total cases in this region. On the other hand, Nicaragua did not report cases of MPVX to WHO until October 31, 2022. Even though Belize is shown on the map, it is a simple illustration, but it was not considered in the analysis of this work.

In order to trace what was the domain of opinion during the inflections, the number of tweets and the most frequently appearing words in each week were obtained. Right away, word clouds from the most frequent terms were generated. Thus, we were able to identify what Twitter users think and feel about MPVX in Central America.

For the explore data period the most important findings are described as follows: From week 22 to week 44, the predominate public terms were: "viruela/smallpox", "mono/monkey", "simica/ape", "primer/first", and "caso/case". As can be seen in Fig. 6, this behavior remains constant during the 23 weeks explored, even when there is variability in the number of tweets published. Unlike the different labeled inflection points (A-D:F-J), the inflection point labeled as "E" corresponding to week 31, reported a different performance. The number of published tweets was increasing considerably since week 29, reaching its peak at week 31, and next the number of tweets is significantly reduced in the following three weeks (32,33, and 34). The international health emergency declaration respect MPVX by WHO [47] is considered the main cause of the increment in the number of tweets in week 31. Unlike Mexico, the Central America region maintained the increase in publications related to MPVX for longer before the peaking of tweets in week 31.

South America Region. With respect to the South American region, the countries that make it up are Argentina, Colombia, Venezuela, Bolivia, Chile, Ecuador, Peru, Uruguay, and Paraguay. Approximately 8,696 MPVX cases were confirmed in this region by WHO, until October 31, 2022. The top 6 countries in South America region with a high number of confirmed cases are Colombia, Perú, Chile, Argentina, Ecuador and Bolivia with 3298, 3048, 1163, 675, 243 and 241 cases respectively, together representing 99.67% of the total cases diagnosed

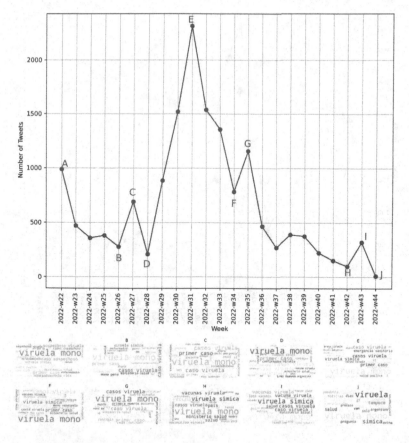

Fig. 6. Published tweets about MPVX and clouds generated from most frequent terms used each week in Central America region.

in the region. The first case was diagnosed in Argentina on June 03, 2022 [7]. However, Colombia and Peru are who maintains first and second position with the highest number of confirmed cases, both representing 72.97% of total cases in this region. On the other hand, Paraguay did not report cases of MPVX to WHO, until October 31, 2022.

In the same way that the analysis was done in the regions of Mexico and Central America, to trace what was the domain of opinion during the inflections, the number of tweets and the most frequently appearing terms in each week are obtained. After, we generate word clouds from the most frequent words. In this way, we were able to identify the opinions and the main concerns about MPVX of South America Twitter users.

The most important findings are described as follows: From week 22 to week 44, the predominate public terms were: "viruela/smallpox", "mono/monkey" and "simica/ape". As can be seen in Fig. 7, this behavior remains constant during

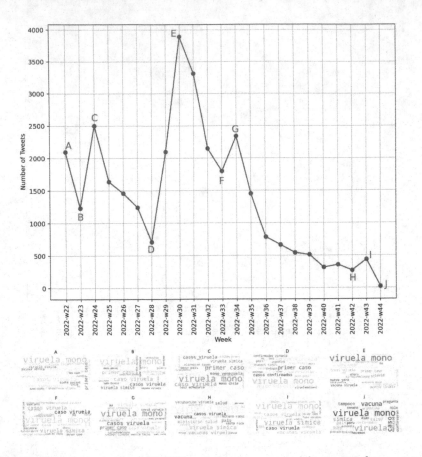

Fig. 7. Published tweets about MPVX and clouds generated from most frequent terms used each week in South America Region.

the 23 weeks explored, even when there is variability in the number of tweets published. Unlike the different labeled inflection points (A-D:F-J), the inflection point labeled as "E" corresponding to week 30, reported a different performance. The number of published tweets was increasing considerably since week 29 until its peak at week 30. Subsequently, the number of tweets was decreasing the following three weeks (31,32 and 33). As in previous regions, the increase in the number of tweets is due to the declaration of the MPVX international health emergency realized by WHO [47]. In general, the South America region reported a performance similarly to Mexico.

Latin America Twitter Sentiment Analysis Polarity. Figure 8 displays the sentiment opinion about MPVX of the Latin American Twitter users per week from May 31, 2022, to October 31, 2022. In general, Twitter users published more negative tweets than positive ones during the 23 weeks analyzed, which represents 91.57%. During week 30, Twitter users published mostly negative tweets, accounting for 11.32% of total negative tweets. It is important to point out that the percentage of negative tweets always predominated over the positive ones from week 22 to week 44, on average 90% more over the course of 23 weeks.

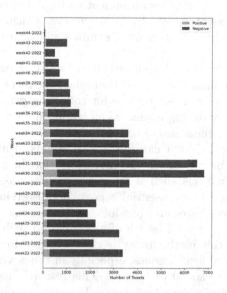

Fig. 8. Sentiment analysis of tweets about MPVX in Latin America.

Expanding on the sentiment analysis, Fig. 9 shows a heatmap with the most common terms with the emotional value used by Latin America Twitter users. It is worth mentioning that "viruela/smallpox," "mono/monkey", "simica/ape", "casos/cases" "oms/who", "salud/health", and "emergencia/emergency" are among the top 10 negative words used by Latin American Twitter users. It is interesting that NLP automatically categorized them as negative words.

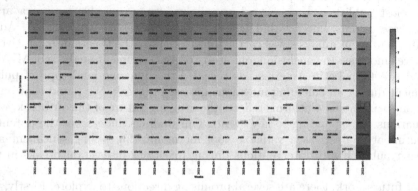

Fig. 9. The top 10 terms per week of the Latin America.

4   Final Thoughts

Being able to draw these conclusions regarding possible health risks in the Latin American population during the wave of Monkeypox shows us the great potential that text mining has, that it was extensive in its data collection and brief in time of treatment and generation of useful indicators for decision-making, compared to other studies that seek the same by using surveys, which, in spite of collecting more detail, their deficiency is their small samples and the time of data collection and processing.

This study presents a novel approach using social networks to monitor, in real-time, information linked to feelings that affect the mental health of the population, besides providing an alternative for collecting primary data on mental health issues, especially during a time when traditional research methodologies may be constrained by measures of social distancing.

Text mining showed that it can find useful trends in line with the current situation, which can be converted into indicators that help make useful public health decisions in situations, such as Monkeypox, since adequate access to accurate health information is an essential aspect, because reliable and up-to-date information on recovery cases and possible treatments may reduce anxiety and stress, and, with it, the mental health of a population such as the Latin America one. In addition, this methodology is shown as an alternative to collecting primary data on mental health issues, especially in times when information cannot be collected due to social distancing. This research also shows that social media have the potential as an alternative data source for public health research, although future studies are needed to improve the relationships of words with feelings that affect mental health.

5   Conclusions and Future Work

This work presented a study to identify the opinions and feelings of Twitter users during the propagation of the MPVX in Latin America. The tweets posted were collected from May 31, 2022, to October 31, 2022. In a first data exploration, the results report that in the outbreak of the MPVX, the top of terms most published were: "viruela/smallpox," "mono/monkey", "simica/ape", "casos/cases" "oms/who", "salud/health", and "emergencia/emergency". Additionally, sentiment analysis was carried out to classify the tweets into positive or negative emotions. In conclusion, our study on the sentiment analysis of MPVX-related tweets in Latin America has revealed the dynamic landscape of public sentiment during an emerging infectious disease outbreak. We found that sentiment on social media platforms reflects the evolving nature of the outbreak, with fluctuations corresponding to key events. Our findings underscore the potential of sentiment analysis as a valuable tool for monitoring public sentiment and tailoring public health interventions during infectious disease outbreaks in the region.

For future work, there are several promising directions to explore. Firstly, the incorporation of geospatial analysis can provide insights into regional variations in sentiment and help prioritize resources for targeted interventions. Secondly, the integration of user demographics and behavioral data could enhance our understanding of how different demographic groups perceive and respond to outbreaks. Lastly, improving the detection of misinformation and fake news in real-time sentiment analysis would contribute to mitigating the infodemic. These avenues for future research can further advance our ability to harness sentiment analysis for effective public health response in Latin America and beyond.

Acknowledgements. The authors thank to Research4tech, an Artificial Intelligence (AI) community of Latin American Researcher with the aim of promoting AI, build science communities to catapult and enforce development of Latin American countries supported on science and technology, integrating academic community, technology groups/communities, government and society. This work was sponsored in part by the Tecnológico Nacional de México/Instituto Tecnológico de Matamoros and by the Consejo Nacional de Humanidades, Ciencias y Tecnologías de México (CONHACyT).

References

1. Alhajji, M., Al Khalifah, A., Aljubran, M., Alkhalifah, M.: Sentiment analysis of tweets in Saudi Arabia regarding governmental preventive measures to contain covid-19 (2020)
2. BBC: Viruela del mono: detectan el primer caso en venezuela (2022). https://www.bbc.com/. Accessed 08 Oct 2022
3. Bengesi, S., Oladunni, T., Olusegun, R., Audu, H.: A machine learning-sentiment analysis on monkeypox outbreak: an extensive dataset to show the polarity of public opinion from twitter tweets. IEEE Access **11**, 11811–11826 (2023)
4. Buitinck, L., et al.: API design for machine learning software: experiences from the scikit-learn project. In: ECML PKDD Workshop: Languages for Data Mining and Machine Learning, pp. 108–122 (2013)
5. Bunge, E.M., et al.: The changing epidemiology of human monkeypox-a potential threat? A systematic review. PLoS Negl. Trop. Dis. **16**(2), e0010141 (2022)
6. Clark, E.M., et al.: A sentiment analysis of breast cancer treatment experiences and healthcare perceptions across twitter. arXiv preprint arXiv:1805.09959 (2018)
7. CNN: Argentina confirma su primer caso de la viruela del mono (2022). https://cnnespanol.cnn.com/. Accessed 08 Oct 2022
8. Di Giulio, D.B., Eckburg, P.B.: Human monkeypox: an emerging zoonosis. Lancet. Infect. Dis **4**(1), 15–25 (2004)
9. Dixon, S.: Most popular social networks worldwide as of January 2022, ranked by number of monthly active users (2022). https://www.statista.com/. Accessed 27 Aug 2022
10. Dubey, A.D.: Twitter sentiment analysis during covid-19 outbreak. Available at SSRN 3572023 (2020)
11. ELECONOMISTA: Panamá confirma primer caso de viruela del mono (2022). https://www.gob.mx/salud/. Accessed 08 Oct 2022
12. Gabarron, E., Dechsling, A., Skafle, I., Nordahl-Hansen, A., et al.: Discussions of asperger syndrome on social media: content and sentiment analysis on twitter. JMIR Formative Res. **6**(3), e32752 (2022)
13. Gabarron, E., Dorronzoro, E., Rivera-Romero, O., Wynn, R.: Diabetes on twitter: a sentiment analysis. J. Diabetes Sci. Technol. **13**(3), 439–444 (2019)

14. Garcia, K., Berton, L.: Topic detection and sentiment analysis in twitter content related to covid-19 from brazil and the USA. Appl. Soft Comput. **101**, 107057 (2021)
15. Hofman, E.: Senti-py. GitHub, Inc (2022)
16. Hu, N.: Sentiment analysis of texts on public health emergencies based on social media data mining. Comput. Math. Methods Med. **2022** (2022)
17. Hunter, J.D.: Matplotlib: a 2D graphics environment. Comput. Sci. Eng. **9**(3), 90–95 (2007)
18. INFOBAE: Ecuador detecta primer caso de viruela del mono (2022). https://www.infobae.com/. Accessed 08 Oct 2022
19. ISO 8601:2004. Data elements and interchange formats-Information interchange-Representation of dates and times 3 (2004)
20. Jahanbin, K., Jokar, M., Rahmanian, V.: Using twitter and web news mining to predict the monkeypox outbreak. Asian Pac J Trop Med **15**(5), 236–238 (2022)
21. Kausar, M.A., Soosaimanickam, A., Nasar, M.: Public sentiment analysis on twitter data during covid-19 outbreak. Int. J. Adv. Comput. Sci. Appl. **12**(2) (2021)
22. LaNación: Salud pública confirma primer caso de viruela símica en paraguay (2022). https://www.gub.uy/. Accessed 08 Oct 2022
23. LATIMES: El salvador confirma su primer caso de viruela símica (2022). https://www.latimes.com/. Accessed 08 Oct 2022
24. Madanian, S., Airehrour, D., Samsuri, N.A., Cherrington, M.: Twitter sentiment analysis in covid-19 pandemic. In: 2021 IEEE 12th Annual Information Technology, Electronics and Mobile Communication Conference (IEMCON), pp. 0399–0405. IEEE (2021)
25. Magnus, P.V., Andersen, E.K., Petersen, K.B., Birch-Andersen, A.: A pox-like disease in cynomolgus monkeys. Acta Pathologica Microbiologica Scandinavica **46**(2), 156–176 (1959)
26. Martinez-Valle, A.: Public health matters: why is Latin America struggling in addressing the pandemic? J. Public Health Policy **42**(1), 27–40 (2021)
27. McCollum, A.M., Damon, I.K.: Human monkeypox. Clin. Infect. Dis. **58**(2), 260–267 (2014)
28. McKinney, W., et al.: Data structures for statistical computing in python. In: Proceedings of the 9th Python in Science Conference, Austin, TX, vol. 445, pp. 51–56 (2010)
29. MINSA: Minsa confirma primer caso de la viruela del mono en el perú (2022). https://www.gob.pe/. Accessed 08 Oct 2022
30. MINSAL: Minsal confirma el primer caso de viruela del mono en chile (2022). https://www.minsal.cl/. Accessed 08 Oct 2022
31. MINSALUD: Minsalud e ins confirman tres casos de viruela símica en colombia (2022). https://www.minsalud.gov.co/. Accessed 08 Oct 2022
32. MSC: Salud confirma primer caso por viruela símica (2022). https://www.ministeriodesalud.go.cr/. Accessed 08 Oct 2022
33. MSP: Primer caso importado de viruela símica en uruguay (2022). https://www.lanacion.com.py/. Accessed 08 Oct 2022
34. MSPAS: Mspas confirma primer caso de viruela del mono en el país (2022). https://dca.gob.gt/. Accessed 08 Oct 2022
35. Mueller, A.: A little word cloud generator in python. Contribute to amueller/word_cloud development by creating an account on GitHub (2018)
36. Naseem, U., Razzak, I., Khushi, M., Eklund, P.W., Kim, J.: Covidsenti: a large-scale benchmark twitter data set for covid-19 sentiment analysis. IEEE Trans. Comput. Soc. Syst. **8**(4), 1003–1015 (2021)

37. Oliphant, T.: Guide to NumPy (2006)
38. World Health Organization: Monkeypox outbreak: Global trends (2022). https://worldhealthorg.shinyapps.io/mpx_global. Accessed 30 Sept 2022
39. World Health Organization: Multi-country outbreak of monkeypox. External situation report, vol. 9 (2022)
40. PL: Bolivia alerta por primer caso de viruela símica (2022). https://www.prensalatina.cu. Accessed 08 Oct 2022
41. Saxena, S.K., et al.: Re-emerging human monkeypox: a major public-health debacle. J. Med. Virol. **95**(1), e27902 (2023)
42. Shofiya, C., Abidi, S.: Sentiment analysis on covid-19-related social distancing in Canada using twitter data. Int. J. Environ. Res. Public Health **18**(11), 5993 (2021)
43. Srinath, K.: Python-the fastest growing programming language. Int. Res. J. Eng. Technol. **4**(12), 354–357 (2017)
44. SSA: Informe técnico semanal de vigilancia epidemiológica de viruela símica en méxico (2022). https://www.gob.mx/salud/documentos/informes-semanales-para-la-vigilancia-epidemiologica-de-viruela-simica-en-mexico. Accessed 01 Nov 2022
45. SSM: México confirma primer caso importado de viruela símica (2022). https://www.gob.mx/salud/. Accessed 08 Oct 2022
46. Stefanis, C., et al.: Sentiment analysis of epidemiological surveillance reports on covid-19 in Greece using machine learning models. Front. Public Health **11** (2023)
47. Taylor, L.: Monkeypox: who declares a public health emergency of international concern. BMJ Br. Med. J. **378**, o1874 (2022)
48. TELESURTV: Honduras confirma primer caso de la viruela del mono (2022). https://www.telesurtv.net/. Accessed 08 Oct 2022
49. Thakur, N.: Monkeypox2022tweets: the first public twitter dataset on the 2022 monkeypox outbreak (2022)
50. Vélez, C.M., et al.: An analysis of how health systems integrated priority-setting in the pandemic planning in a sample of Latin America and the Caribbean countries. Health Res. Policy Syst. **20**(1), 1–16 (2022)

Stock Market Prediction with Artificial Intelligence Techniques in Recession Times

David Valle-Cruz[1]([⊠]) [iD], Vanessa Fernandez-Cortez[2] [iD], Asdrúbal López-Chau[3] [iD],
and Rafael Rojas-Hernández[3] [iD]

[1] Unidad Académica Profesional Tianguistenco, UAEMéx, Paraje el Tejocote, San Pedro
Tlaltizapan, 52640 Santiago Tianguistenco, México
davacr@uaemex.mx
[2] Facultad de Contaduría y Administración, UAEMéx, Cerro de Coatepec S/N, Ciudad
Universitaria, 50110 Toluca, Edo. de México, México
vfernandezc@uaemex.mx
[3] Centro Universitario UAEM Zumpango, UAEMéx, Zumpango de Ocampo, México
{alchau,rrojashe}@uaemex.mx

Abstract. This study contributes to the literature on AI-based stock market forecasting by highlighting the potential of AI-based stock market forecasting in identifying investment opportunities in uncertain times. Globalization and internet access have facilitated portfolio diversification across regions and this paper examines the application of artificial intelligence (AI) in identifying the best global market indices for investment during a recession. The study evaluates markets such as China, the United States, and Japan, as well as emerging markets such as Brazil and Mexico with the aim of making an immediate investment decision. The results suggest that support vector machine and random forest techniques are effective for stock price forecasting, and the S&P BMV IPC Index has been identified as an attractive option. However, real-time data may influence this result, and NASDAQ may offer a better outlook. The research highlights the value of AI-based forecasting in enabling informed investment decisions, portfolio diversification, and capturing opportunities across geographies during downturns.

Keywords: Stock Market · Prediction · Artificial Intelligence · Machine
Learning · Recession · Emerging Markets

1 Introduction

Increased globalization and easy access to information via the Internet create opportunities for investors to build diversified portfolios across multiple geographies. Technology investment platforms allow investors to gain greater perspective on stock selection and reduce risk through global diversification of investments. However, recent events such as the COVID-19 pandemic and the war between Ukraine and Russia have caused unexpected stock market movements and losses for some companies [1]. Still, certain sectors have thrived during these crises, and understanding strategies for navigating uncertain

M. A. Jabbar et al. (Eds.): AMLDA 2023, CCIS 2047, pp. 246–263, 2024.
https://doi.org/10.1007/978-3-031-55486-5_18

times can give investors a competitive edge. Even in the current recession, well-informed investors with the right tools can still find opportunities for success in the stock market. Predicting stock prices for portfolio construction is of primary interest to investors [2]. Stock market prediction uses various methods, including data analysis and machine learning, to forecast future stock market movements. Its goal is to help make informed investment decisions by predicting whether stock prices will rise, fall, or stay stable. It involves analyzing historical data and economic indicators but is inherently uncertain due to market complexity.

Mathematical and computational models, including AI and big data techniques, help investors build portfolios efficiently. Traditionally, technical analysis and expert opinion have been used, but AI and machine learning (ML) techniques are gaining traction by automating and improving stock market investments [3]. In this regard, machine learning is a branch of AI where computers learn from data to improve their performance on specific tasks. Timing is critical to generating the best returns, so rapid analysis is essential to making informed and immediate decisions. Although mathematical statistical models based on historical data can provide useful forecasts, some economic phenomena have special characteristics that prevent accurate forecasting. However, the predictive model generated higher returns and reshaped the exchange's trading model, so it was worth it for investors [4].

Understanding the behavior of global market indices and their constituents can help to measure performance and make investment decisions. Equity market movements are difficult to understand, and numerous studies focus on methods for more accurate forecasting, including both traditional statistical models and AI techniques such as genetic algorithms, artificial neural networks, and exponential smoothing [3]. Forecasting methods include quantitative methods and qualitative methods, and there are quantitative methods based on statistics and qualitative methods based on expert judgment. In recent years, AI predictive models using techniques such as LSTM, RNN, SVM, Random Forest, DNN, and Transformer architecture have been used to analyze large amounts of data [5]. Despite these advances, stock market analysis and forecasting remain challenging due to the complex dynamic and unpredictable nature of data, especially during periods of recession and uncertainty caused by events such as pandemics and wars. It is important to find useful techniques and consider all available information to make an immediate data-based decision-making.

This study evaluates markets such as China, the United States, and Japan, as well as emerging markets such as Brazil and Mexico with the aim of making an immediate investment decision in order to form efficient investment portfolios during a recession To achieve this goal, the study combines a systematic literature review guided by the PRISMA methodology [6] with AI techniques for predicting world stock market performance. In this way, relevant literature on the study topic, as well as the techniques used and the context, is identified. In this regard, this research is guided by the following questions: RQ1: Which AI techniques are commonly used in the literature to predict world market indices and their components? RQ2: What are the most efficient global stocks, including emerging markets, for forming investment portfolios during recessionary times? The paper is organized into five sections, including the current introduction. The second section presents a systematic literature review of the state of the art of stock market prediction during times of recession, using the PRISMA methodology. The third section describes the experimentation for predicting the components of world market indices using AI techniques. The fourth section presents the results. The last section includes conclusions and suggestions for future research.

2 Systematic Literature Review

A systematic literature review allows for comprehending the current state of a topic. Specifically, the PRISMA approach is extensively utilized for conducting literature reviews, thereby mitigating biases in the analysis and selection of documents [6].

2.1 Stock Analysis Methods

Investors use a variety of methods to select stocks, including fundamental analysis, technical analysis, and news analysis [7]. Fundamental analysis examines financial statements to predict the impact on future earnings and stock prices. Technical analysis evaluates price trends, trading volumes, and market indices to predict price movements. News analysis considers external factors that influence stock prices. These methods have limitations, but ML techniques can complement the limitations by providing insights based on historical and real-time data. Combining AI-based stock price forecasting with traditional techniques results in more efficient portfolios and better results. This research focuses on technical analysis as a quantitative and empirical approach to stock selection that is particularly valuable during uncertain and volatile times.

2.2 Diversification and the World Market Indices: A Brief Overview

Markowitz's diversified portfolio theory is a widely used model in investment portfolio management aimed at minimizing risk and maximizing expected return. Diversification, which spreads investment across uncorrelated assets, protects investment and reduces risk if assets underperform. Global diversification has the following benefits: (1) risk reduction, (2) improved returns by identifying undervalued and high-growth stocks; and (3) resilience to changes in the global economy. Investing in various global market indices facilitates this strategy. World market indices reflect the development of stock markets and economic conditions of countries [8]. Analyzing a stock's price history provides insight into its performance. The return on an investment (r_i) in a financial instrument, based on its prices over successive periods, is defined as $n + 1$ (See Eq. 1). Successive time periods are defined by:

$$r_i = \frac{S_i - S_{i-1}}{S_{i-1}} \tag{1}$$

where:

$$i = 1, 2, \cdots, n$$

$\{S_0, S_1, ..., Sn\}$ is the sequence of stock prices and $\{r_1, r_2, ..., r_n\}$ is the sequence of returns.

Many companies or stocks in the world market are listed in different sectors or activities. According to Investing.com, some of the most important world market indices include: Dow Jones Industrial Average, S&P 500, NASDAQ Composite, US Small Cap 2000, CBOE Volatility Index, S&P/TSX Composite, Bovespa, S&P/BMV IPC, DAX, FTSE 100, CAC 40, Euro Stoxx 50, AEX, IBEX 35, FTSE MIB, SMI, PSI 20, BEL 20, ATX, OMX Stockholm 30, OMX Copenhagen 25, MOEX Russia, RTSI, WIG20, Budapest SE, BIST 100, TA 35, Tadawul All Share, Nikkei 225, S&P/ASX 200, Dow Jones New Zealand, Shanghai Composite, SZSE Component, FTSE China A50, Dow Jones Shanghai, Hang Seng, Taiwan Weighted, SET Index, KOSPI, Jakarta Stock Exchange Composite Index, Nifty 50, BSE Sensex 30, PSEi Composite, Karachi 100, and VN 30.

Analysis of these indices can also help investors identify specific sectors that perform well or poorly during a recession. By identifying which global market indices are the most suitable to invest in during certain financial market situations, investors can create more efficient investment portfolios and potentially achieve better investment results.

2.3 A Literature Review Using the PRISMA Approach

The PRISMA approach process [6] is described below (see Fig. 1).

Stage 1: Identification in Scopus, Web of Science, ACM Digital Library, IEEE Xplore, and Wiley Online Library.

As the authors' interest was to find scientific articles on financial market prediction with artificial intelligence techniques, the keywords were 1) "stock market", "market exchange". 2) "Artificial Intelligence", "Machine Learning", "Deep Learning", "Neural", "Networks". 3) "forecasting", "prediction". The authors included the term "Fintech" to select some papers regarding the research topics. The authors performed a logical search in Scopus, Web of Science, ACM Digital Library, IEEE Xplore, and Wiley Online Library, because they are sources that contain influential papers in the research topic (Table 1).

Table 1. Logical search on digital platforms

Platform	Logical search
Scopus	TITLE-ABS-KEY-AUTH (("Stock market" OR "Stock exchange") AND ("Artificial intelligence" OR "Machine learning" OR "Deep learning" OR Neural AND Networks) AND (Forecasting OR Prediction) AND Fintech)
Web of Science	(("Stock market" OR "Stock exchange") AND ("Artificial intelligence" OR "Machine learning" OR "Deep learning" OR Neural AND Networks) AND (Forecasting OR Prediction) AND Fintech)

(continued)

Table 1. (*continued*)

Platform	Logical search
ACM Digital Library	[[All: "Stock market"] OR [All: "Stock exchange"]] AND [[All: "Artificial intelligence"] OR [All: "Machine learning"] OR [All: "Deep learning"] OR [[All: Neural] AND [All: Networks]]] AND [[All: Forecasting] OR [All: Prediction]] AND [All: Fintech]
IEEE Xplore	(("All Metadata":"Stock market") OR ("All Metadata":"Stock exchange")) AND (("All Metadata":"Artificial intelligence") OR ("All Metadata":"Machine learning") OR ("All Metadata":"Deep learning")) AND ("All Metadata": Forecasting) AND ("All Metadata": Fintech)
Wiley Online Library	The following terms were included in the advanced search: "Stock market" OR "Stock exchange"; "Artificial intelligence" OR "Machine learning" OR "Deep learning" OR "Neural networks"; "Forecasting" OR "Prediction", "Fintech"

In the selection process, the search was refined by selecting only scientific articles. As a result, 48 articles were found. Three repeated articles were excluded.

Stage 2: Eligibility, screening, and downloading.

In this phase, 45 scientific articles related to predicting financial markets with AI techniques remained. Titles and abstracts were reviewed. Thirteen papers that were not related to the prediction of financial markets with AI techniques were omitted, resulting in 32 scientific papers that were downloaded for in-depth analysis.

Stage 3: Included in the systematic literature review.

After analyzing the downloaded papers, we discarded 1 document because it was unrelated to this research's central topic. Therefore, the state of the art of financial market forecasting with AI techniques consists of 31 scientific papers.

2.4 State-of-The-Art Characteristics

The existing literature on AI-based stock market forecasting mainly focuses on specific regions such as China, Taiwan, US [7, 9–19], Japan, Malaysia, Iran, Turkey [20–23], and UK [24]. However, research examining the use of AI techniques in European and Latin American stock markets is lacking. LSTM networks have emerged as the most widely used technique [7, 13, 15, 17, 19, 22, 24–28], followed by random forests, support vector machines, recurrent neural networks, and multilayer perceptron [19, 21, 22, 28, 29]. Other techniques include Decision Trees, Extreme Gradient Boosting, Naive Bayes, Logistic Regression [21, 28, 29], and various optimization algorithms [12, 16, 19, 20, 30–33]. Performance evaluation techniques such as RMSE, MAE, MAPE, MSE, and R-square are commonly used to assess the accuracy of AI techniques in stock market forecasting [12, 14, 22, 24, 25, 27, 32, 34]. Overall, the literature review highlights the need for further research comparing different techniques and exploring AI-based stock market forecasting in the context of Europe and Latin America.

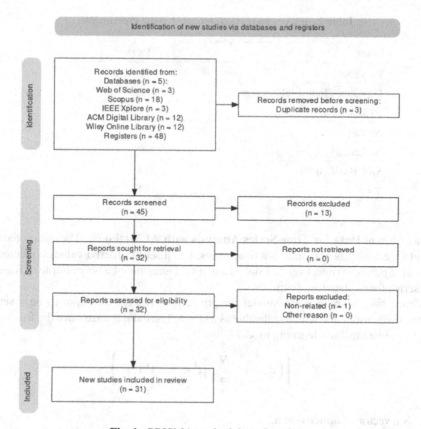

Fig. 1. PRISMA methodology flowchart

3 Experimentation

3.1 Data Collection

For this experiment, we used historical data from 6 indices (BOVESPA, Dow Jones Industrial Average, FTSE China, Nasdaq, Nikkei, S&P/BMV) from 01/01/2000 to 08/31/2022. The author predicts the stock price on September 1, 2022, based on historical values. The analysis covered financial markets in China, the United States, Japan, Brazil, and Mexico. Stocks with very short market lives were excluded from the experimental phase. Table 2 provides an overview of the index and the number of stocks analyzed.

3.2 Models for Predicting Stock Values

ML models can be used to predict stock prices, but they require a structured training dataset consisting of vectors. These datasets should contain the target variables that the algorithm uses to fit a model. For numeric targets, regressors are used as predictors. Below is the process to create a labeled dataset for financial indicator forecasting.

Table 2. Indices and actions included in the experiments

Index	Stocks
BOVESPA	51
Dow Jones Industrial Average	30
FTSE China	37
Nasdaq	63
Nikkei 225	209
S&P BMV (IPC)	34
Total	424

Preparation of Data for Time Series Analysis with AI Methods. The data for stock market forecasting is obtained as a time series, i.e., a set of ordered values collected at successive points in time. Figure 2 shows a non-real example of a very simple univariate time series for explanatory purposes.

Meanwhile, training a ML model for prediction requires the input to be a set of vectors, each associated with a real value as a target. The dataset must have the following form to train a machine-learning model:

$$X = \left\{ \left(x^i, y^i\right) \Big|_{i=1}^{N} \Big| x^i \in \mathbb{R}^n, y^i \in \mathbb{R} \right\} \tag{2}$$

where:

x^i is a vector of dimension n.

y^i is a real number that has a (hidden) relationship to the vector x^i.

N is the number of instances.

The goal of a trained ML model is to predict the value of y^j given a previously unseen vector x^j. Because a time series does not have the form shown in Eq. 2, a proper transformation is required.

The vector x^i is formed as with the series' values with indices from $i \times n$ to $(i+1) \times n$, whereas the target y^i is the value at time $(i+1) \times n + 1$. The number of time-steps of the time series used to form a tuple $\left(x^i, y^i\right)$ is called window size. For some applications, there is more than one-time series to analyze simultaneously. In these cases, the problem is called multivariate. The transformation of them for ML is very similar. ML models perform well on independent samples but may not perform well on continuous data such as the stock market. However, predictive models that use historical information are better suited for such applications. The three most used AI techniques for predicting financial metrics are LSTMs, RF classifiers, and SVM. Because these ML techniques differ greatly in structure.

LSTM. Recursive Neural Networks (RNNs) are one model type that considers the model's current data input and previous states (historical information) to make predictions. RNNs can process inputs of any length (such as time-series) without requiring changing the number of components (layers).

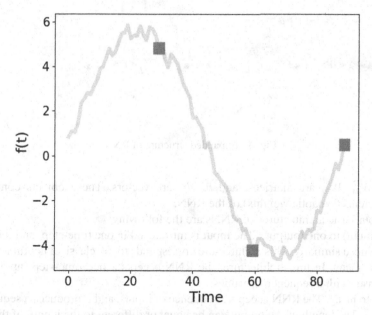

Fig. 2. Example of a simple time series

Figure 3 shows the general elements of an RNN. This recursive structure can be explained more easily in the expanded form, shown in Fig. 4, where:

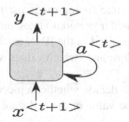

Fig. 3. Basic structure of an RNN

- $a^{<0>}$ is the initial input to the RNN. This is set to zero or other specific value in many applications.
- $x^{<t>}$ is the input at time t.
- $a^{<t>}$ is the value of activation function at time t,. This is an output of the RNN, which is interpreted as the state of the network at time t:
- $a^{<t>} = g_1(W_{aa}a^{<t-1>} + W_{ax}x^{<t>} + b_a)$
- $y^{<t>}$ corresponds to the output or response of the RNN at time t:
- $y^{<t>} = g_2(W_{ya}a^{<t>} + b_y)$
- $g_1(\bullet)$ and $g_2(\bullet)$ are activation functions. Usually, the former is the *tanh* function, and the latter is the sigmoid or softmax function.

Fig. 4. Expanded structure of RNN

- W_{aa}, W_{ax}, W_{ya} are matrices, and b_a, b_y are vectors. These objects contain the coefficients (synaptic weights) of the RNN.
- The four basic architectures of RNNs are the following:
- One (input) to one (output). The input is introduced in one time-step, and the output is produced similarly. This architecture corresponds to the classical neural networks.
- One to many. In this architecture, the RNN accepts a one time-step input and its responses with a sequence of values.
- Many to many. The RNN accepts a sequence of inputs, and it produces a sequence of outputs. The length of the output can be equal or different to the length of the input.
- Many to one. The RNN accepts a sequence of inputs and produces an output.
- RNNs are prone to exploding or vanishing gradient problems, especially for large hidden layers or long input lengths. This is caused by multiplication during weight calibration in the backpropagation optimization process. Techniques such as gradient clipping and second derivatives can be used to combat gradient explosion. A gate that modifies the RNN's cell state (memory) is used to prevent the gradient from going to zero. These gates consider previous states and current inputs to produce the appropriate response. The gates used in the RNN are:
- Gateway or update gateway. Computes which values will be updated, and which will remain unchanged.
- Oblivion gate. Its function is to decide whether a piece of information is discarded.
- Output gate. Computes the next value of the cell state (hidden state) of the RNN.

GRU (Gated Recurrent Unit) and LSTM (Long Short-Term Memory) are key units that improve RNN performance by allowing them to deal with long-term temporal dependencies. LSTM is specifically designed to work with long-term sequences, and GRU addresses the issue of gradient leaks. In LSTMs, input and forget gates determine what is saved or removed from long-term storage, while in GRU update and reset gates perform similar functions. Update gates control what information is passed to the next stage, and reset gates determine how information is forgotten. Figure 5 shows a simplified representation of his LSTM unit elements used in this work.

Main LSTM Parameters in the Keras Library. The main parameters used to create an LSTM layer in Keras are shown in the following list. In other libraries, the parameters for creating predictive models are quite similar.

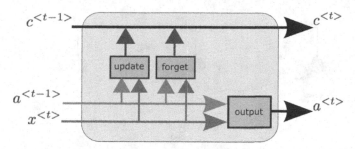

Fig. 5. Simplified explanation of the LSTM's architecture

- **Units**: the number of cells in the LSTM, i.e., the dimensionality of the outer space or the number of features.
- **Activation**: The most common function is the hyperbolic tangent; however, the linear or other function can also be used.
- **Return sequences**: If this parameter is set to true, then the model returns a prediction for each input entered in the model; otherwise, it returns the prediction once the last time step has been reached.

Random Forest. The RF regressor is an ensemble method that consists of multiple decision trees as base regressors. By aggregating the predictions of these base classifiers through a voting scheme, the RF regressor improves performance. This ensemble approach is effective when the errors made by each classifier are uncorrelated with the errors of other classifiers within the ensemble, and when each classifier has an error rate below 0.5. The RF regressor demonstrates strong performance across various applications and exhibits robustness to data noise. Figure 6 illustrates the structure of the RF regressor.

Randomization is often applied to reduce or avoid correlation between the error rates of decision trees in a RF. Randomly select a subset of attributes to compute the best split point in decision tree training; linear combinations of randomly chosen attributes can be used. For example, each base classifier can be trained with a (randomly chosen) subset of samples from the training data set.

Support Vector Machines. SVM are commonly used in ML for classification and regression tasks. SVM was originally designed for classification, but now has additional implementations for regression, clustering, and transductive learning. The key concept of SVM is to find a linear decision boundary with maximal margins to give geometric inspiration. This involves solving an optimization problem called a quadratic programming problem (QPP) to compute the optimal separating hyperplane. Practical classification problems often require nonlinear data transformations using kernels. It is also important to consider some misclassifications during model building to prevent overfitting.

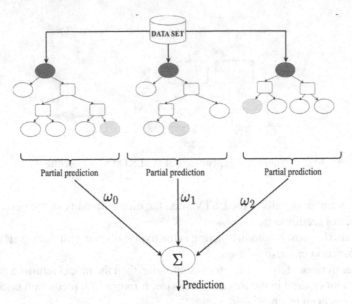

Fig. 6. Random forest regressor

The given data set $X = \{(x_i, y_i) | x_i \in \mathbb{R}^p, y_i \in \{+1, -1\}, i = 1 \cdots N\}$. The optimization problem to solve is the following (Eq. 3).

$$max_{\alpha_i} - \frac{1}{2} \sum_{i,j=1}^{N} \alpha_i y_i \alpha_j y_j \left[K(x_i, x_j) + \frac{1}{C}\delta_{ij} \right] + \sum_{i=1}^{l} \alpha_i \qquad (3)$$

where:

α_i is a Lagrange multiplier.

C is the penalty factor.

One of the most notable disadvantages of SVM is that it requires many resources for tuning. Another problem with SVM is that the selection of the kernel and parameters represents a high computational burden.

3.3 Technical Analysis and Performance Comparison

One approach to selecting stocks for investment portfolios is to select stocks that outperform their respective indices. This ensures that selected stocks outperform the average of similar stocks in financial indices. For example, consider the performance of Nike, Inc. Shown in Fig. 7. Nike's performance was sluggish due to the recession, it has achieved high performance (1,769.33%) compared to the Dow Jones Industrial Average index (189.32%) to which the company belongs.

The approach of selecting stocks based on their performance relative to the index is commonly employed to identify stocks with the potential for above-average returns. However, it's important to acknowledge that past performance does not guarantee future results. Therefore, it is crucial to complement this approach with other stock selection

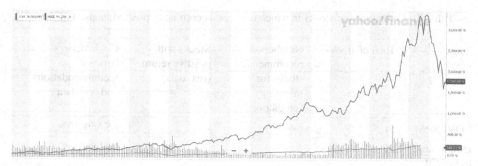

Fig. 7. Technical analysis to select a stock. Source: Extracted from Yahoo Finance

techniques, such as fundamental and technical analysis, to ensure a well-diversified and effective investment portfolio. Using this criterion, the best stocks to invest in during the recession were chosen. Additionally, it was verified that these stocks exhibited positive returns when comparing the predicted value (09/01/2022) with the previous day's value (08/31/2022). In cases where certain companies did not trade on the day of the prediction (09/01/2022), the following day (09/02/2022) was used to compare the predicted value with the actual value. Although this situation occurred in a few stocks, it did not pose any issues for the experimentation.

4 Results

The appendix (Table 4) presents the results of our AI-based forecasting model, which recommends investable stocks with high potential returns. These models showed varying levels of performance, with RF and SVM slightly outperforming Long Short-Term Memory (LSTM) models. The relatively poor performance of LSTM may be due to the need for more data. It is important to note that the model's predicted returns were generally higher than the observed returns, highlighting the risks of relying solely on AI-based predictions for investment decisions. Therefore, it is important to combine these models with other stock selection techniques such as fundamental and technical analysis to ensure a well-diversified and efficient investment portfolio. The results of this study provide valuable insight into the benefits of combining a systematic literature review and AI-based forecasting techniques to identify good global market indices for investment during recessions.

With the systematic literature review, we identified the regions where there is a prevalence and a lack of studies on stock market prediction. Additionally, we identified the most used techniques, as well as the findings and performance metrics. The results demonstrate how AI models can improve stock performance analysis and provide insight into potential investment opportunities amid economic uncertainty and market volatility. The S&P BMV IPC Index initially appeared to be the most attractive investment destination according to our forecast model (see Table 3). However, looking at the actual data, it turned out that the Nasdaq index has more companies that are profitable for portfolio construction. The best-performing forecasting model was the Nasdaq Index, while the Nikkei Stock Average and S&P BMV Index performed relatively poorly. Table 3 shows

Table 3. Comparison of stocks in which to invest according to prediction and real data

Index	Total of stocks	Number of recommended stocks for investing (prediction)	Stocks with positive return (real data)	Coincidences between recommendations and real data
BOVESPA	51	6	4	66.66%
Dow Jones Industrial Average	30	5	2	40.00%
FTSE China A 50	37	2	1	50.00%
S&P BMV (IPC)	34	24	6	25.00%
NASDAQ Composite	53	11	8	72.72%
Nikkei	209	12	3	25.00%
Total	414	60	24	40.00%

the number of investment recommendations based on projections and the number of investments that yielded positive returns. The percentage of matches is also shown in the last column of the table.

5   Conclusions and Future Work

This study contributes to the literature on AI-based stock market forecasting by highlighting the potential of AI-based stock market forecasting in identifying investment opportunities in uncertain times. The outcome consists of showcasing the benefits of AI-based stock market forecasting, offering insights into sector-specific performance, and suggesting directions for future research to enhance predictive models in stock market analysis. Stock market prediction could be improved by integrating external data sources such as social media and news, macroeconomic indicators, political events, and worldwide trends, among other factors. Findings provide insights for stock market participants and show that companies in the consumer staples sector, as well as certain technology and transportation companies, tend to outperform during economic downturns. This study bridges the gap by analyzing European and Latin American stock markets and highlighting the potential of AI technologies in these regions. Combining strategies that consider stocks through market indices and price forecasts to handle the complexities of stock selection. AI technology can identify high performing stocks and their future trends, facilitating decision making. However, this approach has limitations, such as its focus on short-term forecasts and its reliance solely on stock market data. Future research should consider more holistic models that incorporate additional data sources, consider long-term trends, and incorporate different factors and events.

AI technology has practical applications in stock market forecasting, particularly in identifying stocks that can outperform or mimic the performance of respective market indices. This could allow investors to make more efficient and accurate stock selection. AI-based forecasting can also help reduce risk and improve investment decisions by predicting future stock prices. Recent global events such as recessions, wars, pandemics, and inflation have had a major impact on the stock market, prompting investors to sell their stocks. However, not all stocks underperform in times like these, and AI-based forecasting can help spot opportunities, especially in sectors such as technology. The purpose of this study was to identify stocks that are outperforming the index and predict the next day's price for short-term gains. Our analysis finds that companies that provide essential goods and services have performed well during the economic crisis, suggesting safer strategies for investing in basic needs. Additionally, technology and transportation companies were recommended by the AI approach, highlighting their medium- to long-term potential. Insights gained include benefits of his AI technology in navigating the stock market, such as faster response times and simultaneous analysis of multiple indices. Improving predictive models requires more robust methods that incorporate data from financial indicators and other sources such as social media and news. Determining the best performing predictor for a given dataset depends on the complexity of the data and model hyperparameters. Generative AI may offer better results, but more research is needed in this area.

Appendix

Table 4. World market indices and stocks in which to invest in times of recession

Index	Stock	Accuracy	Best prediction (09/01/22)	Real value (09/01/22)	Best Method	Prediction return	Invest (prediction return)	Real return	Invest (Real return)
1	BRASIL ON	97.87	42.40	42.05	RF	2.38%	Yes	1.55%	Yes
1	COSAN ON	96.30	20.17	19.67	RF	0.94%	Yes	−1.55%	No
1	Energisa	98.52	42.94	43.55	SVM	1.54%	Yes	2.98%	Yes
1	HYPERMARCAS ON	96.10	42.91	43.42	RF	0.32%	Yes	1.52%	Yes
1	JBS ON	98.00	29.84	29.08	RF	0.86%	Yes	−1.72%	No
1	LOCALIZA ON	97.30	62.34	62.23	RF	3.11%	Yes	2.93%	Yes
2	Apple	96.96	161.42	157.96	SVM	2.67%	Yes	0.47%	Yes
2	Caterpillar	98.24	185.65	182.44	RF	0.51%	Yes	−1.23%	No
2	Salesforce.com	98.25	156.22	153.53	RF	0.06%	Yes	−1.66%	No
2	Microsoft	97.90	265.87	260.4	RF	1.68%	Yes	−0.41%	No
2	Nike	98.67	107.59	106.18	RF	1.36%	Yes	0.03%	Yes

(*continued*)

Table 4. (*continued*)

Index	Stock	Accuracy	Best prediction (09/01/22)	Real value (09/01/22)	Best Method	Prediction return	Invest (prediction return)	Real return	Invest (Real return)
3	Anhui Conch Cement	99.97	30.51	30.5	RF	0.03%	Yes	0.00%	No
3	China Minsheng Banking	99.98	3.61	3.61	RF	0.30%	Yes	0.28%	Yes
4	Alsea	97.76	36.87	36.35	SVM	0.85%	Yes	−0.57%	No
4	Bimbo	96.39	72.81	70.27	SVM	9.95%	Yes	6.12%	Yes
4	Grupo Elektra	98.67	1052.66	1,038.84	SVM	0.78%	Yes	−0.54%	No
4	GAP B	97.96	291.14	285.29	RF	1.50%	Yes	−0.54%	No
4	Grupo Carso	97.64	71.70	68.14	RF	3.42%	Yes	−1.72%	No
4	Grupo Financiero Banorte	97.70	121.28	119.97	RF	1.94%	Yes	0.83%	Yes
4	Grupo Mexico	97.24	77.47	74.5	RF	1.56%	Yes	−2.33%	No
4	Gruma SAB de CV	98.34	228.05	221.51	RF	3.88%	Yes	0.90%	Yes
4	Kimberly – Clark A	98.27	27.48	27.42	RF	0.71%	Yes	0.48%	Yes
4	Orbia Advance	98.01	39.91	38.36	RF	5.38%	Yes	1.29%	Yes
4	PINFRA	98.61	143.79	140.45	RF	3.38%	Yes	0.99%	Yes
5	Apple	95.79	159.27	157.96	RF	1.30%	Yes	0.47%	Yes
5	Alaska Air	95.92	44.79	43.69	RF	2.82%	Yes	0.30%	Yes
5	Caterpillar	97.98	185.92	182.44	RF	0.65%	Yes	−1.23%	No
5	CH Robinson	97.97	116.62	114.88	RF	2.66%	Yes	1.13%	Yes
5	CSX	96.27	31.82	31.61	RF	0.54%	Yes	−0.13%	No
5	Expeditors Washington	96.76	103.16	103.81	RF	0.26%	Yes	0.89%	Yes
5	Home Depot	98.45	290.12	293.37	SVM	0.59%	Yes	1.72%	Yes
5	JB Hunt	98.00	174.16	173.77	RF	0.08%	Yes	−0.14%	No
5	Landstar	98.45	147.93	148.41	RF	0.89%	Yes	1.21%	Yes
5	Microsoft	95.28	265.61	260.4	SVM	1.58%	Yes	−0.41%	No
5	UnitedHealth	98.43	521.75	522.36	SVM	0.78%	Yes	0.90%	Yes
5	Visa A	98.45	200.82	200.13	SVM	1.06%	Yes	0.72%	Yes
6	Aeon	97.81	1484.82	1,453.00	SVM	3.47%	Yes	1.25%	Yes
6	Asahi Group Holdings	98.55	4730.61	4,663.00	SVM	1.23%	Yes	−0.21%	No
6	Credit Saison	97.08	1792.87	1,742.00	SVM	2.33%	Yes	−0.57%	No
6	DeNA Co	98.25	1933.25	1,900.00	SVM	1.32%	Yes	−0.42%	No

(*continued*)

Table 4. (*continued*)

Index	Stock	Accuracy	Best prediction (09/01/22)	Real value (09/01/22)	Best Method	Prediction return	Invest (prediction return)	Real return	Invest (Real return)
6	Ebara Corp	98.08	5353.92	5,210.00	SVM	0.64%	Yes	−2.07%	No
6	Eisai	96.48	5752.29	5,556.69	SVM	2.18%	Yes	−1.30%	No
6	Isetan Mitsukoshi Holdings	97.33	5600.61	1,100.34	SVM	410.84%	Yes	0.36%	Yes
6	Isuzu Motors	96.03	1736.87	1,670.55	SVM	2.35%	Yes	−1.56%	No
6	Komatsu	97.32	2908.25	2,832.34	SVM	1.09%	Yes	−1.55%	No
6	Kubota Corp	98.22	2179.62	2,141.50	SVM	0.19%	Yes	−1.56%	No
6	Kyowa Hakko Kirin	97.02	3202.68	3,110.00	SVM	2.16%	Yes	−0.80%	No
6	Marui Group	96.87	2533.25	2,456.37	SVM	2.27%	Yes	−0.84%	No
6	Meiji Holdings	98.68	6608.30	6,522.21	SVM	1.01%	Yes	−0.30%	No
6	Mitsui O.S.K. Lines	96.56	3220.67	3,113.56	SVM	0.53%	Yes	−2.82%	No
6	Nichirei Corp	97.61	2513.46	2,454.79	SVM	2.02%	Yes	−0.36%	No
6	Shimizu Corp	98.46	762.39	750.83	SVM	1.01%	Yes	−0.52%	No
6	Shionogi	96.46	6865.02	6,630.31	SVM	1.81%	Yes	−1.68%	No
6	Shiseido	98.14	5297.74	5,201.00	SVM	0.05%	Yes	−1.78%	No
6	Suzuki Motor Corp	97.88	4967.39	4,864.27	SVM	2.81%	Yes	0.68%	Yes
6	Tokai Carbon	96.49	1045.45	1,010.00	SVM	2.09%	Yes	−1.37%	No
6	Tokyo Tatemono	93.97	2207.54	2,082.00	SVM	5.37%	Yes	−0.62%	No
6	Tokyu Corp	94.61	1725.72	1,637.46	SVM	4.50%	Yes	−0.84%	No
6	Toto	98.32	4888.88	4,655.78	SVM	2.18%	Yes	−2.69%	No
6	Yamaha Corp	96.54	5660.66	5,284.06	SVM	4.38%	Yes	−2.56%	No

1. Bovespa, 2. Dow Jones Industrial Average, 3. FTSE China A50, 4. IPC, 5. NASDAQ Composite. 6. Nikkei 225

References

1. Choi, S.-Y.: Analysis of stock market efficiency during crisis periods in the US stock market: differences between the global financial crisis and COVID-19 pandemic. Phys. A Stat. Mech. Appl. **574**, 125988 (2021)
2. Mohamed, E.A., Ahmed, I.E., Mehdi, R., Hussain, H.: Impact of corporate performance on stock price predictions in the UAE markets: neuro-fuzzy model. Intell. Syst. Account. Financ. Manag. **28**, 52–71 (2021)
3. Rout, N., et al.: Stock market prediction using machine learning techniques: a decade survey on methodologies, recent developments, and future directions. Electronics **10**, 2717 (2021)
4. Granger, C.W.J.: Forecasting stock market prices: lessons for forecasters. Int. J. Forecast. **8**, 3–13 (1992)
5. Kim, K., Han, I.: Genetic algorithms approach to feature discretization in artificial neural networks for the prediction of stock price index. Expert Syst. Appl. **19**, 125–132 (2000)
6. Page, M.J., et al.: Others: the PRISMA 2020 statement: an updated guideline for reporting systematic reviews. Syst. Rev. **10**, 1–11 (2021)

7. Day, M.-Y., Lin, J.-T.: Artificial intelligence for ETF market prediction and portfolio optimization. In: Proceedings of the 2019 IEEE/ACM International Conference on Advances in Social Networks Analysis and Mining, pp. 1026–1033 (2019)
8. Kalyoncu, S., Jamil, A., Karatas, E., Rasheed, J., Djeddi, C.: Stock market value prediction using deep learning. Data Sci. Appl. **3**, 10–14 (2020)
9. Kim, K.-J.: Artificial neural networks with feature transformation based on domain knowledge for the prediction of stock index futures. Intell. Syst. Accounting, Financ. Manag. **12**, 167–176 (2004)
10. Wong, S.Y.K., Chan, J.S.K., Azizi, L., Xu, R.Y.D.: Time-varying neural network for stock return prediction. Intell. Syst. Account. Financ. Manag. **29**, 3–18 (2022)
11. Li, H., Yu, J.-L., Zhou, Q., Cai, J.-H.: Forecasting firm risk in the emerging market of China with sequential optimization of influence factors on performance of case-based reasoning: an empirical study with imbalanced samples. Intell. Syst. Account. Financ. Manag. **20**, 141–161 (2013)
12. Wang, F., Tang, S., Li, M.: Advantages of combining factorization machine with Elman neural network for volatility forecasting of stock market. Complexity **2021**, 1–12 (2021). https://doi.org/10.1155/2021/6641298
13. Day, M.-Y., Lin, J.-T., Chen, Y.-C.: Artificial intelligence for conversational robo-advisor. In: 2018 IEEE/ACM International Conference on Advances in Social Networks Analysis and Mining (ASONAM), pp. 1057–1064 (2018)
14. Uddin, A., Tao, X., Yu, D.: Attention Based Dynamic Graph Learning Framework for Asset Pricing. In: Proceedings of the 30th ACM International Conference on Information & Knowledge Management. pp. 1844–1853 (2021)
15. Lee, M.-C., Chang, J.-W., Hung, J.C., Chen, B.-L.: Exploring the effectiveness of deep neural networks with technical analysis applied to stock market prediction. Comput. Sci. Inf. Syst. **18**, 401–418 (2021)
16. Dingli, A., Fournier, K.S.: Financial time series forecasting-a deep learning approach. Int. J. Mach. Learn. Comput. **7**, 118–122 (2017)
17. Bansal, G., Chamola, V., Kaddoum, G., Piran, M.J., Alrashoud, M.: Next generation stock exchange: recurrent neural learning model for distributed ledger transactions. Comput. Netw. **193**, 107998 (2021)
18. Chao, C.-H., Ting, I.-H., Tsai, T.-H., Chen, M.-C.: Opinion mining and the visualization of stock selection in quantitative trading. In: 2019 International Conference on Technologies and Applications of Artificial Intelligence (TAAI), pp. 1–6 (2019)
19. Ma, Y., Han, R., Wang, W.: Prediction-based portfolio optimization models using deep neural networks. IEEE Access **8**, 115393–115405 (2020)
20. Kohara, K., Ishikawa, T., Fukuhara, Y., Nakamura, Y.: Stock price prediction using prior knowledge and neural networks. Intell. Syst. Account. Financ. Manag. **6**, 11–22 (1997)
21. Ismail, M.S., Noorani, M.S.M., Ismail, M., Razak, F.A., Alias, M.A.: Predicting next day direction of stock price movement using machine learning methods with persistent homology: evidence from Kuala Lumpur Stock Exchange. Appl. Soft Comput. **93**, 106422 (2020)
22. Demírel, U., Handan, Ç.A.M., Ramazan, Ü.: Predicting stock prices using machine learning methods and deep learning algorithms: the sample of the Istanbul Stock Exchange. Gazi Univ. J. Sci. **34**, 63–82 (2021)
23. Rikukawa, S., Mori, H., Harada, T.: Recurrent neural network based stock price prediction using multiple stock brands. Int. J. Innov. Comput. Inf. Control. **16**, 1093–1099 (2020)
24. Nikou, M., Mansourfar, G., Bagherzadeh, J.: Stock price prediction using DEEP learning algorithm and its comparison with machine learning algorithms. Intell. Syst. Account. Financ. Manag. **26**, 164–174 (2019)
25. Serrano, W.: The random neural network in price predictions. Neural Comput. Appl. **34**(2), 855–873 (2021). https://doi.org/10.1007/s00521-021-05903-0

26. Santhappan, J., Chokkalingam, P.: An intelligent market capitalization predictive system using deep learning. In: 2018 International Conference on Advanced Computation and Telecommunication (ICACAT), pp. 1–9 (2018)
27. Dey, P., et al.: Comparative analysis of recurrent neural networks in stock price prediction for different frequency domains. Algorithms. **14**, 251 (2021)
28. Nabipour, M., Nayyeri, P., Jabani, H., Shahab, S., Mosavi, A.: Predicting stock market trends using machine learning and deep learning algorithms via continuous and binary data; a comparative analysis. IEEE Access **8**, 150199–150212 (2020)
29. Roy, S.S., Chopra, R., Lee, K.C., Spampinato, C., Mohammadi-ivatlood, B.: Random forest, gradient boosted machines and deep neural network for stock price forecasting: a comparative analysis on South Korean companies. Int. J. Ad Hoc Ubiquitous Comput. **33**, 62–71 (2020)
30. Liu, C., Fan, Y., Zhu, X.: Fintech index prediction based on RF-GA-DNN algorithm. Wirel. Commun. Mob. Comput. **2021**, 1–9 (2021). https://doi.org/10.1155/2021/3950981
31. ShahvaroughiFarahani, M., RazaviHajiagha, S.H.: Forecasting stock price using integrated artificial neural network and metaheuristic algorithms compared to time series models. Soft. Comput. **25**, 8483–8513 (2021)
32. KumarChandar, S.: Grey Wolf optimization-Elman neural network model for stock price prediction. Soft. Comput. **25**(1), 649–658 (2020). https://doi.org/10.1007/s00500-020-05174-2
33. Zhou, W., Zhao, Y., Chen, W., Liu, Y., Yang, R., Liu, Z.: Research on investment portfolio model based on neural network and genetic algorithm in big data era. EURASIP J. Wirel. Commun. Netw. **2020**, 1–12 (2020)
34. Prabin, S.M., Thanabal, M.S.: A repairing artificial neural network model-based stock price prediction. Int. J. Comput. Intell. Syst. **14**, 1337–1355 (2021)

Self-regulated and Participatory Automatic Text Simplification

Thorben Schomacker[✉] [iD], Michael Gille[iD], Marina Tropmann-Frick[iD],
and Jörg von der Hülls

Hamburg University of Applied Sciences, Hamburg, Germany
{thorben.schomacker,michael.gille,marina.tropmann-frick,
joerg.vonderhuells}@haw-hamburg.de

Abstract. This contribution draws upon conceptual and theoretical insights that
have emerged from the authors' research project (Open-LS) aiming at the development of an application-oriented framework for comprehensibility enhanced
text formats tailored to individuals with low literacy level mainly due to cognitive impairments. We address general and domain-specific regulatory model
requirements for text-simplifying Neural Language Models for use in assistive
applications in German. Against this background, we position ourselves as advocates of an accessibility-by-hypertext approach. Further, we put forward for discussion building blocks for an AI Act-compliant self-regulated framework for
participation-driven text simplification systems.

Keywords: Text simplification · AI Act · Plain language · Easy language · DIN
SPEC-33429 · Artificial Intelligence for Social Good (AI4SG)

1 Introduction

To understand complex texts, people with cognitive, sensory and learning disabilities
depend on text conversions into accessible language. With comprehensibility-enhanced
texts from the legal domain, being sine qua non for inclusion and social participation, these texts pose a particular challenge [6]. In the following we focus on German
and distinguish "Easy Language" (Leichte Sprache) and "Simple Language" (Einfache
Sprache). "Easy Language" refers to a comprehensibility-improved and rule-based form
of German, whereby "Simple Language" is used to describe simplified varieties in the
grey area between standard language and easy language [28]. Easy Language is roughly
equivalent to level A2 of the Common European Framework of Reference for Languages.

Public entities in the EU are often required by law to provide an intra-lingual translation of information and communication texts into an Easy Language version [4]. According to a report by the German government to the EU Commission on the implementation

---

This paper is based on the "Proposal for a Regulation of the European Parliament and of the
Council Laying Down Harmonised Rules on Artificial Intelligence (Artificial Intelligence Act)
and Amending Certain Union Legislative Acts" (5662/24 – 2024/01/26). https://artificialintellig
enceact.eu/documents/?utm_source=substack&utm_medium=email.

M. A. Jabbar et al. (Eds.): AMLDA 2023, CCIS 2047, pp. 264–273, 2024.
https://doi.org/10.1007/978-3-031-55486-5_19

of the EU Web Accessibility Directive, German public authority practice falls significantly short of the legal requirements to provide communication and information texts in comprehensibility-enhanced language [1]. The low portion of public sector websites translated into accessible text versions confirms this assessment [4]. The use of automated text simplification through Neural Language Models (NLM) comes with the promise of considerable leverage through more efficient and cost-effective provision comprehensibility-optimized texts versions.

In this contribution we assess building blocks for an AI Act (AIA)-compliant framework for Text Simplification (TS). The analysis focusses on risk-mitigation for a particularly vulnerable target audience of text simplification. We argue in favor of an accessibility-by-hypertext approach in combination with a soft law-compliant output generation.

After a brief review of related work (Sect. 2), the accessibility and participation orientation of published German datasets and approaches is assessed (Sect. 3). We outline the relevance of the EU´s self-regulatory approach for non-high-risk AI (Sect. 4), sketch out an accessibility-optimized hypertext approach for use in assistive technologies (Sect. 5) and conclude with an outlook (Sect. 6).

2 Related Work

Text simplification (TS) can be described as a machine task translation, converting texts intra-lingually from one level of difficulty to less difficult versions. The first German simplification corpus was introduced in 2012 [22] and consisted of articles from GEO (similar to National Geographic) and GEOlino (GEO's edition for children) and was later improved and enlarged by [43]. The first automatic text simplification system for German was released [41] in 2016. It was based on statistical rules, probably because there was a lack of training data for a machine learning approach at that time. In 2020 the first parallel corpus for German and simple German was published [33], combine with a first investigation of the use of a neural machine translation system for this problem. This investigation concluded in fact, that the corpus was not large enough to sufficiently train such a model. The same neural machine translation architecture was later used on a larger dataset [37]. In 2021 [32] adapted mBART [27] with Longformer Attention [3] and applied it to the task of document-level text simplification. This approach was further improved by [13] and was expanded to a larger number of specific datasets [38] in 2023 and applied to novel domain (narrative documents) [35]. Figure 1 illustrates central model elements. More recently, a decoder-only approaches were presented [1, 10], which can be trained with monolingual data (simple language) only.

Automatic simplification of legal documents has only recently emerged with the works of [7, 9, 17, 29]. These works had to rely on monolingual datasets and state that the task is still underinvestigated. To this day, there is no dataset with parallel legal documents (standard → simple language). In Sect. 4 we will further discuss features and domain-specific constraints of legal texts.

Survey Studies: The automatic simplification of German texts is attracting increasing academic attention. As of August 2023, three surveys have been published about the current data sets and approaches in German text simplification [1, 34, 38]. Prior to this year, no surveys were published at all.

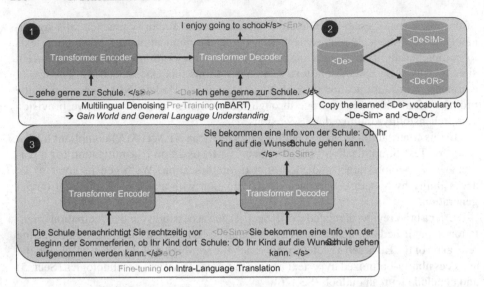

Fig. 1. Training a Multilingual mBart Model with Longformer Attention (as described in [32].

Tools: [39] published a web-tool to make the creation and modification of simplification corpora less difficult. However, it offers only limited options of automatic sentence-alignment.

Our assessment includes considerations regarding a later use for assistive technologies, somewhat in response to the view expressed by [20]. Conceptually, our research can be characterized as participatory [42] and is in line with essential AI for Social Good (AI4SG) criteria [15]. In this context, the study of [23] regarding self-regulation and government oversight forms the basis for some of our deliberations concerning the EU´s risk-oriented soft law approach.

3   (Non-)Consideration of Accessibility in Existing Datasets

Based on the literature review of [34], we created a graphical overview in Fig. 2. With a percentage of 73% News is the largest domain. The more practical and life-oriented categories Government, Disability and Medical are forming together less than 10% of the available data. A significant proportion of 20% of the available simple data is targeted to children. Training machine learning models with children-oriented simple language could lead to a bias.

There are some text genres that are not represented at all in previous datasets. Each genre brings its own challenges. In this paper, we will showcase selected specifics that legal texts bring about.

Legal texts include a broad variety of different text types ranging from formal laws over court decisions to legal interpretations and information texts in the different legal sub-domains. All these types of texts in the various legal sub-domains share similar linguistic characteristics, such as the use of legal terminology, a high degree of formalization, long and complex sentences, formative and omnipresent intertextuality, often

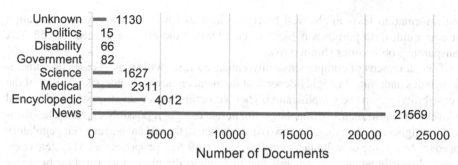

Fig. 2. Comparing the available parallel datasets for German text simplification. Based on the data from [34]

mixed authorship, a wide range of addressees and a characteristic tension between accuracy and vagueness [2]. Moreover, many legal texts establish and organize legal relationships by being legally binding and by creating rights and obligations. These texts are fundamentally different from statements of fact that are subject of most intralingual and monolingual corpora. Texts with legal content differ considerably from texts in standard language. The training of neural language models (NLM) for the legal domain must therefore build on domain-specific German-language training materials. Cross-jurisdictional applicability is limited by the respective national legal context.

4 (Self-)Regulation of Output-Related Requirements

The EU pursues a risk-sensitive approach throughout its AI package. From an institutional theory point of view, risks are transformed uncertainties that allow for actuarial management in the form of insurance [31]. Liability law creates disincentives by defining liability risks that AI system operators will seek to minimize [25] and to insure. The EU´s forthcoming liability framework for AI is based on risk assessment as an essentially non-legal concept. In other words, liability law sends the signal that great care is expected for the party controlling the risk source and thereby has a preventive effect [8]. The requirements introduced by the AIA directly impact design choices at all risk levels. The AIA relies on four levels of criticality, unacceptable, high, limited and minimal risk, and resorts to self-regulation, risk assessments and risk management. A text simplifying AI system is in most areas of application likely to be classified as a non-high-risk AI system. AI systems posing limited risks, including those that interact with natural persons (e.g., chatbots), must abide by the transparency obligations according to Art. 52 AIA, in particular, users should be informed that the texts they read are AI-generated, unless this is clear from the circumstances.

The classification of risks related to text-simplifying NLMs also must consider the relevant text functions (see above Sect. 3). Text functions of the input text must be considered when converting texts into (monofunctional) Easy Language output information texts [12, 18, 34]. In consideration of the vulnerability of the addresses, even in the case of mere information texts, the inclusion-relevance touches upon fundamental rights without posing significant risks, unlike TS in the medical domain. Thus, the conversion into information texts might well be categorized as low-risk, whereas simplification for communication purposes is likely to come under the aforementioned Art. 52 AIA transparency obligations (limited risk).

The addressees of comprehensibility-enhanced texts will in most cases be vulnerable persons and, thus, be highly dependent on the accuracy and understandability of the accessibility-driven text simplification. Their vulnerability is likely to result in additional risk-related requirements within the pertinent risk category, possibly even a reclassification to a higher risk category. For low-risk AI systems, the EU envisages a self-regulatory approach by relying on voluntary compliance: Art. 69 AIA proposes that AI system operators voluntarily adhere to standards that implement the mandatory rules for high-risk AI systems (Art. 8 - 15 AIA). These hard law rules should be converted into *"codes of conduct intended to foster the voluntary application to AI systems other than high-risk AI systems"*. This way, considerations of responsible AI [19] come into play for low-risk AI systems, drawing on ethical notions of the High-Level Expert Group on AI (European Commission, 2022). A risk management system (Art. 9 AIA) must be set up [36], also with particular focus on the vulnerability of the target users.

Any TS aiming at a broader (vulnerable) audience with a one-translation-fits-all approach must come to terms with a built-in homogeneity bias due to the heterogeneity of the target group. This homogeneity bias impacts design decisions and could be monitored in a risk management system. In view of the importance of the quality of training, validation and testing of data sets, data and data governance must conform to high standards (Art. 10 (2) - (4) AIA). Further requirements concern documentation, record-keeping, human oversight etc. (Art. 11 seq. AIA).

The criteria that determine what constitutes an accessible Easy Language text is subject to formal guidelines and legally non-binding standardization [26] and must be reflected in the context of self-regulation. Examples are ISO 24495–1:2023 Plain language [24], EN 301 549 [14] and, in Germany, DIN SPEC 33429 concerning Leichte Sprache (Easy Language) [12]. These standardization efforts do not directly deal with automatic TS, but taking the German standard as an example, they can be a useful reference when it comes to creating a framework as well as defining criteria for annotation, validation, evaluation and testing for standard-compliant outputs [18].

Further, these soft law requirements (codes of conduct, standards) are not generally binding (hard) law, but often come with a *de facto* obligation to observe the content of the standard when assessing conformity and risks, e.g. under German tort law [44]. In terms of liability law, non-compliance with standards can lead to a breach of the duty of care, even if liability depends on the existence of further preconditions. Conversely, the manufacturer or operator of an AI enjoys an *"administrative presumption of conformity"* [44] if the standard is complied with, without being automatically exempt from liability.

In the Open-LS[1] research project, the German Institute for Standardization´s DIN SPEC-33429 is used as a basis for the development of a framework for the annotation of training texts, for validation and for the definition of requirements for the evaluation of the simplified output text in Easy Language (Leichte Sprache). The analysis of DIN SPEC-33429 has produced a preliminary catalogue of 50 + requirements for standard-compliant TS, which can be used for annotation and evaluation [12, 18].

---

[1] https://open-ls.entavis.com.

Further, qualitative and participatory evaluation criteria and evaluation process requirements can be derived from this standard. Text conversions based on DIN SPEC-33429 are created with a comprehensibility assessment by way of a standard-compliant participatory involvement of specially trained proofreaders who themselves belong to the Easy Language target group [12]. The DIN standard itself was developed with the involvement of stakeholders including addressees of simplified texts [11]. By training the NLM based on criteria derived from this soft law standard, the influence of relevant stakeholders on the simplification process is embedded in line with the principles of AI for Social Good (AI4SG) [30] (Table 1).

Table 1. The original criteria will be written in German. Since the DIN-SPEC is also in German. This table provides an excerpt, which was translated into English.

DIN SPEC 33429		Evaluation			
Level	Rule	Constraint	Language Tool	Manual	Participative
Word	Metaphor	-	METAPHORS	-	-
Sentence	Negation	-	NEGATION	-	-
	Punctuation	Compare to character white list	-	-	-
Text	Coherence	-	-	-	YES
Situation	Situation of use	Always assume a specific situation of use and annotate it			

5 Increasing Accessibility with Non-Linear Text Formats

Against the background of the heterogeneity of the target group described above and the risks associated with this homogeneity bias, which vary in intensity and characteristics, we recommend a differentiating design approach for reasons of risk minimization. [34] sheds some light on the current discussion about German Easy Language rulebooks and guidelines. In this debate, we position ourselves as advocates of an accessibility-by-hypertext approach. In accordance with [5], we argue that hypertexts are superior to linear texts (such as printed paper or pdf-files) in terms of accessibility. Hypertexts are characterized by [5, 40]: (a) having non-linear structure, (b) being managed by computer technology, (c) using multi-model representations, (d) being dynamic and (e) interactive, and (f) supporting computer communication. These aspects can be used to increase the accessibility of a document. Like hypertexts, we propose a non-linear text format for LS documents in Fig. 3.

To develop such a hypertext approach, we pursue a participatory approach and collaborate with a large service provider and stakeholder of easy language recipients. Finally, we propose the following four-level complexity hierarchy (Fig. 3):

1. A **short version in easy language** of the underlying standard language /legal document, which has a pre-defined maximum length. It should convey the central meaning of the underlying document in a quickly accessible way.

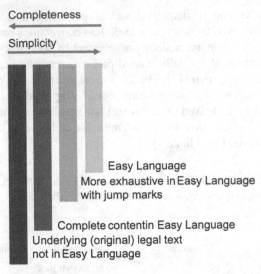

Completeness

Simplicity

Easy Language
More exhaustive in Easy Language
with jump marks

Complete content in Easy Language
Underlying (original) legal text
not in Easy Language

Fig. 3. A Non-linear text-format, proposed in [34]

2. An **exhaustive version in easy language with jump markers** that refer the reader to a glossary. This version especially implements the advantages of the hypertext approach. This allows readers with different reading levels to understand the text at their reading level. Following the debate in [5, 16, 20, 21].
3. A **complete version in easy language** that should only reduce the linguistic complexity and not the complexity of content. This version could exceed the length of its original text.
4. The **original text in standard language**.

6 Outlook

In this contribution, we outlined requirements for text-simplifying AI systems and point out consequences for the development and training of a TS NLMs including a tentative view on the EU´s risk-focused approach and design aspects derivable therefrom. We advocate an implementation- and applicability-conscious approach to the design and development of TS models that embed hard law requirements as well as the already existent or soon to be introduced soft law standards regarding rule-based Easy Language. These rules and standards must be applied when assessing the design and quality of comprehensibility-enhancing TS.

Using the example of a German soft law standard for Easy Language, the article demonstrates that standardization in this field can not only create yardsticks for assessing the quality of TS output but can also play a role in the operator-related liability context. Further, such standards can support the embedding of participatory elements into relevant standardization processes.

In future work, non-linear text formats for more target group-oriented communication need to be assessed with regard to its mitigating effect on a built-in homogeneity bias. In addition, even when compiling data sets only consisting of linear texts, future research should provide information on whether the data targets a specific group and possible limitations. Furthermore, in the future, text simplification should be understood as a participatory task. This participation can take many forms. For example, through the participation of proof-readers, or by basing the research on existing standardization of accessibility-enhanced language that has emerged in a participatory manner. Moreover, proof-readers should not be understood as mere data evaluators, but should also be given the opportunity to take on stakeholder roles. Through them and other stakeholders, such as larger organizations that advocate for the needs of people with disabilities, future research can be better tailored to meet those needs.

References

1. Anschütz, M., et al.: Language Models for German Text Simplification: Overcoming Parallel Data Scarcity through Style-specific Pre-training. http://arxiv.org/abs/2305.12908 (2023)
2. Baumann, A.: Rechtstexte als Barrieren – Einige Merkmale der Textsorte "Gesetz" und die Verständlichkeit. In: Maaß, C., Rink, I. (eds.) Handbuch Barrierefreie Kommunikation, pp. 679–702. Frank & Timme, Berlin (2020)
3. Beltagy, I. et al.: Longformer: The Long-Document Transformer. http://arxiv.org/abs/2004.05150 (2020)
4. BGG: § 11 Disability Equality Act BGG (2022)
5. Bock, B.M.: Leichte Texte schreiben. Zur Wirksamkeit von Regellisten Leichter Sprache in verschiedenen Kommunikationsbereichen und im World Wide Web. trans-kom. **8**, 79–102 (2015)
6. Bundesgesetzblatt Jahrgang 2008 Teil II Nr. 35: Gesetz zu dem Übereinkommen der Vereinten Nationen vom 13. Dezember 2006 über die Rechte von Menschen mit Behinderungen sowie zu dem Fakultativprotokoll vom 13. Dezember 2006 zum Übereinkommen der Vereinten Nationen über die Rechte von Menschen mit Behinderungen (2008)
7. Cemri, M., et al.: Unsupervised Simplification of Legal Texts. http://arxiv.org/abs/2209.00557 (2022)
8. Chamberlain, J.: The risk-based approach of the European union's proposed artificial intelligence regulation: some comments from a tort law perspective. European J. Risk Regul. **14**(1), 1–13 (2023). https://doi.org/10.1017/err.2022.38
9. Collantes, M., et al.: Simpatico: a text simplification system for senate and house bills. In: Proceedings of the 11th National Natural Language Processing Research Symposium, pp. 26–32, Manila (2015)
10. Deilen, S. et al.: Using ChatGPT as a CAT tool in Easy Language translation. http://arxiv.org/abs/2308.11563 (2023)
11. DIN Deutsches Institut für Normung e. V.: Geschäftsplan für ein DIN SPEC-Projekt nach dem PAS-Verfahren zum Thema "Empfehlungen für Deutsche Leichte Sprache" (2022)
12. DIN-Normenausschuss Ergonomie: Empfehlungen für Deutsche Leichte Sprache (DINSPEC 33429) (2023)
13. Ebling, S., et al.: Automatic text simplification for German. Front. Commun. **7**, 706718 (2022). https://doi.org/10.3389/fcomm.2022.706718
14. ETSI: EN 301 549: Accessibility requirements for ICT products and services. https://www.etsi.org/deliver/etsi_en/301500_301599/301549/03.02.01_60/en_301549v030201p.pdf (2021)
15. Floridi, L., et al.: How to design AI for social good: seven essential factors. Sci. Eng. Ethics **26**(3), 1771–1796 (2020). https://doi.org/10.1007/s11948-020-00213-5

16. Fröhlich, W.: Leichte Sprache. Ein Konzept für alle? (2014)
17. Gallegos, I., George, K.: The Right to Remain Plain: Summarization and Simplification of Legal Documents. CS224N: Natural Language Processing with Deep Learning Stanford / Winter 2023 Final poster session. , Stanford (2022)
18. Gille, M. et al.: Der Einsatz von Neural Language Models für eine barrierefreie Verwaltungskommunikation: Anforderungen an die automatisierte Vereinfachung rechtlicher Informationstexte. In: GI Edition Proceedings Band 341, Fachtagung Rechts und Verwaltungsinformatik (RVI 2023) (2023). https://doi.org/10.18420/rvi2023-013
19. Brumen, B., Göllner, S., Tropmann-Frick, M.: Aspects and views on responsible artificial intelligence. In: Nicosia, G., et al. (eds.) Machine Learning, Optimization, and Data Science: 8th International Conference, LOD 2022, Certosa di Pontignano, Italy, September 18–22, 2022, Revised Selected Papers, Part I, pp. 384–398. Springer Nature Switzerland, Cham (2023). https://doi.org/10.1007/978-3-031-25599-1_29
20. Gooding, S.: On the Ethical Considerations of Text Simplification. http://arxiv.org/abs/2204.09565 (2022). https://doi.org/10.48550/arXiv.2204.09565
21. Gooding, S., et al.: Word complexity is in the eye of the beholder. In: Proceedings of the 2021 Conference of the North American Chapter of the Association for Computational Linguistics: Human Language Technologies. pp. 4439–4449. Association for Computational Linguistics, Online (2021). https://doi.org/10.18653/v1/2021.naacl-main.351
22. Hancke, J., et al.: Readability classification for German using lexical, syntactic, and morphological features. In: Proceedings of COLING 2012, pp. 1063–1080 The COLING 2012 Organizing Committee, Mumbai, India (2012)
23. Hoffmann-Riem, W.: Artificial intelligence as a challenge for law and regulation. In: Wischmeyer, T., Rademacher, T. (eds.) Regulating Artificial Intelligence, pp. 1–29. Springer International Publishing, Cham (2020). https://doi.org/10.1007/978-3-030-32361-5_1
24. ISO/TC 37: ISO 24495–1:2023. https://www.iso.org/standard/78907.html (2023)
25. Li, S., et al.: Liability rules for AI-related harm: law and economics lessons for a European approach. Eur. J. Risk Regul. **13**(4), 618–634 (2022). https://doi.org/10.1017/err.2022.26
26. Lindholm, C., Vanhatalo, U. eds: Handbook of Easy Languages in Europe. Frank & Timme, Berlin (2021). https://doi.org/10.26530/20.500.12657/52628
27. Liu, Y., et al.: Multilingual denoising pre-training for neural machine translation. Trans. Assoc. Comput. Linguist. **8**, 726–742 (2020). https://doi.org/10.1162/tacl_a_00343
28. Maaß, C.: Easy Language – Plain Language – Easy Language Plus: Balancing Comprehensibility and Acceptability. Frank & Timme, Berlin (2020). https://doi.org/10.26530/20.500.12657/42089
29. Manor, L., Li, J.J.: Plain English summarization of contracts. In: Proceedings of the Natural Legal Language Processing Workshop 2019, pp. 1–11. Association for Computational Linguistics, Minneapolis, Minnesota (2019). https://doi.org/10.18653/v1/W19-2201
30. Mökander, J., et al.: Conformity assessments and post-market monitoring: a guide to the role of auditing in the proposed European AI regulation. Mind. Mach. **32**(2), 241–268 (2022). https://doi.org/10.1007/s11023-021-09577-4
31. North, D.C.: Institutions, Institutional Change and Economic Performance. Cambridge University Press, Cambridge (1990). https://doi.org/10.1017/CBO9780511808678
32. Rios, A. et al.: A new dataset and efficient baselines for document-level text simplification in German. In: Proceedings of the Third Workshop on New Frontiers in Summarization, pp. 152–161. Association for Computational Linguistics, Online and in Dominican Republic (2021). https://doi.org/10.18653/v1/2021.newsum-1.16
33. Säuberli, A. et al.: Benchmarking data-driven automatic text simplification for German. In: Proceedings of the 1st Workshop on Tools and Resources to Empower People with REAding DIfficulties (READI), pp. 41–48. European Language Resources Association, Marseille, France (2020)

34. Schomacker, T. et al.: Data and approaches for German text simplification - next steps toward an accessibility-enhanced communication. In: Proceedings of the 19th Conference on Natural Language Processing (KONVENS 2023) (2023). https://aclanthology.org/2023.konvens-main.6.pdf

35. Schomacker, T. et al.: Exploring automatic text simplification of german narrative documents. In: Proceedings of the 19th Conference on Natural Language Processing (KONVENS 2023) (2023). https://aclanthology.org/2023.konvens-main.14.pdf

36. Schuett, J.: Risk management in the artificial intelligence act. Eur. J. Risk Regul. 1–19 (2023). https://doi.org/10.1017/err.2023.1

37. Spring, N., et al.: Exploring German multi-level text simplification. In: Proceedings of the International Conference on Recent Advances in Natural Language Processing (RANLP 2021), pp. 1339–1349. INCOMA Ltd., Held Online (2021)

38. Stodden, R. et al.: DEPLAIN: a German Parallel Corpus with Intralingual Translations into Plain Language for Sentence and Document Simplification. http://arxiv.org/abs/2305.18939 (2023). https://doi.org/10.48550/arXiv.2305.18939

39. Stodden, R., Kallmeyer, L.: TS-ANNO: an annotation tool to build, annotate and evaluate text simplification corpora. In: Proceedings of the 60th Annual Meeting of the Association for Computational Linguistics: System Demonstrations. pp. 145–155. Association for Computational Linguistics, Dublin, Ireland (2022). https://doi.org/10.18653/v1/2022.acl-demo.14

40. Storrer, A.: Hypertextlinguistik. In: Janich, N. and Brinker, K. (eds.) Textlinguistik: 15 Einführungen, pp. 315–322 Narr, Tübingen (2008)

41. Suter, J., et al.: Rule-based automatic text simplification for German. In: Proceedings of the 13th Conference on Natural Language Processing, pp. 279–287 (2016)

42. Vaughn, L.M., Jacquez, F.: Participatory research methods – choice points in the research process. JPRM. **1**, 1 (2020). https://doi.org/10.35844/001c.13244

43. Weiß, Z., Meurers, D.: Modeling the readability of german targeting adults and children: an empirically broad analysis and its cross-corpus validation. In: Proceedings of the 27th International Conference on Computational Linguistics. pp. 303–317. Association for Computational Linguistics, Santa Fe, New Mexico, USA (2018)

44. Wilrich, T.: Rechtliche Bedeutung von DIN-Normen und technischen Regelwerken - beck-online.pdf. 1400ff. (2023)

Author Index

M. A. Jabbar et al. (Eds.): AMLDA 2023, CCIS 2047, pp. 275–276, 2024.
https://doi.org/10.1007/978-3-031-55486-5

Printed in the United States
by Baker & Taylor Publisher Services